ALCOHOL AND DRUGS ARE WOMEN'S ISSUES

Volume One:
A Review of the Issues

edited by

PAULA ROTH

Women's Action Alliance
and
The Scarecrow Press, Inc.
Metuchen, N.J., & London
1991

British Library Cataloguing-in-Publication data available

Library of Congress Cataloging-in-Publication Data

Alcohol and drugs are women's issues / edited by Paula Roth.
    p. cm.
   Includes index.
   Contents: v. 1. A review of the issues.
   ISBN 0-8108-2360-8
   1. Women—United States—Alcohol use. 2. Women—United
States—Drug use.   I. Roth, Paula.   II. Women's Action Alliance.
HV5137.A38   1991
362.29′12′082—dc20   90-49988

Contents

Acknowledgements

Many women have contributed to this book. An author of one of the chapters, who is also a member of the national advisory board to the project, said to me during one of our many long-distance telephone conversations, "This is such a collective process . . . a rare experience." It was, indeed. I'm especially grateful to all of the chapter authors who took time away from their already overextended work schedules and time with their families and friends to contribute to the book. Their chapters reflect their areas of expertise and often, areas of deep personal concern to them. Without them, there would be no book.

My special appreciation and thanks to Sylvia Kramer, who recognized that alcohol and drugs were women's issues that needed to be addressed by a national women's organization with activist roots, and to Judy Rowley, who knew alcohol and drugs were women's issues and who, together with Sylvia, developed the original concept for the project.

I'm very grateful to the funders of the Women's Alcohol and Drug Education Project. Without their confidence and support, this book would not have been possible. They are: The New York State Division of Alcoholism and Alcohol Abuse, The New York Community Trust, The Pew Charitable Trusts, the Metropolitan Life Foundation, the J.C. Penney Company, Inc., The J.M. Foundation, The New York Times, The Hearst Foundation, The Hyde and Watson Foundation, Murdoch Magazines, The Leonard N. Stern Foundation, New York Telephone, the Patrolman Edward R. Byrne Fund, the Altman Foundation, The New York State Division of Substance Abuse Services and The New York State Task Force on Integrated Projects.

Invaluable help and support was given by many members of the national advisory board to the project. Many contributed ideas for the book, and some are chapter authors. My thanks to Marilyn Aguirre-Molina, Keven Bellows, Frances L. Brisbane, Joan Buxbaum, Diane Canova, Vivian P.J. Clarke, John B. Evans, Rosa Gil, M. Jean Gilbert, Eda Harris-Hastick, Jean Kilbourne, Barbara King, Cassie Landers, Christine Lubinski, Lynne McArthur, Juana Mora, Mari Nobles-daSilva, Yvonne Pagan, Beth Glover Reed, Marian Sandmaier, K. Santiago-Vasquez, Carole Sneddon, Judith E. Stevenson, Kate Sullivan, Jean Kennedy Tracy, Brenda Underhill, Sharon Wilsnack, Theresa Zubretsky and to Joyce Burland and Sally Peterson of the Women's Action Alliance Board, who served as liaison advisory board members.

I appreciate the encouragement and support of the Board of Directors of the Women's Action Alliance and the staff of the Alliance and women's centers who took the time to comment on drafts of the manuscript: Gerry Pearlberg, Tree Swartzlander, Rosa Maria Bramble, Safiya Bandele, Dominique Treboux, Robin Blynn, Ellen Leuchs, and particularly, Ashaki Taha-Cissé.

I want especially to thank Susan Galbraith and Nancy Griffin for their help in organizing and editing this book. Their consultation, encouragement and friendship were invaluable.

Finally, I am particularly grateful to Sharon Griffiths for her help in designing, organizing, editing and proofreading this manuscript. We spent many weekdays, evenings and weekends reviewing and re-reviewing each of the chapters. Her dedication and expertise made the completion of this book possible.

—P.R.

Introduction

Few national prevention efforts have focused on reaching women regarding alcohol and drugs and their impact on women's lives. Few efforts have focused on linking alcohol and drug problems with other women's issues, such as domestic violence, incest and sexual abuse, teen pregnancy, underemployment and poverty. Issues of sexism and racism and the alcohol and drug connection have received little national attention. Women who are low income, single parents or who are African American or Latino have received particularly inadequate attention.

In response to this need, the Women's Alcohol and Drug Education Project was established by the Women's Action Alliance in 1987. A model program was developed and tested at six women's centers nationwide. The goals of the program were to assist the centers in integrating an alcohol and drug focus into the work they were already doing with women and to help each center implement specific substance abuse prevention and intervention activities. The centers served predominantly Latino, African American or low-income women and their children. The women who received services spanned a range of ages. Most were in their late teens through their thirties.

Our experience with the six women's centers has clearly indicated that it is both helpful and necessary to place alcohol and drug problems within the context of other women's issues. We believe that alcohol and drugs are critical women's issues, whether the woman needs help because she is questioning her own use of addictive substances or is being affected by her spouse's, partner's or child's use of alcohol or other drugs. Women have been tragically underserved, both in prevention and treatment programs. It has been our experience that the sparse information available on a national level has not reached many populations of young and adult women in need. Although articles on women and alcoholism published in "mainstream" or "upscale" magazines reached middle-class women in need of the information, many women who are Latino,

African American or poor do not buy or read these magazines. To date, there has been little or no relevant information with which they can identify to counter the "pro-use" messages that inundate their communities.

The Women's Movement of the 1970s increased public awareness and concern about inequalities in our system affecting women and helped mobilize women around the articulated issues. While the movement focused national attention on a range of issues important to women, including reproductive rights, violence towards women and equal pay for equal work, it did not focus on alcohol and drugs as critical issues affecting women's lives. It also demonstrated an insensitivity to the multicultural and economic issues of large groups of women. In the 1970s, many alcohol and drug treatment programs opened around the country. They were, in large part, designed to treat male alcoholics who were predominantly White. At the same time, many coeducational, hospital-based programs opened, serving those with insurance coverage or with the economic resources to pay for services. Once again, there was an insensitivity to the economic and multicultural issues of large groups of both men and women.

From the mid-1970s to 1980, the National Institute on Alcohol Abuse and Alcoholism (NIAAA) awarded over 40 grants for treatment programs specifically for women. This initiative was aided by a 1976 hearing on "Alcohol Abuse Among Women: Special Problems and Unmet Needs," held by a Congressional Subcommittee on Alcoholism and Narcotics. In 1981, NIAAA sponsored a conference that brought together all the directors from the new federally-funded women's programs. One of their key recommendations was that more services were urgently needed for women's programs nationwide. None of the recommendations were fulfilled, however, since 1981 witnessed the advent of block grants to states. Because of the change to block grants, NIAAA's role was reduced to funding research initiatives in lieu of direct funding for service programs. States had a great deal of discretion on how to spend block grant funds, and some women's programs closed their doors for lack of support. In 1984, women's advocates aided the passage of new federal legislation that mandated states to spend 5 percent of their alcohol, drug abuse and mental health block grant funds on new and expanded prevention and treatment services for women. This block grant "set-aside" was increased to 10 percent in 1988. States have interpreted the set-aside in a variety of ways. Some have not used the funds in a manner consistent with the spirit of the legislation.

To date, the alcohol and drug field has not met the range of women's needs in either prevention or treatment programming. There are few programs designed specifically for women, and it is rare to find a program that offers women the basic service of child care. Most alcohol and drug programs are still designed by and for men, and are based on a male model of treatment. Many women who are poor or who don't speak English as their first language have appalling difficulty finding services. Addicted women who are pregnant are being refused needed services at treatment centers, and institutions in some states are reporting women to law enforcement agencies for drug use during pregnancy. Women who are African American or poor are being reported in disproportionate numbers. A national commitment to women and children must be re-examined in the face of these major barriers to women seeking and obtaining treatment and quality health care.

In 1986, federal legislation authorized the formation of The Office for Substance Abuse Prevention (OSAP). Grants were given to projects to prevent substance use among high-risk youth and, in 1988, the first in a series of grants were awarded to demonstration projects aimed at reducing drug use during pregnancy. In addition, some foundations began taking a leadership role in the prevention of addiction-related problems in women, youth and children. Of current concern to many foundations are issues and problems relevant to underserved groups of women and their children.

Alcohol and drug prevention and treatment providers can learn a great deal from women's centers and women's service organizations. Women's advocates have expertise in issues such as domestic violence, incest, sexual abuse, parenting skills and job skills training, legal and housing advocacy, counseling to troubled youth and educational opportunities. Support and empowerment of women is key to the successful treatment of women who have problems with addictive substances. Community-based women's centers and organizations which take on alcohol and drug issues need referral resources for women that are both gender- and culture-sensitive. Women's advocates and

those working in the alcohol and drug field are in a position to forge a new partnership to both prevent and reduce alcohol and drug-related problems in women and to meet the needs of women in treatment programming. Women's service organizations are uniquely equipped to join concerned individuals in the alcohol and drug field to advocate for states to appropriately spend their set-aside funds for new and expanded prevention and treatment services for women and their children.

A broad range of issues impacting women's lives is explored in Volume One of this two-volume set of books. We believe an understanding of the issues that affect African American women, Latino women, Native American women, Asian American women and lesbians is critical to effectively educate each group of women. Although our gender may be the same, different approaches must be used to reach us regarding alcohol and drugs, since different issues have affected our lives. The linkages between alcohol and drug problems in women and other women's issues such as violence, incest and sexual abuse are addressed. Since almost 70 percent of women in treatment for alcohol and drug problems are survivors of incest, rape or other sexual abuse, a focus on these issues as risk factors for alcohol and other drug problems is key to successful prevention efforts for both young and adult women.

Familial and environmental influences affect women's use of alcohol and other drugs. Poverty, access to medical care and adequate treatment, raising children as a single parent, the impact of AIDS on women, civil rights and workplace issues, problems related to homelessness, the effects of drug use during pregnancy and current efforts to criminally penalize women who use drugs during pregnancy, living with an alcoholic or growing up with an alcoholic or drug-dependent parent, and the effect of advertising on women are all critical issues that have an impact on the lives of women and their children, families and friends. The linkages between alcohol and drug problems and other issues affecting women are examined in this book, and recommendations for those working with diverse groups of women are offered. Self-help groups for women with alcohol and drug problems are assessed, as is the importance of women advocating for women to generate gender-sensitive alcohol and drug prevention and treatment services. Issues relevant to adolescent girls and young women are included in several of the chapters.

At a time when both young and adult women are using cocaine, crack, alcohol and prescription drugs at alarming rates, and the number of young female drinkers is increasing more rapidly than the number of young male drinkers, there is cause for concern. Recent research on the effects of alcohol on women's bodies indicates clearly that women's bodies are more vulnerable to the effects of alcohol than are men's. Women are also twice as likely as men to use mood-altering prescription medications in combination with alcohol, a potentially lethal combination. In the coming decade, we hope to see specific research on the effects of drugs other than alcohol on women's bodies and gain a better understanding of why different ethnic and cultural groups may be affected differently by legal and illegal drug use.

If vast groups of women are not receiving adequate information on the health and social consequences of alcohol and drug use, they are unable to talk with their sons or their daughters about alcohol and drugs. Many surveys suggest that a parent's attitude and behavior regarding alcohol use can have a significant impact on the drinking habits of children. Since three of the biggest killers of adolescents and teens are accidents, homicide and suicide—often drug- and alcohol-related —it is critical that women receive adequate information and education for both themselves and their children.

Some studies indicate that more than 60 percent of children born today will be raised by a single parent. Families headed by single-parent women continue to increase and are among the poorest families in the country. Over 50 percent of families headed by African American or Latino women live in poverty. These are the very women most in need of publicly funded gender- and culture-relevant alcohol and drug prevention and treatment services. Unfortunately, they and other low-income women are the women who have been most neglected. To demonstrate a commitment to women and their children, it is important that alcohol- and drug-related services be available to women independent of their role as mother. Concern for women as individuals beyond the gestatory function is critical if programs are to reach women and provide the range of services they need.

Women's centers and women's service organizations are ideal settings to reach underserved groups of women and their children. Women trust the services and the staff providing the services. Approaches are culturally relevant to the populations served. Whether the center is community-based or community college-based, the principal goal is to empower women. These organizations are in a position to advocate for a broad range of issues that affect women's lives. They have a history of doing so. Their advocacy efforts can have an enormous influence—community by community, state by state, and on the national level—to help women, and particularly underserved groups of women, receive the prevention, education, intervention and treatment services that they and the people they love need. The settings also offer a non-stigmatizing environment for women and their children to talk about the impact of

alcohol and other drugs on their lives. The centers that tested our model program have told us incorporating a focus on alcohol and drugs has enhanced their ability to empower the women they serve and is consistent with their holistic approach to women's health and social issues.

Centers and organizations throughout the country have expressed an interest in replicating the Alliance model program. The extraordinary response tells us an approach that integrates these issues into the principal focus of a center or organization is an approach whose time has come. We hope the publication of these books will enable women's advocates to offer early preventative information and education to women regarding addictive substances. The Women's Alcohol and Drug Education Project is committed to reaching women early, before their lives and the lives of their children are devastated by alcohol- and drug-related problems.

Volume One of this two-volume set of books focuses on the key issues for different groups of women and the linkages between the issues. Twenty-four chapters written by outstanding women committed to helping women are included. Authors were chosen based on their expertise in and concern about the issues addressed in their respective chapters. The opinions expressed are the authors' and do not necessarily reflect the opinions of the Women's Action Alliance. We do, however, respect the opinions of each author.

Volume Two is a step-by-step guide to replicating the model program that provides content for staff training sessions, content for six educational classes for center or organization participants, an evaluation of the test of the model at the six original sites, each center's experiences in implementing the program, suggested resources and where to find them, and funding resources.

We recommend that any center or organization interested in addressing issues related to alcohol and drug problems in women's lives read both Volume One and Volume Two. Whatever the choice of the reader, it is our hope that alcohol and other drug problems in women will be viewed in a new light. And viewed for what they are, critical women's issues.

About the Women's Action Alliance

The Women's Action Alliance was established in 1971 as a national organization committed to furthering the goals of all women regardless of race or economic status. The Alliance has worked towards this goal by providing information on a range of women's issues, building networks among women's organizations committed to empowering women, and developing innovative programs in areas of importance to women. Programs have focused on critical issues in the lives of young and adult women that were being ignored or underaddressed.

Among the achievements of the Alliance was the formation of the National Women's Agenda Project in 1975. A coalition of over one hundred women's organizations promoted a national women's agenda and produced the *Women's Agenda Magazine*. In the late 1970s, the Alliance cosponsored the Institute on Women's History with the Smithsonian Institution. The Institute brought together leaders of national women's organizations and led to the establishment of national Women's History Month. In the 1980s, the Alliance was instrumental in the creation of the National Association of Women's Centers. The Associa-

tion held its first national conference in May, 1986. The interest many centers had at the 1986 conference in addressing alcohol and drug problems among women and the Alliance's recognition of these problems as underaddressed women's issues led to the Alliance's development of the Women's Alcohol and Drug Education Project and this two-volume set of books.

Paula Roth
Director
Women's Alcohol and Drug Education Project
Women's Action Alliance
June 1, 1990

1 American Women and Polydrug Abuse

Dooley Worth, Ph.D.

"Polydrug use among American women has a long history that is linked to social, economic and political oppression. Drugs of choice, combinations of drugs, modes of administration and levels of use have changed over time, but the institutions and attitudes that support or encourage addiction in women have remained remarkably constant."

The term "polydrug user" is being applied with increasing frequency to women in a manner that implies it is a new phenomenon. Generally, when researchers use the term "polydrug use" they are referring to the simultaneous or sequential use of more than one legal and/or illegal drug. A preliminary examination of the literature on women and drug use indicates that, although the context of multiple drug use by women has shifted over time, the problem is not new. In fact, there is a long history of the combined use of legal and illegal drugs by American women. Polydrug abuse among women is perceived as a new problem because Americans have such a poor sense of their own history.

The 18th Century

The information on patterns of drug use by women prior to the late 18th century is meager. The drug most used by women before the 18th century was alcohol.[1] Indian hemp was planted in the American colonies, but for commercial purposes only. Opium had been available in the United States since the 17th century (in crude form, it was used in extracts—usually in combination with alcohol), but the extent of its use by American women is poorly documented. Most social documents concentrate on the effect of men's alcoholism on their wives and families.

It is clear, however, that both alcohol and drugs were

consumed by 18th-century women, most often in the form of patent medicines.[2] Patent medicines were promoted as treatments for a wide range of medical problems, particularly "female" medical problems. As medical practices in the eighteenth century were fairly primitive, there being few medications effective in altering the course of most ailments, nostrums which made the patient "feel" better were widely accepted. Physicians employed such nostrums to treat patients for anxiety and for illnesses they couldn't cure.

Women consumed alcohol-based elixirs containing opiates for dental problems, painful menstruation and "female organ" problems, and used opiate-based cough suppressants. The elixirs and remedies were manufactured and promoted by largely unregulated medical "practitioners."[3,4]

The 19th Century

Opiates

The pattern of drug consumption established in the late 18th century escalated during the first half of the nineteenth century as women increased their use of opium derivatives such as laudanum.

Examining the social context in which female opiate addiction flourished, it becomes apparent that prevailing social values attributed physical and intellectual inferiority to women. These values supported a social and economic status for American women greatly inferior to that enjoyed by men.[5]

Women were divorced from the centers of power which were dominated by men. They had no legal right to political participation, they were denied voting rights and they lacked legal access to economic resources by law, as they were not "separate" from their husbands. Women also lacked legal control over

This chapter is the outgrowth of an ongoing conversation with Dr. Stephen Sorrell, the Medical Director of St. Luke's/ Roosevelt Medical Center's Substance Abuse Program, New York City, whose expertise helped to provide the conceptual framework on which the work is based.

their children's destiny and had little access to educational opportunities. Moreover, they were required to live in accordance with repressive social codes of behavior which promoted an ideal of women as wives and mothers who put aside their own needs to address those of others.[6]

In reality, few American women could readily conform to this ideal. This placed them at risk of feeling "culturally non-competent"—of becoming frustrated, disappointed and angry. American women's emerging perception of "cultural non-competence" and male-dependence during this period can be linked both to their being drugged (by so-called medical practitioners) and their drug abuse. The link between the widespread perception of women as culturally non-competent and drug abuse is evident in periods where there is a florescence of heavy multiple-drug abuse by American women. By the mid-19th century, technological advances in chemistry and medicine led to variations in both the drugs being used by American women and in their routes of administration. Alkaloids were synthesized providing refined opium (morphine), which was discovered by Friedrich Serturner in 1806. The syringe was developed and improved by Alexander Wood in 1853.[7]

Following these advances, the use of morphine as well as the smoking of opium increased between 1860 and 1900. Morphine imports to the United States grew as the drug gained in popularity due to its low price, standardized production, and the fact that it could be easily and effectively administered by injection. Morphine was often first administered to women by their physicians for the treatment of pain in childbirth. The highest rate of opiate addiction among women was in the South, where opiates were widely prescribed not just to ease pain but to treat gastrointestinal and infectious illnesses. As physicians could not always be present when an injection might be needed, they resorted to leaving the patient the syringe so that the drug could be self-administered, opening the way for potential abuse. Syringes could also be obtained by mail order and were relatively inexpensive, costing $1.50 to $2.75 in the 1890s.[8]

One study of addicted women, undertaken in 1880, showed that women using opiates outnumbered men by two to one. One-third of the women studied were prostitutes, 39 percent were between the ages of 30 and 40, and 22 percent were between the ages of 40 and 50. Most of the women were married, American born, White, and housewives.[9] The majority of women in the study used noninjected morphine, which they mixed with chloral hydrate or chloroform.[9]

As many of the women using opiates were of childbearing age, their children were not exempt from the effects of widespread opiate use. Some were born addicted while others became addicted through the prescribing of opiate-laced medications, such as cough medicines, to infants.

Alcohol

Although alcohol abuse by women was a problem in the nineteenth century, it was not always easily identified. There was a stigma attached to women's drinking which was perceived as "offending" cultural expectations of female behavior. Women who abused alcohol were often referred to in literature as female "hysterics."[10] Female hysteria can be seen as a chosen behavior, a means for some women to express their "malaise, discontent, anger and pain" related to male expectations of stereotyped female behavior.[11]

While women played a central role in the Temperance Movement throughout the 19th century, their anti-alcohol-consumption efforts concentrated not on alcoholism among women but on the impact of men's alcoholism on their wives and families.[12] Their temperance efforts were often ridiculed by males.[6]

The Temperance Movement did, however, have some effect on women's alcohol consumption, even if that was not its primary goal. By creating pressure on women who drank excessively to move away from consuming alcohol, it contributed to women's increasing use of laudanum and morphine, drugs whose use could be more easily hidden and, therefore, would not "offend" cultural expectations.[6] For instance, in the latter part of the 19th century, Southern women began using "respectable substitutes for alcohol," such as patent medicines, more heavily.[13] Ironically, one of the main ingredients of a popular elixir, Lydia Pinkham's Tonic, was alcohol.

Alcohol consumption among women did not disappear. In addition to the use of alcohol-based patent medicines, women in the lower socioeconomic classes abused gin, while middle and upper-class women combined consumption of whiskey with opiates.[8] A contributing factor to continuing alcoholism among women was the habit on the part of physicians of prescribing alcohol for "female" conditions—to relieve discomfort during pregnancy, to relieve premenstrual tension, or to prevent post-partum infection. Beer, for instance, was frequently prescribed for nursing mothers.[10]

Analgesics and Hallucinogens

The second half of the 19th century also witnessed the spread of the abuse of chloral hydrate ("knock-out drops"), a drug developed in 1868. Upper-class women used chloral hydrate believing it made them appear more "brilliant" while attending social events.[8] Chloral hydrate was also used by middle- and upper-class women, along with ether and bromides, to treat exhaustion, anxiety and sleep problems. During this period, marijuana was also prescribed for women who suffered from venereal disease, pain, insomnia or migraines.[14]

Cocaine

In addition to alcohol, analgesics and opiates, cocaine was developed and was touted by Freud and other physicians as a wonder drug. The principal alkaloid in cocaine was isolated by Albert Niemann in 1859.[7] Cocaine was promoted for treating toothaches, digestive disorders, neurasthenia and other medical ailments as well as for promoting strength and stimulation.[15] It was consumed by American women mostly in patent medicines.[16] The manufacturers of patent medicines were U.S. newspapers' major advertisers during the Civil War.

Women of all classes used cocaine-laced products. Parke-Davis and Company marketed coca products such as Coca Cordial (which was recommended for persons with "delicate nervous organizations") and coca cigarettes.[16] Cocaine was taken as a "wine," Vin Mariani being the most famous. In addition, cocaine was found in over-the-counter or mail-order sprays, ointments, tablets and injections, and in hay fever remedies.[1,15] Nyalls Compound Extract of Damina was marketed to help restore the reproductive organs. Cocaine pills were touted by Sharpe and Dohrn as aphrodisiacs. The use of cocaine by women in the 19th century was not limited to its inclusion in patent medicines. Dr. William Hammond, a former U.S. Surgeon General, advocated using cocaine to anesthetize a woman's clitoris to prevent her from masturbating.[15] Hammond was a cocaine addict himself.

Other cocaine-based products were advertised as "brain food" and general cure-alls.[16] The use of these and other coca products by women was promoted by celebrity endorsements, books, posters, music and plays.

The promotion of cocaine was not limited to improving health and vitality. It was also promoted as a cure for morphine addiction.[15] Morphine-addicted women were prescribed the equivalent of modern day "speedballs," mixtures of morphine and cocaine. Parke Davis, which was manufacturing cocaine products, advertised cocaine as a cure for "morphinism" and also for alcoholism.[15]

Patterns of Addiction

Vicious cycles of addiction were created throughout the second half of the 19th century, often unwittingly, by physicians who gave women injections to "make them feel better" or prescribed sedatives when women couldn't sleep. They then treated the resulting headaches with powders containing opiates.[1]

From 1850 to 1880 the number of American women addicted to legal "remedies," alcohol, opiates,

analgesic and coca products, outnumbered men by two to one. Official records of female opiate addicts in the period 1878 to 1914 indicate that 62.2 percent of opiate addicts in Michigan in 1878, 71.9 percent of opiate addicts in Chicago in 1880, 63.8 percent of opiate addicts in Iowa in 1885, 58.9 percent of opiate addicts in Florida in 1913 and 66.9 percent of opiate addicts in Tennessee in 1914 were women.[3]

Because female addiction was highly stigmatized and thus "hidden," the true extent of female addiction in the late 1800s is difficult to gauge. It is clear the majority of addicted women were White, middle-aged, middle- or upper-class women. They had become addicted through drugs dispensed by their physicians or through self-medication.[13] Physician's wives were particularly at risk for heavy drug use or addiction, as were physicians themselves.

In the latter part of the nineteenth century, middle-class women were believed to be susceptible to vague nervous complaints. Being nervous was equated with social "fineness." A high rate of female anxiety was, however, not a social characteristic of middle-class women. Anxiety was a symptom of the effects on women of the momentous social and economic changes taking place in late nineteenth century America which were not accompanied by rapid enough change in the social expectations of gender-specific behavior.

Socioeconomic Change and Drug Use

The entire nation was on the move during the latter part of the nineteenth century. Easterners moved West. Foreign immigration to the United States from Europe increased substantially and women living on farms moved to the cities to work.

Starting in 1848 with the Seneca Falls Conference, small groups of American women began addressing the social, political and economic issues affecting them, issues which were related to the widespread drug addiction found among American women of all classes.

End-of-the-century American women continued to be portrayed as the guardians of moral "purity" and social standards, but these standards were being challenged by the rapid economic and demographic changes the country was experiencing.[14] Changes in family structure resulted in women assuming the major role as the socializers of children. This role became more pronounced as their husbands became increasingly occupied with employment outside the home.[14] This trend was begun in the 18th century and escalated following the Civil War.[5]

The combination of rapid change in social expectations and roles and increased leisure time (related to the Industrial Revolution) created new social tensions. Drugs were prescribed to help middle-class women cope with these tensions, with the inhibitions they had incorporated from their upbringing and with the social restraints placed on them. Drugs also provided self-administered relief for women's anger, frustration, boredom and anxiety.[14] Some women—rich women, women who earned their living through prostitution and "show girls"—continued to smoke opium and inject morphine for pleasure or to assist them in their work.

Opium-smoking was indulged in by socialites who visited opium dens. Opium-smoking was also prevalent among prostitutes, who learned from the Chinese who frequently settled in or next to red-light districts in American cities.[3]

In the second half of the nineteenth century, American women began observing the connection between constant social and economic change and the tension it generated in their lives. It was this tension which increased their vulnerability to drug addiction.

By the 1890s, changes in drug consumption patterns among women occurred that would become more pronounced in the twentieth century. There was a decline in the per capita consumption of opiates. Although the overall consumption of opiates declined, the smoking of opium increased.[2] This decline was related to an increase in immigration, an aging population of addicted women and a growing awareness of the dangers of narcotic overuse. In response to the growing awareness of these dangers, state laws emerged to regulate the labeling and sale of patent medicines and the prescribing of morphine.

Pre-World War II

In the period before the First World War, drugs were still employed to calm women's nerves, society women continued to use opiates, and bromide salts gave way to barbiturates as a treatment for anxiety.[3,17] In the 1928 study by Terry and Pellens, they state that the simultaneous use of morphine, cocaine and alcohol was not uncommon among male addicts in the early 1900s, but they do not comment on the extent of such polydrug use by female addicts.[3] There is evidence, however, of major changes in drug abuse patterns by American women occurring during this period, as increasing restrictions were placed on the sale and use of opiates because of the growing social disapprobation of drug use. The Pure Food and Drug Act of 1906 required labeling of over-the-counter products containing opiates, cocaine, marijuana or chloral hydrate. Although the Act reduced narcotic sales by about a third, women could still easily obtain narcotics. In 1909 the importing of prepared smoking opium was banned.[18] That was followed by the passage of the Harrison Narcotic Act in 1914, which taxed the non-medical use of opiates and resulted in a further drop in female consumption.[18]

Liquor availability also decreased in some states as the Temperance Movement gained momentum in the first decades of the twentieth century. This contributed to an increase in the consumption of cocaine-laced "cola" drinks, particularly in the American South. Cocaine use itself was, however, also under attack in the South, where it became a fulcrum of the expression of Whites' fears of Black male sexuality and anger.[18] The Committee on the Acquirement of the Drug Habit, in 1907, issued a report which worried that "women were particularly vulnerable to cocaine," as were Blacks.[18] Although there is no evidence that cocaine use was more prevalent among Blacks (although most Black prostitutes in the 1890s were believed to use cocaine), Whites feared that the use of the drug by Black males would result in their anger being loosed upon White women in the form of sexual assaults.[18] Similar racially-based fear of the Chinese had resulted in outcries for the control of opium.

The reform movements which followed the First World War, many of them advocating health improvements, worked to establish a social climate where the tolerance for open drug addiction was reduced. The smoking of opium was banned in 1919. Women who were addicted to smoking switched to injecting morphine or heroin. The sale and use of heroin increased as drug laws made it more difficult and expensive to obtain morphine and opium.[19] Heroin (from the German word for heroism) was not only cheaper and faster acting than opium or morphine, but it could be snorted. Snorting was, however, soon supplanted by injecting. The popularity of heroin led to its increasing adulteration, necessitating its injection to get a "good hit."[3]

With the enactment of the Harrison Narcotic Act, the treatment of opiate addiction passed out of the control of physicians. Federal action against the sale of narcotics increased and clinics which had dispensed drugs were closed. The treatment of opiate addiction was increasingly relegated to the criminal justice system, where it remained until the 1960s when new medical and psychiatric models of drug addiction emerged.

These changes in regulations resulted in a decrease in opiate use over the next several decades. Programs to help individuals addicted to opiates were first opened in cities with large populations of addicts. They maintained addicts on these drugs while gradually decreasing their dosage until they were no longer drug-dependent. At the New York City Department of Health's clinic at 125 Worth Street, 18 percent of addicts seen in 1919 were women. By 1920, women made up 20 percent of the addicts.[18]

Not all middle-class female addicts were cut off from access to narcotics. Nurses and others who could obtain narcotics at work continued to use and inject opiates. After the New York City Narcotic Relief Station opened at Bellevue in 1919, the majority of women seen there were nurses (others were working mothers, college students and adolescents).[20] Nurses have continued to represent a small percentage of female addicts. They vary from other female polydrug users in that they tend to be older (the average age in the 1970s was 42) and addicted to a single substance such as Demerol which can be obtained on the job.[13]

Yet most addicts who entered narcotic relief programs in New York City in 1919 were men (81%). What happened to all the female addicts? Some continued to be treated privately by their doctors, especially those who could be maintained on small doses thus not attracting too much attention to the doctor.

As has been mentioned, female narcotic addicts at the turn of the century were primarily middle-aged women, many of them in poor health. It is believed that the number of female addicts decreased sharply as this generation of addicts died and was not replaced by a younger generation of addicts. Furthermore, public awareness of the detrimental effects of narcotic use had grown and physicians were increasingly held accountable for administering narcotics to women too easily. In 1919, the U.S. Supreme Court ruled that under the Harrison Act, physicians could be restricted in the prescribing of narcotics.[18]

Upper-class addicts, treated discreetly by their doctors, continued to use their drugs of choice, since they had access to them without fear of social retribution. Other women who continued to use narcotic and other illicit drugs became social outcasts as they were forced to seek the now-illegal drugs in the "underworld," the only place where these drugs were still readily available. This experience of being on the social margin or "edge" has not changed over time. Women pulled into the drug subculture become unemployed and become dependent on the subculture for survival. They engage in criminal behavior and are at increased risk for psychological, emotional, and sexual problems.[21] Female addicts from the lower socioeconomic classes were the hardest hit by changes in narcotic laws. In 1915, the price of street heroin in New York City rose from $6.50 an ounce to $100 an ounce because of the restrictions on legal sales of opiates.[18]

The availability of cocaine also increased in the "underworld" in the 1920s, where it was employed by women working in brothels. They alleviated the feelings of "coming down" from cocaine with heroin.[3] In Paris, it was estimated that one-half of all prostitutes working in Monmartre in 1913 were using cocaine, given to them by their pimps who thought it made them more "attractive" to their customers.[15] The belief

that cocaine makes women more "animated" or sexually accessible persists today. Female addicts report being given cocaine by their boyfriends or pimps to "get them in the mood for sex." "Johns" picking up street prostitutes often offer to buy them cocaine as payment for sexual transactions.[22]

As "visible" drug use among women shifted from middle-class women to lower-class women and women who frequented the "underworld," attitudes towards women's drug use changed. When most addicted women were in the middle class they were seen as physiologically addicted or diseased. Now women using opiates and cocaine were increasingly viewed as socially deviant or pathological.[3] Women who used opiates were increasingly identified as "addicts," and physicians no longer wanted to "treat" them.[18]

The social roles of American women were also changing. Starting at the turn of the century, women's work increasingly took place outside the home. In 1900, one out of three women worked outside the home. Many of these women were poor immigrants employed in textile factories in the Northeast, where they worked for 13½ hours a day.[6] The need for labor had been expanding since the Civil War, opening the opportunity for more women to become employed outside the home. Many young women preferred to work in factories than to stay at home and be pressured into early marriages and childbearing, indicating their dissatisfaction with the "American ideal of womanhood."[5]

In addition to changes in women's employment patterns, there were other important changes in the first decades of the 20th century. Women gained more access to education, but the gap between social classes grew. The rich grew richer, and a greater distance developed between the middle and lower classes.[6]

The First World War resulted in many reform movements springing up to address social problems, some of which affected women's health (such as birth control). However, female addiction was not identified as a major social issue. Social problems, such as alcohol and drug abuse, tended to be submerged by the economic depression which followed the stock market crash in 1929. These problems did not disappear, however. Throughout the 1930s, middle-class women continued combining the consumption of alcohol with prescription drugs such as sleeping medications. The alcohol was cheaper than the medications and enhanced the potency of the medicines.

Upper- and lower-class women used illegal drugs such as opium, morphine, heroin and cocaine as they had in the past. Marijuana use increased, especially among Mexican Americans in the southwestern United States. Like their middle-class female counterparts, the use of drugs among this group of women remained "hidden" unless they had an encounter with the criminal justice system.[4] Overall, women had less money available to spend on hard drugs during the Depression and the drugs themselves, particularly narcotics, became scarce.

World War II and its Aftermath

The Second World War, although it had an impact on expanding drug use in males, created little immediate change in patterns of "illicit" polydrug use among women. The most important changes in patterns of multiple drug use by women would result from war-related research which led to the development of new types of drugs and from the expansion of employment opportunities for women, which opened up new social roles and mobility for them.[6]

The war and its aftermath led to a reappraisal of the American ideal for female behavior. Women were now expected to be competent in multiple roles, including mothering and full-time employment outside the home. Following the war, competency in the home was stressed although many women still remained in the work force.[6] Women had increased personal opportunities. Birth control technology improved and women had more access to education. However, they continued to earn less than men and to be restricted in their career choices and advancement.

Women's increased social participation led to the involvement of some middle-class women in the Civil Rights movement in the 1960s. As these women addressed the oppression of Blacks in American society, they also began to readdress the issue of their own continued oppression in a male-dominated society. As a result, women came to be seen as a new "minority" and traditional American gender-role behavior was called into question.

This led to feminists challenging the American social and economic systems which had been built on concepts that included dependence and the inferiority of women and other minorities. Women began working to change sex-role stereotypes and to gain sexual and reproductive freedom. One component of this work was the establishment of alternative health care for women to address those needs that continued to be unmet by the medical system.[6] The availability of the birth control pill, combined with the empowerment of women fostered by the Women's Movement, helped to destroy traditional sex-role behavior and open women to sexual experimentation. The 1960s "love" culture encouraged both men and women to explore new lifestyles. The social disapproval of open drug use by women gave way to social approval of experimentation with drugs, at least among young middle-class women. However, these new "lifestyles" and sexual norms were still driven by male expectations and desires. Women continued to be seen, even in radical subcultures, as sexual objects.

Sexual liberation did not result in gender liberation. In some cases, drug use enabled women to participate in lifestyles which were, in fact, uncomfortable for them.

The World Health Organization redefined drug abuse in the post-war period to include the use of tranquilizers, antidepressants, diet pills and other medications. The primary users of these medications were women.[13] With this redefinition came the realization that a large number of middle-class American women were addicted to multiple drugs, many of them legally prescribed by their physicians.

Not only did the definition of drug abuse change in the postwar period, but there were major changes in actual drug use patterns starting in the 1960s. A new class of drugs—aniolitics or anti-anxiety drugs, such as the benzodiazepines (Valium, Librium, Ativan, Xanax, Dalmane, Halcion), were developed and widely marketed to women through their physicians.

Simultaneously, many women began experimenting with unconventional lifestyles which included legal and illegal drug use.[4] As middle-class women experimented with combinations of benzodiazepines, amphetamines, hallucinogens and alcohol, more women became cross- or poly-addicted. Levels of drug use among women also increased and by the 1970s women accounted for two-thirds of psychoactive drug users.[23]

Increasing amphetamine use in the 1960s (much of it in the form of diet pills) introduced women to "speed," a racy high. The use of amphetamines helped open the door to subsequent widespread cocaine use (a not-dissimilar high) among women in the late 1970s and early 1980s.[17] Researchers had already documented a high degree of polydrug use in the United States, when a new epidemic of cocaine abuse began in the United States in the early 1970s.[24] Cocaine use among 18- to 25-year-olds in the United States tripled between 1972 and 1979.[25] The use of marijuana by women also escalated in the 1970s and approached the levels of male use of the drug. This issue is key, since early marijuana use has been shown to be a significant predictor of cocaine abuse. There was also an increase in the use of non-medical stimulants among women. By the late 1980s, the levels of women abusing cocaine were close to the number of men.[26]

The escalation in polydrug use by women has been accompanied by a drop in the median age for the onset of alcohol and cigarette use among women to 14 1/2 years. This brings women closer to onset rates for men for both cigarette and alcohol use.[26] This is particularly important, as there is a strong correlation between alcohol and cigarette use and cocaine use. Among high school seniors who use cocaine, 84 percent use marijuana, 80 percent drink alcohol and 50 percent smoke.[27]

Not only has the prevalence of cocaine and other drug use increased since 1974, but the routes of administration and the levels of use have changed. This has resulted in a more destructive pattern of cocaine use among women.[28] Today, two-thirds of female cocaine addicts are poly-addicted.[17] Overall, cocaine users are more heterogeneous in their drug use than users of other drugs.[29]

American Women and Polydrug Use: 1800-1980

If we carefully examine the use of multiple licit and illicit drugs by American women over the last 180 years, there is evidence that critical changes in drug abuse patterns and their intensity are linked to major upheavals in the lives of American women. These occurred primarily in three periods: 1840 to 1880, when the country underwent rapid industrialization; 1890 to 1930, when major upheavals occurred in world political and economic systems; and 1960 to 1980 following World War II when rapid social change in the United States had profound effects on the American family.

All three were periods of major national transition and in all three there was a significant increase in drug use among American women. Between 1840 and 1880, the United States experienced the Civil War and massive immigration, and underwent industrialization. Most American women found themselves unable to affect their changing world since they lacked the political, social and economic means to express their needs or desires.[6] The periods leading up to and following the First and Second World Wars were also marked by major social, economic and political up-heaval, not just in the United States but internation-ally. In all three periods, American women re-experienced their social inferiority. In all three per-iods, significant increases in female drug addiction are documented. In all three periods, there is evidence that American medical, social, economic and political institutions failed to meet the needs of American women to express their individual, social, political and health concerns. Conversely, other periods such as the 1920s and 1940s, when drug abuse among American women apparently declined, were periods in which women organized to fight for political rights, enter the work force in larger numbers and assume new social roles.

Meeting the needs of many American women today, particularly women who are poor, will require *changing the institutional structures which control women's lives.* It will require a lessening of the tensions in American society between employer and employee, Whites and ethnic minorities, parents and children,

natives and immigrants, rich and poor, men and women.[6] Polydrug abuse among American women has a long history that is linked to social, economic and political oppression. Drugs of choice, combinations of drugs, modes of administration and levels of use have changed over time, but the institutions and attitudes that support or encourage addiction in women have remained remarkably constant.

The question facing us as we enter the 1990s is what particular social, economic and political circumstances are contributing to the current epidemic of polydrug abuse among American women. Once again, the United States is undergoing a technological and social revolution. The creation of a global economy has set in motion changes that may indirectly contribute to an increase in poverty in American inner cities. Some of these changes may be related to the rise in a service economy and the decline in manufacturing. Shifts in the United States tax system have redistributed wealth upward, widening the gap between rich and poor. Educational opportunities, the traditional route for social mobility in the United States, have diminished for the most disenfranchised as the deterioration of inner city school systems continues. The lack of educational, and therefore employment, opportunities for minority men has resulted in heavier social pressures on minority women, who often head families living in poverty.

In studying female polydrug abusers, Hagan found that 67 percent had one or two alcoholic parents, 8 percent had one alcoholic parent, and 8 percent had at least one alcoholic older sibling. An intergenerational addiction pattern is strikingly pervasive, with 87 percent of polyaddicted women overall coming from chemically dependent families. Over 50 percent of the women had left school before completing the eleventh grade and most had poor or limited work histories, although many had post-high-school vocational training.[30] Many female polydrug users were abused children. In Hagan's study 67 percent of the polydrug abusing women had been sexually assaulted as opposed to 15 percent of the controls. Of the women who had been sexually assaulted, 75 percent had been raped before the age of 16, some of them by more than one man. Of the women who had been raped, 25 percent were abused by a father, grandfather or brother. Another study showed a higher rate of parental sexual abuse among Black female addicts.[21] For women who have been sexually abused, drugs may be the only escape from memories or feelings of guilt with which they cannot cope.

Social change related to economic and technological change has been accompanied by changing social expectations. Impoverished young boys and girls are no longer content to be promised a small piece of the pie should they struggle and sacrifice for years, toiling at boring, low-paid jobs with little chance for advancement. Television shows them the "good life," while daily realities deprive them of any access to or hope of achieving it. Many turn to using drugs to forget or to selling them to obtain the money for the "good life."

Middle-class children with material comforts often find they have nothing to strive for. They may fear being unable to provide such affluence for themselves and their future families. They find they have been ignored by parents who are absorbed in their own pursuit of material wealth. These children often turn to drugs as a way of chemically "dropping out" or to blunt the pain of what seems to be a meaningless or over-pressured life.

Similar pressures are found in both lower- and middle-class women who are experiencing increased levels of polydrug abuse as they are pressured into full-time employment outside the home to help their families maintain the "good life." Since a significant amount of their husbands' real wages have dropped over the last decade, more women are experiencing these pressures. Most women lack support for child care. They have to manage parenting, housekeeping and full-time jobs. Cocaine seems uniquely suited to addressing the chronic exhaustion of today's middle-class "super mothers." It also seems uniquely suited to addressing the feeling of despair and lack of "cultural competency" experienced by young mothers who are single heads of households in inner-city minority neighborhoods.

There has been an increase in cocaine-related polydrug abuse among both middle-class and lower-class women. In New York City alone in the period 1983 to 1984, there was an 18 percent increase in the number of women using cocaine regularly.[31] This is partly due to the increased availability of the drug. The United States has been inundated with cheap cocaine from Latin America, where failed economies have been replaced by cocaine economies. Crack (free base cocaine), processed in the United States, has become available at a price which even schoolchildren can afford.

It is important not to attribute the new patterns of polydrug use among women to increased cocaine use and availability. History has shown us that polydrug use among American women is not just driven by increased amounts and types of drugs, whose availability and popularity have ebbed and flowed over time. Rather, it is more reflective of America's power structure, which places women in repressive sexual and social roles and which confines the majority of women to low-paying and unsatisfying, or high-paying and high-pressure jobs. It is more reflective of a male-dominated medical system which has prescribed drugs for women rather than addressing the anxiety generated by oppressive social roles or the despair and illness connected to poverty. This is a system which silences and controls rather than heals. It is reflective of racism, which allows drugs to proliferate in impoverished minority neighborhoods and where the drug abuse problem is addressed only when it spreads to White middle-class neighborhoods, and even then with more rhetoric than resources. It is reflective of the corruption which allows drug trafficking and production to flourish here and abroad, often replacing entire national economies in countries destroyed by oppressive foreign debt. And finally, it is reflective of a cultural apprehensiveness— the feeling that as a culture we are not in control of our destiny.

All of these factors, combined with rapid changes in sex-role behavior, have left many women feeling anxiety-ridden, fearful, angry, powerless and "culturally non-competent." Polydrug use is one manifestation of these tensions and of women's unfulfilled desire to achieve full participation in a society that continues to promote cultural values that support their oppression.

References

1. Mayor LaGuardia's Committee on Marijuana. 1973. *The Marijuana Problem in the City of New York*, Scarecrow Reprint Corporation, Metuchen, N.J. (original publication 1944), pp. 2-14.
2. Musto, David. 1987. *The American Disease, Origins of Narcotic Control*, Oxford University Press, New York, pp. 1-158.
3. Terry, Charles E. & Pellens, Mildred. 1928. *The Opium Problem*, The Committee on Drug Addiction in collaboration with The Bureau of Social Hygiene, Inc., New York, pp. 98-481.
4. Sorrell, Stephan J., M.D. 1988. Personal communication on the history of women's drug use.
5. Brownlee, W. Elliot & Mary M. 1976. *Women in the American Economy: A Documentary History*, 1675 to 1929, Yale University Press, New Haven, Conn., p. 10.
6. Papachriston, Judith. 1976. *Women Together: A History in Documents of the Women's Movement in the United States*, Alfred A. Knopf, New York, pp. xi-246.
7. Castiglioni, Arturo, M.D. 1958. *A History of Medicine*, Alfred A. Knopf, New York, p. 744.
8. Morgan, H. Wayne. 1974. *Yesterday's Addicts, American Society and Drug Abuse 1865-1920*, University of Oklahoma Press, Norman, Okla., pp. 3-15.
9. Earle, Charles W. 1974. "The Opium Habit: A

Statistical and Clinical Lecture (1880)," in *Yesterday's Addicts*, Morgan, H.W., ed., University of Oklahoma Press, Norman, Okla., pp. 53-57.

10. Hornick, Edith Lynn. 1977. *The Drinking Woman*, Association Press, New York, p. 20.

11. Smith-Rosenberg, Carol. 1985. *Disorderly Conduct, Visions of Gender in Victorian America*, Oxford University Press, New York, p. 198.

12. Levine, H.G. "Temperance and Women in 19th-century United States," *Alcohol and Drug Problems in Women: Research Advances in Alcohol and Drug Problems*, Kalant, O.J. ed., Vol. 5, Plenum Press, New York.

13. Cushey, Walter R., Premkumar, T. and Sigel, L. 1983. "Survey of Opiate Addiction Among Females in the United States Between 1850 and 1970," in *Psychotherapy and Drug Addiction I: Diagnosis and Treatment*, NYC, abstracted in *Women and Drugs, Research Issues*, Number 31, NIDA, Washington, D.C., pp. 58-59.

14. Morgan, H. Wayne. 1981. *Drugs in America, A Social History, 1800-1980*, Syracuse University Press, Syracuse, N.Y., pp. 15-128.

15. Grinspoon, Lester & Bakalar, James B. 1976. *Cocaine, A Drug and Its Social Evolution*, Basic Books, Inc., New York, pp. 20-21, 24-107.

16. Chitwood, Dale D. 1985. "Patterns and Consequences of Cocaine Use," in *Cocaine Use in Americans: Epidemiologic and Clinical Perspectives*, NIDA Research Monograph No. 61, DHHS, Washington, D.C., p. 111.

17. Mondanaro, Josette. 1989. *Treatment of Women with Chemical Dependency Problems*, Lexington Press, Lexington, Mass., p. 233.

18. Musto, David. 1977. "Historical Highlights of American Drug Use (1800-1940)," in *Americans and Drug Abuse*, Kryder, C. and Strickland, S.P. eds., Aspen Institute for Humanistic Studies, Aspen, Colo., pp. 3-8.

19. Courtwright, David T. 1982. *Dark Paradise*, Harvard University Press, Cambridge, Mass., pp. 84-90.

20. Graham-Mulhall, Sara. 1926. *Opium: The Demon Flower*, Harold Vinal, New York City, pp. 17-162.

21. Cushey, Walter R. & Wathey, Richard B. 1982. *Female Addiction*, Lexington Books, Lexington, Mass., p. 139.

22. Worth, Dooley. 1990. *Ethnographic Research on Crack Using Heroin Addicted Women*, Montefiore Medical Center, Bronx, N.Y., unpublished data.

23. Wesson, Donald R., Carlin, Alert S., Adams, Kenneth M. & Beschner, George, eds. 1978. *Polydrug Abuse*, Academic Press, New York, pp. xix-128.

24. Clayton, Richard R. 1985. "Cocaine Use in the United States: In a Blizzard or Just Being Snowed," in *Cocaine Use in America: Epidemiologic and Clinical Perspectives*, NIDA Research Monograph No. 61, DHHS, Washington, D.C., pp. 8-34.

25. HHS News. 1980. "Report Shows Dramatic Increase in Use of Marijuana and Cocaine," Department of Health and Human Services, Washington, D.C., pp. 1-4.

26. Clayton, Richard R. , Voss, Harwin L., Robbins, Cynthia & Skinner, William F. 1986. "Gender Differences in Drug Use: An Epidemiological Perspective," in *Women and Drugs*, NIDA Research Monograph No. 65, DHHS, Washington, D.C., pp. 80-99.

27. O'Malley, Patrick M. 1985. "Cocaine Use Among American Adolescents and Young Adults," in *Cocaine Use in America: Epidemiologic and Clinical Perspectives*, NIDA Research Monograph No. 61, DHHS. Washington, D.C., pp. 50-75.

28. Adams, Edgar H. & Kozel, Nicholas J. 1985. "Cocaine Use in America: Introduction and Overview," *Cocaine Use in America: Epidemiologic and Clinical Perspectives*, NIDA Research Monograph No. 61, DHHS, Washington, D.C., pp. 1-7.

29. Mendelson, Jack H. & Mello, Nancy K. 1986. "Clinical Investigations of Drug Effects in Women," in *Women and Drugs*, NIDA Research Monograph No. 65, DHHS, Washington, D.C., pp. 21-30.

30. Hagan, T. 1988. "A Retrospective Search for the Etiology of Drug Abuse: A Background Comparison for a Drug Addicted Population of Women and a Control Group of Non Addicted Women," in *Problems of Drug Dependence 1987*, Proceedings of the 49th Annual Scientific Meeting, The Committee on Problems of Drug Dependence, Inc., NIDA Research Monograph No. 81, DHHS, Washington, D.C., pp. 254-261.

31. Gold, Mark S., Washton, Arnold M. & Dackis, Charles A. 1985. "Cocaine Abuse, Neurochemistry, Phenomenology and Treatment," in *Cocaine Use in Americans: Epidemiologic and Clinical Perspectives*, Kozel & Adams, eds., NIDA Research Monograph No. 61, DHHS, Washington, D.C., pp. 130-150.

2 The Spirit of the Czar: Selling Addictions to Women

Jean Kilbourne, Ed.D.

"Ads for alcohol and cigarettes stress freedom, independence, control and power because it is exactly these things that addiction takes away. The major symptom of addiction is dependence and powerlessness. To divert attention from this fact, the ads often portray the smoker or drinker as the independent man or woman who dares to defy public opinion, to stand on his or her own."

Heavy drinking and smoking used to be considered the province of men, indeed emblems of masculinity. It did not take the alcohol and tobacco industries long to realize that they could greatly increase their profits if they could expand the market to include women.

In 1929 Edward Bernays, the "father of public relations," was hired by American Tobacco to promote cigarette smoking by women. He did an excellent job. He hired ten women to march with the suffragists in the Easter Parade in New York and to smoke Lucky Strikes, asserting that their cigarettes were "torches of freedom." This was reported as news, rather than as an advertising campaign, and the spurious link between cigarettes and female independence was born, with lethal consequences for women.[1]

Bernays did not *create* the link between cigarette smoking and emancipation for women, but he certainly did more than simply reflect it. The cigarette was a symbol of liberation and independence for women in the 1920s for many political and cultural reasons. However, the advertising did a great deal to legitimize, normalize and promote this theme. It will probably never be possible to determine exactly the effects of advertising on smoking or drinking. There is no comparison group, no group that has not been affected by the bombardment. There are also too many co-varying events. It seems safe to say, however, that advertising played an important role in creating a climate in which cigarette smoking by women was seen as normal, acceptable, and even desirable, thereby encouraging more women to smoke. Some scholars believe that advertising was responsible for bringing women into the cigarette market.

Women took up smoking in greater and greater numbers. Today the only group in the society in which cigarette smoking is increasing is young girls. The American Cancer Society reports that girls under the age of eleven have become the largest new group of smokers in the country.[2] Twenty percent of young women graduating from high school smoke, versus 10 percent of the men.[3]

The health consequences of smoking are severe. Lung cancer has recently overtaken breast cancer as the leading cancer killer of women. Smoking increases a woman's chance of heart disease two to six times, increases her chance of lung cancer two to six times, and doubles her chance of cervical cancer.[4]

In addition to the personal risks to women who smoke, their babies run extra risks of low birth weight, fetal death, prematurity, fetal distress and other complications. According to the American Lung Association, the risk of miscarriage is 170 percent higher for heavy smokers (10 or more cigarettes a day), the risk of premature birth 300 percent higher and the risk of stillbirth 55 percent higher.[5]

Alcohol-related problems are also escalating among young women (and young men). The average age at which people begin to drink today is twelve. A recent national *Weekly Reader* survey found that 30 percent of 4th-graders have experienced peer pressure to drink alcohol. As many as 1 in 5 American teenagers (aged 14 to 17) may be a problem drinker.[6]

Regular drinking is common among high school girls and a sizeable number engage in heavy drinking. Teenage girls are drinking more like boys and thus, of course, experiencing more problems. Even the heavy drinkers who do not become alcoholic may well experience adverse consequences, such as accidents, suicide, sexual violence, eating disorders and teenage pregnancy.

Although alcoholism is an equal opportunity illness that seems to afflict women as often as men, there are some special problems for women. There is still a powerful double standard, and the consequences of alcohol abuse for women are often even more grim than for men. Most men leave their alcoholic wives, whereas most women stay with their alcoholic husbands. This, of course, has more to do with sex roles than with alcohol. Women are still often economically dependent on men and therefore cannot leave even desperate situations. Women are also socialized to be self-sacrificing. Men are much freer to leave, economically and and psychologically, and leave they do.

Recent research has found that women suffer greater physiological consequences from alcohol than do men. Women do not metabolize alcohol as well as men. Male and female alcoholics do not metabolize alcohol as well as nonalcoholics. Among alcoholic women, gastric metabolism is almost nonexistent.[7]

Most alcohol research has focused on White men. More research is urgently needed on all women and specifically on underserved groups such as women of color, older women and lesbians. Women of color are especially affected by alcohol-related problems. Death rates for chronic liver disease and cirrhosis, which are reliable indicators of alcoholism, are twice as high for African Americans of both sexes as for Whites. African American women between the ages of 15 and 34 have cirrhosis rates over 6 times those of White women, and Native American women ages 15 to 34 have a cirrhosis death rate 36 times that of White women.[8] Problem drinking by Hispanic women seems to be increasing with acculturation and is probably seriously underreported because of the strong cultural sanctions against it.

Fetal Alcohol Syndrome (FAS) is one of the top three known causes of birth defects with accompanying mental retardation—and the only preventable cause among those three. There is no known safe dose of alcohol during pregnancy, nor does there appear to be a safe time to drink during pregnancy. Native Americans are 33 times as likely as White women to have a child with FAS; for African American women, the rate is 6.7 times as high as for White women.[9]

Women who become alcoholic are likely to be cross-addicted, usually to legal prescription drugs. Alcoholism in women is often misdiagnosed by physicians and therapists. Symptoms of alcohol problems such as depression, anxiety, mood swings and irritability are usually treated with tranquilizers. These medications have a synergistic effect in combination with alcohol—and, of course, the underlying problem is neither diagnosed nor treated. Women consume two-thirds to three-quarters of all psychotropic drugs,

and tend to take them for much longer periods of time than do men.[10]

Although ads in medical journals rarely stereotype women as blatantly as they used to, they still usually show the doctor as male and the patient as female —and, of course, they offer drugs as solutions to all problems. This attitude is common in the popular media too. "Life got tougher. We got stronger" was a slogan for aspirin a few years ago, as if the proper response to difficulty in life is to take a stronger drug. Another ad features a door marked "Pharmacy" and the headline "Have you discovered the pain relief behind this door?" No wonder Americans spend an estimated $1.7 billion annually on nonprescription painkillers. Drug companies spend far more than $5,000 a year per doctor to introduce them to products.[11]

Alcohol, cigarettes, and other drugs are among the most heavily advertised products in the nation. Both the alcohol and tobacco industries spend well over two billion tax-deductible dollars a year on advertising. Anheuser-Busch's annual budget for just one brand, Budweiser, is greater than the entire federal budget for the National Institute on Alcohol Abuse and Alcoholism.[12] Less than one million dollars is spent by the government on public service announcements and pamphlets informing people of the dangers of smoking.

Advertising does not cause addiction. Addiction is complex and its etiology is uncertain. However, alcohol and cigarette advertising do create a climate in which dangerous attitudes toward alcohol and cigarettes are presented as normal, appropriate and innocuous. One of the chief symptoms of addiction is denial. It is often not only the addict who denies the problem but also his or her family, employer, doctor, etc. In general, as a society we tend to deny the disease and to support the alibi system of the addict. Advertising can encourage this denial. It can create a world in which myths about addiction are presented as true and in which signs of trouble are erased or transformed into positive attributes. It is difficult to get health messages taken seriously in such a climate, especially by young people, the major targets of advertisers.

Advertising is a powerful educational force in American society and one of the major health educators. A recent television commercial featured an actor who said, "I'm not a doctor, but I play one on TV," and then proceeded to peddle a drug. The average American is exposed to over 1,500 ads a day and will spend a year and a half of his or her life watching television commercials. The influence of advertising is cumulative and mostly unconscious. Each week TV reaches 90 percent of all children and 92 percent of all teenagers.[13]

Advertising creates a climate in which certain attitudes are presented as normal and therefore acceptable. In some instances, advertising creates needs; in others, it embellishes them. For example, human beings may have a need to be clean, but the American abhorrence of body odors is largely a result of advertising. It is not "natural" to prefer that the human body smell like a lemon or leather or flowers, but that attitude is *presented* as "natural" and thereby legitimized by advertising.

Advertising clearly has played a role in creating the current national obsession with excessive thinness for women. Women's magazines are filled with ads and articles featuring very rich food, articles on dieting, ads featuring very thin models and ads for diet products. This obsession supports a multi-billion-dollar diet industry, but it also ruins a lot of women's lives. A recent survey of 4th-grade girls found that 80 percent of them were on diets.[14] This in itself should be regarded as a major public health problem.

A primary reason that many women start and do not quit smoking is their terror of gaining weight. Ads have played upon this fear for a long time. In 1928 the Lucky Strike ads said, "To keep a slender figure, no one can deny . . . Reach for a Lucky instead of a sweet."

The advertisers probably couldn't get away with such an overt message today. They can, however, use extremely thin models and advertising copy that includes word such as "slim" or "slender," e.g., Virginia Slims. A recent campaign for Capri cigarettes features an attractive young woman and the heading, "The slimmest slim in town." This pitch is one major reason that cigarette smoking is on the increase among preteen and teenage girls, a group especially susceptible to obsession with weight.

Most advertising is essentially myth-making. The point of almost all national advertising is not to give us information about a product but rather to establish an image for the product. Advertising does this by linking the product with a quality or attribute. The jeans will make you sexy, the detergent will save your marriage, the car will give you confidence. An article in *Advertising Age* on liquor marketing stated that "product image is probably the most important element in selling liquor. The trick for marketers is to project the right message in their advertisements to motivate those often motionless consumers to march down to the liquor store or bar and exchange their money for a sip of image."[15]

The links are generally false and arbitrary but we are so surrounded by them that we come to accept them, to believe that they are logical and natural. This myth-making is always deceptive and often harmful. In the case of alcohol and tobacco advertising, however, it can be truly dangerous. It further convinces the addict (and often those around him or her) that the drugs are benevolent and essential. Most important, the adver-

tising spuriously links cigarettes and alcohol with precisely those attributes and qualities—happiness, wealth, prestige, sophistication, success, maturity, athletic ability, virility, creativity, sexual satisfaction and others—that addiction usually diminishes and destroys.

A central premise of the mythology is that alcohol is a magic potion that will make the user *powerful*. Sometimes the ads imply that alcohol will transform the user into a king or czar or other form of ruler (never a queen or czarina, however). Ironically, delusions of grandeur are often symptomatic of alcoholism. "The spirit of the Czar," one ad proclaims—and there he stands, in full regalia, lord and master of his surroundings. The woman is at his feet just like the dog (and indeed has a similar hairstyle). [See Figure 1.] The submissive pose of the woman is an important part of this message. Most men have little power in the society but can at least dominate women.

In fact, most czars were ruthless dictators who broke the spirit of the multitudes. Drugs, including alcohol, generally forestall revolutionary sentiments, deflect political energy, and make people feel that what is really social and political is "only personal." This is especially true for the powerless. The ads offer them a stone instead of bread. Alcohol offers a spurious route to power at the same time that it blocks real power. It gives the illusion of power instead, just as it sometimes gives the illusion of contact and intimacy while destroying relationships.

"Not every man can handle Metaxa," boasts another ad, implying again that powerful men drink heavily. Drinking becomes a way to prove one's manhood. Power is defined as success (as measured by wealth), control over others (especially women) and violence. These ads often feature a very dominant, ruthless image of masculinity. When this image of masculinity is linked with heavy drinking, violence is often the result. Women are often the victims of this violence. This is sometimes alluded to in the ads. One famous campaign featured a closeup of a woman's face and the headline, "Hit Me With a Club." Another ad featured a woman marching to the liquor store saying to herself, "This time I won't forget. When Ed says Scotch, he means Johnny Walker Red, Johnny Walker Red, Johnny Walker Red."

In addition to offering White men alcohol as a way to maintain and expand their power, the alcohol advertisers often target powerless groups in the society and offer alcohol to them as a route to power. Young people are heavily targeted and are told that alcohol can transform them into sophisticated and mature adults. Sometimes the alcohol is linked with very risky activities, as if to imply that it will give them courage and the ability to deal with challenges.

FIGURE 1.

People of color are told that alcohol can turn them into winners and can help them to "beat the system." Of course, when members of oppressed groups use alcohol in an attempt to beat the system, it isn't usually the system that ends up beaten. The life expectancy of White Americans is increasing while that of Black Americans has fallen. The decline is due to deaths from types of cancer linked to drinking and smoking, as well as AIDS and homicide. The death rate for cirrhosis of the liver is nearly twice as high for Blacks as for the rest of the population. Blacks also suffer disproportionately from cancer of the esophagus, which is linked with drinking and smoking, and from a high rate of alcoholism.[16]

At the same time, alcohol and tobacco companies spend millions of dollars supporting Black organizations (and women's organizations) such as the National Black Caucus, the National Association of Hispanic Journalists and the National Women's Political Caucus. In 1989, Philip Morris was the second largest advertiser in the Hispanic media; not surprisingly, it was named company of the year by the National Association of

BEEFEATER GIN
Se distingue claramente.

Beefeater tiene un sabor perfectamente balanceado, suave, seco...
de carácter extraordinario. Saboréelo con naranja, toronja,
tónico...con lo que sea.

Después de todo, cuando usted toma Beefeater, se distingue claramente.

Beefeater Gin. 94 grados prueba. 100% espíritus neutros. © 1987 Importado de Inglaterra por Kobrand Corp., N.Y., N.Y.

FIGURE 2.

Hispanic Publications.[17] The alcohol and tobacco companies also sponsor events such as the Kool Jazz Festival and the Ebony Fashion Fair. Many critics feel the companies are buying the silence of these organizations on health issues.

Billboards for alcohol and cigarettes are especially prevalent in low-income neighborhoods. Children are prime targets of these billboards, many of which are placed outside of schools. Cigarettes are the single most advertised product on billboards and alcohol is the second. A third of all billboards nationwide sell alcohol and cigarettes; in inner-city Black neighborhoods, this percentage doubles.[18]

Women and girls of color are doubly targeted and doubly oppressed. The health statistics are particularly grim for them. Black women contract heart disease 50 percent more often and lung cancer 50 percent more often than White women. Figures for Hispanics are even worse.[19] A 1989 report from the Center for Science in the Public Interest, entitled *Marketing Disease to Hispanics,* found that, "Hispanics are suffering from an ever-increasing number of health problems related to drinking and smoking. Traditionally, Hispanics have generally had lower rates of drinking and smoking than Whites, but recent studies indicate that Hispanics are catching up and even overtaking Whites in some categories. Most troubling, it appears that Hispanic youths—particularly female teenagers—are becoming increasingly hooked on alcoholic beverages and tobacco."[20] Not surprisingly, the report found that the alcohol and tobacco companies are increasing their efforts to target this group.

Some of the ads aimed at Hispanics trivialize and exploit important aspects of Hispanic culture. One features a priest and a monk gazing toward a light shining from above while holding glasses of brandy. Translated, the Spanish copy reads, "To drink it is not a sin." Some of the campaigns are tied into Hispanic celebrations such as Mexican Independence Day and Cinco de Mayo.[21] The beer industry also advertises heavily on Spanish-language radio and television stations, with many of the commercials featuring Hispanic sports figures and other celebrities. According to Juana Mora, research analyst at the University of California at Los Angeles (UCLA), "In the case of alcohol advertising to Latinos, there is a deliberate practice of influencing beliefs and behaviors by appealing to 'cultural nostalgia'—traditions, images and norms that many of us grew up with. . . . These powerful advertising companies totally undermine the educa-

tional efforts of families, schools, and non-profit organizations."[22] [See Figure 2.]

Women of color are also exploited in alcohol ads aimed at men. [Figure 3.] An Olde English malt liquor campaign links seductive images of women with wild animals and the "power" of malt liquor (a reference to the fact that malt liquor has 10 to 50 percent more alcohol than most other beers). These ads, which also run in Spanish and feature Latino models, have been criticized by Hispanic leaders for their blatant attempt to capitalize on the "macho" Latin stereotype.[23] One example is a billboard featuring a seminude Black woman (another version features a Latina) riding a tiger with the bold headline "It is the power!" [See Figure 4.] This is a similar promise to the "spirit of the Czar" ads and perhaps even more misleading.

This malt liquor ad also exemplifies the commonplace use of women in alcohol advertising as a symbol of the alcohol. For years the Black Velvet whisky campaign has featured a woman dressed in black velvet

FIGURE 3.

FIGURE 4.

saying something suggestive, such as "Try Black Velvet on tonight." The woman is the alcohol and the alcohol is the woman—they merge and become one and the same. The advertiser promises the male drinker that the alcohol will deliver sexual fulfillment.

Many ads use such double entendre. One college poster features a closeup of a woman's derriere with a can of beer next to it and the headline, "The best little can in Texas." Another alcohol ad pictures a very young woman in a white dress with the heading, "Put a little cherry in your life." Many sexualize the bottle and/or the drink itself. One campaign features extreme closeups of drinks with headlines such as "Seduce a slice" and "Arouse an olive." An ad for Miller beer features a closeup of a six-pack and the headline "Six Appeal." The copy says, "The next time you make eye contact with a six-pack of Cold-Filtered Miller Genuine Draft Longnecks, go ahead and pick one up. You won't be disappointed." Alcohol is offered as a replacement for as well as a route to intimacy.

Perhaps the most blatant example is a product called Nude Beer. The label features a woman in a bikini. The bikini top can be scratched off, revealing her bare breasts. [See Figure 5.] The objectification and dehumanization of women is commonplace in advertising for all kinds of products, but perhaps nowhere is it more blatant or insidious than in alcohol ads. This objectification creates a climate in which sexual harassment and other forms of violence against women flourish. Turning a human being into a thing is almost always the first step toward justifying violence against that being.

The alcohol ads generally emphasize hard-core sex to men and love and romance to women. This is particularly insidious given that alcohol abuse often leads to sexual dysfunction and to damaged relationships. "The romance never goes out of some marriages," coos an ad for a liqueur. The sad truth is that people with drinking problems are seven times more likely to be separated or divorced than the general population. [24]

In addition to promising love and romance to women, alcohol advertisers often promise power and freedom. "Break tradition," proclaims a series of rum ads that feature women in athletic gear. "Now that you're bringing home the bacon," another ad proclaims, "don't forget the Chivas."

These ads are analogous to the long-running and infamous Virginia Slims campaign, "You've come a long way, baby," which astonishingly equates liberation with addiction, freedom with enslavement to tobacco. [See Figure 6.] This equation is particularly ironic, given that nicotine is the most addictive drug of all, and that at least 85 percent of all smokers wish they could quit. [25] The only equality that smoking has given women is that they are now getting lung cancer at the same rate as men. One can only consider cigarette smoking liberating if one considers death the ultimate freedom.

The proof of women's progress is that we now have our own cigarette. However, there is never any hint in the Virginia Slims ads of the wider world, the world in which women are still making 70 cents or less for every

FIGURE 5.

dollar men make, the world in which a woman is beaten every 15 seconds, the world in which one of every three women can expect to be raped in their lifetime. The vignettes in the background of the ads picture the dismal past, those distant times in which women were oppressed, juxtaposed with today's skinny, liberated woman, flaunting her very own cigarette. Who needs equal rights?

In a very subtle way, however, the ads themselves acknowledge that there has been no real change. Although the model seemingly is proclaiming that she is liberated, her pose, dress, makeup and demeanor are always stereotypically feminine. There is never a hint of feminism. The model is never shown *doing* anything except laughing, holding a cigarette and wearing stylish clothes. She is never working or in any way demonstrating her liberation and independence. She's playing at being liberated. And she's still a "baby."

It is also telling that the Virginia Slims ads that feature women of color leave out the vignettes. [See Figure 7 and Figure 8.] A vignette showing an oppressed woman of color would not be funny or ironic nor would it seem to belong to the past. It would be a striking statement that there has been very little progress and the symbolic cigarette, the "torch of freedom," would seem like a mockery. It is a mockery, for White women as well, but this is far more obvious in the case of women of color.

One of the most insidious aspects of the promise of power via the drugs offered in the ads is that it is often feelings of powerlessness that lead people to rely on drugs in the first place. For example, the lower one's status, income and educational achievements today (i.e., the less powerful one is in the society), the more likely one is to smoke.[26]

Far from being a route to power, addictions rob individuals of power and deprive the whole group of some of the collective energy necessary to achieve real power and status in the society, instead of the illusory power offered in the advertising. Addictions lead to increased feelings of helplessness, powerlessness, dependence and despair. Effective action for social change requires clarity, energy and a sense of purpose, qualities that addictions diminish.

Advertising could be considered the propaganda of American society. It is both a creator and perpetuator of the dominant attitudes, values and ideology of the culture, the social norms and myths by which most people govern their behavior. Advertising performs much the same function in industrial society as myth performed in ancient and primitive societies (and with a similar conservative effect). Advertising often reduced complex sociopolitical problems to personal ones, thereby both trivializing the issues and diverting energy and attention from a search for genuine solutions.

Advertising generally co-opts and trivializes any movement for profound change in the society. ERA is a laundry detergent and New Freedom is a maxipad. Sometimes the co-optation can seem trivial, as when an ad proclaiming to women, "So you're out to change the world, we can do it together," turns out to be for shoe coloring. When the product is a drug, however, and

FIGURE 6.

when members of oppressed groups are told that this drug can help them to "beat the system" and "break tradition," then the whole issue becomes profoundly political. It may well be that there is more at stake here than simply increased profits for the alcohol and tobacco industries. "The spirit of the Czar" indeed.

Increased drinking and smoking among women is advertised as and often believed to be a symbol of liberation. In reality, these products are drugs which diffuse energy, mask continuing inequality and its effects, and distract many women from the real struggle. Women are particularly likely to use drugs to numb their anger. Anger is such a taboo emotion for women that we are not even supposed to feel it, let alone act on it. Far better to take a tranquilizer or a drink, smoke a cigarette or eat another piece of cake. Research indicates that it is far more difficult for women than men to quit smoking because women are more likely to use cigarettes to cope with negative feelings such as anger, stress and depression.[27]

You've come a long way, baby.

MENTHOL

VIRGINIA SLIMS

Menthol: 15 mg "tar," 1.1 mg nicotine—Lights Menthol:
5 mg "tar," 0.7 mg nicotine av. per cigarette by FTC method.

SURGEON GENERAL'S WARNING: Quitting Smoking
Now Greatly Reduces Serious Risks to Your Health.

Slimmer than the fat menthol
cigarettes men smoke. And rightly so.

FIGURE 7.

Ads for alcohol and cigarettes stress freedom, independence, control and power because it is exactly these things that addiction takes away. The major symptom of addiction is dependence and powerlessness. To divert attention from this fact, the ads often portray the smoker or drinker as the independent man or woman who dares to defy public opinion, to stand on his or her own.

Teenage girls are especially vulnerable to this pitch. An American Cancer Society report found that cigarette smoking among teenage girls was highly identified with an anti-authority, rebellious syndrome in terms of the adult world. One Lucky Strike campaign features very defiant-looking young women with the caption, "Light my Lucky."

Virginia Slims cleverly plays on this attitude in many of their ads. In one ad, an older, rather Victorian looking woman is complaining about young women, "Shocking, absolutely shocking, the way young women cavort about these days," and another says, "Tsk. Tsk. Proper decent women shouldn't have fun in the sun. In fact, they shouldn't have any fun at all." A young

woman replies, "Well, shame on me, 'cause I really like to have fun." Certainly these older women are meant to represent mothers, teachers and other adults who might tell young women, among other things, not to smoke. A rebellious adolescent might hear this as an edict against having fun.

The tobacco industry is attempting to get even more mileage from this image by portraying public health advocates as anti-smoking fanatics who want to tell everybody else what to do and setting them against the courageous, independent, free-thinking smoker. Their extraordinary public relations campaign equates smoking with freedom and the criticism of smoking with totalitarianism. The alcohol industry has jumped on this bandwagon too. Philip Morris (makers of Miller Beer and Virginia Slims and other cigarettes) has a new campaign linking itself with the Bill of Rights.

The tobacco and alcohol industries have insidiously positioned themselves on the side of autonomy and freedom. Their critics need to expose the truth—that cigarette smoking and alcohol abuse are dangerous addictions deliberately promoted by callous industries that care only for profit. We also need to help people, especially the young, realize that by smoking and drinking they are giving in to conformity rather than expressing their individuality. They are allowing themselves to be manipulated by two very powerful industries. The most effective incentives against smoking and drinking for young people involve an emphasis on the importance of physical well-being and the need to be an independent thinker.

Advertising is an over $130 billion industry.[28] Although the individual ads are stupid and trivial, the consequences of their cumulative impact are often serious. Advertising, of course, is not solely responsible for any of the problems in the society. It is by no means the only source of sex-role stereotyping or of anti-health messages, perhaps not even the most important one. The power of an endless barrage of images should not be underestimated, however.

We also should not underestimate the true role of advertising in our society. The primary purpose of the mass media is to deliver audiences to advertisers. Everything else is secondary. Magazines court the

FIGURE 8.

Figure 9.

alcohol and cigarette industries' advertising in full-page ads placed in *Advertising Age* and other publications aimed at advertisers. "Attention alcoholic beverage marketing executives," proclaims an ad for *Family Circle* magazine, "American women make up 48% of your market. You need to reach our 16 million to earn your market share." An ad placed in *Advertising Age* by *Cosmopolitan* magazine says, "Cosmopolitan readers drank 21,794,000 glasses of beer in the last week. . . . Isn't it time you gave Cosmopolitan a shot?"[See Figure 9] An ad for *Ebony* magazine features a

champagne bottle bursting open and the headline, "Uncork the Black market." Needless to say, these magazines (and television programs) rarely give us accurate information about these drugs.

Alcohol and tobacco industry money buys more than advertising. It all too often buys silence throughout the media on these major drug problems. It is no coincidence that the "war on drugs" is routinely silent on the two major killers. The "war on drugs" leads people to believe that cocaine is America's major drug problem. However, in 1988, cocaine and crack killed about 3,300 people. Alcohol is linked with ten percent of all deaths in the nation (at least 100,000 deaths a year). Cigarettes kill 1,000 people every day.[29]

It is important to examine and be aware of advertising and to call for bans and counterads not only because of the message of such advertising but because of this censorship. We shouldn't get involved in the argument about whether such ads increase consumption or not; at the very least, they create a climate in which two major drugs are seen as benevolent and and they prevent the media from doing an honest job of discussing these drugs.

Those of us who sincerely care about the health of women and of others in the society must work to expose this form of censorship and these marketing strategies. We should insist on counteradvertising and increased taxation of alcohol and cigarettes. We must work to change the conditions in our society that so often lead to despair and addiction—poverty, racism, sexism, violence, the collapse of our educational system, the destruction of our environment. We must stop valuing corporate profits more than human needs. We must encourage women and other people who have been conditioned to feel powerless to develop authentic routes to power. Above all, we must work together to create the kind of society that would welcome such advances.

References

1. Barnouw, E. (1978). *The Sponsor*. NY: Oxford University Press.
2. *National NOW Times* (1982, June/July).
3. "In college more women smoke than men." (1986, July 8). *New York Times*, p. C8.
4. National Women's Health Network News Release (1986, June 16).
5. Rovner, S. (1985, January 25). "The wooing of the woman smoker." *The Times-Picayune* (New Orleans), p. D-3.
6. National Council on Alcoholism (1986). *Alcoholism and other alcohol-related problems among children and youth*.
7. "The alcohol gender gap." (1990, January 22). *Newsweek*, p. 53.
8. National Council on Alcoholism (1987, August). *A federal response to a hidden epidemic: Alcohol and other drug problems among women*, p. 35.
9. Harbison, G. (1989, August 28). "Alcohol's youngest victims." *Time*, p. 3.
10. Lee, B.L. (1982, June 1). "What price tranquility?" *The Journal*, p. 16.
11. Diamant, A. (1986, April 4). "What doctors recommend most is . . ." *Boston Globe*, p.35.
12. *The Alcoholism Report* (1987, March 17), vol. 15, no. 10, p.3.
13. Center for Science in the Public Interest, Washington, DC (1985). Project SMART pamphlet.
14. "Can low-cal Gerbers be far behind?" (1986, June). *New Age Journal*, p. 12.
15. Nathanson-Moog, C. (1984, July 26). "Brand personalities undergo psychoanalysis." *Advertising Age*, p. 18.
16. "Alcohol, tobacco and Black Americans." (1990, Winter). *Prevention File*, p. 81.
17. Ibid., p. 22.
18. McMahon, E. (1988, February 21). Killer billboards. *The Washington Post*.
19. "Why big tobacco targets minorities." (1990, January 29). *Adweek's Marketing Week*, p. 21.
20. Maxwell, B. and Jacobson, M. (1989, September). *Marketing Disease to Hispanics*. Washington, DC: Center for Science in the Public Interest, p. ix.
21. Ibid, p. 31.
22. Ibid, pp. 36-37.
23. "Alcohol, tobacco and Black Americans." (1990, Winter). *Prevention File*, p. 8.
24. *Harvard Medical School Health Letter*. (1987, July), p. 1.
25. Rothschild, B. (1985, November 20). "Smokeout targets women." *USA Today*, p. 3A.
26. Blair, G. (1979, January). "Why Dick can't stop smoking." *Mother Jones*, p. 40.
27. Jacobson, B. (1982). *The Ladykillers: Why Smoking is a Feminist Issue*. NY: Continuum.
28. *Special Events Report* (1989, December 25), vol. 8, no. 24.
29. Lapham, L. (1989, December). "A political opiate." *Harper's Magazine*, p. 45.

3 Coyote Returns: Survival for Native American Women

Robin A. LaDue, Ph.D.

"The loss of cultural ties and values contributes greatly to Indian alcoholism. Women who are away from their traditional centers of support, be it familial, spiritual or communal, appear to be at higher risk for alcohol abuse."

Introduction: When Coyote* Was There

It has now been almost five hundred years since Columbus first set sight on the "New World." It may be safe to say that the myths and misconceptions about Native American people started at that time. The first error was that Columbus "discovered" a world already inhabited by millions of people who had lived there for thousands of years.[1,2] The second myth, a precursor to the negative stereotypes of Native people today, was the concept of Indian people as "savages," noble or otherwise. Another damaging notion was the concept of "Manifest Destiny" which stated that the "New World" was open to conquest by war, plunder and religious conversion due to the lower status of the Native inhabitants. None of these myths acknowledged the humanness, dignity, cultural richness and diversity or achievements of the people already living in the "New World." In addition, such attitudes permitted the near annihilation of the millions of aboriginal people living in the Americas.[3-6]

Because of past and present attitudes towards Native

---

* Coyote (Trickster) was often used as an example to teach Native children how to survive in the world, the rights and wrongs, and the way of the People.

The critical issue facing American Indian women today is the same issue that has always existed: survival. With this in mind, this chapter is written to help people become more aware of the pluses and negatives of being a Native woman in the 1990s. The author says, "*I write from a singular perspective, drawing on my years of working in Indian communities and from watching my own tribe attempt to survive the onslaught of contemporary society. I do not purport to speak for all Native women or to imply that my own perceptions and experiences define any 'universal' truth about Native women. If the information in this chapter helps make even one more person more aware of the struggles and successes faced daily by Native women, I will have accomplished what I intended.*"

The author wishes to thank Herbert J. Cross, Ph.D., Ann P. Streissguth, Ph.D.; Sandra P. Randels, MSN; Alicia Ellis; Gerald and John-Paul Carriveau and especially, Dr. William Willard.

people, the critical issue facing American Indian women as we approach the 500th anniversary of Columbus's arrival is survival; as individuals, as cultural entities, as tribal groups and as contributing partners in contemporary American society. For American Indian people life is a circle—a connection of all things and all people, of the physical, spiritual and emotional world.[3-5] Critical problems facing Native women today include the particularly high rate of alcoholism and the increasing rate of drug abuse found in Indian communities. Substance abuse in the Native population breaks the circle of life and contributes to other problems such as an increased risk of alcohol-related birth defects, family disruption, community disruption and health, education and economic problems. Native groups have experienced extreme family and cultural disruption over the past two hundred years. The current levels of drug and alcohol abuse are contributing factors to the continuing destruction of Native communities. As long as the high level of substance abuse continues, the survival of many Native people remains tenuous.[7-10] Sad to say, while a substantial body of alcoholism research exists, there is still little concrete information on the current level of drug use in Indian communities. There are few cultural-specific prevention and treatment programs.[11] This chapter will focus primarily on alcohol abuse as an obstacle to survival and present information regarding drug use and interacting issues such as high school dropout rates, economic deprivation, cultural disintegration and the loss of effective role models for Native youth.

The Loss of Coyote

The majority of the health and social problems facing American Indian women today have their roots in history. It is difficult to fully understand and appreciate the issues of contemporary life for Indian women without becoming familiar with historical events. Contrary to popular belief, there is no "typical" Indian.[1,2] There are over three hundred tribes in the lower forty-eight states and close to two hundred Native organizations in Alaska, each with its own language, culture, history, government and values.

The Time of the Survival Pact

Prior to the time of contact between Native people and Europeans (ranging from the later fifteenth century to the mid-nineteenth century, depending on geographic location), there was a close tie between the environment and social rules. This interdependence has been described as the "Survival Pact."[12] The central concept of the Pact is that the survival of the entire community depends upon individuals within the community obeying the particular rules of the Pact and fulfilling their expected roles.

The stringency of Pact rules was largely dependent upon the harshness of the physical environment. The West Coast, where resources were abundant, had more relaxed rules than the Arctic. The laws of the Pact touched on all aspects of life including marriage, medicine, food gathering, hunting and fishing, religious practices and social encounters. Pact laws were passed from generation to generation. Children were socialized into their expected roles as they grew. Failure to comply with the rules of the Pact resulted in a variety of punishments ranging from social ridicule or ostracism to death.

Tribal structure centered around kinship groups and included cousins, aunts and uncles, as well as siblings and grandparents. It is impossible to make any completely accurate generalizations regarding the status of women, given the cultural diversity of the Native groups. In some tribal groups, women had leadership roles and there are cases where women participated as warriors. Taboos regarding women's roles did exist in many tribal groups, but varied from community to community. As might be expected, many of these taboos and accompanying rituals centered on menstruation and childbirth.[3,4,6]

Certain tribal groups were matrilineal with family identification passed to the next generation through the mother.[13] Whether leadership positions were held by males or females, both genders had significance in the established cultural practices and values that allowed for a continuity of child-rearing practices and permitted the community to survive and prosper.

Deviant behavior was frequently defined in spiritual terms such as "soul loss" or "object intrusion" where the spirit had to be healed to help the body mend.[5,12] The practice of healing was ritualistic and often involved the patient's entire family and/or community. Many tribal groups had both male and female shamans (healers). A woman could gain status in her tribe as a practitioner of medicine.[13]

Religious practices and spiritual beliefs were defined within the guidelines of the Survival Pact. Coyote (Trickster) stories were often used to illustrate what happened to people when they failed to follow the Survival Pact rules.

Much of the information available about precontact life comes from ethnographic accounts and from post-contact collections of myths and legends. The knowledge that is available points to a way of life that was closely linked to the physical world and one that required each individual in the community to fulfill an expected role for the survival and benefit of the entire group. The roles of women varied greatly from tribe to tribe and region to region with women having equal or near equal status to men in specific groups.[3,4,6,13]

The Time of Manifest Destiny

"Manifest Destiny" is the term used to define the doctrine of possession of the entire North American continent. The period of Manifest Destiny describes the time between contact until just after the Spanish American War in the early years of the 20th century. Consequences of this era include the decimation of Native people and their cultures. The devastation took many forms, such as the destruction of the buffalo on the Plains, starvation, widespread smallpox, influenza, and measles epidemics, tuberculosis, forced removal from their lands, war, and ultimately, alcohol and drug abuse.[14,15] The negative consequences and attitudes so prevalent during the era of Manifest Destiny remain today and continue to shape the lives of Native women.[16,17]

Formal policies of relocation of Indian people from their ancestral lands began at this time. It was in 1829, under the direction of Andrew Jackson, that this policy was most cruelly demonstrated. Jackson's policy of Indian removal resulted in the forced march of the five civilized tribes from the southeast region of the country to Indian Territory, later to become the state of Oklahoma. The conditions of this march were severe and contributed to the deaths of thousands of members of these tribes. The route taken during the removal of the tribes has became known, quite appropriately, as the Trail of Tears.[12,14]

The practice of forced removal of Indian people continued with the development of the reservation system, a much-debated point of contention at the time of implementation. The elimination of many reservations, placement of rival bands on the same reservation, poverty, starvation, disease, the forced removal of Indian children from their families to boarding schools, loss of population and tribal leadership, disintegration of traditional practices and the passage of legislation prohibiting the practice of Indian languages, religion and customs led to the crushing of the spirit of Indian people.[18,19] The boarding schools, run by both the Federal government and Christian religious denominations, were intended to remove any trace of Indianness from Native children and to facilitate assimilation.[20]

The imposition of Christianity on Indian people was part of a larger social attitude that denigrated the dignity and usefulness of Indian traditions and customs. It led to thousands of Indian children being taken from their parents and communities and raised in an environment (the boarding schools) that devalued and condemned their Indianness. Parenting skills, formerly passed from generation to generation, were lost, as were the knowledge and social roles that had been an integral part of the Survival Pact. The devaluing of Indian culture and practices, separation of children from their families, loss of language and disruption of knowledge that led to healthy functioning resulted in enormous problems for Indian communities and individuals. If communities cannot raise their own children in healthy ways, whether because of the removal of children by outside forces or due to poor parenting skills, they have little on which to build their future. Indeed, this is often the case for Indian people as the 1990s begin.

The Time of Assimilation

Military resistance on the part of Native peoples ended with the massacre of over two hundred Indian people at Wounded Knee, South Dakota in 1890, marking the beginning of the "official" policies of assimilation, termination and relocation. The psychological state of American Indians during this time has been described as "helplessly low," with depression, alcoholism, violence and disease occurring in epidemic proportions on reservations and among Native people who had been relocated.[21,22]

Overall, the situation for both urban and reservation Indians during the time period from the late 1800s to the mid-1970s was grim and inevitable given the historical events previously described. It is highly unlikely that any group of people who had suffered the conquest, oppression and genocide of the American Indian could continue to exist were not some coping mechanisms developed. Unfortunately, alcoholism, depression, violence, suicide, and more recently, drug abuse have all too often become the coping skills of "choice."[23]

The Time of Self-Determination and Renewal

Relief from the continuing despair seen in Indian people came in the form of the Indian Self-Determination Act of 1975, the Indian Health Care Improvement Act of 1976, the Indian Child Welfare Act of 1978 and the Indian Religious Freedom Act of 1978. The Indian

Self-Determination Act reaffirmed the rights of Indian people to choose their own form of government and destiny. The Indian Health Care Improvement Act brought the deplorable state of Indian health to the forefront and, for a brief period of time, there was an increase in badly needed health programs and services.

The Indian Child Welfare Act helped stop the flow of Indian children from their families and communities into non-Indian foster and adoptive care. It gave Indian tribes the right to make decisions for their children when placements were needed and established in formal policy that Indian children have the right of access to their native culture. It is only if an appropriate Indian home cannot be found that Indian children are to be placed in a non-Indian home. The impetus for this legislation came from the mass removal of Indian children to boarding schools and the failure to acknowledge the rights of Indian parents.[19,20]

The Indian Religious Freedom Act gave Native people back the right to practice their religious beliefs and customs.[24-26] These customs formed the backbone for traditional Indian life and the acknowledgment of their validity has helped spark a spiritual renewal. Many of these practices have "come out of the closet" and are now used in conjunction with Western medical practices.[12]

Searching for Coyote: Into the 1990s

There are approximately 1.4 million American Indians in this country according to the 1980 census, double the number since the 1970 census. Half live in urban areas and the rest on reservations in rural areas. Because American Indians are the only minority group in this country that has a government-to-government relationship with the Federal government, there are now recognized and nonrecognized tribes. Recognized tribes are those with a formal relationship with the Federal government and their lands may have trust status. People enrolled in federally recognized tribes are eligible for services through the Indian Health Services (IHS) and the Bureau of Indian Affairs (BIA). Other Indians belong to nonrecognized and/or terminated tribes. Terminated tribes previously had a formal relationship to the Federal government which was later abrogated.

Many tribes follow Federal precedent and enroll on the basis of blood quantum, usually one-quarter or more. Some tribes, due to declining populations, are electing to enroll on the basis of descendency rather than quantum. Splits and legal definitions have led to innumerable arguments between and within tribes as to who is and who is not an Indian. However, the legal status of Indian people carries serious implications, particularly in the delivery of critically needed health and social services.

Alcoholism and American Indian Women

The triad of alcoholism, violence, and depression has been cited as the most serious social and health problem facing Indian women.[24] The rates of these three problems have greatly increased in both urban and reservation Indian communities in the past twenty-five years.[9] A vicious circle exists between the problems of alcohol and drug abuse and other social and health issues present in Indian country, such as diabetes, high dropout rates, domestic violence and child abuse. The high use of alcohol and drugs can be seen as indicative of underlying social and mental health problems as well as a problem in and of itself. At some point, the "chicken-egg" argument becomes moot. What is critical is how alcohol and drugs contribute to the breaking of the circle of life.

Why Do Indian Women Drink?

Studies to determine *why* American Indian women drink are few although alcoholism, as an Indian problem, has been studied in great detail and several theories have been postulated.[8,27,28] A common notion, supported by the popular myths of the "drunken Indian and her firewater" is that Indians literally cannot safely drink. Some researchers argue that Indians have a deficiency in their ability to metabolize alcohol. Other studies do not support this idea, and the definitive answer to a biological component of Indian alcoholism has not been found. The hypothesis that many Indian people learned to consume alcohol rapidly before they went back onto "dry" reservation land and, thus, learned to drink to get drunk has also been put forth.[24-26]

Other researchers feel that there is an intricate pattern of social and historical factors that lead to a cultural-specific pattern of drinking. This pattern evolves from the historical breakdown of traditional family and community life through the boarding schools and relocation programs, increasing cultural identity problems, exposure to alcohol at a very early age and often within the family setting, a high social pressure to drink, loss of clear roles, low self-esteem and models of excessive drinking.[10,21] A "typical" pattern of drinking among Indian women is dissimilar to what may be found among other groups of women. For example, Indian women may be more likely to drink in bars with their men, to drink to intoxication each time alcohol is consumed, to begin drinking at a very early age and to experience significant peer pressure to drink. Furthermore, there may not be strong community and/or family sanctions against drinking.[27]

It should be remembered that drinking is *not* a traditional Indian value or behavior and that many Indian people do not drink at all. Alcoholic beverages are not allowed at traditional ceremonies and alcohol consumption is contrary to the practice of traditional Indian values. The loss of cultural ties and values contributes greatly to Indian alcoholism. Women who are away from their traditional centers of support, be it familial, spiritual or communal, appear to be at higher risk for alcohol abuse. Native women still drink less than their male counterparts but available data indicates that they suffer from alcohol-related illnesses, such as cirrhosis, at a rate 37 percent higher than their non-Indian agemates.[29] Unfortunately, biology is still destiny and the use of alcohol by Indian women, particularly those in their child-bearing years, is significantly more dangerous than for their male counterparts.[28,30]

Health Problems Among Native American Women: Diabetes, Obesity and Alcohol

It is somewhat ironic to note that the problems associated with alcohol abuse and alcoholism, such as cirrhosis, hepatitis, gout and malnutrition, are the same as many of the health concerns that plague Native women. Diabetes is a significant health problem among American Indian women and contributes to other physical difficulties such as renal failure, disorders of the eyes, cardiovascular accidents and high-risk pregnancies. Researchers have explored the high rate of diabetes among American Indians and possible causal factors. Heredity, environment, diet, alcoholism and obesity are all cited.

Obesity seems to be the most important factor in the causation of diabetes and is common among American Indian women for a variety of reasons. Native people have traditionally depended upon a subsistence way of living, such as hunting and fishing. A cash economy was forced upon Native people along with the implementation of the reservation system and relocation programs. The change from a subsistence to cash economy created a high level of poverty among Native women and dependence upon surplus commodities such as flour, butter and milk that continues today. A diet based on commodities, coupled with a woman's inability to purchase healthy food for her family, increases the risk for future health problems.

Poor nutrition, whether it be due to poverty or alcohol and drug use, is also a problem among pregnant Indian women. Infant mortality rates among Indian populations appear to have dropped in recent years, but this may not be true for reservation communities because of the deficit of services that occurred during the 1980s. American Indian women get pregnant before the age of twenty at a rate twice the national average.[24-26] Teenage mothers are high-risk mothers not only due to their age, but also because of their poor nutrition practices, low participation in prenatal care and the increased probability of substance use and abuse.[23,28] Teenage mothers are more likely to be single, school dropouts and dependent upon welfare for support. These factors, particularly for young women who are away from family and community, contribute to a higher risk of child abuse, neglect, and foster placements for Indian children.[22]

Fetal Alcohol Syndrome and Fetal Alcohol Effects among Native Women

Fetal Alcohol Syndrome (FAS) is a cluster of lifelong birth defects resulting from the mother's prenatal abuse of alcohol. The diagnostic criteria for FAS include growth deficiency, a characteristic pattern of physical malformations, central nervous system dysfunction and mental retardation. Studies have shown that FAS occurs at the rate of 1 in 750 births for the general population.[31] However, the incidence of FAS in some Native populations may be as high as 1 in 50 births.[32] The presence of FAS and FAE (Fetal Alcohol Effects) are tragic symptoms of the alcoholism problem found among Native women and reinforce the notion of the "drunken Indian" which so many Native people themselves believe.

Alcoholic women who have children with FAS and FAE die at a much higher rate than mothers of children with other disabilities. Data from a 1987 study indicated that 60 percent of the mothers who had given birth to children with either FAS or FAE were dead at the time of follow-up, usually by the time the child was five years of age.[33] Children with FAS/FAE who are raised in alcoholic homes during their early years are at increased risk of neglect, physical and sexual abuse, sexual promiscuity and abandonment.[34] Alcoholic mothers are more likely to have difficulties maintaining a calm, nurturing and healthy environment. This is not because alcoholic women do not love their children, despite the societal picture of drunken women, but more from the debilitating effects of alcoholism.

American Indian communities need healthy children to ensure the necessary leadership and survival of their communities and traditions. Alcoholic Indian women producing affected children compromise this goal and compromise the health of the entire Native community.[35] An inability to maintain sobriety has frequently resulted in the termination of maternal rights for Indian women.[24-26,33] Foster placements, prior to the enactment of the Indian Child Welfare Act in 1978, were usually outside the Indian community.[22] The rights of the affected child to have a safe, nurturing home are particularly important since it is difficult for these children to overcome the psychosocial problems that result from alcoholic and/or abusive, neglectful homes. It is critical that Indian people be allowed to raise their own children, given the historical consequences of the forced removal of Indian children from their homes, but these homes need to be safe and nurturing. This is a major problem, given the rate of alcoholism among Indian women and the long-term and serious difficulties associated with FAS and FAE.

Alcohol's Impact: Depression, Domestic Violence, Child Abuse, and Neglect

The contribution of alcoholism to depression and domestic violence is frequently postulated and seems to be supported by the available data.[24-26] However, it is too simplistic to say that alcoholism is *the* cause of depression or violence among Indian women.[27,36] The loss of cultural identity, lack of healthy role models, little community support, poverty, a high level of personal and community loss and the sense of no future have led to depression among Native women. Alcohol is used to "treat" the depression, but ultimately leads to more depression and subsequent self-destructive behavior such as suicide. A vicious circle of depression and alcohol leads many Indian women to feel that a sad, unhealthy life is inevitable.[27]

Depression, frustration, few community resources, a sense of personal failure, a family history of violence and a higher level of community acceptance of violence coupled with excessive alcohol use creates an atmosphere where violence becomes "normal" and an "acceptable" way to solve family disputes.[9] Alcohol tends to lower behavioral inhibitions and increases the risk of violence.

Some sources indicate that child neglect and abuse occur in Indian homes at twice the national average.[24-26] This may or may not be true. Factors that do seem to contribute to child abuse and neglect include poverty, parental alcohol abuse and poor parenting skills. Single mothers are particularly vulnerable to the cycle of alcohol abuse and child neglect because of their lack of financial resources, parental skills and family and community support.

Sexual abuse was also "taboo" in traditional Indian culture, but has become a problem in some Indian communities.[13] Sexual abuse is more likely to occur in families where such behavior has become "acceptable" and where women are unable to provide protection for their children.[37] A mother who is unable to maintain her sobriety is less likely to be able to provide a safe environment.[33] Children who grow up in a violent and/or sexually abusive home are more likely to repeat the same patterns, and the circle of life remains broken.

Alcohol's Impact on Education and Economics

The high school dropout rate among both urban and reservation Indian youth is a major concern for Indian women. The percentage of Indian youth who fail to graduate from high school is often over 50 percent.[22] Reasons cited for why Indian youth drop out of school include teacher insensitivity to Indian culture, hostility and prejudice towards Indians, curricula which emphasize majority culture values and beliefs and the lack of Indian personnel in schools.[22] In addition, lack of supportive role models in the education process has a negative impact on self-concept among Indian youth. Poor self-concept leads to low self-esteem and an increased risk of drug and alcohol use.[11] Indian youth who drop out of school frequently find themselves at "loose ends" and unable to compete in the job market. Pregnancy and motherhood may give Indian girls a sense of identity and value, but without adequate resources the cycle of poverty, depression and alcoholism continues.

American Indian women are frequently the head of the household. Family and community support, access to traditional subsistence forms of living and access to commodities to help feed the family may be more available in reservation communities. Indian women in urban settings may have to turn to the welfare system for financial aid. Indian women are apt to have a distrust of "helping" agencies and a reluctance to accept aid from "strangers." Many Indian mothers are young and may not have enough knowledge to wend their way through the tangle of red tape that so often accompanies receiving welfare, food stamps and medical care.

Indian women who do graduate from high school and/or college find few jobs available on reservations where the unemployment rate may run as high as 80%. They may have to relinquish traditional Indian values and practices to fit into the "9 to 5" world. They may find themselves caught between two worlds of conflicting priorities. It is not uncommon for Indian women to be the only Native person in their place of employment (unless it is in an Indian agency or on a reservation). The sense of isolation they may feel can lead to an increased risk of self-doubt, depression and alcohol abuse.[22]

Many Indian women have never formally entered the job market. They practice subsistence living or are seasonally employed in areas such as fishing and timber. Indian women often feel they face racial discrimination in hiring practices, although there are laws prohibiting such actions. It is difficult to document discrimination in hiring but it is true that there are very few qualified Indian women in upper management or in advanced training and education programs.

Several programs have been started (and terminated) to help Indian women receive job training. The now defunct CETA program was an example. Unfortunately, few programs have been implemented in a meaningful way in Indian country. Tribal input has not been sought and there seems to be little commitment from outside agencies to continue these programs.[22]

Drug Abuse

Alcohol use among Indian youth has been high for many years and the level of drug use is beginning to increase. Marijuana and other substances such as crack, amphetamines, sedatives and barbiturates are now being used along with alcohol.[38] Most of the information about drug use among Indian youth is anecdotal, as there are very few studies available regarding this problem.

Alcohol and drug use among Indian youth contribute to difficulties with other family members, a loss of healthy, nondrug-using friends, lower academic achievements and poor social adaptation. The reasons cited for drug use parallel those given for alcohol use *and* for dropping out of school. These include feelings of low self-worth and powerlessness, as well as the stress of being caught between two conflicting cultures.[39]

Coyote Returns

Service Delivery Recommendations: Alcoholism and Mental Health

Health programs for Indian women are typically publicly funded and administered by the Indian Health Service (IHS), a branch of the Public Health Service. Programs in urban areas are available through the local Indian Health Boards. These programs were cut dramatically when Ronald Reagan took office in 1980.

Indian communities and urban Indian centers are attempting to build outreach programs to prevent, treat and rehabilitate Indian women and youth with drug and alcohol problems. A significant problem with many treatment programs is that there are no cultural components addressing the special values of Indian women. The majority of programs have few or no Indian staff members.[22] The following recommendations are offered to increase the ability of programs to serve Indian women:

1. Early and intensive education programs to teach Indian children their own value and the value of their culture, and how alcohol takes these strengths away.
2. Acknowledgment of the cultural traditions, strengths and values that Indian people possess.
3. Integration of mental health services, drug treatment and alcoholism programs, and the inclusion of traditional healers in these programs.
4. Respect for the spiritual beliefs and practices of each client.
5. Flexibility in where, when and how services are provided, such as home visits, and provision of services other than during "office hours."

6. Awareness of individual and cultural differences between Indian women.
7. A willingness to include family members in any treatment program.
8. Training and hiring of Indian women as service providers for other Indian women.
9. Treatment facilities that provide care to pregnant Indian women.
10. An increase in research on drug abuse among Indian women and youth, and research that focuses on the unique issues and patterns of Indian women who drink.

Service Delivery Recommendations: Fetal Alcohol Syndrome and Fetal Alcohol Effects

Because FAS and FAE are critical problems for Indian women, specific recommendations which address these issues are offered:

1. Intensive education programs for Indian children about the effects of alcohol on the unborn.
2. Community education and early identification programs for Indian women through urban Indian centers, tribal health facilities and nutrition and prenatal care programs.
3. Evaluation of the prevalence of affected children in Indian communities.
4. Screening programs in community and tribal hospitals for newborn infants, and an FAS registry to help track affected children.
5. Full psychosocial and medical examinations of affected children on a regular basis to ensure that each child receives adequate care.
6. Development of community-based programs that utilize nondrinking Indian women as foster and adoptive parents, including the integration of traditional Indian values and parenting skills.
7. Development of tribal policies that address the special needs and problems of affected children including the termination of maternal rights if necessary, and support services for the caretakers of affected children, such as counseling, respite care and subsidized adoption.
8. A strong commitment on the part of Indian women to abstain from alcohol during pregnancy, and the formal adoption of such values on the part of tribal leadership.

Service Delivery Recommendations: Domestic Violence, Child Abuse and Neglect

For Indian women to have healthy relationships, marriages and children, steps need to be taken to bolster self-esteem, redefine roles and increase community support for Indian mothers. To help obtain these goals, the following are recommended:

1. Development of community-based programs that teach mothers healthy parenting skills that include traditional values and practices.
2. Programs that link young Indian women to Indian "grandmothers" who can help teach these skills and provide support for young mothers.
3. Education programs aimed at young women to bolster their self-esteem and to help them develop options that might help prevent both teenage pregnancy and substance abuse. Such programs should include classes, vocational skills training and child care.
4. Culture-specific, nonjudgmental treatment programs to help Indian women who themselves have been abused and/or are at high risk to be abusive.

Service Delivery Recommendations: Education and Economics

The connections between alcoholism, low levels of education and high rates of unemployment are strong. More culture sensitivity is needed in the development of academic curricula and training and employment programs. Programs need to encourage and promote both education and economic activities that involve traditional Indian crafts, such as beadwork, artwork and rug weaving. Indian leadership needs to renew its commitment to ensure any non-Indian employers on reservations adhere to proper Indian preference employment policies. The following are recommended:

1. The employment of Indian women as teachers and, particularly, the use of Indian elders as role models and educators.
2. Tribal schools where Indian children are taught their native languages and values.
3. Vocational training programs that acknowledge and help develop the inherent skills of each Indian child and are adapted to the specific community where the child resides.
4. The development of more accurate curricula to be used in all schools to present American Indian history in a more accurate light and allows Indian children to feel valuable for who and what they are.

Conclusion

That Indian people have managed to survive is a testimony to the inherent strength to be found in Indian culture. Indian women have traditionally taken on the responsibility for home and family, often at a young age. This responsibility today frequently includes financial obligations as well as major decision making. Indian women need to work with their men to help build healthy families and healthy communities.

No longer can Indian people afford to let their individual differences divide them. Indian tribes need to put aside their traditional divisions and look to the future where all Indian people can move beyond survival and into a positive future. Healthy Indian women need to form a network to preserve their skills and to provide a foundation for leadership.

Positive change is linked to a return to the spirituality and strengths that have always been the mainstays of Indian people. Indian women are in a unique position to provide a network of support and education to their communities and their children. Indian women must dedicate themselves to sobriety, safety, an end to abuse and violence and to the spiritual growth of themselves and their children. No longer can Indian women afford to be passive and invisible. The return of Coyote means a return to the traditional values of family, community and harmony. This can be accomplished in part by advocating for appropriate legislation to ensure their aboriginal rights, advocating for improved health programs, and, above all, by not drinking, so that a better future is ensured for themselves, their children and the generations of Indian people to come.

References

1. Brandon, W. *The American Heritage Book of Indians.* New York: Dell, 1961.
2. Garbarino, M.S. *Native American Heritage.* Boston: Little, Brown, 1976.
3. Allen, P.G. *The Woman Who Owned the Shadows.* San Francisco: Spinsters, Ink, 1983.
4. Allen, P.G. *The Sacred Hoop.* Boston: Beacon Press, 1986.
5. Bierhorst, J. (Ed.) *The Sacred Path: Prayers & Power Songs of the American Indians.* New York: William Morrow and Company, 1983.
6. Cameron, A. *Daughters of Copper Woman.* Vancouver, B.C.: Press Gang Publishers 1984.
7. Berlin, I.N. *Suicide among American Indian Adolescents.* Washington, D.C.: National American Indian Court Judges Association, 1984.
8. Blume, S.B. "Women and alcohol: A review." *Journal of the American Medical Association* (1986) 256: 1467-1470.
9. Frederick, C.J. *Suicide, Homicide and Alcoholism Among American Indians: Guidelines for Help,* Rockville, MD: National Institute of Mental Health, 1973.
10. Lurie, N.O. "The world's oldest ongoing protest demonstration: American Indian drinking patterns." In *The American Indian.* N. Hundley (Ed.) Santa Barbara, CA: CLIO Books, 1974.
11. Carpenter, R.A., Lyons, C.A., Miller, W.R. "Peer-managed self-control program for prevention of alcohol abuse in American Indian high school students: A pilot evaluation study." *The International Journal of the Addictions* (1985) 20: 299-310.
12. Walker, R.D., LaDue, R.A. "An integrative approach to American Indian mental health." In *Ethnic Psychiatry.* C.B. Wilkinson (Ed.) New York: Plenum Press, 1986.
13. Neithammer, C. *Daughters of the Earth.* New York: Collier Books, 1977.
14. Brown, D. *Bury My Heart at Wounded Knee.* New York: Bantam Books, 1971.
15. Beal, M.D. *I Will Fight No More Forever.* New York: Ballantine Books, 1971.
16. Kalant, O.J. *Alcohol and Drug Problems in Women.* Toronto: Plenum Press, 1980.
17. Metcalf, A. "From schoolgirl to mother: The effect of education on Navajo women." *Social Problems* (1976) 23: 533-544.
18. National Geographic Society *The World of the American Indian.* Washington, D.C.: National Geographic Book Service, 1974.
19. Wilkinson, C.F. *American Indians, Time, and the Law.* New Haven: Yale University Press, 1987.
20. Gidley, M. *With One Sky Above.* New York: Putnam, 1979.
21. O'Sullivan, M.J., Handal, P.J. "Medical and psychological effects of the threat of compulsory relocation for an American Indian tribe." *American Indian and Alaska Native Mental Health Research* (1988) 1: 3-20.
22. Sorkin, A.L. *The Urban American Indian.* Lexington, MA: Lexington Books, 1978.
23. Dinges, N.G., Joos, S.K. "Stress, coping, and health: Models of interaction for Indian and Native populations." *American Indian and Alaska Native Mental Health Research* (1988) 1:8-64.
24. Swinomish Tribal Mental Health Project *Overview of the Mental Health Status of Indian Communities: Needs and Barriers: Booklet I.* 1989.
25. Swinomish Tribal Mental Health Project *Cultural Considerations for Tribal Mental Health: Booklet II.* 1989.
26. Swinomish Tribal Mental Health Project *A Tribal Mental Health Program: The Skagit County Experience: Booklet III.* 1989.
27. Leland, J. "Women and alcohol in an Indian settlement." *Medical Anthropology.* (1978) 2:85-119.
28. Sandmaier, M. *The Invisible Alcoholics: Women and Alcohol Abuse in America.* New York: McGraw-Hill Book Company, 1980.
29. Johnson, S. "Cirrhosis mortality among American Indian women: Rates and ratios, 1975 and 1976." Presented at the Tenth Annual Medical-Scientific

Conference of the National Council on Alcoholism/American Medical Society on Alcoholism/Research Society on Alcoholism. Washington, D.C., 1979.

30. Youcha, G. *Women and Alcohol: A Dangerous Pleasure.* New York: Crown Publishers, 1978, 1986.

31. Abel, E.L., Sokol, R.J. "Incidence of Fetal Alcohol Syndrome and economic impact of FAS-related anomalies." *Drug and Alcohol Dependence,* (1987) 19:51-70.

32. May, P.A., Hymbaugh, K.J. "A pilot project on Fetal Alcohol Syndrome among American Indians." *Alcohol Health and Research World* (1983) 7:3-9.

33. Streissguth, A.P., LaDue, R.A., Randels, S.P. "Indian Adolescents and Adults with Fetal Alcohol Syndrome." *The IHS Primary Care Provider* (1987) 11: 89-91.

34. Streissguth, A.P. "The behavioral teratology of alcohol: Performance, behavioral, and intellectual deficits in exposed children." In J. West (Ed.) *Alcohol and Brain Development* New York: Oxford University Press, Inc., 1986.

35. Dorris, M. *The Broken Cord.* New York: Harper and Row, Publishers, 1989.

36. Lewis, R.G. "Alcoholism and the Native American—A review of the literature." *Alcohol and Health, Monograph 4; Special Population Issue.* Rockville, Md: National Clearinghouse for Alcohol Information, 1982.

37. Walker, C.E., Bonner, B.L., Kaufman, K.L. *The Physically and Sexually Abused Child.* New York: Pergamon Press, 1988.

38. Loretto, G., Beauvais, F., Oetting, E. "The primary cost of drug abuse: What Indian youth pay for drugs." *American Indian and Alaska Native Mental Health Research.* (1988) 1: 21-32.

39. Gilchrist, L.D., Schinke, S.P., Trimble, J.E., Bell, C.S. Preventing drug abuse with American Indian teenagers, unpublished paper, 1984.

4 Recent Research: Alcohol and Women's Bodies

Sandie Johnson

"Overall, both the extent and the effect of alcohol and other drug abuse on women's lives and on women's bodies are not fully understood because addiction has traditionally been regarded as a problem for men rather than for women. Studies regarding the human body's reaction to alcohol often use only male subjects. The results are then assumed to apply to both sexes. This phenomenon has been called the 'Adam's Rib Syndrome.' The tendency of researchers to behave 'as if women are identical to men is a deterrent to including women in research.'"

"Women go downhill faster," my Uncle Frank used to say, observing women from the vantage point of 25 years of sobriety in Alcoholics Anonymous. This same idea is espoused in more academic terms by some of the most respected researchers in the alcohol and other drug abuse fields. They say, for instance, that women are more vulnerable to certain medical consequences, such as liver cirrhosis.[1-4] They say that women have a "telescoped" progression of their addiction, meaning that women begin drinking and abusing alcohol at a later age than men but appear for treatment at about the same age as men.[5,6] To some, "more rapid progression" and "women just go downhill faster" both sound suspiciously like "women are just the weaker sex." And therefore, it is time for a re-examination of the research. Although women are not the "weaker sex," research indicates that women's bodies are, indeed, more vulnerable to the effects of alcohol than are men's.

This chapter will examine long-held assumptions while summarizing the most current findings in research concerning physical consequences of alcohol use and misuse on women's bodies. Ways in which these effects on women's bodies differ from the effects on men will be discussed. The following areas will be covered: state of the research, rates of alcohol use, blood-alcohol levels, menstrual cycle effects, obstetric/gynecologic problems and sexual function, and the relationship of alcohol use and abuse to breast cancer,

heart disease and liver cirrhosis. Finally, areas where more research is needed will be suggested.

Research on fetal alcohol syndrome has been excluded from this chapter because, essentially, it has become a separate body of research and is included in other chapters. In fact, research on the effects of alcohol and other drugs on the fetus often wins the lion's share of the funding and attracts more publicity than research on the effects of alcohol on women's nonpregnant bodies. Following the same pattern of the past, in 1989, the National Institute on Alcohol Abuse and Alcoholism (NIAAA) allocated $9.1 million for research on the effects of drinking on the fetus. Only $3.1 million was allocated for prevention research and treatment research on women. One author has commented that "alcoholism [is] seen only through the prism of . . . motherhood."[7] Clemmons states that "the concern is for her effect on society in a moral arena or a maternal arena; it is not the woman as person who is valued but rather the role she is fulfilling for society."[8] This chapter, therefore, will focus on research on the woman herself.

State of the Research on Women

Overall, both the extent and the effect of alcohol and other drug abuse on women's lives and bodies are not fully understood because addiction has traditionally been regarded as a problem for men rather than for women. Studies regarding the human body's reaction to alcohol often use only male subjects. The results are than assumed to apply to both sexes. This phenomenon has been called the "Adam's Rib Syndrome." The tendency of researchers to behave "as if women are

The author wishes to thank Susan Galbraith for providing sections on alcohol for use in this chapter.

identical to men is a deterrent to including women in research."[9] Even when studies include both men and women, treatment outcome results are typically not reported separately by sex.[10]

Frequently the effects of alcohol have been tested only on men or male animals with the thought that females would respond in the same manner if their cyclic hormonal fluctuations were held constant. Hormonal cycles "complicate any type of research with women, hence they are 'too messy and complicated' to deal with."

Another way of stating this is that women show a greater variability of responses, and the results are less conclusive, more difficult to interpret. This greater variability of responses among women occurs in many research areas: physiological, psychological and socio-logical. It is one of the major reasons researchers tend to limit their research subjects to males or to discard data on females. The difficulty with female subjects lies with being able to draw conclusions when research results are quite variable. However, greater variability can be regarded as a strength rather than a weakness. It is a truism in psychology that individuals possessing a greater variability of responses exhibit greater coping ability.

Only 8 percent of the subjects in studies of alcoholism and drug dependency treatment published between 1970 and 1984 were women.[11] Hamilton has observed that "when specialized treatment programs were first being established for the female alcoholic [in the 1970s], no research was available to validate the need for specialized treatment or for the best directions for specialized programs to take."[12] When Johnson and Garzon published one of the first reviews of the literature on women in 1978, there were only 66 journal articles.[6] By 1984, the number had more than doubled. This change came about because women began "asking some crucial questions in the hope that data has emerged during the last decade that will aid in making solid funding decisions about the forms of treatment that best serve her."[12]

However, the path that researchers took in their quest for data in the 1970s and early 1980s was actually a well-worn path defined in earlier times. A vast amount of information began to be published concern-ing women's drinking and drinking problems, but the research agendas had actually been set in the 1930s, 1940s and 1950s, and, therefore, they arose "from a social milieu in which gender relations of power went unquestioned."[13,14]

How could this happen in the latter half of the 20th century, a time when a strong wave of feminism was occurring? It happened because investigators followed established research procedures and drew upon the published literature. The published literature in the

case of women and alcohol was extremely conservative, often viewing women's drinking or alcoholism as psychopathology or due to marital disruption.[8] Other frequently cited causes were "grown children leaving home" or "obstetrical and gynecological problems."[6] Alcoholic women were often reported as behaving in a "masculine manner," according to Gomberg.[15] Morris-sey observed that "scientific discourses produced from a feminist perspective in this area have, with few exceptions, been conspicuous by their absence."[13]

Had scholars examined the changing world of women and their relationship to alcohol, they might have established the link between access to power and access to alcohol sooner than they did. Morrissey succinctly argues that there is a symbolic link between the use of alcohol and power in Western society.[13] She concludes that "strategies developed for the medical control of women's drinking problems were based on research formulations originally proposed between 1937 and 1963. These formulations suggest . . . that the development of alcoholism and drinking problems among women is associated with the loss of traditional female gender roles. The implication of this formula-tion is clear. To avoid experiencing drinking problems or to recover from alcoholism, women should accept traditional feminine productive and reproductive func-tions."[14]

In the last 15 years, women began to be represented "in a field of research and policy analysis previously dominated by male investigators and policy makers."[13] The body of knowledge expanded in order to create alcoholism programs for women, and therefore "it was necessary for these women to demonstrate that drink-ing by women was a special, and increasing, problem. In order to produce the necessary literature, differ-ences between the sexes were emphasized and the biology of women, women's vulnerability to stressors and the acceptance of non-traditional (masculine) roles became risk factors which would lead women to abuse alcohol. This emphasis on differences between men's and women's drinking provided a justification for the expansion of the control of women's drinking, for the funding of further research on the link between paid employment and drinking, female hormones and drinking, pregnancy and drinking and the rejection of femininity and drinking."[13]

The situation regarding research on alcohol and women has not improved since Morrissey's papers were published. The most recent report to Congress on alcohol problems from the National Institute on Alcohol Abuse and Alcoholism summarizes the most up-to-date and significant research findings in the field.[16] In recapitulating research by Drs. Sharon and Richard Wilsnack, it is reported that women develop drinking-related problems due to "role deprivation rather than from role overload or conflicts resulting from multiple roles." "Role deprivation" is defined as a "loss or lack of family roles"—being divorced or separated or having children who have left home. Research on women's drinking continues to define women by their relationship to men and motherhood. Any deviation from the wife and mother role is defined as "nontraditional." For example, one of the criteria for a "nontraditional" woman in recent research is "having an advanced degree."[16] Therefore, relying on the published literature has its limitations. Research by women, defined by women, conducted by women, with the conclusions interpreted by women researchers is only now beginning to emerge.

Nevertheless, there is evidence of male-female differences in the way our bodies handle alcohol and other drugs. These differences have important implications for prevention and treatment. As Morrissey pointed out, the differences also have serious political implications. The knowledge is evolving and must be questioned at each step. This body of knowledge is power—power to denigrate or power to strengthen women's lives. A review of the research is presented in this chapter with the hope that it will be used to empower women in prevention and treatment settings.

Rates of Alcohol Use

Alcohol is a powerful and potentially addictive drug. It is a central nervous system depressant and acts to slow down all of the body's major functions. A small amount of alcohol has a relaxing effect. Larger quantities can interfere with judgment, coordination, emotional control and reasoning. Excessive drinking over time can lead to addiction and a range of physical problems including stroke, heart attacks, liver disease, gynecological problems, gastrointestinal problems and many types of cancers.[17] If too much alcohol is consumed in a short period of time, it can be fatal.

Alcohol is the most widely used and misused drug in America.[17] Two-thirds of the adult population drinks. Surveys show that women are less likely to drink and less likely to report drinking-related problems than men. Sixty percent of adult women 18 and over drink, while almost 40 percent abstain. Fifty-five percent of the adult women who drink do so moderately—which is defined as less than 60 drinks per month by some survey researchers.[18] Five percent of the women who drink are considered heavy drinkers—defined as more than 60 drinks per month.[18]

Drinking practices among women have changed in this century. According to Dr. Sheila Blume, "Estimates of the relative prevalence of female and male alcohol problems have varied widely over time and in relationship to populations studied, but there is little doubt that both drinking and alcohol problems have

increased considerably in women since the end of World War II."[19] Dr. Kaye Fillmore of the University of California at Berkeley believes that female drinking patterns in this country have remained fairly consistent since the end of World War II and that "society at one point in time minimizes or understates the alcohol problems of women while at another point it maximizes those problems," depending on the political and moral climate and the "threat to society of the perceived role shifts among women."[20] Her view is supported by an analysis of trends over a 9-year period: no increases were detected for women in the national surveys funded by the National Institute on Alcohol Abuse and Alcoholism.[18]

The first full-scale survey on women's drinking patterns did not occur until 1981.[17] Conducted by research psychologist Dr. Sharon Wilsnack and her colleagues, the survey also revealed no evidence of a major increase in alcohol consumption by women over a 20-year period. However, the survey did identify several subgroups of women with relatively high rates of drinking problems. These include women who are unemployed and looking for work, women who are divorced or separated, women who are unmarried but living with a partner, women in their twenties and early thirties, and women with heavy-drinking husbands or partners.[16]

The targeting of women by the advertisers of alcoholic beverages is heavier today than at any other time. According to a recent industry newsletter, women are expected to spend $30 billion on alcoholic beverages in 1994, compared with $20 billion in 1984.[21]

Regular drinking is now common among high school girls, and a sizeable number drink heavily. In a 1983 survey, 31 percent of 12th grade girls had consumed at least five or more drinks at least once in the preceding two weeks.[22] Drinking patterns between boys and girls are growing more similar. Moreover, the number of young female drinkers has been increasing more rapidly than the number of young male drinkers.[22] The highest percentage of drinkers is in the 21-34 age group.[18]

There is little research on the drinking patterns of women of color. Furthermore, assessments of the drinking practices of ethnic groups are often based on generalizations and do not take into account the great variation within groups. Although the available information remains inadequate, it is known that Hispanic and African American women are more likely to abstain from drinking alcohol than White women.[17,18] Extremely limited data is available for Native American and Asian women. Research also indicates that women of lower educational status are more likely to abstain from alcohol.[17]

Although women consume less alcohol on average

than men, the effects of drinking on women can be devastating. Women alcoholics are more likely to suffer from suicide, anemia, circulatory disorders and liver cirrhosis than alcoholic men. Alcoholic women are more frequently disabled and for longer periods than alcoholic men, and women alcoholics have a higher death rate.[23]

Definitions of Alcoholism

Drinkers display many different patterns of alcohol use, including social drinking, alcohol abuse and alcoholism. Evidence is mounting to suggest that alcoholism represents the interaction of environmental factors with specific biological factors.[16] Two distinct forms of problematic drinking exist: alcohol abuse and alcohol dependence. Alcohol abuse is heavy drinking associated with impairment of social, psychological or health functioning. Alcohol dependence is alcohol abuse plus physical dependence, which is often felt in craving and in the development of tolerance (a condition in which it takes more alcohol to obtain the same effect). Both of these can be thought of as alcoholism.

The current medical trend is toward this dual classification system, which differentiates between nondependent problem drinking and alcohol dependence. In other words, the trend is toward defining alcoholism by what it does to you rather than in terms of how much you drink. In the research studies cited below, alcoholism was usually defined as "being in a treatment program" or by an individual's self-definition. Survey research, on the other hand, examines amounts and frequency of drinking, and definitions of heavy drinking vary from survey to survey. Amounts and definitions have been noted where relevant.

Blood-Alcohol Levels

Women reach higher peak levels of alcohol in the blood than men even when they are given the same amount of absolute alcohol per pound of body weight.[24] This occurs in part because women's bodies have more fat content and less water than men's bodies. Therefore, the alcohol consumed by women is dissolved in less total body water. Because women attain a higher peak blood-alcohol level than men on the same dose of alcohol, women should not depend on the usual estimates for the amount you can drink before you can drive safely. Most of these charts are published by the alcohol industry and calculated on men's biology. Women who are taking oral contraceptives have been found to metabolize alcohol more slowly than women not taking oral contraceptives.[25] That means alcohol may be present longer in the bodies of women "on the pill," and this factor needs to be taken into consideration by women planning to drive or operate machinery.

New information from research in this area is emerging. One explanation for sex-related differences in blood-alcohol levels was recently proposed by a team of researchers using alcoholic and nonalcoholic men and women in Italy.[26] As with previous studies, women were found to have higher blood-alcohol concentrations than men after ingesting an equivalent dose of ethanol. This difference was found in both the alcoholic and nonalcoholic men and women, but no such difference was found when alcohol was administered intravenously.

This team of researchers found differences in the capacity of the stomach to oxidize ethanol. Because the oxidation process depends upon alcohol dehydrogenase, or enzyme activity, the researchers measured stomach enzymes. They found that the women subjects had less of a particular stomach enzyme, and therefore more of what they drank entered the bloodstream in the form of pure alcohol.

They found women get about 30 percent more alcohol into the blood than men of similar weight who drink the same amount. The findings, according to the *New York Times*, may explain why women often say they feel the effects of alcohol more than men, even if they drink the same amount relative to body size.[27] It may also explain the observation that women are more susceptible than men to liver damage when they become alcoholics.

Menstrual Cycle Effects

In studies of blood-alcohol levels, women show a great deal of day-to-day variability in peak blood-alcohol levels.[24] This variation appears to be connected in part with the phases of the menstrual cycle, with high peaks occurring in the premenstrual phase, although alcohol is eliminated more rapidly during this phase.[28,29] Overall, this means that women in general may be less able to predict accurately the effect on their bodies of a given amount of alcohol consumed because of the greater variability in peak blood-alcohol levels and elimination times.

Schaefer and Evans believe there may be a link between alcohol craving and hormonal status. As clinicians, they note that "women in recovery are at the highest risk for relapse during the premenstrual phase of their cycles."[30] In fact, alcoholic women in treatment report a higher degree of total menstrual distress than nonalcoholic women, including severity of premenstrual syndrome (PMS).[31,32] In an early study Beckman noted higher rates of drinking among premenstrual women,[33] but others have found that frequency of alcohol use is unrelated to the menstrual cycle phase.[34] The subsequent research that would offer us some insights remains to be done.

Schaefer and Evans (1987) note the similarity

between the symptoms of low blood sugar (hypoglycemia) and PMS. They believe that PMS may simply be an exacerbation of the hypoglycemic condition that certain women experience throughout the month. Because alcoholics seem to experience disproportionately high rates of hypoglycemia,[35,36] the implication for treatment is simply to screen for and then address that condition through diet, exercise, and vitamins. Because the current medical treatment for PMS is virtually the same as the treatment for hypoglycemia, it is suggested that treatment of hypoglycemia and PMS simultaneously with alcohol and drug rehabilitation may help prevent relapse among the subgroup of women who suffer from these conditions.

Obstetric/Gynecological Problems

A link between chronic alcohol consumption and reproductive difficulties has been found, although the exact reasons and mechanisms are not known at this time.[19,37,38] The association between drinking and ob/gyn problems exists for heavy drinkers, as well as for alcoholic women. In fact, high alcohol intake has been associated with infertility, amenorrhea (irregular periods), failure to ovulate and higher rates of gynecological surgery, miscarriages, stillbirths and premature births.[39] It is well documented in the literature that alcoholic women have a higher incidence of gynecological problems than do nonalcoholic women. The problems include sterility, repeated miscarriages, irregular periods and pelvic pain. As high as 78 percent of alcoholic women have reported experiencing gynecological disorders, compared to 35 percent of a control group.[40]

In fact, women who drink more heavily visit their physicians more frequently, especially ob/gyns. In one study, 12 percent of White gynecologic outpatients who came for routine care were heavier drinkers.[41] (Heavier drinking was defined as having 5 or more drinks on one day or having 3-4 drinks 15 or more days per month.) Fifteen percent of African American gynecologic outpatients were heavier drinkers. The highest rates of heavier drinking were among gynecologic patients who were unemployed and looking for work (19 percent African American and 23 percent White, respectively).

We need to examine this research closely and ask additional questions. Does it mean that alcohol has a direct effect on the uterus, ovaries, fallopian tubes and vagina, leading to gynecological problems? Other questions include: Do alcoholic women simply seek help more often for ob/gyn problems? Do reproductive difficulties precede and perhaps lead to increased drinking?

Wilsnack, Klassen and Wilsnack asked these questions in conducting a retrospective analysis of changes in women's drinking behavior over time.[42] For those women who reported experience with depression or reproductive problems and also with heavier drinking, it was found that heavy drinking was not an antecedent. Rather, it began after the occurrence of the health problem, often after a lag of several years. These findings suggest that, although heavy drinking may lead to a variety of adverse reproductive consequences, the reverse may also be true: problems with depression or reproductive disorders may precede and possibly contribute to the onset of heavy drinking.

Some suggestions are offered to healthcare providers. Healthcare staff regularly meeting with or working with women who report depression, miscarriages, infertility and other ob/gyn problems should ask more questions to detect alcohol dependency, during regular meetings or the history-taking, because it may be possible to detect problems earlier. In these cases, early intervention should be considered.

Sexual Function

Although the fact that chronic alcohol consumption interferes with reproductive function is well established, researchers have only recently begun to examine the specific effects of alcohol on hormones and on sexual behavior. Again, most research has been done with male subjects. The few studies of female hormone levels and alcohol consumption have used a small number of subjects, which weakens the findings.

Testosterone, a powerful chemical previously believed to be present only in males, has now been found to be associated with sexual arousal in both sexes.[43] In men, testosterone supplies the major chemical basis for sexual behavior and secondary sexual characteristics. In women, however, sexual behavior is more complex and is dependent upon several hormones. Testosterone is only one of several, and only a small amount of it is present in women. The responsiveness of the clitoris, the primary erotic zone of the female, is dependent upon testosterone. Incidently, no evidence suggests that because women have less testosterone than men, they have lower sexual interest.[43]

Research shows that when males drink, testosterone levels are significantly reduced.[17,44,45] There is little research to measure testosterone levels in women, but one study is interesting. When healthy women were given a heavy dose of alcohol in a laboratory situation, hormone levels increased for about 4 hours. Estradiol, progesterone, and testosterone increased in a "small but significant" manner.[45] So, it appears that alcohol may increase hormone levels in women, including testosterone levels, but decreases them in men. Ellingboe is puzzled by several conflicting reports of alcohol on male and female hormones and merely concludes that "alcohol affects sex hormones differently in men and women."[45] The National Institute on Alcohol Abuse and Alcoholism's Sixth Report to Congress agrees.[17]

In another set of experiments, actual physiological arousal was measured in college-age women and men as they drank alcohol separately and viewed sexual stimuli.[46] In women, there was a conflict between what they reported and their actual physiological responses. Women who thought they had received an alcoholic beverage said they felt more aroused, whether or not they had actually consumed alcohol. However, actual alcohol consumption depressed physical arousal (as measured vaginally), even when the women thought they were more stimulated and reported feeling aroused. At higher blood alcohol levels, men and women showed the same reaction—that is, decreased sexual arousal.

A substantial number of women, with or without alcohol problems, report using alcohol as an aphrodisiac and report experiencing increased sexual enjoyment when drinking.[47] Despite the fact that women report experiencing increased sexual enjoyment and enhanced sexual feelings when drinking, the physiological research denies it. Perhaps researchers have not yet measured the right variable. Wilson and Lawson measured women's physiological response vaginally; they did not measure clitoral response.

This brings us to looking at the myth of promiscuity as it relates to alcoholism. Although women report experiencing enhanced sexual feelings when drinking, research does not show that drinking leads to "promiscuity." Nor is there evidence that women who are drinking become less discerning about their choice of a sexual partner.[48] Although information on sexual behavior is generally sparse, this question was addressed in a 1981 national survey of drinking behavior among women. Klassen and S. Wilsnack report that "stereotypes linking women's drinking with sexual 'promiscuity' are . . . not supported by our data." The survey indicates that women, on the other hand, are often targets of drinking-related sexual aggression from men who had been drinking.

Many studies have referred to sexual dysfunction in alcoholic women.[38,39] According to Roman, up to 70 percent of alcoholic women report sexual dysfunction. According to Stephanie Covington, 85 percent of the alcoholic women in her study reported some type of sexual dysfunction as compared to 59 percent of the nonalcoholic women.[49] Sexual dysfunction included lack of orgasm, lack of erotic feelings or interest, lack of sexual arousal or pleasure, painful intercourse and lack of lubrication. Sexual dysfunction among the alcoholic group of women could not be attributed to problem drinking alone. In the Covington study, seventy-nine percent reported having experienced sexual dysfunc-tion before alcoholism.[49] Wilsnack, Klassen and Wilsnack also found women report that sexual difficulties preceded their drinking problems, and that sexual satisfaction deteriorated further after the onset of excessive drinking.[39]

In Covington's study, the group of alcoholic women did not report greater satisfaction with sexual responsiveness. They reported less satisfaction than the control group with their sexual relations. Looking into the women's history, researchers found sexual abuse was a common life experience for both alcoholic and nonalcoholic women. The sexual abuse was usually perpetrated by a male known to them. Seventy-four percent of the alcoholic group reported at least one instance of sexual abuse in their lives, compared to 50 percent of the nonalcoholic women. Over 90 percent of the sexual abuse reported by alcoholic women was rape or incest.[49]

In a study on the sexuality of women alcoholics in Germany, Heiser and Hartmann found no significant group differences in the frequency of sexual activity between alcoholic women and that of a matched sample.[50] However, there were important differences in the histories of the women and in their feelings toward sex. More alcoholic women had severe feelings of depression linked to sexuality, stating that sexual desire had decreased during the course of their lifetime. More women alcoholics tried to avoid sexual contacts. More alcoholic women felt disgusted by their first menstruation, and their first intercourse more often caused feelings of fear. Women alcoholics felt it more difficult than the nonalcoholic women to communicate with their partners about sexual desires and feelings. They quarreled more often with their partners, and reported that their partners suppressed them, hurt their feelings and were more violent. The women alcoholics reported a significantly stronger fear of being abandoned by their partner. They reported that physical contact made them tense, and they reported more masturbation guilt. The group of women alcoholics reported that drinking made them feel less lonely, more self-confident, and more independent of their partners. These findings have far-reaching implications for prevention and treatment. It is probable that sexual dysfunction is both cause and consequence of excessive drinking. We need to recognize the vicious circle that drinking can create in this area.

We also need to address the set of stereotypes that every drinking woman has internalized. This involves the myth of promiscuity mentioned above. It involves the assumption that there is a one-to-one correlation between drinking and "being loose." This stereotype is pervasive in the offices of professionals, and is well illustrated in an anecdote that Marian Sandmaier tells in her book, *The Invisible Alcoholics*.[7] She describes a commercial artist in her mid-thirties who "summoned the courage" to tell her doctor that she thought she had a drinking problem. He replied, "I hope you're on the pill, and if you're not, you better start thinking about it."

The myth of promiscuity has a devastating impact on women who fear they might have a drinking problem. They often hesitate to seek help or to enter treatment for fear people will think they are "loose." They have often internalized the myth to the extent that they feel "I'm worthless" and therefore not worthy of a better life. If and when they finally enter a treatment program, they often are eager to assure counselors that "I did my drinking only at home, not in bars." The myth of promiscuity engenders guilt as well as fear.

This is the point where we as women need to start thinking about the myth . . . and acting to overthrow it. The reality is that women are more often the targets of sexual aggression. When 50 percent of a control group has suffered from sexual abuse, and is the social norm against which we measure alcoholic women's even higher rates of sexual abuse, there is a reason for concern. There is a serious problem in a society that tolerates this behavior on the part of males as normal. The use of alcohol by women often seems to be a way of numbing feelings after the abuse. Women need to recognize and address the complex relationship between alcohol use, sexuality, and sexual abuse if our goal is to assist women in developing full lives without the abuse of alcohol.

Breast Cancer and Other Cancers

There is considerable epidemiologic evidence that alcohol abuse is associated with increased risk of certain kinds of cancers, especially those involving the liver, esophagus, nasopharynx and larynx.[16] In Hill's extensive review of the biomedical literature, she reports that cancer of the mouth and esophagus are related more to drinking than to smoking in both men and women.[23]

Research findings linking alcohol with breast cancer have been inconsistent. Reports indicate that the risk of breast cancer is increased by 30 percent even for women who drink as little as three alcoholic drinks per week compared to abstainers.[51,52] A new statistical technique has permitted researchers to pool the data from 21 studies. This team of researchers found that about two drinks a day increases the risk of breast cancer about 40 percent.[53] In addition, they found compelling evidence in favor of a dose-response relation between alcohol consumption and the risk of breast cancer. In brief, this means that the more you drink, the greater the risk of breast cancer. The NIAAA takes the conservative view that more research is needed to provide definitive information on the relationship between alcohol use and breast cancer.[16]

Heart Disease

The risks and benefits of moderate alcohol intake have long been debated, and nowhere have they been debated as strongly as in the arena of heart disease research. Because alcohol can increase the risk of high blood pressure and, thus, hypertension, it would be logical to assume that it would increase the risk of stroke and heart attack, but the findings have been inconsistent.

However, a recent study of over 87,000 nurses suggests that moderate alcohol consumption among middle-aged women decreases the risk of coronary heart disease by 40 percent.[54] Moderate consumption is defined as three to nine drinks per week. Drinking also appeared to protect against strokes caused by blood clots, but increased the risk of strokes caused by bleeding into the brain. This study has received much attention in the media, and women often express bewilderment at the conflicting claims of alcohol giving "protection against heart disease" and "increased risk of breast cancer." A group of researchers in New Zealand studying the relationship between alcohol consumption and sudden coronary death in men and women found that leisure time physical activity may be as important as hypertension, cigarette smoking, and alcohol consumption.[55]

Heavy alcohol consumption causes numerous biochemical changes in the heart muscle, and many studies show that alcohol can change the ability of the heart muscle to contract.[16] There is evidence of problems, not only while drinking heavily, but during the withdrawal period. Often seen in chronic drinkers, this "holiday heart syndrome" is characterized by irregular heart rhythms.[16]

Hill cites a study in which White women with no prior history of heart disease died within 24 hours after the onset of symptoms.[23] Of the women who died suddenly, over 25 percent were heavy drinkers, compared to 6.3 percent of the control group. So, despite the large study of nurses, we caution against thinking of drinking as "protective" factor on the strength of the available evidence.

Liver Cirrhosis

Alcohol-related liver cirrhosis interests prevention, research, and treatment personnel because there is a mathematical relationship between the number of alcoholics in a population and the number of cirrhosis cases.[56] Of course, not every alcoholic contracts liver damage, but the proportion of alcoholics who die from alcohol-related cirrhosis can give us some idea of the total number of alcoholics in any given population.

Therefore, cirrhosis has been studied widely as an indicator of alcoholism.

One finding emerges again and again worldwide —women appear to develop alcoholic liver disease more readily than men.[4,16,23,38,57,58] Over 25 studies suggest that women may be at greater risk of developing alcohol-related liver damage, according to Norton and Batey.[3] This is despite the overall higher liver cirrhosis death rates of men.[16] Women appear to develop more severe forms of liver disease than their male counterparts, and they are said to develop them more rapidly.[16,23] Women appear to incur liver damage with shorter drinking histories and at lower levels of alcohol intake (even accounting for differences in body weight) than men.[16,23]

This is one research area where we have reliable data by race as well as by sex. Any scientific explanation needs to take racial differences into consideration and, to date, there has been far too little research. African Americans of both sexes have cirrhosis and chronic liver diseases rates twice that of Whites.[60] Native Americans have the highest rate of cirrhosis mortality, followed by African Americans.[58] In general, males of all races have a higher rate than females.[16] Native American females, however, have a higher rate of deaths attributable to alcoholic cirrhosis than either African American or White males.[58]

This, then, is one of the areas where women are said to show "telescoped" development of alcoholism and alcohol-related problems. They are said to be more biologically vulnerable.[6,23] Some of the reasons thought to play a major role in women's biological vulnerability are life event stressors, poorer nutrition, differences in metabolism, more continuous drinking as compared to binge drinking, body weight or body water content, hormonal factors (especially estrogen), genetic factors, the use of oral contraceptives, and/or the greater use of over-the-counter drugs than men.[4,23,57] Robyn Norton, a researcher from Australia, suggests more than one factor my be important, and that future research should consider all the factors in combination.

The recent research by Frezza and his colleagues in Italy points to differences in metabolism and enzymes as a possible explanation.[26] However, they examined only male-female differences, not cirrhosis rates among varied ethnic groups. African American males have extremely high cirrhosis death rates, as do Native American males.[58] Any explanation will eventually have to take these differences into account. We need to examine research findings with a critical eye, and we need to search for more plausible interpretations of the data—explanations other than "women go downhill faster." If White and male are the standards by which we are measured, significantly more research is needed.

Conclusion

Twenty years after the new wave of feminism began, women generally have come to accept that "the personal is political," and nothing is more personal than our health. We need now to see that science relating to health is political—that scientific explanations and interpretations are political, and that addictions are political. Addictions keep oppressed people oppressed. People who are drinking heavily or who are addicted are not working to change the status quo. Their potential, their gifts, their contributions to humanity are lost.

If you have any doubt that alcohol is political, think about the way it was used to subdue Native Americans. It was used in the fur trade and to take their land in less than fair ways.[61,62] Then it was banned. Drinking for Indians in the United States only became legal in 1953, twenty years after prohibition ended for other Americans.

The pattern of control for women seems to be the reverse of the American Indian experience. Throughout history, women were "protected" by being kept away from alcohol. In the last century, a woman was not permitted to pour liquor even in her own business establishment.[8] Now, women are often offered drinks by men during seduction attempts.

In a study of alcohol, drugs and sexual seduction, the most common drug involved was alcohol.[63] Alcohol was used by males to make their partners "more sexually willing or responsive." A look at popular liquor ads shows sexual seduction as major themes. Advertising companies spend an extraordinary amount of money promoting liquor sales to women and ethnic minorities.[64,65]

Those who hold the power in our society (i.e., mainly White men) currently hold the power (and make large amounts of money) in liquor companies and in the advertising field. In government and public health, it is predominantly White men who are defining the research questions and the policies surrounding alcohol use, distribution, taxing, research, funding, treatment and rehabilitation. Real change will take place only after there has been a transformation in social values and a redistribution of power.

For women, the first step may be to become familiar with the research upon which policies and research initiatives are based. As part of becoming familiar, we can work with the concepts in women's centers, women's programs, and in the living laboratory of our lives. And then we can begin to reframe new and different research questions.

References
1. Morgan, M.Y., and Sherlock, S. Sex-related differences among 100 patients with alcoholic

liver disease. *British Medical Journal* 1:939-941, 1977.

2. Saunders, J.B., Davis, M., and Williams, R. Do women develop alcoholic liver disease more readily than men? *British Medical Journal* 282:1140-1143, 1981.

3. Norton, R., and Batey, R. Why do women appear to develop liver disease more readily than men? *Australian Alcohol/Drug Review* 2(2):48-52, 1983.

4. Norton, R., Batey, R., Dwyer, T., and MacMahon, S. Alcohol consumption and the risk of alcohol-related cirrhosis in women. *British Medical Journal* 259:80-82, 1987.

5. Johnson, S., and Garzon, S.R. Alcoholism and women. *American Journal of Drug and Alcohol Abuse* 5(1):107-122, 1978.

6. Hill, S.Y. A vulnerability model for alcoholism in women. *Journal of Addictions and Health—Focus on Women* 2(2):68-91, 1981.

7. Sandmaier, M. *The Invisible Alcoholics: Women and Alcohol Abuse in America.* New York: McGraw-Hill, 1980. (287 pages)

8. Clemmons, P. Reflections of social thought in research on women and alcoholism. *Journal of Drug Issues* 15(1):73-80, 1985

9. Kumpfer, K.L., Prazza, A.H., and Whiteside, H.O. Etiology of alcohol and other drug problems: nature vs nurture. In R.C. Engs (ed), *Women; Alcohol and Other Drugs.* Iowa: Kendall/Hunt Publishing, 1990, pp. 31-40.

10. Annis, H.M., and Liban, C.B. Alcoholism in Women. In Kalant, O.J. (ed), *Alcohol and Drug Problems in Women.* New York: Plenum Press, 1980, pp. 385-422

11. Harrison, P.A., and Belille, C.A. Women in treatment: beyond the stereotype. *Journal of Studies on Alcohol* 48 (6): 574-578, 1987.

12. Hamilton, G. "Alcoholism & Women." Unpublished manuscript, prepared for Division of Extramural Research, National Institute on Alcohol Abuse and Alcoholism, March 13, 1984. 22 pages.

13. Morrissey, E.R. Power and control through discourse: the case of drinking and drinking problems among women. *Contemporary Crisis* 10:157-179, 1986a.

14. Morrissey, E.R. Contradictions inherent in liberal feminist ideology: promotion and control of women's drinking. *Contemporary Drug Problems,* Spring:65-88, 1986b.

15. Gomberg, E.A. Alcoholism in Women. In B. Kissin and H. Begleiter (eds), *The Biology of Alcoholism,* Vol. 4. New York: Plenum, 1976.

16. National Institute on Alcohol Abuse and Alcoholism (NIAAA). *Seventh Special Report to the U.S. Congress on Alcohol and Health.* Rockville, MD: National Institute on Alcohol Abuse and Alcoholism, 1990.

17. National Institute on Alcohol Abuse and Alcoholism (NIAAA). *Sixth Special Report to the U.S. Congress on Alcohol and Health.* Rockville, MD: National Institute on Alcohol Abuse and Alcoholism, 1987.

18. Clark, W., and Midanik, L. Alcohol use and alcohol problems among U.S. adults: Results of the 1979 national survey. In: National Institute on Alcohol Abuse and Alcoholism. *Alcohol Consumption and Related Problems.* Alcohol and Health monograph No. 1 DHHS Pub. No. (ADM 82-1190). Washington, DC: Supt. of Docs., U.S. Govt. Print. Off., 1982, pp. 3-52.

19. Blume, S.B. Women and alcohol: a review. *Journal of the American Medical Association* 256(11):1467-1470, 1986.

20. Fillmore, K.M. "When angels fall": Women's drinking as cultural preoccupation and as reality. In S.C. Wilsnack and L.J. Beckman (eds) *Alcohol Problems in Women.* New York: Guilford Press, 1984.

21. "Betty Briefcase Buys More Bottles," *Advertising Age,* Thursday, September 12, 1985.

22. Thompson, K., and Wilsnack, R. Drinking problems among female adolescents: patterns and influences. In S. Wilsnack and L. Beckman (eds), *Alcohol Problems in Women.* New York: Guilford Press, 1984. (pp. 37-65).

23. Hill, S.Y. Vulnerability to the biomedical consequences of alcoholism and alcohol-related problems among women. In S.C. Wilsnack and L.J. Beckman (eds) *Alcohol Problems in Women.* New York: Guilford Press, 1984.

24. Jones, B.M., and Jones, M.K. Women and alcohol: Intoxication, metabolism, and the menstrual cycle. In M. Greenblatt and M. Schuckit (eds.), *Alcohol Problems in Women and Children.* New York: Grune and Stratton, Inc., 1976.

25. Jones, M.K., and Jones, B.M. Ethanol metabolism in women taking oral contraceptives. *Alcoholism: Clinical and Experimental Research* 8(1):24-28,1984.

26. Frezza, M., Di Podova, C., Pozzato, G., Terpin, M., Baraona, E., and Lieber, C.S. High blood alcohol levels in women. *New England Journal of Medicine.* 322 (2):95-99, 1990.

27. Kolata, G. Study tells why alcohol is greater risk to women. *New York Times,* January 11, 1990.

28. Jones, B.M., and Jones, M.K. Alcohol effects in women during the menstrual cycle. *Annals of the New York Academy of Science* 273: 576-587, 1976b.

29. Sutker, P.B., Goist, K.C., and King, A.R. Acute

alcohol intoxication in women: Relationship to dose and menstrual cycle phase. *Alcoholism: Clinical and Experimental Research 11(1):74-79, 1987.*

30. Schaefer, S., and Evans, S. Women, sexuality and the process of recovery. *Journal of Chemical Dependency Treatment* 1(1):91-120, 1987

31. Shelley, S. Relationship of menstrual distress to craving for alcohol in alcoholic women. *Proceedings of the 31st International Institute on the Prevention and Treatment of Alcoholism, Volume I.* Rome, Italy: 2 June-7 June 1985, pp. 305-327.

32. Price, W.A., DiMarzio, L.R., and Eckert, J.L. Correlation between PMS and alcoholism among women. *Ohio Medicine* 83(3):201-202, 1987.

33. Beckman, L.J. Reported effects of alcohol on the sexual feelings and behavior of women alcoholics and non-alcoholics. *Journal of Studies on Alcohol* 40(3):272-282, 1979.

34. Griffin, M.L., Mello, N.K., Mendelson, J.H., and Lex, B.W. Alcohol use across the menstrual cycle among marihuana users. *Alcohol* 4:457-462, 1987.

35. Milam, J.R., and Ketcham, K. *Under the Influence.* Toronto and New York: Bantam, 1981.

36. Ryan, K. Alcohol and blood sugar disorders: An overview. *Alcohol Health and Research World* 8(2):3-7,15, 1983/84.

37. Pratt, O. Alcohol and the woman of childbearing age: a public health problem. *British Journal of Addictions* 76:383-390, 1981.

38. Roman, P.M. *Women and Alcohol Use: A Review of the Research Literature.* Rockville, MD: National Institute on Alcohol Abuse and Alcoholism, 1988 (64 pages) [DHHS No. (ADM) 88-1574].

39. Wilsnack, S.C., Klassen, A.D., and Wilsnack, R.W. Drinking and reproductive dysfunction among women in a 1981 national survey. *Alcoholism: Clinical and Experimental Research* 8:451-458,1984.

40. Wilsnack, S.C. Sex-role identity in female alcoholism. *Journal of Abnormal Psychology* 82:253-261, 1973.

41. Russell, M. Alcohol use and related problems among Black and white gynecologic patients. *Alcohol Use Among U.S. Ethnic Minorities: Proceedings of a Conference on the Epidemiology of Alcohol Use and Abuse Among Ethnic Minority Groups, September 1985 (Research Monograph 18).* Rockville, MD: National Institute on Alcohol Abuse and Alcoholism, 1989.

42. Wilsnack, R.W., Klassen, A.D., and Wilsnack, S.C. Retrospective analysis of lifetime changes in women's drinking behavior. *Alcohol and Substance Abuse in Women and Children* 5(3)9-28, 1986.

43. Masters, W.H., Johnson, V.E., and Kolodny, R.C. *Masters and Johnson on Sex and Human Loving.* Boston and Toronto: Little, Brown and Co., 1986.

44. Cole-Harding, S., and Wilson, J.R. Ethanol metabolism in men and women. *Journal of Studies on Alcohol* 48(4):380-387, 1987.

45. Ellingboe, J. Acute effects of ethanol on sex hormones in non-alcoholic men and women. *Advances in Biomedical Alcohol Research: Third Congress of the International Society for Biomedical Research on Alcoholism. Alcohol and Alcoholism Supplement No. 1.* Helsinki, Finland: 8 June-13 June 1986. 765 pages (pp. 109-116).

46. Wilson, G.T., and Lawson, D.M. Effects of alcohol on sexual arousal in women. *Journal of Abnormal Psychology* 85:489-497, 1976.

47. Covington, S. Misconceptions about women's sexuality: Understanding the influence of alcoholism. *Focus on Family* 9(2):6-8, 1986.

48. Klassen, A.D., and Wilsnack, S.C. Sexual experiences and drinking among women in a U.S. national survey. *Archives of Sexual Behavior* 15(5):363-391, 1986.

49. Covington, S. Chemically dependent women and sexuality. *Proceedings of the 31st International Institute on the Prevention and Treatment of Alcoholism, Volume I.* Rome, Italy: 2 June-7 June 1985, pp. 197-210.

50. Heiser, K., and Hartmann, U. Disorders of sexual desire in a sample of women alcoholics. *Drug and Alcohol Dependence* 19(2):145-157, 1987.

51. Willett, W.C., Stampfer, M.J., Colditz, M.B., Rosner, B.A., Hennekens, C.H., and Speizer, F.E. Alcohol consumption and the risk of breast cancer. *The New England Journal of Medicine* 316:1174-1179, 1987.

52. Schatzkin, A., Jones, D., Hoover, R.N., Taylor, P.R., Brinton, L.A., Zeigler, R.G., Harvey, E.B., Carter, C.L., Licitra, L.M., Dufour, M.C., and Larson, D.B. Alcohol consumption and breast cancer in the epidemiological follow-up study of the first national Health and Nutrition Examination Survey. *The New England Journal of Medicine* 316:1169-1173, 1987.

53. Longnecker, M.P., Berlin, J.A., Orza, M.J., and Chalmers, T.C. A meta-analysis of alcohol consumption in relation to risk of breast cancer. *Journal of the American Medical Association* 260(5):652-656, 1988.

54. Stampfer, M.J., Colditz, G.A., Willett, W.C., Speizer, F.E., and Hennekens, C.H. A prospec-

tive study of moderate alcohol consumption and
the risk of coronary disease and stroke in women.
New England Journal of Medicine 319(5):267-273,
1988.

55. Scragg, R., Stewart, A., Jackson, R., and Beagle-
hole, R. Alcohol and exercise in myocardial
infarction and sudden coronary death in men and
women. *American Journal of Epidemiology*
126(1):77-85, 1987.

56. Coakley, J., and Johnson, S. *Alcohol abuse and
alcoholism in the United States: Selected recent
prevalence estimates.* Alcohol Epidemiologic
Data System (Working Paper #1). Rockville,
MD: National Institute on Alcohol Abuse and
Alcoholism, March 27, 1978.

57. Grant, B.F., Dufour, M.C., and Harford, T.C.
Epidemiology of alcoholic liver disease. *Seminars
in Liver Disease* 8(1):12-25, 1988.

58. Johnson, S. Cirrhosis mortality among American
Indian women: Rates and Ratios, 1975 and 1976.
In M. Galanter (ed). *Currents in Alcoholism*
7:455-463, 1980.

59. Petersen, J., Skinhos, P., and Thorsen, T. An
epidemic of cirrhosis in Danish women revisited
(abstract). *Scandinavian Journal of Social Medicine* 14:171-178, 1986.

60. Leland, J. Alcohol use and abuse in ethnic
minority women. In S. Wilsnack and L. Beckman
(eds) *Alcohol Problems in Women.* New York;
Guilford Press, 1984.

61. Ray, A.J. *Indians in the Fur Trade.* Toronto:
University of Toronto Press, 1974.

62. Westermeyer, J., and Baker, J.M. Alcoholism
and the American Indian. In N.J. Estes and M.E.
Heinemann (eds) *Alcoholism: Development, Consequences and Interventions (Third Edition).* St.
Louis, MO: C.V. Mosley, 1986 (pp. 273-282).

63. Bowker, L.H. The relationship between sex,
drugs, and sexual behavior on a college campus.
Drug Forum 7(1):69-80, 1978.

64. Hacker, G.A., Collins, R., and Jacobson, M.
Marketing Booze to Blacks. Washington, DC:
Center for Science in the Public Interest, 1987.

65. Jacobs, M., Atkins, R., and Hecker, G.A., *The
Booze Merchants.* Washington, DC: Center for
Science in the Public Interest, 1983.

5 Issues for Latinas: Mexican American Women

Juana Mora, Ph.D. and M. Jean Gilbert, Ph.D.

"Until recently, it was believed that Mexican American women were unique in their abstinence and freedom from problems related to alcohol. The strong cultural sanctions against women's alcohol use and the segregation of social life along gender lines in traditional Mexican society were well known. . . . In the last decade, however, research has shown that the patterns of alcohol use among Mexican American women are more complex than had been supposed."

Latinos are presently the second largest and, because of high fertility and immigration rates, also the fastest growing ethnic group in the United States. Recently released data from the U.S. Bureau of the Census show that between 1980 and 1988, the U.S. Latino population grew from 14.5 million to 19.4 million, representing a 34 percent increase, compared to a 7 percent growth rate for non-Latinos during the same period.[1] In 1988, Latinos accounted for 8.1 percent of the total United States population, compared to 6.4 percent in 1980.

Mexican Americans represent the largest Latino group in the United States. Roughly 63 percent of all U.S. Latinos are of Mexican descent. While Mexican Americans represent the largest number of Latinos in the United States, they have some unique historical, cultural and regional characteristics which influence their specific problems and experiences with alcohol and other drugs.

Much of the early research literature on alcohol and other drug use among Latinos was problematic because data for the various Latino groups were collected and analyzed as aggregate data. This combining or "lumping" of data under a generic "Latino" or "Hispanic" label did not allow an examination of across-group differences in drinking styles and related problems. For this reason, this chapter will focus specifically on drinking patterns and other drug use among Mexican American women.

Mexican Americans

The current and projected growth of the Mexican American population is magnified by well-documented indications that Mexican Americans suffer dispropor-

tionately from problems of poverty, low educational attainment, under- and unemployment, low adult literacy and lack of general health care factors associated and exacerbated by alcohol and other drug use. Moreover, Mexican Americans may be at an elevated risk for alcohol and other drug use because of their concentration in large metropolitan urban centers and inner cities, known for a higher prevalence of alcohol and drug use and associated conditions.[2]

An additional risk factor associated with the population increase among Mexican Americans is that so many are very young. For example, the median age for Mexican Americans is 23 compared to 33 for the general population. As the Mexican American population grows, primarily through natural increase, it is expected that in the next 20 years a very large proportion of the total United States youth population will be of Mexican American ancestry.[3] Alcohol and other drugs are implicated in many of the social problems facing young Mexican Americans, including teenage pregnancy, school drop-out and criminal behavior.

Mexican American women also have all the characteristics of a high-risk group for alcohol-related problems. They are overrepresented in the lower socioeconomic levels and are having children at younger ages as well. They also have lower educational levels than other women and are over-represented among those women who are single heads of households. These conditions, combined with issues of language differences, substandard and overcrowded housing, immigration status and discrimination, compound the stresses created by alcohol abuse within the family.

Mexican American Women and Alcohol Use

Until recently, it was believed that Mexican American women were unique in their abstinence and freedom from problems related to alcohol. The strong cultural sanctions against women's alcohol use and the segregation of social life along gender lines in traditional Mexican society were well known. Mexican Americans are known for their loyalty to cultural norms and so it was assumed that women maintained these norms and the behaviors that went along with them when they immigrated to the United States. In the last decade, however, research has shown that the patterns of alcohol use among Mexican American women are more complex than had been supposed. The most important variations in alcohol use among women in this very large ethnic group are associated with generational status, age and acculturation. Let's look at these factors one by one.

It *is* true that women in Mexico are more likely to be abstainers than women in the United States. A recent study which compared Mexican and U.S. women disclosed that many more Mexican women than women in the U.S. general population are abstainers—that is, they report that they don't drink at all. And in the United States, women who drink tend to drink more and to drink more frequently than female drinkers in Mexico. Unlike U.S. women, Mexican women are most likely to do their drinking during private family celebrations, whereas U.S. women drink in a much wider range of settings, both public and private. On the other hand, Mexican and U.S. men tend to drink similar amounts of alcohol, but the *way* they drink is very different: Mexican men don't drink as often as U.S. men, usually only once or twice a month compared to the weekly drinking typical of male drinkers in the United States. However, when they drink, Mexican men consume much larger quantities of alcohol. Much Mexican male drinking takes place at bars and *cantinas* outside the home. These different male and female drinking patterns, generated out of the cultural mores of Mexico, are one of the important influences shaping the alcohol "ecology" or environment of Mexican American women.

Upon immigration to the United States, however, some fascinating changes begin to occur among both men and women. Very shortly after immigration, mostly within the first five years, Mexican men begin to drink at a higher frequency, more like that of other U.S. men, but they also keep the higher quantity-per-occasion patterns they developed in Mexico. The reasons for this rapid increase in drinking frequency among immigrant men are as yet unknown. Some researchers hypothesize that the increase occurs because men are trying to cope with the stresses of adaptation to a strange society. Others feel it occurs

because men have more disposable income. Whatever the reasons, the result is that many immigrant men have heavy drinking patterns, and this has serious implications for their wives, partners and families.

Interestingly, immigrant women do not show much of a change in their drinking habits when they come to the United States. In fact, if anything, they are more abstinent than the women they left behind in Mexico, and this doesn't change much throughout their lifetimes. Again, we do not know precisely why immigrant Mexican women maintain very high rates of abstinence, but some good guesses have been made. Immigrant women are often quite isolated from family and friends, and as a result do not have occasion to consume even moderately at family gatherings. They are somewhat less likely than their husbands to be in the labor force and consequently less likely to speak English and to associate with persons not of their culture. The result of these male/female differences is that first-generation (immigrant) women are much more likely to be coping with problems generated by spouse alcohol abuse than by their own misuse of alcohol. And many are attempting to cope under very difficult conditions—poverty, language barriers, lack of information about services and a terrible isolation from family and friends.

However, for their second-generation daughters who are born and raised in the United States, the situation is very different. It is among Mexican American women in this second generation that the most dramatic change in drinking patterns occurs: abstinence rates plummet and light-to-moderate drinking greatly increases. Every study that has examined Mexican American women's drinking patterns has uncovered this same generational pattern. In the third generation (U.S.-born daughters of U.S.-born parents), there are even fewer non-drinkers.

One doesn't need to look far to understand what is happening. Studies of teenage drinking show that Mexican American girls now in school are beginning to experiment with alcohol at around age thirteen and are only slightly more likely to be abstainers than Mexican American boys. One large, recent study of California youngsters showed that 76 percent of 9th grade Chicanas and 60 percent of their male counterparts had been introduced to alcohol. Forty-one percent of the Chicanas reported that they had been intoxicated at least once. This still isn't quite as high as the rates among non-Hispanic girls, 78 percent of whom had tried alcohol and 57 percent who reported having been intoxicated. However, these are pretty high figures for 9th graders, and, as with all teenagers, an even higher proportion are drinking in late adolescence. Studies of Mexican American adolescents in Texas and Colorado show similar figures. Most research has shown that one

of the strongest predictors of teenage drinking is having
friends who drink, and this seems to be the case among
Mexican American girls as well. Overall, then, it isn't
surprising that it is the younger generation of Mexican
American women who are most likely to be drinkers
(though not necessarily the most likely to be abusive
drinkers). And, given the drinking rates and the
increases we're seeing in the adolescent Mexican
American population, we can project much higher
drinking rates for young adult women in the next
decade.

The Mexican American woman who has developed
an abusive drinking pattern is very likely to be
U.S.-born. And, she is likely to be acculturated, a
useful term that needs some explanation here. Acculturation is a process that involves giving up some of the
customs and ways of thinking that are learned in an
individual's culture of origin and adopting some of the
behaviors and ideas prevalent in the society to which
she has immigrated. This is not a simple or systematic
process because it is affected by many other factors—
changes taking place in the newly adopted culture
(e.g., in recent years U.S. society has become more
permissive in its attitudes toward women's drinking),
the customs unique to the part of the United States to
which the woman has immigrated, class and occupational factors and the degree of exposure an immigrant
has to persons outside her own culture. The process of
acculturation goes on for several generations following
immigration because people rightly value the norms
and behaviors transmitted to them as part of their
cultural heritage. Many second- and third-generation
Mexican American women are bicultural, that is, they
have integrated into their world view aspects of both
U.S. and Mexican culture.

Although alcohol-related norms are just one aspect of
a culture's value system, it is the aspect we're
concerned with here. U.S. society is much more
permissive with respect to women's access and right to
drink than are most Latin cultures, including Mexico.
The more a woman of Mexican heritage is exposed to
the majority society culture through school, the
workplace, friendship and intermarriage, the more she
will be exposed to situations in which it is normatively
appropriate for her to drink. Interviews with numerous
Mexican American women conducted by one of the
authors (Gilbert) provide some examples. One woman
born and raised in Mexico and now a bilingual teacher's
aide commented on how surprised she was when the
women at her school (both Latino and non-Latino) gave
a shower for a colleague and served alcohol-spiked
punch. The idea of an all-female group consuming
alcohol together was new to her. On the other hand,
this practice was commonplace to other Mexican
American women who had gone to school in the United

States and graduated into the workforce. Another
woman, U.S.-born, reported that she found the holiday
dinner for husbands and wives given by her husband's
employer an unusual experience. She was surprised
that men were expected to bring their wives and that at
the event men and women stayed in mixed-sex groups,
drinking together. In traditional Mexican culture and
among some Mexican Americans, mixed-sex social
drinking in non-family settings is uncommon.

There are clearly more opportunities and more
pressures for a Mexican American woman to drink as
she adopts aspects of the majority culture. The
pressures will come from both non-Latinos and Latinos
who are more acculturated than she. Further, the
opportunities to drink and her willingness to accept
drinking as an appropriate behavior for herself will
increase as increased educational and financial status
allow her to go to new places and interact with new
people.

Against this backdrop, it is not surprising that a small
but growing number of acculturated Mexican American
women with heavy drinking patterns is being reported.
It is also probable that these women carry a particularly
heavy burden of guilt over excessive drinking because
their behavior conflicts with at least some of their
culturally based ideas of how a "good" woman is
supposed to behave. Certainly there will be people
around her who, ascribing to more traditional Mexican
drinking norms, will level criticism at her "shameful"
behavior. The recovery process for these women is
made more difficult because it is traditionally the
people most critical of her drinking who have provided
the social and emotional support common in extended
families. Now these same family members, if they are
to remain a source of support, will have to be educated
and incorporated into the recovery process. Sometimes
it is not possible to do this and difficult decisions
regarding recovery from alcohol addiction and family
loyalty will have to be faced. Helping professionals who
counsel or work with Mexican American women must
be aware of the guilt and culture conflict issues which
may surround women's use of alcohol. Dealing with
attitudes of more traditional family members will often
be an issue in treatment as will the need to uncover and
work with the individual's own confusion about conflicting cultural values in this and other life arenas.

There is danger in the speed at which changes in
alcohol-related norms and behaviors are taking place in
Mexican American women's lives. A youthful Chicana
may not have the opportunity to have moderate drinking
modeled for her by older women in her family because
they are quite likely not to drink at all. She may,
however, often be surrounded by heavy-drinking male
family members. Her questions, if she discusses the
issue of drinking with family members, may be met with

a flat statement that it is not appropriate for girls/women to drink. This will be of little help to her in view of the contradictory models and pressures she is encountering in her social world and in the media. Prevention programs targeted to adolescent and young adult Mexican American women need to realistically address the issues of learning how to drink moderately and assessing appropriate and safe contexts for drinking.

Use of Drugs Other Than Alcohol by Mexican American Women

There is very little specific information on the extent to which adult Mexican American women use illegal drugs or misuse prescription drugs. The scarcity of information is due to several factors. First, the published information on many large-scale studies, such as the National Household Survey, fails to desegregate Mexican Americans from other Latinos.[4] Additionally, some drug studies fail to break down ethnic data by gender. Further, most drug use prevalence studies have been concerned with adolescent rather than adult drug use.

Bearing these limitations in mind, however, several general findings can be extrapolated from available data. First, Mexican American women are less likely than their male counterparts to use drugs of all types. Data from the Hispanic Health and Nutrition Exam Survey (HHANES), for example, shows that 28 percent of the Mexican American women surveyed had ever used marijuana, compared to 36 percent of the men. The comparable percentages for cocaine were 6 percent and 17 percent and for inhalants, 3 percent and 10 percent.[5] A study of patients coming to emergency rooms with drug involvement revealed that 25 percent of the Latino males but only 9 percent of the Latinas mentioned heroin as contributing to their presenting difficulties. In general, too, Mexican American women are less likely than Puerto Rican or Anglo women to use illegal drugs, according to the HHANES and the Epidemiological Catchment Area studies of selected urban populations.[5,6]

Secondly, all studies that have looked at the relationship between drug use and level of acculturation among Mexican American women have shown greater drug use among acculturated as contrasted with less acculturated women, just as with alcohol use. For example, the HHANES showed that English-speaking Mexican American women were more than twice as likely to have used marijuana than non-English-speaking women and, similarly, women born in the United States were almost twice as likely to have used this drug than immigrant women. This is no doubt linked to the finding appearing in numerous studies of adolescents that drug use among Latinas is on the increase and is occurring at progressively younger ages.

Finally, there appears to be very substantial regional and local variability in the degree to which Mexican American women and girls are involved in illegal drug use. Reports from Texas, for example, show Mexican American girls in several south Texas locations as being much more likely to use illegal drugs than Latinas in national adolescent samples. Girls in *barrio* settings tend to use more drugs than other Latinas, and there is some indication that Mexican American girls in rural Southwestern settings equal and sometimes exceed the drug use of Anglo girls.

These general findings, while not as definitive as we might wish, do support the concept that drug prevention programs for Mexican American women and girls need to be grounded in good knowledge of the characteristics of Mexican American women in specific locales. Issues such as the general level of acculturation and the relative proportion of U.S.-born to Mexican-born women in a given locale need to be considered if programs are to be effective.

Developing Alcohol and Drug Services for Mexican American Women

Alcohol and drug use become a problem for Mexican American women when they develop problem drinking and drug use behaviors or are married to, living with, or related to someone who drinks excessively or takes illegal drugs. Mexican American women perhaps suffer greater alcohol- and drug-related health and social consequences than any other member of the family. Because of the traditional female role of "caretaker" and central figure in the family, the responsibility of maintaining a family under combined poor, unsafe and alcoholic or drug-using conditions is a tremendous psychological and physical burden. Immigrant women, especially, may not have the social and family networks that are often helpful and they will most likely lack the financial and language resources necessary for seeking help. Many of these women may also be debilitated by alcohol-related depression and other health problems. The more acculturated, second-generation woman may encounter other difficulties in seeking assistance with her own or another's alcohol or drug problem. Language will most likely not be a barrier, but financial problems and other cultural barriers may still apply.

Mexican American women, especially immigrant women, will be reluctant to ask sources external to the family for help. If they do seek help it is more likely that they will speak to a trusted neighbor, a *comadre*, a priest or a close family member. These sources may be helpful in some cases but may not be able to help in chronic situations or when women have a drinking problem of their own. When some women are ready to seek help outside of the family, they may not know where to go or what resources are available to them in their surrounding communities. Too often, there are few options for confidential, affordable, accessible and culturally compatible alcohol or drug treatment services for Mexican American women.

In order to be effectively utilized, a program must be committed to serving Mexican American women at all program levels. For a program to reproduce a safe, family-like environment conducive to reaching these women, it must adopt a philosophy that will support ongoing and specific outreach efforts, home visits, family involvement and a commitment to hiring bilingual, bicultural, recovering Mexican American women. The development of these services depends on support from the Board of Directors and adoption of language into the agency by-laws defining the program philosophy, services, facility planning and staff appropriate to these services.

Effective service programs in Mexican American communities are woven into the life of the community and become important to the community as they build credibility. Continuity of staff over time is an important element in developing credibility. An important element in establishing community support is networking with important community institutions such as the local churches, Head Start programs and health clinics. Developing these relationships also serves to establish strong and ongoing cross-referral links with other agencies and avoids the kind of referral process that often results in the recycling of individuals in need of services.

Other program elements which are important to the development of culturally appropriate services for Mexican American women are the availability of child care and a "children are welcome" attitude at the facility, the free use of Spanish at the facility, the availability of Spanish Alcoholics Anonymous and Al-Anon meetings at the facility and in the community, and continuous community education and involvement.

Support groups for Mexican American women are important for the women's development of positive coping mechanisms and self-empowerment. These help create safe environments where these women, perhaps for the first time, learn to trust someone outside of the family and find out that they are not alone in experiencing these problems. They learn to cultivate trusting and mutually supportive relationships in a cultural framework that is familiar and acceptable to them.

Conclusion

Changes taking place within the Mexican American population make it clear that the perception of the Chicana as an alcohol abstainer and a non-user of drugs is no longer accurate across the entire subcultural group. Rather, drinking and drug use patterns among Mexican American women is highly variable and is dependent on a number of factors including generational status, acculturation level, social class and place of residence. The changes in gender-related cultural norms, usually across just one generation, from strong sanctions prohibiting women's substance use to pressures encouraging women's substance use, creates value conflict, guilt and stigma surrounding the use and abuse of alcohol and drugs. Providers of services need to be very sensitive to this range of issues when assessing the need for substance-related services for Mexican American women. The design of services offered to Chicanas also should be sensitive to the range of factors influencing their lives.

References

1. U.S. Bureau of the Census, Current Population Reports, Series P-20, No. 431 (1988), *The Hispanic Population in the U.S.: March 1988 (Advance Report)*. Washington, D.C.: U.S. Government Printing Office.

2. Report of the Secretary's Task Force on Black & Minority Health (1986), *VII: Chemical Dependency and Diabetes*. Washington, D.C.: U.S. Department of Health and Human Services.

3. Santiesban, H. & Santiestevan, S., (eds)(1984), *The Hispanic Almanac*. Washington, D.C.: The Hispanic Policy Development Project.

4. National Center for Health Statistics (1985). *Plan of the Hispanic Health and Nutrition Exam Survey 1982-84*. U.S. Department of Health and Human Services, Series 1, No. 19, DHHS Pub. No. (PHS) 85-1321. Washington, D.C.: Government Printing Office.

5. National Institute on Drug Abuse (1989). *National Household Survey on Drug Abuse: Population Estimates 1988*. (DHHS Pub. No. (ADM) 89-1636. Washington, D.C.: Gov't Printing Office.

6. *Hispanic Health and Nutrition Examination Survey (1985)*. DHHS Pub. No. 85-1321. U.S. Dept. of Health and Human Services. Nat'l Center for Health Statistics. Sept. 1985.

7. Carno, M., et al. Lifetime Prevalence of Specific Disorders Among Mexican Americans and non-Hispanic Whites in Los Angeles. *Journal of General Psychiatry*, Vol. 44 p. 695-701 (1987).

6 Civil Rights and the "War" on Alcohol and Drugs

Ellen Weber, J.D.

"Drug testing programs have raised significant questions regarding a woman's privacy and due process rights. For example, a drug test subjects women to the intrusive and humiliating experience of providing urine samples to an employer and, in some cases, being observed in the process of doing so. In addition, women have been subjected to drug tests without first being told that they were being tested for drugs or asked to consent to the intrusive procedure."

Introduction

This nation's efforts to fight the ravages of alcoholism and drug dependence have placed tremendous strains on individual rights and civil liberties. While professionals working with alcohol- and drug-dependent people have long recognized that addictions can and must be treated, policy makers in federal and state governments and public and private employers have emphasized law enforcement activities and punishment of persons with drug and alcohol problems more than treatment. We are witnessing an alarming trend in which basic rights of privacy and fair and equal treatment have been sacrificed in the name of fighting the "war" on drugs and alcohol. It is important that women's centers and women's service organizations have an understanding of the current political climate as they begin to take on the work of advocating for women with alcohol and drug problems.

This chapter will provide an overview of the important civil rights issues that are related to alcohol and drugs and discuss how individual rights have been compromised in those areas. It will first examine drug testing in the workplace and the use of drug tests in other areas of life. It will then examine the protections that exist to prevent employment discrimination against persons with alcohol and drug problems and how the United States Congress may change those protections. Finally, it will examine recent efforts to fight drug-related activity in public and private housing and the impact on family life. Although this chapter focuses on individual rights and civil liberties as they pertain to women, many of the same issues apply to men.

Drug and Alcohol Testing in the Workplace

Background Information About Drug Testing Programs

One of the most controversial measures that has been adopted by employers to fight drug use in the workplace is drug testing. A drug test is a laboratory procedure that identifies the presence of alcohol or drugs in body fluids such as urine and blood. Drug tests determine whether a woman has used illegal drugs or prescription medications in the past. Drug tests cannot identify the frequency or pattern of use, the time of use or whether the individual was ever impaired as a result of the drug use.

Like all laboratory tests, drug test results can be inaccurate. Both over-the-counter and prescription medications have been misidentified as illegal drugs. Laboratory errors, such as mixing up samples and failure to follow accepted laboratory procedures, also lead to incorrect test results. As a result, women who do not use drugs may be falsely charged with drug use and those who do use drugs may never be detected.[1]

Drug tests can also reveal medical conditions totally unrelated to drug use. They can, for example, be used to determine whether a woman is pregnant or is taking medications to treat any number of medical conditions from epilepsy to depression.[2]

Drug and alcohol treatment programs have used drug tests for many years as one way to monitor whether recovering individuals are abstaining from drug use. But in the early 1980s, employers around the country began to use drug tests as a way to identify applicants and employees who were using drugs and to remove them from the workforce. Many employers instituted drug testing programs even though they did not have a drug problem in their workforce. Many have claimed that drug testing deters drug use and creates a safer workplace. However, little evidence exists that drug testing accomplishes either goal.[3]

Drug testing programs vary considerably among employers. Many employers test all job applicants, but test employees on a more limited basis, such as when there is reason to believe that a person has been using drugs or when an individual in a safety-related job has an annual physical examination. Other employers conduct unannounced random drug tests of all or selected categories of employees. Generally, employers only test for drug use and ignore alcohol use, even though most experts agree that alcohol dependence is a more significant problem within all workforces.

Drug testing programs have raised significant questions regarding a woman's privacy and due process rights. For example, a drug test subjects women to the intrusive and humiliating experience of providing urine samples to an employer and, in some cases, being observed in the process of doing so. In addition, women have been subjected to drug tests without first being told that they were being tested for drugs or asked to consent to the intrusive procedure. Moreover, in most cases, women are tested without any evidence that they have used drugs or have had a work problem that might be linked to drug or alcohol use.

In addition, many employers have used inexpensive and sloppy laboratory procedures to test the urine samples and others have not monitored laboratory testing to ensure that test results are accurate. Nevertheless, many employers have relied exclusively on the laboratory test result in making job decisions and many of those decisions have been based on inaccurate test results. People have been fired or disciplined and rejected from jobs solely on the basis of their test results. Many individuals who have never used drugs and were excellent employees have been falsely accused of drug use, stigmatized and have had their careers ruined.

Legal Challenges and Legislative Activity
The extensive and often inappropriate use of drug tests has generated two responses. First, many individuals have filed lawsuits challenging both the right of employers to conduct drug tests and the adequacy of the test procedures that have been used. Second, some states have enacted legislation limiting drug testing by employers and establishing standards to govern how drug tests are to be conducted and providing protections for employees who test positive.

Litigation
Most drug testing cases have challenged testing in the public sector—by schools, police and fire departments and public transportation authorities—under the Fourth Amendment to the United States Constitution and similar state constitutional provisions. The Fourth Amendment protects an individual's privacy against unreasonable searches and seizures that are performed by the government.

Courts have ruled that taking and analyzing urine samples for drugs is a search, and that a public

employer must, in general, have "reason to believe" that an individual has used drugs before requiring her to submit to a drug test. In other contexts, the courts have held that the government must have "probable cause" to believe that an individual is involved with unlawful activities and must obtain court approval to conduct the search. Thus the standard applied in drug testing cases is weaker and strips citizens of protections that the Fourth Amendment has given historically. Courts have reasoned that it is unrealistic to require employers to obtain court approval to conduct a drug test and that the individual's right to privacy is protected adequately if the government employer has some reason to believe that an individual has used drugs.

For individuals who work in safety-related and law enforcement jobs, the United States Supreme Court has gone further to remove privacy protections.[4] It has ruled that public employers can test employees in safety-related transportation jobs after accidents. Women who apply for jobs in law enforcement that involve narcotics or guns or deal with certain classified information can also be tested without any evidence that the applicant has used drugs or is impaired. However, the Supreme Court did emphasize that the drug test procedures must be accurate and the invasion of personal privacy must be as limited as possible.

Fourth Amendment limitations do not apply to private employers. Therefore, in many states private employers have broad discretion in determining when and who to test. In most cases, individuals who have been subjected to a drug test by a private employer have no way to challenge this practice. Some states, such as California, have a state constitutional right of privacy that many individuals have used to challenge unfair drug testing programs. But in most cases, a woman will not be able to challenge the requirement to take a drug test. Often the only available legal recourse is for women who have been falsely accused of using drugs: they may be able to sue an employer for negligent testing.

Legislation
The limited protection for employees in the private sector has led twelve states to enact laws to regulate drug testing by private employers. The states include Connecticut, Iowa, Louisiana, Maine, Maryland, Minnesota, Montana, Nebraska, Oregon, Rhode Island, Utah and Vermont. While each law differs, they generally specify when employees or applicants can be tested, what test procedures must be used, and what action can be taken against persons who test positive. For example, Maine, Vermont, Rhode Island and Montana impose strict limits on when employees can be tested. Most of these states, in addition to

Minnesota, Connecticut, and Nebraska, require employers to use the most accurate test procedures
available to ensure reliable testing. Finally, Iowa,
Maine, Minnesota and Vermont prohibit employers
from taking disciplinary action against a person who has
tested positive without first giving the employee a
chance to complete a treatment program.

It seems clear that drug testing will be part of
employment practices for the foreseeable future. This
has serious implications for whether women with drug
problems will be employable and have a chance to
receive treatment. Widespread use of drug tests is also
troublesome because of recent trends, discussed
below, to weaken protections against discrimination for
people who have drug dependence problems.

Drug Testing As a Condition for Receiving AFDC Benefits

Drug testing has reared its head in other important
areas of life. The United States Congress recently
considered a bill that would have required women to
take and pass a drug test in order to receive Aid to
Families with Dependent Children (AFDC) benefits.
Under the bill a woman who tested positive for drugs
would have had to enter a treatment program in order
to receive benefits. Refusal to register for a treatment
program would have resulted in the denial of benefits.
The bill would have also required random testing of
women currently receiving AFDC benefits.

The rationale for this troublesome proposal was that
women who receive public benefits should be held
accountable for the funds and should be required to get
treatment if they wish to continue to receive public
funds. Significantly, the bill was defeated by the Senate
and was never considered in the House of Representatives.[5]

This proposal, along with existing employment drug
testing programs, demonstrates the extent to which
drug tests may be used to deny women who have drug
problems the most basic means of survival.

Laws Protecting Alcohol- and Drug-Dependent Women From Employment Discrimination

The Rehabilitation Act of 1973 and State Disability Rights Laws

One of the most important laws that protects women
with alcohol and drug problems against discrimination
and promotes treatment for such problems is the
federal Rehabilitation Act of 1973.[6] This Act protects
women against discrimination on the basis of handicap
in a variety of areas including employment. Alcoholism
and drug dependence are among the medical conditions that are considered handicaps under the Rehabilitation Act.

The Rehabilitation Act protects three categories of
women: those who are currently handicapped, those
with a history of a handicap and those erroneously
regarded as being handicapped. Women who have had
a drug- or alcohol-dependence problem in the past and
have recovered from it are protected against employment discrimination under the last two categories
because they have a history of a handicap and are often
erroneously regarded as continuing to have a handicap.
The law also protects women who currently have an
alcohol- or drug-dependence problem as long as they
are able to perform the duties of the job and do not pose
a direct threat to property or the safety of others as a
result of current drug or alcohol use.

The Rehabilitation Act's prohibition on employment
discrimination applies to three groups of employers.
First, private employers who contract with a federal
agency for the supply of goods and services in excess of
$2,500 are bound by the Act. Second, any institution
that receives federal financial assistance, such as
schools, hospitals, social service agencies and state and
local governments, is prohibited from discriminating
under the Act. Finally, the federal government is
subject to the antidiscrimination provisions.

The Rehabilitation Act prohibits discrimination in all
aspects and conditions of employment—both pre-
employment and post-employment. It requires employers to make employment decisions based on
job-related criteria, not on stereotypical attitudes about
what an employer believes a woman with a disability is
able to do.

The Act prohibits employers from using blanket
policies to deny employment or advancement to entire
groups of individuals, such as all women who were
formerly dependent on drugs or alcohol. It also
prohibits employers from asking questions about handicaps that are not job-related and from conducting
medical examinations unless the applicant has been
given a conditional offer of employment. Thus, an
employer cannot require a job applicant to answer
questions concerning prior drug or alcohol use during
the preliminary employment process, and cannot ask
her to provide information about addiction-related
illness or treatment unless she has already been offered
employment.

An employer is, of course, entitled to consider the
applicant's prior work record in assessing her suitability
for employment. And applicants must meet all the
requirements for the job, which may include receiving
a particular educational degree or passing a competitive
examination. Similarly, employees must meet the same
non-discriminatory standards as any other employee in
seeking a promotion and may be disciplined for rule
violations and poor performance even if her drug or
alcohol problem contributed to the work performance

problem. What an employer *cannot* do is reject an
applicant or fire an employee simply because she was
once dependent on alcohol or drugs or is currently in a
treatment program.

The Rehabilitation Act is important not only because
it prohibits discrimination by many employers, but also
because it has served as a model for many state laws
protecting women against discrimination based on
handicap or disability. Virtually all states have passed
laws that prohibit discrimination by private employers
and a substantial number have followed the federal law
by including alcoholism and drug dependence as
covered disabilities.[7] These state laws are an important
source of protection because they go beyond the reach
of the Rehabilitation Act by prohibiting discriminatory
actions by virtually all private employers.

Congressional Action To Weaken Antidiscrimination Laws

The antidiscrimination protections that have been in
place for over fifteen years are now under attack in the
United States Congress. In previous years, the Congress has attempted to amend the Rehabilitation Act to
exclude persons with alcohol and drug problems from
protection. Those efforts have all been unsuccessful
until now.

The Congress is currently (March, 1990) debating a
new civil rights law known as the Americans With
Disabilities Act that will protect persons with disabilities against discrimination in the private employment
sector, in public accommodations, in transportation
and telecommunications. The Americans With Disabilities Act is very important because it will significantly
expand the employment opportunities of persons with
all types of disabilities. In addition, the Americans
With Disabilities Act will prohibit discrimination
against persons with AIDS and HIV infection.

One of the key points of debate surrounding this bill
has been whether persons with alcohol and drug
problems will be included within its protection. The
Bush Administration has indicated that it will not
support the Americans With Disabilities Act if persons
who use drugs illegally are among the individuals
protected. The Administration set this policy because it
believes that all individuals who use drugs must be held
"accountable" for their illegal activity and that people
will stop using drugs if they are denied benefits.

As a result, the Senate passed a bill (S.933) that does
not protect women who currently use illegal drugs.
This means that if an employer learns that a woman
uses or is addicted to drugs, the employer can fire or
not hire her regardless of whether she is able to do the
job. The Senate, however, went beyond the Administration's position and also removed protection for
women who are dependent on alcohol and women who

have been in recovery but still have physical and
mental conditions that resulted from alcohol or drug
dependence.

The House of Representatives is now voting on the
Americans With Disabilities Act. It appears that
several improvements will be made in the House
version of the bill. First, all women who have
recovered from alcohol and drug problems and those in
treatment will be protected. In addition, women who
have current alcohol problems will also be protected.
Finally, the House bill will protect women with current
drug problems from discrimination when they seek
health and social services. It is expected that the House
will continue to exclude women with current drug
problems from protection in employment. If the House
of Representatives passes a bill that contains different
protections than the Senate bill, as is expected, the two
bodies will have to reach an agreement on the scope of
protection for women with alcohol and drug problems.

Permitting employers to discriminate against women
who have current drug problems—simply because of
the drug problem—has serious implications. It is likely
that women who have drug problems and want to enter
treatment will be deterred from seeking it because of
the fear that their employer, upon learning of their
condition, will fire them. As a result, women will try to
hide their problems and workplaces may become more
dangerous. Once they have lost their employment,
drug-dependent women will have a more difficult time
obtaining treatment and other employment and living
a stable life.

Protection Against Discrimination in Housing

The Fair Housing Amendments Act of 1988

Housing, like employment, is fundamental to a
fulfilling and stable life. But, as with employment,
women with disabilities are often denied housing
simply because they are perceived to be dangerous or
unable to live safely and independently. In 1988, the
Congress passed the Fair Housing Amendments Act to
deal with senseless discrimination on the basis of
disability.[8]

The Fair Housing Amendments Act is an expansive
act that reaches every housing practice that results in
the segregation of people with disabilities. The Act
prohibits discrimination in the sale, rental or advertising of public and private dwellings, in the provision of
brokerage services, in the availability of residential real
estate loans and other financial assistance and in the
implementation of zoning laws.

The Fair Housing Act is modeled directly after the
Rehabilitation Act in defining who is protected against
discrimination. It protects women who have a current
disability, those with a history of a disability and those

regarded as having a disability. And the physical and mental conditions that constitute a "handicap" under the Rehabilitation Act generally constitute a "disability" under the Fair Housing Act.

Protection for persons with alcohol and drug problems was a key issue in the debate surrounding the Fair Housing Act. Many in Congress opposed protecting individuals who use drugs because of the serious safety threat in public housing projects that exists because of drug-related criminal activities. While the Act would have protected only those individuals who were qualified to reside in the dwelling and not a drug user whose activities created such a threat, Congress decided to eliminate all protections for persons who currently use or are addicted to illegal drugs.

Thus, a landlord can now evict a woman who uses drugs even if she is a good tenant and creates no problems. This provision eliminates protections that are essential to recovery. Women cannot be expected to recover from a drug problem if they do not have housing. Moreover, eliminating these protections was simply not necessary to create safe dwellings since persons who present a threat can be evicted from housing.

The Fair Housing Act does, however, prohibit landlords from discriminating against women who have recovered from a drug problem or who are in treatment. Just recently, the federal Justice Department filed several lawsuits alleging discrimination under the Fair Housing Act by several apartment management companies that refused to rent apartments to a drug treatment program. The treatment program attempted to rent the apartments for individuals who had successfully completed a residential treatment program and were required to live together as they made the transition back into society.

Eviction From Public Housing On The Basis of Drug-Related Criminal Activity

The serious threat posed by drug-related activity in public housing has led to increased efforts by federal and local officials to evict persons involved in such activity. Yet, like other efforts to deny rights to persons with drug problems, the eviction procedures have gone too far and have affected innocent individuals.

In 1988, the Congress passed a law that permitted public housing authorities to evict a public housing tenant and the tenant's entire household if the tenant or any member of the household or any guest engages in drug-related criminal activity on or near the public housing premises.[9] To speed up the eviction process, the Department of Housing and Urban Development instituted regulations that removed the tenant's right to an automatic administrative hearing before eviction. A court stopped the Department from implementing

these regulations on the ground that it violated the tenants' due process rights.[10]

Nonetheless, the Department has accomplished the same result by relying on a 1983 law to waive the obligation of city housing authorities in over twenty-nine states to follow federal eviction grievance procedures. As a result, landlords can bypass the administrative procedures and go directly to court to remove tenants arrested for—not convicted of—selling or using drugs. This process has had a serious affect on many poor families. In most cases, the families of the accused tenant have also lost the right to housing. For example, a grandmother and her four young grandchildren were evicted because another grandson who didn't live in the apartment but was named on the lease was arrested on cocaine charges. In another case, a mother was evicted because her son was arrested for cocaine use *off* the public housing premises.[11] The "family eviction" procedure is one more example of how policies to fight drug use have gone overboard and impinge on principles of fairness.

Conclusion

It is alarming that the federal government has advocated for the retrenchment in civil rights and privacy protection as a way to fight drugs. This policy is certainly inconsistent with the government's recent efforts to pump more federal dollars into drug and alcohol treatment and prevention activities, and it increases the stigma that is attached to drug and alcohol dependence. This shortsighted approach will certainly discourage treatment and will result in many more casualties in the "war on drugs."

References

1. For example, a grandmother was removed from her job as a school bus attendant because a drug test erroneously detected marijuana in her urine. The Court found that the drug test procedure was inadequate. *Jones v. McKenzie;* 628 F. Supp. 1500 (D.C.C. 1986).
2. One of the first lawsuits that challenged a drug testing program was brought by a woman who was fired after refusing to take a drug test. It was reported that she did not want to submit to the medical test because she was pregnant and did not want to reveal her medical condition. A jury awarded her $485,000 for the incorrect discharge and infliction of emotional distress. *Luck v. Southern Pacific Transportation Co.,* no. 843230 (Calif. Super. Ct., Oct. 30, 1987).
3. "Evidence is Skimpy That Drug Testing Works, But Employers Embrace Practice," *Wall Street Journal,* Sept. 7, 1989. B1.
4. In *National Treasury Employees Union v. Von*

Raab, 109 S. Ct. 1384, the Supreme Court upheld the Customs Service mandatory testing program of employees who seek promotions to positions involving drug interdiction or use of firearms. In *Skinner v. Railway Labor Executives Association,* 109 S. Ct. 1402, the Supreme Court upheld the mandatory post-accident testing of railroad employees in safety-sensitive positions.

5. 132nd Congressional Record 512736-39 (Oct. 5, 1989).

6. 29 U.S.C. section 701-794.

7. The disability laws of Connecticut, District of Columbia, Florida, Illinois, Iowa, Maine, Massachusetts, Minnesota, Missouri, Nebraska, New Hampshire, New Jersey, New York, North Dakota, Ohio, Oklahoma, Oregon, Rhode Island, South Dakota, Utah, Vermont, West Virginia, Wisconsin and Wyoming have been interpreted by either courts or administrative agencies to protect individuals with drug and alcohol problems against discrimination. In addition, the laws of Arizona, Michigan, Montana, New Mexico, Tennessee and Virginia protect individuals who have recovered from a drug or alcohol problem and are not currently using substances.

8. Pub. L. No. 100-430, 42 U.S.C., section 3601 *et seq.*

9. The provision was passed as part of the Anti-Drug Abuse Act of 1988 and is codified in the United States Housing Act of 1937, 42 U.S.C., section 1437d(1).

10. "In Antidrug Drive, Alexandria May Test Housing Eviction Rules," *The Washington Post,* March 25, 1989, A1.

11. "Public Housing Aides Push to Evict Drug Users, Sometimes Violating the Rights of Other Tenants," *Wall Street Journal,* July 6, 1989, A14.

7 Issues for African American Women

Ashaki H. Taha-Cissé

"The African American woman has emerged from a history of oppression. Stigmatized for being Black in a racist society, female in a sexist society, poor in an affluent society and frequently, a single parent in a traditionally two-parent society, African American women are resistant to owning yet another problem—alcohol and drug abuse."

Alcohol and drugs constitute a health crisis for African American* women in the United States. African American women are disproportionately affected by alcohol and drugs, whether through their own use of substances or that of family members, life partners, children, friends or others. This chapter provides an overview of the historical, socioeconomic, political and cultural factors affecting African American women and their relationship to alcohol and drug use. The chapter brings an Africentric** perspective to the field of alcohol and drug prevention and treatment, challenging long-held assumptions and stereotypes that continue to function as barriers to effective interventions for African American women. Finally, it offers recommendations for culturally specific components of prevention and treatment initiatives for African American women and their children.

African American women share a cultural and historical legacy that encompasses both our African heritage and the consequences of centuries of exploitation and oppression, whether through colonization, enslavement, codified apartheid, de facto segregation or other expressions of individual and institutional racism.[1] Although we share these common experiences, African American women are not a monolith.

Rather, we reflect southern, northern, urban, suburban and rural American sensibilities, Caribbean (West Indian), Latin American and African nuances from varied regions of the continent. We also reflect an extensive array of educational, occupational and economic diversity. To be effective, therefore, prevention and treatment initiatives must acknowledge both our similarities and our differences through gender-specific, culturally relevant service models, staffing patterns, educational materials and referral networks.

Historical Overview

Like other health and social problems among African Americans, alcohol and drug problems are rooted in history. Unlike Europeans, Africans did not import drinking customs or problems from Old World settings. Rather, alcohol was thrust upon Africans by slave traders who bartered their lives for whiskey and rum and by American slave owners who utilized alcohol as a tool of control to pacify slaves and thwart insurrection.[2] Alcohol was introduced on plantations and distributed generously to slaves on holidays as a reward for hard work.[2] On these occasions, drunkenness was considered normal and acceptable, even desirable. Patterns of alcohol consumption today are consistent with this historical use of alcohol, such as weekend drinking after working all week.

Following Nat Turner's Revolt in 1830, a major shift in the perception of drunkenness from being benign or desirable to being a preceptor of revolt occurred.[2] As a result, many laws were passed that imposed rigid restrictions on alcohol use among African Americans.[2]

Herd attributes the low rates of alcohol-related problems among African Americans throughout most of the 19th century to their strong identification with the Temperance Movement, which was closely linked with

*Within this chapter, African American is an inclusive identifier of all women of African ancestry in the Americas, i.e., African Americans (born in the U.S.), African Caribbeans, African Latinas and African nationals living in the U.S. as part of the African Diaspora.

**Africentric refers to a world view based upon African values and sensibilities in contrast to the Eurocentric perspective of the dominant American culture.

The author wishes to thank Denise Herd, Ph. D., Lee Brown-Corbin, J.D., Marsha Russell, Ph. D., Brenda Underhill, M.S.W., Clarissa Chandler and Autherine Walker. Special thanks to Denise Mahnken for her assistance in the preparation of this chapter.

the Anti-Slavery movement.[3] Following the abolition of slavery, African American organizations advocated for a "Colored Temperance Movement."[4] African American women were in the forefront of such efforts through the Colored Women's Club Movement, and the African American church continued to promote temperance well into the beginning of the 20th century. At that time, the southern-based Temperance Movement became steeped in the politics of white supremacy, supportive of "Jim Crow" laws and the political disenfranchisement of African Americans.[4] As a result, African Americans effectively distanced themselves from the temperance issue.[5] The 20th century also witnessed major shifts in population among African Americans from the south to the north. In these urbanized and often alienated settings, still faced with social and economic inequality, African American alcohol consumption and involvement in the illegal trafficking of alcohol increased dramatically, as did alcohol-related problems.[4]

Throughout the twentieth century, African American expectations for major political and socioeconomic justice have been raised and dashed with regularity. This pattern is reflected from World War I to the post-Civil Rights Movement expectations of the 1960s. Indicators of quality-of-life issues in the African American community reveal that the majority of African Americans continue to live in poverty and have diminished access to quality health care, housing, education and employment opportunities. For many, the response to these conditions is alcohol and drug use. However, alcohol and drug use in the African American community should not be seen solely as an individual response to societal stresses. Deliberate efforts have been made by different groups to increase dependence on legal and illegal drug use among African Americans. A widely-held belief in the African American community, supported by anecdotal reports, is that undercover agents infused virtually uncut heroin into the African American community during the 1960s to subvert grassroots political activity.

As for legal drugs, the alcohol industry now inundates African American communities with pro-use advertising messages on billboards, in magazines and the broadcast media that link power, sexuality and affluence with drinking.[6,7] Whether politically or economically motivated, these efforts share responsibility for high levels of alcohol and drug use within the African American community.

Alcohol and Drug Consumption and Related Problems

Two devastating new drug-related epidemics have assaulted African American women and their children. The first is crack use, which is both enslaving and killing large numbers of women and children. The second is the incidence of AIDS resulting from sharing needles, increased sexual activity due to crack use or having unprotected sex with partners who are intravenous drug users. Nationally, 52 percent of the women and 57 percent of the children with AIDS are African American.[8] African American and Latino women comprise more than 70 percent of women diagnosed with AIDS.[9]

It is also estimated that women may comprise about one-fourth of all persons addicted to heroin. However, lack of national interest, sparse research and inadequate funding resources for communities hardest hit by heroin addiction has resulted in little current data.

Alcohol is the number one cause of health problems among African Americans.[10] Alcohol is the most commonly abused drug in the African American community.[10] It is estimated that 14-16 percent of African Americans are alcoholic.[10] Alcohol is the leading cause of death among African American men between 25 and 44 years of age and has been linked to violent behaviors that include homicide, automobile crashes, criminal assaults, violence against women, child abuse and suicide.[10,11] After prescription drugs, alcohol is the drug most often abused by African American seniors.[12] African American adolescents are at high risk for alcohol use, often in combination with other drugs, and children begin experimenting with alcohol at about age nine.[12] The risk of Fetal Alcohol Syndrome to African American infants is seven times greater than among White infants who receive the same prenatal alcohol exposure.[13] Seventy percent of all African American adults drink to some extent, with men twice as likely as women to drink heavily.[14]

Sex differences are diminishing, however, with the greatest increase in drinking occurring among women in the 15-29 age group and among African American women under 35 who are divorced or separated.[14] According to the National Institute on Alcohol Abuse and Alcoholism, African American women "suffer disproportionately from the health consequences of alcoholism, including cancer, obstructive pulmonary disease, severe malnutrition, hypertension and birth defects."[10] Twice as many African American women as men report alcohol-related health problems.[15] African American women between the ages of 15 and 34 have rates of cirrhosis of the liver more than six times the White rate and have a high incidence of death once the liver has been damaged.[15] The incidence of esophageal cancer, promoted by both alcohol and cigarette use, is three to seven times greater for African American women than for White women.[16] Drinking patterns among African American women appear to be polarized. They reflect both higher rates of abstinence and higher rates of heavy drinking than do White women.[17]

African American women who do drink heavily tend to become alcoholic more rapidly and those who enter treatment are significantly younger than their White counterparts.[18,19]

Cultural Considerations

It is virtually impossible to develop effective prevention interventions without understanding the culture-bound health beliefs and behaviors of the community. It is essential to work within—rather than counter to—that context so that interventions are consistent with both self- and group esteem. New information must be integrated into ways of behaving that are consistent with the culture. If the new information is in conflict with cultural behaviors, the increase in knowledge is unlikely to cause behavioral change. The health education research of Braithwaite and Lythcott supports this view. "Because health behaviors are culture-bound, primary prevention efforts . . . must emerge from a knowledge of and respect for the culture of the target community to ensure that both the community organization and development effort and any interventions are culturally sensitive and linguistically appropriate."[20] Brisbane and Womble support the significance of treatment that recognizes and addresses issues of gender, race, and sociopolitical and economic realities within a cultural context.[21]

African American culture tends to be permissive toward alcohol consumption, although it is least tolerant concerning alcohol and drug use among women and seniors.[12] Generally, the culture supports alcohol use during an array of events such as family reunions, holidays, birthdays, anniversaries, graduations, christenings and wakes, and attributes weakness to those who can't hold their liquor.[22] As previously mentioned, drinking patterns tend toward heavy weekend consumption. A strong work orientation within the African American family may also account for this alcohol-related behavior.[23] Some studies indicate that women tend to engage in heavy weekend or binge drinking.[24]

The cultural interpretation of alcohol problems is noteworthy. For White, middle- and upper-class men and women, the recognition of alcoholism as a treatable disease with medical and genetic components helped reduce the stigma of being alcoholic. However, the African American community is far more likely to reject the illness concept and refer to someone as "drinking too much" as a result of stress related to the reality of life in America.[12] For African American women, those stresses include having to cope with racism, sexism and, frequently, single parenthood and poverty. Alcohol, then, is perceived as a means of handling problems, something that serves as a buffer between the person and a hostile environment, something used to cope until things get better.[25] Problems with alcohol are viewed in terms of how they affect an individual's relationship with others, not as a physical allergy to alcohol.[24] Further, weekend or binge drinking patterns enable denial of a problem with alcohol to continue. After all, how can there be a problem if a person works every day, holds down one or more jobs and is meeting her responsibilities? Alcohol is perceived as helping her to cope with job pressures and family stresses.[24]

One of the strongest African American cultural patterns is that of the extensive internal helping system found in the extended family, which may include, but is not limited to, blood relatives.[21] In fact, it is far more common for the extended family to be more of a family of choice than of origin. For African American women, the family of choice may be a greater source of support and play a far more prominent role in their lives than does the family of origin. Any prevention and treatment initiative for African American women must include their extended families.

Barriers to Prevention and Treatment for African American Women

The issues that place the African American woman at risk for problems with alcohol and drugs are precisely the issues that affect her ability to seek help for these problems. She is one of the least identified to receive prevention information and adequate treatment, and is most frequently punished for behavior accompanying alcohol and drug abuse.

The African American woman has emerged from a history of oppression.[27-29] Stigmatized for being Black in a racist society, female in a sexist society, poor in an affluent society and frequently, a single parent in a traditionally two-parent society, African American women are resistant to owning yet another problem—alcohol and drug abuse. The ways in which the African American woman continues to be devalued by the larger society affects her perception of self, her relationships, and her ability to maintain sanity and balance in the midst of insanity and disequilibrium. The result is an overwhelming sense of powerlessness, which generates an attitude of self-blame, generalized mistrust, feelings of alienation from resources of social influence, disenfranchisement, economic vulnerability and, finally, a sense of hopelessness.[20] In the face of this reality, the myth of the African American woman as matriarch is particularly cruel. It is a myth that was created not to empower African American women, but to further emasculate African American men. While matriarchy implies the exercise of power by women, African American women have had consistently low status within the society.[30]

The African American woman's ability to adapt, through necessity, to roles traditionally viewed as

male, has resulted in negative labelling. She has been
called both dominating and castrating, and blamed for
the disintegration of the African American family and
community. Conversely, she has been idealized as the
strong, liberated, self-sufficient matriarch who is responsible for the survival of the family and community.
Seen as monuments of strength, African American
women are left little room to admit they have a
problem, engage in help-seeking behaviors or utilize
resources.

It has been suggested that an unresponsive alcohol
and drug service delivery system is a barrier to African
Americans seeking treatment. An insensitivity to
cultural values, such as the extended family, may be
one of the major barriers. The Eurocentric nuclear
family model, which has even begun to break down for
non-African American families, is not relevant or
effective when working with African American family
systems. Failure to understand this has resulted in a
distorted view of the African American family as
dysfunctional. This misperception diminishes the opportunity to tap one of the strongest resources for
prevention and treatment within the culture. African
American women are far more likely to look to their
extended families as a source of strength and protection
and for help with problems than to outside sources.
This tendency is consistent with the cultural notion of
not "putting your business in the street."

There are additional barriers to successful intervention with African American women. Prevention and
treatment models that focus on individual pathology to
the exclusion of sociological and environmental factors
fail to acknowledge the essential links between alcohol
and drug problems, racism, sexism and poverty for
African American women. The concept of rehabilitation
is also not relevant to African American women. To
rehabilitate is to return to a state of well-being. For
African American women, whose entire psychosocial
development has occurred in a hostile environment
that conveys negative messages about who they are and
how they look, the focus must be habilitation. Habilitation requires life-affirming, self-validating program
components that are family focused. This serves to
dismantle distorted ideas of self that have been built on
a European standard of beauty, stereotypical role
definitions and the experience of powerlessness.

The response to African American women by medical, social service and police personnel is more punitive
than to White women. Researchers from the National
Association for Perinatal Addiction Research and Education report that "a minority woman who uses drugs or
alcohol during pregnancy is almost ten times more
likely to be reported to child abuse authorities than is a
White woman."[31] In the light of these findings,
pregnant African American women who are using

alcohol and drugs are understandably reluctant to seek
help. Other barriers to treatment include lack of
third-party insurance coverage and times when services are available. African American women also tend to
not turn to Alcoholics Anonymous, which is perceived
to have a White male orientation. Many A.A. meetings
are held outside the African American community,
which is a barrier to attendance for many women.

Public agencies tend to be seen as intrusive and
punitive and are perceived with distrust. African
American women are reluctant to seek help from
agencies with the power to cut off financial support or
take their children from them.

Women who come to the United States from
countries where communal living is the norm can feel
isolated and alienated. The transition from communal,
group-centered living is a difficult one. The absence of
extended family, especially of older women to provide
support, advice and information regarding marital,
health and child-rearing matters, places these women
at particularly high risk for alcohol and drug use.
Research is needed to assess the relationship between
acculturation and the use of alcohol and other drugs
among women of the African Diaspora. Undocumented
women have additional problems. They may not speak
English, and be unable to read or write. Resources to
assist them with their basic needs and information and
services regarding alcohol and drugs may be particularly inaccessible to them. Thus, the rich diversity of
the African American community brings both special
strengths and special needs to the prevention and
treatment process.

Conclusion
Racism and sexism are persistent, pernicious conditions from which American society continues to suffer
and which serve to doubly oppress African American
women, who share both a rich African past and the
current reality of the African Diaspora. They span a
wide range of geographic, linguistic, economic, educational and social differences. Despite these variations,
African American women are overrepresented in lower
economic levels, among women who are single heads of
households, women who have less access to decent
housing and quality medical care, women addicted to
crack, women suffering from alcohol-related health
problems and women living with AIDS.

The complex issues and influences that affect the
African American community require innovative strategies to help reduce alcohol and drug problems for
women and their children. Comprehensive planning
that involves women from the community is required.
Planning must consider the knowledge, attitudes,
beliefs, cultural values and perceptions of the women to
be served. A sensitivity to educational, socioeconomic

and acculturation issues must also be demonstrated. Innovative prevention and treatment initiatives will then emerge from an understanding of and respect for the varied multicultural and multilingual realities of African American women.

It is essential that African American women and the community-based organizations that serve them acknowledge that alcohol and drugs are women's issues that can and must be addressed now. The survival of the African American community is at stake.

The following recommendations for program planning and prevention and treatment services are offered.

Cultural Considerations for Program Planning
- Recognize that an Africentric perspective values the interpersonal relationship between people above other motivations.
- Spirituality is an important component of the culture. Spirituality does not necessarily mean religiosity, but recognizes the relationships between human and spiritual networks.[26]
- Even some attempts to be "culturally sensitive" reflect a Eurocentric perspective. For example, health educators have been encouraged to look at the way in which a particular culture attributes events to internal or external causes when developing health interventions. The very notion of locus of control is inconsistent with an Africentric perspective that recognizes the interconnectedness of human and spiritual networks, so that nothing is attributed exclusively to either internal or external causes.
- Be sensitive to the resistance to anything that is critical of family, especially that implies that parents are "bad" or "sick." Be aware that messages that are heard as "you have a problem," or language that implies "you are needy" or "you are sick" will also meet with resistance.[12]
- Expand and redefine the concept of family to include the extended family of choice.
- Encourage approaches that support and sustain "independence." The African American cultural context is not individual-oriented. It incorporates interdependence, collectiveness and cooperation for the benefit of the group. It is independence in the sense of being able to "take care of business," as opposed to dependence, but always includes family and community.
- Recognize the cultural role of the elders in the community as the conveyors of information, values and tradition. Securing the participation of seniors offers an opportunity to educate them about their own use of prescription drugs and is

consistent with the multigenerational, cultural concept of extended family.
- Be sensitive to the nuances of non-verbal forms of communicating, such as eye contact. Not looking someone in the eye is a sign of respect ("Don't you eyeball me, boy") in many cultures, including African American culture. Others may misinterpret the avoidance of eye contact as reflecting disrespect, dishonesty or untrustworthiness.[2]
- Be aware of language formalities. Calling an older African American woman by her first name is considered disrespectful. African American sensitivity to language is based on a long history of verbal denigration and racial epithets. Historically, African American women were "girl" until they were old, then became "aunt," but were never Mrs. (Similarly, African American men were "boy" until they became "uncle," but were never Mr.).
- Recognize the oral tradition of African American culture. Prevention interventions can include story-telling and other audio-visual communications, such as rap music on video and audio cassettes, in addition to written materials.

Recommendations for Prevention and Treatment for African American Women
- For many women, it is critical to address basic survival issues first—food, shelter, clothing, legal advocacy, jobs, education and child care. Women's centers and other women's service organizations also have a unique opportunity and a responsibility to provide alcohol and drug education to women they serve. By offering alcohol and drug information in an environment that African American women perceive as safe and supportive, the level of resistance to alcohol and drug information is lowered and constructive messages are likely to be heard.
- The name of the program should be positive. A name that supports self-empowerment will be more acceptable to African American women than one which is "problem-oriented."
- Programs should build on the cultural strengths of African American women and provide counseling that validates their experiences and enhances their self-esteem. Presently, African American women have to contort to fit within existing support systems. Programs should be designed to dismantle negative self- and group concepts by building on inherent cultural strengths.
- Both prevention and treatment initiatives should reflect a holistic approach that focuses on relationship building and demonstrates care for the African American woman in all her roles. The

African American woman must be seen as a whole person, not just in relation to her "problem."

- Prevention and treatment initiatives must reach out to and include extended families, which are as often families of choice as families of origin, and a fundamental source of support.
- Alcohol and drug programs must develop both gender-specific and culturally relevant treatment models and employ bicultural staff representative of the populations served. Staff must be able to relate to the African American experience. It is important to acknowledge that African American women may find it difficult and "off-putting" to seek or obtain support from people they perceive as part of the problem. Women would not be expected to seek rape crisis intervention from a project predominantly staffed by men, no matter how caring and competent they might be. In addition, the effectiveness of messages designed to alter health attitudes and behavior is, to a large extent, determined by the credibility of the individual delivering the message. African American women must be able to see themselves reflected in the service models and the sources of support.
- Child care is a critical component of any program that offers treatment to African American women. Ideally, child care should be more than "baby sitting," offering education to children and helping children explore their own identities as well as feelings related to the drinking and drug use of their parents.
- Flexible hours for service are recommended. They reflect a respect for the working poor who may be unable to take time off from work. Programs should consider offering services on evenings and weekends, including Sundays.
- Network with other community service providers who can further support African American women's efforts toward self-empowerment.
- Education must focus on deglamorizing and demystifying the use of alcohol and drugs as a means of gaining social and economic power and success.
- Prevention initiatives should also focus on children. Network with Head Start teachers, family day care providers, after-school programs and community-based religious groups. This will help counter peer pressure to use drugs and media "pro-use" messages.
- Program materials should be multilingual and multicultural, and should be sensitive to literacy levels and nuances of the same language that have different cultural interpretations of common words or expressions. They must also include an Africentric standard of beauty, color and design.
- For service providers who are not African American, it is essential to acknowledge the cultural variables that determine how effective your interventions can be when working with African American women and their families. It is important to recognize that services designed for the majority population, generally White men, and based upon European American cultural norms cannot be generically applied to African American women, nor should African American women be expected to contort to fit them.
- For African American women working in the alcohol and drug field, the African American "clients" we see are our mothers, aunts, sisters, grandmothers, daughters and nieces—they are ourselves. Professional detachment should be set aside in order to communicate our genuine concern for them as "our own," empower them to draw on their own strengths and encourage them to support one another.

References

1. Carmichael, S. and Hamilton, C.V. 1967. *Black Power*. New York: Vintage Books, p. 4.
2. Davis, F. 1974. "Alcoholism Among Black Americans." *Addiction*, p. 8-16. Quoted in Williams, M. 1982. "Blacks and Alcohol — Issues in the 1980s," *Alcohol Health and Research World*, Summer 1982, pp. 31-40.
3. Herd, D. 1985. "The Epidemiology of Drinking Patterns and Alcohol-Related Problems Among U.S. Blacks, *Alcohol Use Among U.S. Ethnic Minorities*, U.S. Department of Health and Human Services, p. 3.
4. Cheagle, R.U. 1969. *The Colored Temperance Movement*, Moorland-Springain Research Center, Washington, D.C.: Howard University Press, and Quarles, B. 1969. *Black Abolitionists*, New York, Oxford University Press. Cited in Herd, D. "Migration, cultural transformation and the rise of Black liver cirrhosis mortality." *Br. Jour. Addict* 80:397-410.
5. Herd, D. 1983. "Prohibition, Racism, and Class Politics in the Post Reconstruction South", *Jour. Drug Issues*, pp. 149-170.
6. Hacker, G.A., Collins. R. and Jacobson, M. 1984. *Marketing Booze to Blacks*. Center for Science in the Public Interest, Washington DC.
7. McMahon, E.T. and Taylor, P.A. 1990. *Citizen's Action Handbook on Alcohol and Tobacco Billboard Advertising*. Center for Science in the Public Interest, Washington, DC.

8. "HIV/AIDS Surveillance Report—United States, 1989." Centers for Disease Control.

9. Nobles, M. and Jacob, O. 1987. Testimony to the New York State Governor's Advisory Committee for Black Affairs on their preliminary report on the AIDS crisis in the Black community. *Women in Crisis,* October, 1987.

10. National Institute on Alcohol Abuse and Alcoholism. 1987. Sixth Special Report to the U.S. Congress on Alcohol and Health, Rockville, Maryland , Haxer, F.D. 1976. *Alcohol Abuse in Black America.* Alexandria, VA: Douglass Publications, and Womble, M. "Black Women," in Ruth Engs (Ed.), *Women, Alcohol and Other Drugs.* ADPA.

11. National Criminal Justice Information and Statistics Service. 1975. Survey of Inmates of State Correctional Facilities: Advance Report, Washington, D.C., U.S. Department of Justice Law Enforcement Assistance Administration.

12. Jackson, J. 1986. 11th FDCI Chemical Dependency Symposium. Jan. 15-17th, Sacramento, CA., transcript.

13. Sokol, Robert J. et al. 1986. "Significant Determinants of Susceptibility of Alcohol Teratogenicity," *Annals of New York Academy of Sciences Vol 477,* pp. 87-102.

14. King, L. M. 1982. "Alcoholism: Studies Regarding Black Americans. *Alcohol and Health Monograph 4, Special Population Issues,* DHHS publication No (ADN 82-1193), Washington, D.C.: U.S. Government Print Office, pp. 385-407.

15. Leland, J. 1984. "Alcohol Problems in Women: Antecedents, Consequences, and Intervention," in S. Wilsnack and L. Beckman (Eds.) *Alcohol Use and Abuse in Ethnic Minorities,* NY: Guilford Press, pp. 66-96.

16. Herd, D. 1985. op. cit., p. 10.

17. Gary, L.E. and Gary, R.B. 1985. "Treatment Needs of Black Alcoholic Women" in F. Brisbane and M. Womble, M. (Eds.), *Treatment of Black Alcoholics,* NY: The Haworth Press, p. 97-114.

18. Cahalan, D., Cisin, I.H. and Crossley, N.M., 1969. *American Drinking Practices: A National Study of Drinking Behavior and Attitudes,* N.J: Rutgers Center of Alcohol Studies.

19. Amaro, H., Beckman, L., Mays, V., 1986. A Comparison of Black and White Women Entering Alcohol Treatment, *Journal on the Studies of Alcoholism,* vol. 48, no. 3 (1987) p. 220.

20. Braithwaite, R.L. and Lythcott, N. "Community empowerment as a strategy for health promotion for Black and other minority populations." *JAMA,* Vol. 261, no. 2., January 13, 1989.

21. Brisbane, F. and Womble, M., 1985. "Afterthoughts and Recommendations." In *The Treatment of Black Alcoholics,* New York: Hawthorn Press.

22. Bailey, M.B. and Alksne, H. 1965. "The epidemiology of alcoholism in a residential area," *Quarterly Journal of Studies* on Alcohol 26: 19-40.23.

23. Hill, R. *The Strengths of Black Families.* NY: Emerson Hall Publishers.

24. Stern, M. and Pittman, D.J., 1976. *Drinking Practices in the Ghetto,* Vol I and II. IL: St. Louis University, Social Science Institute.

25. "Guideline for Community Prevention of Alcoholism Among Black Women." 1990. California Women's Commission on Alcohol and Drug Dependencies.

26. Nichols, E.J. 1976. "The philosophical aspects of cultural differences," presented at the World Psychiatric Association and Association of Psychiatrists in Nigeria Conference.

27. Lerner, G. 1972. *Black Women in White America.* NY: Vintage.

28. Cade, Toni. 1970. *The Black Woman.* NY: Mentor.

29. Rogers-Rose, L.F. 1980. *The Black Woman.* Beverly Hills, CA: Sage Publications.

30. Ladner, J. 1972. *Tomorrow's Tomorrow: the Black woman.* NY: Anchor Books.

31. National Association for Perinatal Addiction Research and Education. News release, Sept. 18, 1989.

8 Adult Survivors of Childhood Sexual Abuse: Substance Abuse and Other Consequences

Sue A. Russell and Sharon Wilsnack, Ph.D.

"Even using the more conservative definition of sexual abuse, well over one-third of the female children in the United States have experienced sexual abuse by the age of eighteen. There is no excuse for a problem of this magnitude to go unaddressed. . . . We question how there can be any equality between the sexes 'as long as girl children are being sexually violated in such massive numbers.'"

Introduction

Sexual abuse in childhood has been thought to be but one of many unfortunate experiences befalling a few women. Repercussions, if any, were expected to be sexual in nature (e.g., sexual dysfunction in adulthood). Consequently, it may surprise the reader to find a chapter on sexual abuse in a book about alcohol and other drugs. To the surprise of many, there is strong evidence to suggest that a major contributing factor to many of the problems for which women seek assistance (substance abuse, family violence, rape, emotional and economic difficulties, and marital and relational problems) is a history of sexual abuse in childhood. This finding has important implications for persons providing services to women. Attempts to alleviate the consequences of abuse will often meet with limited success until the sexual abuse itself is addressed.

Discovering and treating the sexual abuse is made difficult by the fact that it will seldom be brought to the attention of the caregiver. Women are much more likely to seek help for the *consequences* of abuse, such as depression or alcoholism, than for the abuse itself. This is probably due to many factors. One is that the women survivors, and often their helpers, are unaware that their current difficulties are in any way related to their earlier abuse. Another factor is that the sexual abuse of children is not a topic that most people are comfortable discussing. In addition, some women are unable to recognize and label their childhood experiences as abuse, while others are unable to recall the experiences altogether, probably repressing them in an attempt to cope. Therefore, it is of utmost importance that staff of women's centers and organizations serving women be alerted to just how widespread the sexual

abuse of children is, and to the many interconnections between childhood sexual abuse and the difficulties for which adult women seek help. One can be sure that a number of women seeking help for other problems have a history of sexual abuse complicating a satisfactory recovery.

Prevalence of the Sexual Abuse of Children

The reported prevalence of childhood sexual abuse varies widely and is much debated. In seven major studies reviewed by a leading researcher in the field[1], the rate of sexual abuse varied from as low as 5 percent[2] to as high as 62 percent.[3] Much of the variability depends on how researchers define childhood sexual abuse.

Definition of Childhood Sexual Abuse as Related to Prevalence

There is no standard definition of childhood sexual abuse at this time. The research findings and statistics that are available are meaningful only in the context of how each study defines childhood sexual abuse. In defining abuse, we must grapple with such questions as the relationship of the abuser to the girl (relative vs. nonrelative, type of relative, stranger vs. acquaintance, etc.), the age difference between the victim and her abuser, whether the advances involved physical contact, to what degree the advances were forced, whether the advances caused distress and, if so, how much and how long-lasting.

It is particularly important to determine if the definition of abuse includes sexual abuse by nonrelatives. The rate of prevalence often doubles when extrafamilial abuse experiences are included in the statistics. For the purposes of this chapter, we use the term "childhood sexual abuse" inclusively to refer to both intrafamilial and extrafamilial sexual abuse experiences before the age of eighteen. When we use the term "incest" we are referring exclusively to sexual abuse by a relative before the age of eighteen.

Some definitions of childhood sexual abuse are limited to adult abusers. Childhood peers are not considered as possible perpetrators by some researchers. Other researchers include some sexual experiences with peers in their definition of childhood sexual abuse, arguing that just as adult women can be sexually abused by peers, certainly children can be sexually abused by one another. Since abusive sexual behavior between children may be difficult to distinguish from nonabusive sex play, many researchers, out of convenience, define child sexual abuse as occurring between a child and an adult (the perpetrator being at least five years older than the girl).

Some researchers limit their definition of sexual abuse to actual sexual contact or attempted contact with the child, while other researchers also include behaviors that do not involve actual or attempted sexual contact with the child, such as exhibitionism, voyeurism and verbal propositions. When we informally compared studies listed by a well-known researcher which looked at noncontact and contact experiences separately, the inclusion of noncontact experiences in the statistics tended to increase the rates of abuse by approximately 40 percent.[1]

Research Methodology as Related to Prevalence

Another factor accounting for the large discrepancies in prevalence is research methodology. When studies are designed with sensitivity to childhood sexual abuse, high disclosure rates can be obtained; but where knowledge and sympathy are lacking, low rates of disclosure are the result. For instance, only 2-3 percent of the women studied by Alfred Kinsey reported intrafamilial sexual abuse before the age of 14, compared with 12 percent of the women studied by D. Russell.[1] Kinsey used all male interviewers (Kinsey himself did over half the interviews) and has been criticized for having a bias against recognizing the abusiveness of incest.[4] In contrast, Russell chose all female interviewers and carefully selected out biased, "victim-blaming" interviewers. The remaining women were given an intensive 65-hour training program. Sensitivity to ethnicity, socioeconomic status and age was exercised in interviewer-interviewee matches wherever possible.

Other variations in research methodology which affect prevalence rates include the rigor of the research design, such as the number and randomness of subjects (how well the subjects represent the general population

of women) and the sophistication of the statistical analysis. Due to limited financial means, studies often have few subjects who are drawn mostly from clinical settings (treatment facilities and social agencies), rather than more representative samples of women from the general population.

We are not aware of any *national* probability surveys from which we could estimate the prevalence of childhood sexual abuse most accurately. Our best estimates must come from surveys of specific communities or regions of the country. Because of their methodological rigor, their knowledge of and sensitivity to the survivor of sexual abuse and the representativeness of their samples, Russell's[5] and Wyatt's[3] studies appear to give us the best estimates available at this time.[6] Both researchers took extra care to include women of color in their samples. Russell included all racial and ethnic groups according to their representation in the region from which she drew her sample, and Wyatt's sample consisted of Whites and African Americans. Both studies were conducted in California but during different time periods and using different methodology. Russell's study was a community survey of 930 women living in San Francisco and Wyatt's was a stratified probability sample of 248 women (126 African American, 122 White) living in Los Angeles County. The prevalence rates of childhood sexual abuse reported in the two studies are strikingly similar.

Employing the more conservative definition of abuse which excludes behaviors not involving physical contact, Russell found that 16 percent of the women in her sample had experienced sexual abuse by a relative before the age of 18, compared to Wyatt's 21 percent. When familial and nonfamilial childhood sexual abuse cases were combined, Russell found that 38 percent of the women in her sample reported being sexually abused before the age of 18 compared to 45 percent in Wyatt's sample. When the broader definition of abuse was employed, which included noncontact experiences, Russell's reported rate of abuse jumped to a shocking 54 percent, and Wyatt's rate reached an equally distressing 62 percent.

If these findings reflect the incidence of childhood sexual abuse in other areas of the country, as we believe they most likely do, this means that, even using the more conservative definition of sexual abuse, well over one-third of the female children in the United States have experienced sexual abuse by the age of eighteen. There is no excuse for a problem of this magnitude to go unaddressed. That incest as a child predisposes a girl to "revictimization" as an adult is becoming more widely known.[1] There is reason to believe this is true for extrafamilial childhood sexual abuse as well.[7] Consequently, we agree with D. Russell that "millions of American girls are being socialized into victim roles" and we, like her, question how there can be any equality between the sexes "as long as girl children are being sexually violated in such massive numbers." [1]

Who is Being Abused?

Gender ✓

Not surprisingly, given the extent of sexualization of girls and women in this society, survivors of childhood sexual exploitation tend to be female. One recent reviewer found that the children being abused are four to five times more likely to be girls than boys.[6] In addition, the preponderance (95%) of the abusers of these girls are male, according to another review by two leading figures in the field.[8]

Race and Ethnicity ✓

Women of color have been severely neglected in the study of child sexual abuse. Of the few studies which have compared the prevalence of abuse by ethnicity, some did find more occurrence in particular ethnic groups, especially among Blacks.[1,6,9-11] However, since the samples for these studies were not representative, the studies' conclusions are questionable at best. Several recent studies with better samples and sensitivity to ethnicity found few if any differences in the prevalence of childhood sexual abuse. Gail Wyatt was the first researcher to design a large-scale community study for the express purpose of comparing African American and White women's childhood sexual abuse experiences. She looked at both intrafamilial and extrafamilial abuse and found no difference in prevalence, although African American women reported more severe *consequences* than White women.

Although there are no comparable studies for other women of color, another study looked at the rates of both incest and extrafamilial childhood sexual abuse in a random sample of Texas residents and found Latinas reporting a substantially higher rate of abuse than white women (22% vs. 10%).[13] Russell compared the ethnic groups represented in her random sample and found the occurrence of incestuous abuse was quite similar across races except for a lower rate among the Asian and Filipina group. It is suspected that the lower rate of incest reported by Asians may occur because their culture makes it extremely difficult for these women to talk about such matters.

Although the incidence of incest was similar for all but one of Russell's groups, the *degree* of trauma reported by the women differed significantly across racial and ethnic groups. Eighty-three percent of the Latinas reported severe or considerable trauma, compared to 79 percent of the African Americans, 50 percent of the Asians, 49 percent of the Whites and 71 percent of survivors from other racial or ethnic groups. These differences may be due to many things. Perhaps

White women are more willing to report milder forms of abuse, or perhaps the trauma of incest is increased for some groups because of the greater stigma attached. Or perhaps the women reporting the most trauma were living under more stressful conditions than the other women at the time of the reporting and, consequently, remembered the incest as even more traumatic than it actually was. Until more ethnic-specific research is generated, we cannot begin to answer these and other urgent questions. It is clear, however, that no cultural group has escaped childhood sexual abuse. Therefore, if a women's center or organization is attracting only victims from particular ethnic groups, staff may want to take special measures to reach the survivors from other groups in the locale. It would be a mistake to assume a lack of abuse in the underrepresented groups.

Gail Wyatt is an invaluable model for how to begin to discern the specific effects of childhood sexual abuse on women from particular ethnic groups. Her research provides invaluable information for people who work with African American women. For instance, she suggests several reasons why sexual abuse is reported as more traumatic by African American women than by other women: these women tend to internalize the reasons why they were victimized (e.g., their precocious physical development); as a group, they tend to have highly negative reactions to childhood sexual abuse; and they tend not to disclose the abuse.[3] Similar research with other women of color is urgently needed.

Social Class ✓

It has been assumed for some time by both researchers and the general public that incest is primarily a problem of lower-class families.[1,14] Some research findings support this idea. However, for the most part, the designs of these studies were weak, employing highly selected groups of people and using no control groups for comparison. A more recent well-designed study found incest more prevalent in upper-class families.[1] We wonder if the earlier research may have been biased in favor of the middle and upper classes. The researchers themselves may have been unaware of their bias, which affected how they designed their studies and how they interpreted their results. Another possibility is that the findings from the more recent study reflect in part the education and services available to women in the higher socioeconomic classes, which may have raised their awareness of intrafamilial childhood sexual abuse. The question is in need of clarification. What is clear at this time is that there is no social class, just as there is no racial or ethnic group, untouched by incest.

In contrast to the social class of the families of origin in which the girls were abused, childhood incest experiences have not been found to affect the social class to which the survivor will belong as an adult.[1] In other words, adult women who were incest victims do not appear in one socioeconomic class more than another. This is misleading, however, for when the *degree of trauma* the woman remembers experiencing as a girl is considered, a negative effect on the social class she attains as an adult is found. Therefore, one of the many negative effects of severe childhood incest is that the adult survivor is unable to reach the socioeconomic level of her parents. Perhaps the survivor of severe trauma has found it necessary to employ her energies surviving the abuse and its profound consequences, while her peers were freer to concentrate their energies on the business of upward mobility. It would be important to see if this pattern is true for survivors of severe nonfamilial sexual abuse as well. This finding, if taken seriously by government agencies, could revolutionize our attitudes and actions toward the large female segment of the population who are economically disadvantaged, probably many of them with a history of childhood sexual abuse. One would want to keep this in mind when attending to such women. What may appear as a lack of motivation may be one of the many consequences of sexual abuse in childhood.

The Consequences of Sexual Abuse in Childhood for Adult Women✓

Childhood sexual abuse is clearly not just a girl's issue. Adult women carry the scars of such experiences well into adulthood and often throughout their entire lives. The impact was overlooked or underestimated at best by influential researchers such as Kinsey, who measured the seriousness of consequences of the abuse by the extent of the immediate physical harm incurred.[1,4] Cases involving vaginal bleeding, which today we would consider among the most traumatic, did not concern Kinsey as causing particularly serious damage, since the vagina would heal in a short time.[4,15] Other researchers, as well as major clinicians such as Freud, have been guilty of discounting the seriousness of sexual abuse. Differences in power and dominance between a child and an adult were ignored until the rise of feminist thinking and research in the late 1970s.

Once feminists began educating the research community about the potential damage inherent in sexual relations between adults and children, research findings began to reflect this sensitivity. A multitude of consequences surfaced. Connections were found between childhood sexual abuse and depression, suicide, anxiety, negative self-concept and low self-esteem, difficulties in interpersonal relationships, a tendency toward "revictimization," sexual dysfunction, prostitution and alcohol and other drug abuse in adult women. More information about each of these consequences is presented below. As was the case for the prevalence of childhood sexual abuse, there are very few empirically sound studies addressing the subject of long-term effects (that is, studies that have representative samples and use control groups of nonabused women). For the purposes of this chapter, we present findings, where available, from the better-designed, more recent studies. However, this is not meant to be an exhaustive review, but rather an effort to acquaint the reader with the numerous potential effects of childhood sexual abuse. As before, unless otherwise specified, we use the term "childhood sexual abuse" to refer to both intrafamilial and extrafamilial abuse.

Emotional Effects

Clinical studies have found women with a history of sexual abuse well represented among psychiatric patients.[4,16] One recent study found that 46 percent of chronically institutionalized and actively psychotic women for whom all psychopharmacological and social treatments had failed reported histories of childhood incest.[17] Another study discovered childhood sexual abuse to be among the sexual and physical assault experiences reported by 81 of 100 psychiatric inpatients.[18] The majority of these assault experiences were unknown to the therapists and physicians responsible for treating these women.

One small-scale study did find that specific personality types and disturbances occurred more frequently among incest survivors.[19] More incest survivors were avoidant, dependent and passive-aggressive personality types. A high prevalence of borderline personality disorder occurred among incest survivors. Kovach[20] and Herman and associates[21] suggest that adult incest survivors have a clinical profile of their own which resembles the post-traumatic stress disorder diagnosed in Viet Nam veterans. However, in contrast to that experienced by Viet Nam vets, the trauma resulting from childhood sexual abuse occurs so early in a survivor's life that the stress reaction becomes chronic and integrated into her personality structure. This approach to adult survivors of childhood sexual abuse acknowledges the role of the initial abuse in the development of the disorder, in contrast to assigning traditional diagnostic labels which imply that the disorder is the result of an inherent weakness in the woman herself. We believe that severe sexual abuse is beyond the adaptive capacities of even the strongest and brightest young girls and will regularly produce a long-lasting traumatic syndrome. If a label must be assigned, care should be taken that it reflect this fact.

Depression is the symptom most commonly found among adult survivors of childhood sexual abuse. Comparing rates of occurrence reported by studies in a recent review, we found that women with abuse in their histories are almost twice as likely as nonabused women to have elevated scores on scales measuring depression.[22] They are also more likely to be hospitalized for depression, and, in general, report more symptoms associated with depression than do nonabused women.[22-24] In addition, abuse involving physical contact appears to be associated with a higher incidence of depression and more depressive episodes.[23] When the contributions of sexual abuse and several family background factors were statistically compared, sexual abuse made an independent contribution, adding strength to the evidence that sexual abuse in childhood predisposes adult women to depression.[23]

The second most likely symptom to be found among women sexually abused as children is anxiety. One study found that 59 percent of abused women had symptoms of nervousness and anxiety compared to 41 percent of the controls.[24] Anxiety attacks, difficulty sleeping and nightmares were found to be more common in abused than nonabused women.[24-26] When incest survivors were compared with survivors of nonfamilial abuse, incest survivors reported the higher levels of anxiety.[27]

Another clear finding in the research literature is that survivors of sexual abuse in childhood are more likely to have attempted suicide than nonabused women. One study[26] reported in a recent review[22] found that 51 percent of the abused women sampled had attempted suicide compared to 34 percent of the nonabused women. The same study found that women sexually abused as children were also more likely than nonabused women to have *thoughts* of committing suicide. We found similar results in our recent national survey of a nonclinical sample of women.[7] Self-mutilation and other deliberate attempts at self-harm have also been found to be associated with childhood sexual abuse.[25]

A negative self-concept and lowered self-esteem are longterm consequences of early sexual abuse. One study found that 19 percent of survivors scored in the "very poor" category of self-esteem compared to 5 percent of a control group.[25] The same study found that women with very poor self-esteem were four times as likely to have a history of childhood sexual abuse as other subjects. Adult survivors report feelings of self-loathing, worthlessness, sinfulness and guilt.

There is evidence to suggest that incest, particularly with the primary caregiver, or violent, prolonged abuse, is associated with more severe long-term negative consequences.[21] For instance, in a recent clinical study, incest survivors reported higher levels of depression and anxiety and more suicide attempts than survivors of other types of sexual abuse combined.[27] This pattern is probably true for self-esteem as well.

Effects on Interpersonal Relationships

Women who have been sexually abused as children, especially those with a history of incest, not surprisingly report difficulty in their close relationships. They report difficulties with trust, fear and anger.[22] One study[26] in a recent review[22] found that survivors of childhood sexual abuse were three times as likely as nonabused women to experience both a fear of men (48% vs. 15%) and a fear of women (12% vs. 4%).

Conflicts with parents continue well into adulthood for incest survivors as they often experience feelings of hostility toward both their mother and their abuser. Several studies reveal that survivors experience more hostile feelings toward their mothers than they do toward the male perpetrators.[4,28,29] Some surmise that survivors are angry at their mothers for not protecting them. One may wonder if women may not feel safer experiencing anger toward their mothers than toward their male abusers. Whatever the reason for their anger at their mothers, the result of the incestuous abuse for these women appears to be a loss of respect for themselves and other women.

There is some evidence to suggest that early sexual abuse predisposes a woman to difficulties with parenting and relating to her own children. In one study, 24 percent of 100 mothers of sexually and/or physically abused children had incest histories compared to 3 percent of the control mothers.[30] The molested mothers were found to maintain an emotional and physical distance from their children.

In one clinical study, incest survivors reported more conflicts with or fear of their sex partners—64 percent compared to 40 percent of nonabused women.[29] In our own nonclinical, national survey, we also found that women with a history of child sexual abuse (intrafamilial and extrafamilial) reported more interpersonal conflict with their partners than did nonabused women.[7] These women not only acknowledged their own contribution to the conflicted relationship, but, as a group, ascribed more conflict-inducing behaviors to themselves than to their spouse or partner. When these results are weighed with other findings that sexually abused women are likely to be physically and sexually abused by husbands or other adult partners, one may wonder if this difference is perhaps an artifact of abused women's tendency to self-denigrate themselves.[1,26] Further research is necessary to clarify this; however, what is clear is that women with childhood sexual abuse histories tend to be involved in conflicted and disturbed relationships compared to nonabused women.

Women with a history of incest are also more likely to be divorced or separated than women with no history of incest. One researcher found that 28 percent of incest survivors were divorced or separated compared to 16 percent of the nonincest sample.[1] In addition, she found that the degree of trauma as perceived by the victims appeared to affect marital status. Of those reporting the most extreme trauma, 37 percent were divorced or separated compared to 31 percent reporting considerable trauma, 22 percent reporting some trauma and 7 percent reporting no trauma.

A large number of sexually abused women do not marry. Some studies report that as many as 40 percent never marry.[29,31] An interesting pattern emerges when the severity of the incest as perceived by the victim is taken into account. D. Russell found survivors reporting the most severe trauma were most likely to marry and much more likely to have raised one or more children than survivors reporting only some trauma.[1] The least likely to marry were those reporting only some trauma, with over half of them remaining single. It appears that "the more traumatic experiences of incest increase the likelihood that the victim will accept the traditional female role of both marriage and motherhood".[1] In support of this idea is the finding that women reporting extreme trauma tended to be more traditional than women reporting less extreme trauma.

We do not believe, as do some, that marriage is a sign of mental health in women, and that not being married or being divorced should be viewed as a negative consequence of child sexual abuse. However, the difference in marital status is noteworthy.

Effects on "Revictimization"

Women sexually abused as children are twice as likely as nonabused women to be raped or to experience an attempted rape in adulthood.[1] Incest survivors are even more likely to be raped as adults than those women molested by nonfamily members. In addition, survivors of childhood sexual abuse seem to be more likely to be engaged in physically and sexually abusive relationships. In D. Russell's large-scale, nonclinical study, 27 percent of incest survivors reported having husbands who had been *physically violent* towards them at least once compared to 12 percent of the nonabused women. The same study found that 19 percent of the incest survivors, compared to 7 percent of the nonabused women, had been *raped* by their husbands.

Studies of prostitute populations suggest a link between sexual abuse in childhood and later prostitution. One study found that 55 percent of the prostitutes interviewed reported sexual abuse by someone 10 years older prior to her first intercourse.[32] Another study found that 60 percent of the prostitutes interviewed had been sexually abused before the age of 16 by at least two people for an average of 20 months.[33]

Effects on Sexuality

Sexual problems appear to be linked to a history of early sexual abuse, especially to childhood incest experiences. However, this finding is based solely on data from clinical studies, and the results are not as clear as they are for other long-term consequences.

The percent of adult incest survivors reporting sexual adjustment problems in studies cited in a recent review[22] ranged from 55 percent[4] to 87 percent.[29] In a study including both intrafamilial and extrafamilial sexual abuse, 45 percent of the abused women reported sexual adjustment difficulties, compared to 15 percent of the controls.[26] Another study by Becker and colleagues found that, as a group, 40 percent of survivors of sexual assault (rape, incest and both) reported sexual difficulties.[34] The most prevalent sexual problems among the assault survivors were fear of sex, arousal dysfunction and desire dysfunction. The rape, incest and mixed-assault women did not differ in prevalence of these problems; therefore we can tentatively generalize this finding to incest victims even though the study was not limited to this group. One is not surprised by this and other findings that incest survivors experience more sexual anxiety, more sexual guilt and more dissatisfaction with their sexual relationships than do nonabused women.[35]

However, some findings are more complex. One researcher found that 80 percent of the incest survivors studied reported either an *avoidance* of sex, or the reverse, a *compulsive desire* for sex.[31] Further complicating this unclear picture are our own national survey findings which reveal that women sexually abused as children are more likely to engage in premarital relations and have their first sexual partner (other than the abuser) at an earlier age than do nonabused women.[7] Early sexual abuse does appear to have an impact on adult sexuality, but better-designed studies are necessary to help us understand the complex nature of this impact and its ramifications.

Some studies purport that another consequence of childhood sexual abuse is promiscuity.[4,28,29,31] Doubts have been cast on these findings by an insightful study by Fromuth, who found that having experienced sexual abuse as a child predicted only how a woman would describe herself, not her actual sexual behavior.[36] (Here is another example of the tendency of abused women to assign to themselves negative attributions.)

Some have raised the concern that sexual abuse may predispose a woman to homosexuality. Although a recent review[22] of the more substantial studies concerned with the topic[29,36-38] found little connection between sexual abuse and sexual preference, the authors do mention one study of lesbians which found molestation to be common in their background.[39] In our own national survey, almost one-third of the sexually abused women but only 9 percent of the nonabused women answered "yes" to the question, "If there were no question of right or wrong, would you say that sex with another woman might be enjoyable for you?"[7] Although this is a hypothetical question and not one concerned with actual behavior, it makes sense to us that an abuse experience might cause an adult woman to be more receptive to considering a woman for a sexual partner. Like divorce and remaining single, we would not consider this to be a particularly negative consequence or undesirable outcome of a childhood sexual abuse experience.

Effects on Substance Abuse ✓

Recent evidence suggests that there may be important connections between sexual abuse in childhood and later abuse of alcohol and/or other drugs. This can be inferred from the high percentage of women in treatment for alcoholism and other drug abuse who report histories of childhood sexual abuse. One study[40] cited in an article by Miller and colleagues[41] found that as many as 75 percent of women in treatment for alcoholism reported a history of incest or childhood sexual abuse. Another study reported 44 percent of women in treatment for other drug abuse had histories of either incest or other childhood sexual abuse.[42] Miller and colleagues found that 67 percent of the women in their alcoholic sample had experienced childhood sexual abuse compared to 28 percent of the nonalcoholic group; this study included nonphysical contact experiences (e.g., invitations and exposure) in its definition of abuse.[41] Another study[43] cited by Wilsnack[44] found that 34 percent of the alcoholic women in a middle-class sample reported histories of incest, compared to 17 percent of the controls.

A link between sexual abuse in childhood and alcoholism has also been inferred from the number of women with childhood sexual abuse experiences who report difficulties with alcohol or other drugs at some time in their life. One community study found that 17 percent of abused women had symptoms of alcohol abuse compared to 4 percent of nonabused women, and 27 percent of abused women abused at least one kind of drug other than alcohol, compared to 12 percent of nonabused women.[23] In a clinical study, 27 percent of the sexual abuse survivors had a history of alcoholism compared to 11 percent of the nonabused women, and 21 percent of the survivors had a history of drug addiction compared to 2 percent of the women who were not sexually abused.[26] Our own national survey found that women who reported problems with alcohol were significantly more likely to have childhood sexual abuse histories than women without alcohol problems (23% vs. 10%).[7] In addition, we found that women with histories of childhood sexual abuse also reported more use of drugs other than alcohol than did women with no sexual abuse history. Evidence, still in need of further analysis, suggests that women with a history of sexual abuse, but no history of alcohol-related problems at the time of our first survey (1981), were more likely than women without sexual abuse histories to develop problems with alcohol by the time of the five-year followup interview in 1986. This finding emphasizes the need for research which follows abused women throughout their lives to give us a better understanding of the development of long-term effects over time.

Substance abuse is associated with many of the consequences of early sexual abuse that we have discussed in this chapter. It is difficult to distinguish whether the substance abuse comes first and is a factor in the development of consequences such as depression and sexual dysfunction, or if such consequences come first and alcohol and other drugs follow in an effort to cope. In all likelihood, a vicious cycle exists in which painful consequences of childhood sexual abuse—such as depression, low self-esteem, conflicted relationships and sexual dysfunction—increase a woman's risk of self-medicative use of alcohol and other drugs. Substance abuse in turn can make these consequences worse, leading to increased use of alcohol and other drugs in an effort to cope. When sexual abuse in childhood underlies this painful constellation it may be difficult, if not impossible, to reduce the resulting problems without addressing the underlying sexual abuse experience itself.

How Can Women's Centers Help Adult Survivors of Childhood Sexual Abuse?

One of the major goals of this book is to sensitize staff of women's centers and other organizations that serve women to the important interrelationships between women's use of alcohol and other drugs and a wide variety of other problems women experience. Our purpose in this chapter has been to raise awareness of childhood sexual abuse as an early experience that can increase women's risks not only for alcohol and other drug abuse, but also for many other problems, including depression, anxiety, low self-esteem, suicide, relationship conflict, sexual dysfunction and "revictimization." Many of these adult consequences of childhood sexual abuse cannot be satisfactorily alleviated until the abuse experience itself is recognized and addressed.

Many abused women are themselves unaware of a connection between their current problems and their earlier sexual abuse. Women's centers are in an excellent position to reach such women, most of whom would never find their way to a mental health professional.

What can women's centers do to help the adult victim of childhood sexual abuse? We would like to offer some suggestions. First, staff members should not feel that they must diagnose and treat the effects of childhood sexual abuse themselves. While some centers or organizations may have the experience and training needed to work effectively with sexually abused women, others may not. Sexual abuse has many profound effects and its effective treatment requires professional training and experience dealing with sexually abused women.

Second, staff should recognize that what they *can* do—and very effectively—is to educate women about sexual abuse and its long-term consequences. Information can be provided to center participants, regardless of whether they themselves have been sexually abused.

This information can take many forms—fact sheets and brochures, films and videotapes, workshops and seminars—depending on the resources available. Staff members do not need to be experts at identifying underlying sexual abuse or at initiating discussions of this topic. Simply providing sensitive and accurate educational materials in a non-blaming, supportive atmosphere can help sexually abused women self-identify and self-select themselves into the services they need. An additional benefit of this education may be to sensitize women to the possible presence of *current* sexual abuse of children in their families, for example, with their daughters or other girls they know.

Third, beyond disseminating information, we recommend offering services specific to adult survivors of childhood sexual abuse out of the center itself, if at all possible. Bring in a mental health professional trained and experienced in dealing with sexual abuse and offer a group. (We do not recommend leaderless groups or groups led by a sexual abuse survivor without professional training or supervision. The powerful and pervasive effects of childhood sexual abuse seem to us to require the skills of a professional.) Many women who would find it too stigmatizing or intimidating to seek professional help from a psychiatric clinic or mental health center might accept the same help offered in the familiar and comfortable setting of a women's center.

Finally, if it is not possible to offer sexual abuse groups out of the center itself, be sure that staff members are well informed about such groups or therapists specializing in incest and childhood sexual abuse in the surrounding community, and make this information easily accessible to all women served by the center.

Staff members in women's centers and other women's service organizations, even if they have not themselves experienced overt sexual abuse, may be able to recognize more subtle forms of sexual abuse in their own lives and draw on these experiences to better understand and support center participants who are adult survivors of childhood sexual abuse. We propose

that it may be helpful to conceptualize a *continuum* of sexual abuse upon which *all* women in this culture fall. At one end of the continuum we find severe, overt physical abuse. At the other end, we find more subtle psychological and interpersonal abuse such as is encountered in popular magazine and television advertisements, in sexist jokes at the office, in whistles and "cat calls." We suggest that many problems plaguing women today (e.g., depression, low self-esteem, passivity and vulnerability to victimization) reflect this pervasive, societal exploitation of women which begins at birth. We must come to recognize all forms of sexual abuse of girls and women for what they are, and demand that they be stopped and be replaced with an attitude of honor and respect for the female gender. We as women who help other women can begin this process ourselves by respecting ourselves and endowing our wounded mothers, sisters, friends and daughters with honor and dignity.

References

1. Russell, D. E. H. (1986). *The secret trauma: Incest in the lives of girls and women*. New York: Basic Books, Inc.
2. Sapp, A. D. & Carter, D. L. (1978). *Child abuse in Texas: A descriptive study of Texas residents' attitudes*. Huntsville, Texas: University Graphic Arts Dept.
3. Wyatt, G. E. (1985). "The sexual abuse of Afro-American and white women in childhood." *Child Abuse and Neglect: The International Journal*, 9, 507-519.
4. Herman, J. (1981). *Father-daughter incest*. Cambridge, Mass.: Harvard University Press.
5. Russell, D. E. H. (1983). "The incidence and prevalence of intrafamilial and extrafamilial sexual abuse of female children." *Child Abuse and Neglect: The International Journal*, 7(2), 133-146.
6. Alter-Reid, K., Gibbs, M. S., Lachenmeyer, J. R., Sigal, J., & Massoth, N.A. (1986). "Sexual abuse of children: A review of the empirical findings." *Clinical Psychology Review*, 6, 249-266.
7. Russell, S. A., Wilsnack, S. C., Klassen, A. D., & Deitz, S. R. (November, 1988). *Consequences of childhood sexual abuse among problem drinking and nonproblem drinking women in a U.S. national survey*. Paper presented at the Annual Meeting, American Society of Criminology, Chicago, IL.
8. Finkelhor, D. & Russell, D. (1984). "Women as perpetrators of sexual abuse: Review of the evidence." In D. Finkelhor (Ed.), *Child sexual abuse: New theory and research* (pp. 171-187). New York: Free Press.

9. DeJong, A. R., Hervada, A. R., & Emmett, G. A. (1983). "Epidemiological variations in childhood sexual abuse." *Child Abuse and Neglect, 7,* 155-162.

10. Peters, J. J. (1976). "Children who are victims of sexual assault and the psychology of offenders." *American Journal of Psychotherapy, 30,* 398-421.

11. Weinberg, S. K. (1976), orig. pub. 1955. *Incest Behavior* (rev. ed.). Secaucus, NJ: Citadel Press.

12. Wyatt, G. E. (1984). "The aftermath of child sexual abuse: The victims' experience." Type-script referenced in Russell, D.E.H. (1986), *The Secret Trauma: Incest in the Lives of Girls and Women.* New York: Basic Books, Inc.

13. Kercher, G., & McShane, M. (1984). "The prevalence of child sexual abuse victimization in an adult sample of Texas residents." *Child Abuse and Neglect: The International Journal, 8,* 495-501.

14. Katz, S. & Mazur, M. A. (1979). *Understanding the rape victim: A synthesis of research findings.* New York: John Wiley and Sons.

15. Kinsey, A. C., Pomeroy, W. B., Martin, C. E., & Gebhard, P. H. (1953). *Sexual behavior in the human female.* Philadelphia: W. B. Saunders.

16. Carmen, E., Mills, T., & Rieker, P. P. (1984). "Victims of violence and psychiatric illness." *American Journal of Psychiatry, 141,* 378-383.

17. Beck, J. C. & van der Kolk, B. (1987). "Reports of childhood incest and current behavior of chronically hospitalized psychotic women." *American Journal of Psychiatry, 144,* 1474-1476.

18. Jacobson, A. & Richardson, B. (1987). "Assault experiences of 100 psychiatric inpatients: Evidence of the need for routine inquiry." *American Journal of Psychiatry, 144*(7), 908-913.

19. Wheeler, B. R. & Walton, E. (1987). "Personality disturbances of adult incest victims." *Social Casework: The Journal of Contemporary Social Work,* 597-602.

20. Kovach, J. A. (1986). "Incest as a treatment issue for alcoholic women." *Alcoholism Treatment Quarterly, 3*(1), 1-15.

21. Herman, J., Russell, D., & Trocki, K. (1986). "Long-term effects of incestuous abuse in childhood." *American Journal of Psychiatry, 143*(10), 1293-1296.

22. Browne, A. & Finkelhor, D. (1986). "Impact of child sexual abuse: A review of the research." *Psychological Bulletin, 99,* 66-77.

23. Peters, S. D. (1984). *The relationship between childhood sexual victimization and adult depression among Afro-American and white women.* Unpublished doctoral dissertation, University of California, Los Angeles.

24. Sedney, M. A. & Brooks, B. (1984). "Factors associated with a history of childhood sexual experiences in a nonclinical female population." *Journal of the American Academy of Child Psychiatry, 23,* 215-218.

25. Bagley, C., & Ramsay, R. (1985, February). *Disrupted childhood and vulnerability to sexual assault: Long-term sequels with implications for counseling.* Paper presented at the Conference on Counseling the Sexual Abuse Survivor, Winnipeg, Canada.

26. Briere, J. (1984, April). *The effects of childhood sexual abuse on later psychological functioning: Defining a post-sexual-abuse syndrome.* Paper presented at The Third National Conference on Sexual Victimization of Children, Washington, DC.

27. Hartman, M., Finn, S. E., & Leon, G. R. (1987). "Sexual-abuse experiences in a clinical population: Comparisons of familial and nonfamilial abuse." *Psychotherapy, 24*(2), 159.

28. DeYoung, M. (1982). *The sexual victimization of children.* Jefferson, NC: McFarland.

29. Meiselman, K. (1978). *Incest.* San Francisco: Jossey-Bass.

30. Goodwin, J., Divasto, P., & McCarthy, T. (1981). "Prior incest in mothers of abused children." *Child Abuse and Neglect, 5,* 87-96.

31. Courtois, C. (1979). "The incest experience and its aftermath." *Victimology: An International Journal, 4,* 337-347.

32. James, J., & Meyerding, J. (1977). "Early sexual experiences and prostitution." *American Journal of Psychiatry, 134,* 1381-1385.

33. Silbert, M. H., & Pines, A. M. (1981). "Sexual child abuse as an antecedent to prostitution." *Child Abuse and Neglect, 51* 407-411.

34. Becker, J. V., Abel, G. G., Axelrod, R., Cichon, J., & Skinner, L. J. (1984). "Sexual problems of sexual assault survivors." *Women and Health, 9*(4), 5-20.

35. Langmade, C. J. (1983). "The impact of pre- and postpubertal onset of incest experiences in adult women as measured by sex anxiety, sex guilt, sexual satisfaction and sexual behavior." *Dissertation Abstracts International, 44,* 917B. (University Microfilms No. 3592)

36. Fromuth, M. E. (1983). *The long term psychological impact of childhood sexual abuse.* Unpublished doctoral dissertation, Auburn University, Auburn, AL.

37. Bell, A., & Weinberg, M. (1981). *Sexual preference: Its development among men and women.* Bloomington: Indiana University Press.

38. Finkelhor, D. (1984). *Child Sexual Abuse: New*

theory and research. New York: Free Press.

39. Gundlach, R. (1977). "Sexual molestation and rape reported by homosexual and heterosexual women." *Journal of Homosexuality, 2*, 367-384.

40. Rohsenhow, D. J., Corbett, R., & Devine, D. (1986, April). *Molested as children: The hidden contribution to alcohol and substance abuse.* Paper presented at the annual meeting of the American Medical Society of Alcohol and Other Drug Dependence, San Francisco.

41. Miller, B. A., Downs, W. R., Gondoli, D. M., & Keil, A. (1987). "The role of childhood sexual abuse in the development of alcoholism in women." *Violence and Victims, 2*(3), 157-172.

42. Benward, J., & Densen-Gerber, J. (1975, February). *Incest as a causative factor in anti-social behavior: An exploratory study.* Paper presented at the meeting of the American Academy of Forensic Science, Chicago, IL.

43. Covington, S. S. (1982). *Sexual experience, dysfunction, and abuse: A comparative study of alcoholic and nonalcoholic women.* Unpublished doctoral dissertation, Union Graduate School.

44. Wilsnack, S. C. (1984). Drinking, sexuality, and sexual dysfunction in women. In S.C. Wilsnack and L. J. Beckman (Eds.) *Alcohol Problems in Women* (pp. 189-227). NY: The Guilford Press.

9. The Pain of Invisibility: Issues for Lesbians

Brenda L. Underhill and Suzanne E. Ostermann

"Despite the gains made by the Women's Movement and the Gay Rights movement in the 1960s and 1970s in addressing the issues of sexism and social justice, lesbians continue to be the object of considerable prejudice by the dominant culture. The social factors which every lesbian must contend with, consciously or unconsciously on a daily basis, produce fertile ground for problems with alcohol and other drugs."

When an organization commits to providing effective services to lesbians in an affirmative, healing environment, it is a commitment to creating visibility and acknowledging the worth of a segment of our population that is, for the most part, unseen, unknown and undervalued. Lesbians are truly an invisible minority who exist within a biased and largely hostile environment. Social bias takes various forms, from outright denial that lesbians exist (or exist in any significant numbers) to open hostility and violence against lesbians.

Despite the gains made by the Women's Movement and the Gay Rights movement in the 1960s and 1970s in addressing issues of sexism and social justice, lesbians continue to be the object of considerable prejudice by the dominant culture. The social factors which every lesbian must contend with, consciously or unconsciously on a daily basis, produce fertile ground for problems with alcohol and other drugs.

This chapter will examine some of the ways in which our culture transmits its anti-lesbian messages to individuals. The eroding effects of this discrimination on self-esteem will also be explored. The focus will be on factors such as stigma, denial, alienation and discrimination, which place lesbians at high risk to develop problems with alcohol and other drugs. Some suggestions for guidelines in working with lesbians and incorporating their needs into any project or program will also be presented, along with some of the available resources.

A startling statistic is that while lesbians and gays are estimated to comprise approximately 10 percent of the general population, 25-35 percent of lesbians and gays may have serious problems with alcohol and other drugs.[1-4] Various factors have been suggested as contributing to the large numbers of lesbians and gays affected by alcohol and other drug problems. These factors include the effects of minority group status and discrimination,[5,6] the role of the bars in the lesbian and gay community,[7,8,9] and a denial system which is developed in childhood by many lesbians and gays to survive a hostile world and which later becomes a psychological vulnerability that aids development of an alcoholic denial system. The lack of services designed to meet the needs of lesbians and gays may be an additional factor contributing to their high rate of alcohol and other drug problems. Finally, stress underlies the lives of all lesbians and may be a significant contributing factor as well. Much of the stress of being lesbian begins with the myths and lack of understanding surrounding the lesbian lifestyle. It begins with the issue of who is a lesbian and continues with a general confusion about what sexual orientation involves.

To begin to understand lesbianism, it is important to understand that sexual orientation is defined not only by who you are sexually attracted to, but also by how you live your life. Thus, lesbianism is an issue of lifestyle. A lesbian is a woman whose most fulfilling relationships are with women, and her sexual attractions are primarily or exclusively to other women. It is also important to note that since sexual orientation is not an either/or issue, but rather a continuum as Kinsey documented through research, an individual may be anywhere from exclusively homosexual to exclusively heterosexual in feelings and behavior at any one time.[10]

Finnegan & McNally state: "Although sexual orientation is ordinarily used to designate a person's sexual behavior, its wider, more comprehensive application involves human relationships and emotions. The term refers not just to what people 'do in bed' but who they are as complete human beings."[11] This wider understanding of lifestyle becomes key to understanding issues related to the importance of a lesbian community and its role historically in providing lesbians with support and a sense of "family" in a hostile world. This point, concerning "family of choice," will be discussed later in this chapter.

It is estimated that lesbians and gays constitute 10 percent of the general population. That means in terms of the general population that there are over 10 million lesbians in this country. Among this 10 million, there is enormous diversity. There is no one kind of lesbian. Just as with any woman, a lesbian may be young or old. She may grow up feeling "different," identifying her lesbianism from early youth, and she may even be openly lesbian all her life. On the other hand, she may not have discovered or acted on her feelings for women until she was in her 30s, 40s, or even later. Approximately one-third of lesbians have children. These children may be from a previous heterosexual marriage, artificial insemination or adoption.

Lesbians come from a variety of backgrounds in terms of race, ethnicity and class. Lesbians of color must deal not only with the sexism and racism of the dominant culture but with the racism within the lesbian and gay subculture. All of these social and physical factors combine to make for the same diversity there is in heterosexual women.

One major problem, even today, is that little positive information is available to the general public about lesbians' lives. The word 'lesbian' carries a tremendous stigma and stereotypes continue to characterize lesbians as man-hating, abnormal, unfulfilled and even psychologically sick. The church has historically condemned homosexuals as sinners, often citing the Bible as verification. This interpretation has been taken from a few passages of the Bible that refer to male homosexuality. Diamond comments that it is interesting to note that the Bible also speaks against a woman wearing red and anyone eating shellfish.[12]

Mental health professionals have also added to the systematic discrimination of lesbians. It was not until the mid-1970s that both the American Psychiatric Association and the American Psychological Association removed homosexuality from their classification system as a type of mental illness. Unfortunately, this bias in the helping professions is still alive today. Recently, Rudolph reported that although 52 clinicians and clinical trainees disagreed with the statement "Homosexuals are sick," only slightly more than two-fifths supported the statement "Just as in any other species, homosexuality in humans is a natural expression of sexuality."[13] The fact that there is often little satisfaction or therapeutic success for lesbian and gay clients in counseling becomes particularly relevant when considering that the percentage of lesbians and gays seeking counseling is two to four times higher than the percentage of heterosexuals.[14]

The attitudes of organized religion and mental health professionals are only two examples of institutionalized discrimination that lesbians face in the hands of the systems that our society traditionally turns to for emotional, psychological and spiritual guidance and health. Lesbians encounter rampant heterosexual bias and homophobia from individuals in these professions. Heterosexual bias is the belief that opposite sex relationships are natural and therefore superior to homosexual relationships. Homophobia is the dread of being in close contact with homosexuals.[15] Another definition of homophobia, by Audre Lorde, is "the fear of feelings of love for members of one's own sex and therefore the hatred of those feelings in others."[16] Institutions then reflect and perpetuate heterosexual bias and homophobia at the systemic level.

The internalization of homophobia may be even more deadly and insidious than external social homophobia. When homophobia is internalized, the enemy outside becomes the enemy within. This internalization results in varying degrees of lowered self-esteem, self-loathing and self-hatred. For lesbians, shame, in the sense of feeling defective as a human being, often combines internally with guilt for not meeting heterosexually-defined standards of what it means in this culture to be a woman. Alcohol and other drugs are often used to anesthetize this internal pain.

Since lesbians are usually born to heterosexual families, the pain of lesbian oppression and discrimination is not a feeling easily shared with family members. This can create a situation where there is a lack of family support. A family, upon finding out their daughter is a lesbian, may actually disown her as a family member. Some families try to ignore their daughter's lifestyle, hoping it is simply a passing phase. Families can also often be sources of conflict in a coupleship. The lover/partner may be ignored by the family or even scapegoated as the reason for their daughter's "deviant" behavior. This produces added strain to the couple's relationship. So, rather than being a source of support, the family of origin may be a source of conflict.

Lesbian partnerships are not legally acknowledged. When a death or illness occurs, the lover or partner may be totally shut out unless the couple has taken specific legal steps through power of attorney and wills.

Children and ex-husbands, if there are any, can often further complicate the picture. Lesbian blended families have all the problems of heterosexual blended families without the support of society and usually without the support of the traditional extended family.

A lesbian in most states can be declared an "unfit" mother solely based upon her lesbianism. Thus, a woman with children may not publicly acknowledge her lifestyle to friends or family. This often leads to isolation and living a "double life." One life may be lived at home in the privacy of the couple and another life in the outside world. Leading a double life also happens for many single lesbians and is a source of great stress regardless of a woman's relationship or parental status.

In discussing the issues related to family it is important to understand the concept of "family of choice" for lesbians. Family of choice may include family of origin but is also extended beyond the nuclear family to include present partner, ex-partners, friends and significant others. For many lesbians, their family of choice may be a greater source of support and therefore play a more prominent role on a day-to-day basis than their family of origin. The lack of acceptance and understanding of this "type" of family is another stress to the lesbian lifestyle.

A major issue for all lesbians is the process of "coming out." In general, coming out involves first self-identification as a lesbian and then disclosure to others. This is an identity process with phases. Since lesbianism is so taboo and stigmatized in society, this is another source of stress.

A study by de Monteflores and Schultz differentiated six stages that are basic to the emerging lesbian identity.[17] These stages are represented by an individual's awareness of: 1) same-sex attractions; 2) first homosexual experience; 3) coming out in the gay world; 4) labeling oneself homosexual; 5) coming out to friends, family and co-workers; and 6) coming out publicly. It is important to understand that coming out is a process, not an event, and even after completing all stages, a lesbian finds herself in a constant process of identifying herself as a lesbian as she meets new friends, co-workers and acquaintances. It is also important to understand that some lesbians never come out.

Contrary to popular belief when a lesbian "comes out" by speaking of her personal life as it really is, she is not "flaunting it," as many heterosexuals often accuse. Quite the contrary. Just because lesbian life is so stigmatized and unspeakable, in order to simply assert who she is, state the facts of her existence and *not* be invisible, it is necessary and important to disclose her lifestyle and sexual orientation. Heterosexuals do this constantly as part of the dominant culture, regularly incorporating personal information about themselves in conversation without fear of rejection, but simply as a method of defining themselves to others. Statements beginning with "My wife and I . . . ," or "My boyfriend . . . ," are some of the first

phrases that are used by people when making new acquaintances. These phrases provide the listener with the information that the person is heterosexual, what their marital status is, and even clues as to the level of satisfaction in their existing relationships. This "ease of disclosure" is denied to lesbians.

A point to consider in understanding issues related to lesbians is that the strong and rich history of lesbians and gays is unknown not only to heterosexuals but also to lesbians and gays themselves. As Katz states in his work *Gay American History*: "We have been the silent majority, the silenced minority—invisible women, invisible men. Early on, the alleged enormity of our 'sin' justified the denial of our existence, even our physical destruction. Our 'crime' was not merely against humanity, but against 'nature'—we were outlaws against the universe. Long did we remain literally and metaphorically unspeakable, 'among Christians not to be named—nameless.' "[18]

As a result, there is a lack of visible mainstream role models for lesbians of all ages. Educational information regarding lesbians' history and culture is important in helping lesbians work through their own internalized homophobia and to claim a positive lesbian identity. If lesbian sexual orientation were simply seen in the natural continuum of human sexual expression and dealt with openly as a variation of human sexual expression, lesbians would have access through family, religion and the educational system to the realities of lesbian life and years of pain from denial and fear would be eliminated.

However, this is not the case. Haven, in her research on alcoholism and self-esteem among lesbians, found that the mean age at which subjects had their first intimate contact with another woman was nine years after their first identified attractions and two years after they began self-labeling.[19] This is nine years of isolation and feeling a difference which is not a valued difference in society.

Another social fact of lesbian culture is that bars have served as the traditional social setting for the lesbian and gay community. This may be the only place a lesbian may experience the feeling that she can safely socialize and be open about her sexuality. As McGirr writes: "Straights have the world at large to develop their social network. This is a privilege and a right not available to gays, whose individual rights are still unprotected by the laws. Even with the advent of gay liberation or more public sorts of gatherings and places to meet, the bar still remains a prominent place in the culture, which is fine for those who enjoy bars—not so fine for those who would rather not, yet don't feel these are alternatives suitable to their needs and lifestyles. Very simply, there still remains a need for meeting places out of the public view."[20]

This means that many lesbians spend considerable time in alcohol-saturated environments where the norm is drinking, and often drinking to excess. Fifield noted that lesbian and gay bar users report spending 80 percent of their social activity time at bars or parties where alcohol is served.[21] In addition, bar users reported visiting the bars an average of 19 times per month and drinking an average of six drinks per visit.

It is true that in large urban cities such as Los Angeles and San Francisco, the lesbian community has worked to create some social alternatives to the bars. However, it is important to remember that since lesbians are everywhere, including small towns and rural areas across the nation, in many areas the lesbian/gay bar remains the only place to be openly lesbian and in these places the bars remain the center of the lesbian community.

It is also important to note that many small and/or rural communities have no social gathering places for lesbians. Single lesbians and lesbian couples in these settings have either minimal or no social support for their lesbian identity.

To put all of these realities in a lesbian's life into the framework of the high rate of serious alcohol problems within the lesbian community, it is important to correlate the points covered thus far with known risk factors in alcohol and other drug problems. These risk factors become the basis for the development of effective prevention programs.

Lack of a defined societal role has been shown to be a frequent precedent for alcohol problems in women. The dearth of public lesbian role models, the rejection and denial of lesbians by society and the fear of many "successful" lesbians to be open about their lesbianism are all factors that contribute to confusion about the role of lesbians in our society. Programs serving women should *always* have "out" lesbians on their boards of directors, in key staff positions, and available as resources to service-seekers.

Alcohol and other drugs are frequently used by women to counteract feelings of low self-esteem. Lesbians, combatting negative messages about lesbianism, struggling with a sense of invisibility and reacting to rejection and discrimination from their families, churches, health providers and work places, must constantly remind themselves of their self-worth. The obvious programmatic response to low self-esteem is support groups aimed specifically at internalized homophobia. Just as important, however, is the feeling a lesbian has the first time she enters a new environment. This environment can either say "It's okay to be whoever you are," or "We assume you to be heterosexual." Visual images at the program or center should depict a variety of women (Black, Latina, Anglo, Asian, lesbian, heterosexual, differently-abled, etc.), and

brochures and other literature should include information about and references regarding available lesbian services. Intake forms should be designed to include non-threatening questions about sexuality, lovers/partners and families of choice.

Isolation may cause many women to seek a sense of comfort and well-being through the use of alcohol and other drugs. Prevention services can be designed to reach isolated lesbians, and to provide the opportunity to interact with others. Lapis, a prevention program offered through the Alcoholism Center for Women in Los Angeles, was designed specifically for Black and Latina lesbians.[22] As this population had never before been targeted for services by any alcoholism service provider, outreach and program design were developed by community advisory groups representative of the population to be reached. It was found that this population was so highly stigmatized and understandably wary of traditional providers that outreach needed to be consistent and long-term before participation stabilized and significant numbers of women used the services. The Lapis program offers alcohol- and drug-free cultural, theater and art events, unstructured drop-in rap groups, facilitated workshops, newsletters and networking opportunities in a safe environment, and is a model program for very isolated and disenfranchised populations.

Although Lapis is only three years old, some tentative observations are worth noting. In the development of Lapis, many outreach strategies were tested. It was found that, for this population, the most effective outreach was personal and individual contact. The credibility and accessibility of the individual staff members was more important than that of the agency. Secondly, Lapis has demonstrated that services designed for the "stigmatized of the stigmatized" are very effective when offered to mainstream populations. Since the reverse application (mainstream services applied to underserved populations) is not true, it appears obvious that the development of these types of programs is cost-effective within service delivery systems.

Most of the groups and workshops offered through the Alcoholism Center for Women's Prevention Services focus on specific issues. Alcohol and other drugs are used by most members of our society to lessen the intensity of emotional pain, to cope with life problems and to ease discomfort. As previously noted, being a lesbian in our society can be painful and problematic at times, because of the heterosexual bias within the dominant culture. Workshops that provide validation of these social facts in lesbian's lives and teach skills in assertiveness, using anger effectively and processing grief and loss are key elements in prevention programs as well as recovery services. It is very important that facilitators of these workshops be trained in identifying homophobia and have the ability to recognize subtle homophobic attitudes and behaviors within a group.

Some research has shown that major life transitions are high-risk periods for women. These include such events as: leaving your parents' home (for some lesbians, this life event may be precipitated by parental rejection); getting married (a ritual not legally available to lesbians); having children (lesbian families are not condoned by society as a whole); children leaving home; and divorce, separation, or the death of a spouse (lesbian partnerships are not legally sanctioned, and thus often not viewed as "serious" or "meaningful," as are heterosexual marriages). When the series of transitions that are a natural part of the coming-out process for lesbians are coupled with the major life transitions for all women, it is obvious that lesbians encounter frequent high-risk periods during their lives. Once again, staff training is critical for the delivery of effective services for lesbians. Far too often, service providers minimize the significance of life events in lesbians' lives, thus implying that the pain or confusion that the woman is feeling is out of proportion to the event.

When heavy drinking is the norm within a person's social structure, alcoholism and other alcohol problems are not frequently recognized as problems. The alcohol-infused social life that lesbians and gay men encounter when bars are the focal point of their social lives encourages excessive use of alcohol. Sound prevention strategies for the lesbian community include offering alcohol- and drug-free social events for lesbians, such as women's dances, readings by lesbian authors, hikes, and other recreational activities, and forming all-lesbian sport teams.

Well-designed prevention programs that serve lesbians can often serve as pre-treatment services. Consequently, recovery and treatment programs whose staff are trained in and responsive to the needs of lesbians must be identified and readily available. Effective prevention programs can provide safe environments for lesbians to identify many service needs. The staff of prevention programs have a responsibility to their service-seekers to provide resources that encourage the healing process and validate each woman's life experience.

In addressing the service needs of lesbians, *both* prevention services and effective recovery services must be considered. The Alcoholism Center for Women (A.C.W.) was founded for the purpose of providing residential alcoholism services to the lesbian community. The program has expanded to include a comprehensive non-residential program, aftercare, re-entry and extensive prevention services. A.C.W.

maintains a high-profile presence within the lesbian community in order to be responsive to community needs, and offers services such as lesbian support groups, lesbian mothers groups, adult daughters of alcoholics groups, incest survivors workshops, relapse prevention seminars for women and financial planning workshops. Frequent trainings on lesbian and alcohol issues are provided to community service providers. Sources of referral, including therapists and health professionals, are interviewed and assessed before they are incorporated into A.C.W.'s referral list.

The need for lesbian-only and lesbian-sensitive services cannot be overstated. In designing such services, the beginning and end is staff knowledge and attitudes. Programs and services are only as effective as their staff. The training of staff in lesbian life issues and identifying homophobia plays a critical role in setting a supportive, non-judgmental environment which affirms the identity of each woman.

All of us working in human services and education need to act as advocates for our lesbian clients. We need to work together to end sexism, racism and discrimination based on sexual orientation. The process of change needs to be confronted not only on an individual and internal basis but also on a social and external basis. The myths used to discriminate against lesbians are extensions of those that oppress all women. The terms "queer," "dyke" and "castrating bitch" are labels used when women cross the boundaries of sex roles. The basis of homophobia is sexism, and thus it is in the interest of heterosexual women to make a commitment to change society's perceptions and biases toward lesbians. Working to eliminate stereotypes and legal, economic, social and psychological oppression of all lesbians and gays is essential to building a society where women and men are equal. Lesbian educational and service organizations offer trainers who can train both staff and volunteers in lesbian lifestyles. This is an excellent way to begin the process.

The following suggestions are offered for improving services to lesbians:

1. Staff and volunteers should have regular in-depth trainings on homophobia and lesbian life issues. These trainings should be a combination of educational information and process-oriented groups.
2. Board of directors, key staff positions, volunteers and referral resources should always include "out" lesbians.
3. The physical setting in which services are offered should include visual affirmations that lesbians are included and expected to be in the service populations.
4. Brochures and other literature should include available lesbian services. Where feasible, sepa-

rate brochures targeted to lesbians should be made available.

5. Intake forms should be designed to include non-threatening questions about sexuality, lovers/partners, and families of choice. All language used should be examined for heterosexual bias and homophobic assumptions.

6. Lesbian-only groups and alcohol- and drug-free social activities should be offered.

7. Guidelines should be developed for referral resources to help ensure proof of sensitivity to and knowledge of lesbian issues.

8. Agency non-discrimination policies should include lesbians and gays. Procedures should be available for any lesbians and gays who are the subject of harassment by other staff or participants.

9. Lesbians should not be considered as a homogeneous group. Services need to be relevant to age, race and ethnicity.

10. All services to families should include "family of choice."

11. Providers need to be knowledgeable of the lesbian subculture in each community, so that outreach can be done to lesbians through lesbian publications, networks and organizations.

References

1. Fifield, L. *On My Way to Nowhere: Alienated, Isolated And Drunk.* Los Angeles Gay Community Services Center, 1975.
2. Lohrenz, L., Connelly, J., Coyne, L. and Spare, K. "Alcohol Problems In Several Mid-Western Homosexual Communities." *Journal of Studies on Alcohol,* 39(-11), 1959-63, 1978.
3. Saghir, M. and Robins, E. *Male and Female Homosexuality,* Baltimore: Williams & Wilkens, Co., 1973.
4. Morales, E.S. and Graves, M.A. *Substance Abuse: Patterns and Barriers to Treatment to Gay Men and Lesbians in San Francisco.* San Francisco: Department of Health, 1983.
5. Weathers B. *Alcoholism and the Lesbian Community.* Alcoholism Center for Women: Los Angeles, 1975.
6. Ziebold, T.O. "Alcoholism and the Gay Community." *The Blade,* March 1978.
7. Fifield, L. *On My Way to Nowhere: Alienated, Isolated and Drunk.* op. cit.
8. McGirr, K. "Alcohol Use and Abuse in the Gay Community: A View Toward Alternatives." In K. Jay and A. Youth (Eds.). *After You're Out.* New York: Pyramid Books, 277-278.
9. Weathers, B. *Alcoholism and the Lesbian Community,* op. cit.
10. Kinsey, A., et al. *Sexual Behavior in the Human Female.* Philadelphia: W.B. Sanders Co., 1953.
11. Finnegan, D.G. and McNally, E.B. *Dual Identities.* Center City, MN: Hazelden, 1987.
12. Diamond, L. *The Lesbian Primer.* Salem, MA: Women's Education Media, Inc., 1979.
13. Rudolph, J. "Counselors' Attitudes Toward Homosexuality: A Selective Review of the Literature." *Journal of Counseling and Development,* 67:165-168, 1988.
14. Bell, A.P. and Weinberg, M.S. *Homosexualities: A Study of Diversity Among Men and Women.* New York: Simon & Schuster, 1978.
15. Weinberg, G. *Society and the Healthy Homosexual.* Garden City, New York, 1973.
16. Lorde, A. *The Black Unicorn.* New York: W.W. Norton, 1978. p. 195 .
17. de Monteflores, C. and Schultz, S.J. "Coming Out: Similarities and Differences for Lesbians and Gay Men." *Journal of Social Issues,* 34: 59-73, 1978.
18. Katz, J. *Gay American History.* New York: Avon Books, 1976.
19. Haven, M.J. *Alcoholism and Self Esteem With a Female Sex Object Preference.* Unpublished doctoral dissertation, California School of Professional Psychology, Los Angeles, CA, 1981.
20. McGirr, K. "Alcohol Use in the Gay Community," op. cit.
21. Fifield, L. *On My Way to Nowhere: Alienated, Isolated and Drunk.* op. cit.
22. The Lapis Program is named after lapis lazuli, an azure gemstone believed to bring clarity, capacity and success.

Resources

Campaign to End Homophobia
PO Box 819
Cambridge, MA 02139

Children of Gays/Lesbians
8306 Wilshire Blvd. No. 222
Beverly Hills, CA 90211

Lesbian Herstory Educational Foundation (LHEF)
PO Box 1258
New York, NY 10016

Lesbian Mothers National Defense Fund
PO Box 21567
Seattle, WA 98111

Lesbian Rights Project
1370 Mission Street 4th Fl.
San Francisco, CA 94103

National Association of Lesbian and Gay
  Alcoholism Professionals (NALGAP)
  204 W. 20th St.
  New York, NY 10011

National Gay/Lesbian Task Force (NGLTF)
  1517 4th St. NW
  Washington, D.C. 20009

National Gay Rights Advocates
  8901 Melrose Ave.
  West Hollywood, CA 90069

National Lesbian and Gay Health Foundation
  PO Box 65472
  Washington, D.C. 20035

National Organization for Women, Lesbian Rights Task
  Force
  PO Box 1404
  Sacramento, CA 95807

The World Directory of Meetings of Gay/Lesbian
  Groups of Alcoholics Anonymous, International
  Advisory Council
  PO Box 492, Village Station
  New York, NY 10014

Parents and Friends of Lesbians and Gays
  PO Box 82762
  San Diego, CA 92138

10 Single-Parent Women: What a Mother Can Do

Norma Finkelstein, Ph.D. and Laura Derman

"The ongoing stress experienced by single mothers puts them at high risk for many physical and emotional illnesses. Too often, single mothers neglect their own well-being, choosing to meet their children's needs at the expense of their own."

This chapter combines a research perspective with a hands-on practical approach to the issues of single parenting and substance abuse. Included is a discussion of the stresses in the lives of single mothers and the risks of alcohol and drug abuse. Special issues for the alcoholic or drug-addicted mother are presented. The focus shifts to children in the final section with an examination of how to talk to children about alcohol and drugs.

Single-Parent Families

The past twenty years have seen dramatic changes in both the lives of women and the portrait of the American family. The major change has been the increasing incidence of single-parent families, over 90 percent of which are headed by women.

Between 1970 and 1982, female-headed families increased by 71 percent. This increase has continued so that today 14 percent of all families are headed by women.[1] In 1987, 23.9 percent of all children under eighteen were living with a single parent and estimates say almost 50 percent of all children will live in a single-parent family for a significant period of time.[2] In Black families, the rise in female-headed households has been even more dramatic, showing an increase of 92 percent between 1970 and 1980.[3] While 12 percent of White children live with a single mother, the comparable figure for Black children is 42.5 percent.[4]

While widowhood accounted for a great many female-headed households in years past, the major increase today is due to divorce and out-of-wedlock births. This results in households headed by young mothers with young children to support. According to the United States Census Bureau, 85 percent of families headed by women under age 25 included pre-school children and there were pre-school children present in 50 percent of families headed by a female between the ages of 25 and 34.[5]

While previously viewed as pathological and deviant, it is increasingly clear that the single-parent family has become a major family form in the United States today. In addition to divorce, separation and widowhood, there are women, including lesbian couples, who choose to raise children without fathers and whose families thrive because they have both adequate incomes and strong personal and communal support networks. Families are not necessarily "broken" when a marriage terminates. Whether or not a family unit remains viable and not disorganized depends less on the presence or absence of a father but more on the ability of the mother to cope with her situation. Much of the mother's ability to cope is dependent upon her educational background, financial status and social support systems.[6]

Unfortunately, many single mothers juggle the roles of breadwinner and parent with inadequate social and financial support. In fact, the increase in female-headed families is primarily responsible for the recently-labeled "feminization of poverty." Finances are the most serious issue facing the single mother with young children. In spite of increases in employment and other changes brought about by the women's movement, two out of three poor adults in the United States today are women, and families headed by women continue to experience a consistent decline in their economic status.

For example, female-headed families have a poverty rate six times that of male-headed families, with 34 percent of all families headed by women living in poverty.[7] Women of color fared even worse. While 27.4 percent of White female single parents had incomes below poverty, the comparable figures were

50.5 percent for Black women and 53.1 percent for Hispanic women.[8]

The high numbers of female single parents and their children living in poverty persist even though almost three-quarters of all single mothers are employed. Although the median income for employed single mothers is significantly higher than for non-employed single mothers, it is frequently not enough to keep them out of poverty or very far above the poverty line. Women still earn only an average of 70 percent of what men earn and the work they do is usually low-paying and stressful and provides little opportunity for advancement. While many American families presently rely on the income of two adults to break even or stay ahead of expenses, the female single-parent family must subsist on one income of a usually lower-paid woman.[9]

Single mothers and their children, therefore, pay the "highest" price for the inequitable economic position of women in this society. Being employed, single and raising young children alone too frequently leads to high levels of stress and low levels of well-being. Most research confirms that single mothers have little economic support and experience levels of stress significantly greater than other groups. For example, in a recent study on work and family conducted in two large New England companies, researchers found that 1) female single parents had the lowest salary levels of all categories at all work sites studied; and 2) over one-half reported they received no financial assistance from their child's father. The authors also found that single female parents had both the smallest support networks and the highest levels of depression of all groups.[10]

Other studies suggest that women's primary stress results from their role as mother.[11] Psychological well-being is rarely associated with mothering. Mothering is more often associated with psychological distress, particularly when children are six years of age or younger. For example, in a study by Gore and Mangione in 1983, women with young children reported higher levels of complaints such as difficulty breathing, lack of appetite and sleep disturbances.

It comes as no surprise then, that single parenthood, particularly for poor mothers, too often leads to exhaustion, depression and ill health as mothers struggle to cope with multiple roles and responsibilities; low-paying, high-stress jobs; inadequate child care; lack of child-support payments; escalating housing costs and a society which is not supportive of the needs of women and children.

Alcohol, Drugs and Single Parents

The ongoing stress experienced by single mothers puts them at high risk for many physical and emotional illnesses. Too often, single mothers neglect their own well-being, choosing to meet their children's needs at the expense of their own.

One way a single mother may try to cope with stress, poverty and/or depression is through escape by means of alcohol or other drug use. Turning to alcohol and other drugs to deal with life's problems does not, of course, make them better and too often leads to substance abuse or addiction.

While there are no specific studies regarding the prevalence of alcohol and drug problems among single mothers, most national surveys show separated or divorced women to be both heavier drinkers and to be less likely to abstain from alcohol than other groups of women. In addition, most studies report a high rate of alcohol problems among divorced and/or separated women. A 1981 national survey on women's drinking conducted by Sharon Wilsnack found that separated or divorced and never-married respondents reported higher rates of drinking problems, symptoms of alcohol problems, drinking episodes and intoxication than did married respondents.[12] The Women's Drug Research Project found that 73 percent of addicted women studied had children and were less likely than the non-addicted comparison women to be involved in a supportive relationship.[13] Finally, a recent study by Edith Gomberg of 301 middle-class alcoholic women found there were considerably more disrupted and multiple marriages among alcoholic women than among comparable age groups of non-alcoholic women, a finding consistent with most other studies.[14]

The Balancing Job and Homelife Study by Burden and Googins mentioned earlier found that 27.2 percent of single female parents answered "yes" to the question "Has drinking ever been a cause of trouble in your family?" The average percentage answering affirmatively in this study was 22 percent, or about the national norm. As reported earlier, single mothers also had the lowest amounts of social supports, highest rates of depression and lowest salary levels and, not surprisingly, reported the lowest overall life satisfaction.[15]

Clearly, single female parents are at particular risk for alcohol and other drug abuse. It is difficult, however, to separate whether excessive drinking may be the cause of divorce and multiple marriages or the consequence of an alcohol or drug problem.

A number of other factors may interrelate with both the higher rates of drinking among separated and divorced women and the high risk for developing alcohol problems that is also found in this population. Past research has consistently shown a significant number of alcoholic women have had a pre-existing depression before beginning to abuse alcohol. If low-income single parents are at high risk for depression, as reported by Belle and others, they may also be at high risk for substance abuse.[16]

In addition, the literature on female alcoholism reports that women frequently cite a specific stressful life event, such as divorce or widowhood, when asked about circumstances leading to their problem drinking. Women mention these stresses as contributing to their alcohol problem significantly more often than men. In Gomberg's study, 56 percent of the alcoholic women spontaneously mentioned a life event or crisis, with divorce or the death of a person close to them mentioned most frequently. Alcohol was mentioned by over 50 percent of the women as a way of coping with stressful events and "bad" feelings.[17]

Finally, the role employment plays in women's use and abuse of alcohol and other drugs needs to be examined, particularly since the majority of single mothers are in the labor force. Employed single mothers may find themselves in situations where they are expected to drink alcohol. Opportunity and expectations may combine and lead to increased alcohol consumption. For example, the Wilsnack study found that 41 percent of separated or divorced women who were employed full time drank at a moderate or heavy level.[18]

Parenting and Substance Abuse

Parenting is central to many women's identities and is often the source of much anxiety and guilt. Whatever is "wrong" with the child is assumed to be the fault of the mother. When substance abuse is added to mothering and feelings about self, an already difficult area for many women is magnified and intensified. The guilt of the alcoholic or drug-addicted mother is reinforced both by the stigma of being a substance-abusing woman and by the real problems her drinking or drugging may have caused her family. There are very few people for whom the words "alcoholic or drug-addicted mother" do not evoke some negative image. Many people automatically feel anger at the mother and identify with the helpless child.

Mothering is a difficult task for many women but for substance-abusing women in early recovery, the task can be overwhelming. Their feelings of inadequacy are grounded in the fear that they might fit society's stereotype of "bad mothers." They fear their baby was damaged during pregnancy and their older children were inadequately cared for during their drinking or drugging. These feelings are made worse if women have unrealistic expectations of themselves as parents. Once in treatment, the guilt about parenting that most substance-abusing mothers feel is exacerbated if their children have any serious physical, emotional or learning problems. This guilt can be overpowering and

can lead to feelings of hopelessness and helplessness, and possible relapse.

Many alcohol- and drug-abusing women were raised in substance-abusing families often characterized by conflict, unclear expectations, denial of feelings, inconsistent parenting and mixed messages. The fact that so many alcohol- and drug-abusing women are also adult children of alcoholic or drug-abusing parents can have significant implications for treatment and recovery. They must contend with their own substance abuse and also with years of behavior and role patterns developed in response to growing up with alcohol and other drug abuse.

It is important that a substance-abusing woman in recovery understand that both she and her family have been victims of her illness, not her deliberate or intentional behavior. She needs to understand that parenting is a learned behavior for which many adult daughters of substance-abusing parents never had positive role models, and that during her period of active drinking or drugging she had limited options. It is important that a woman express her profound guilt and shame as well as learn to forgive herself. It is essential for a recovering woman to believe that if she abstains from drugs and alcohol she can regain control of her life and become the mother she would like to be. She also needs reassurance that a caregiver will help her find the tools she needs to take care of her children successfully through such services as parenting classes and mothers' groups.[19]

Having responsibility for children all too often drastically effects both what kinds of treatment a substance-abusing woman can use, such as residential care, as well as how long she can stay in treatment. This is especially true for single parents for whom the difficulty of finding acceptable child care arrangements—particularly if the mother needs in-patient or residential care—can be overwhelming. Single mothers too often face the conflict of choosing between placing their children in the care of foster homes or with relatives or foregoing treatment altogether. Many fear they will lose their children permanently due to their drug or alcohol addiction and therefore are very reluctant to begin involvement with state agencies and foster care programs.

Treating the family unit together would permit a woman to enter a treatment program without forcing her to choose between her own recovery or caring for her children and would enhance her recovery by strengthening her parenting skills by engaging the entire family unit in treatment. This approach would also possibly reduce the child's risk of becoming alcoholic or drug-addicted in the future.

How To Talk With Children About Alcohol and Drugs

Talking with children about alcohol and drugs is not always easy. For some families it can be as hard as talking about sex, sexual abuse, AIDS or nuclear war. Resistance to this topic may stem from concerns about one's own use of alcohol or other drugs or being from raised in a substance-abusing family, causing this topic to evoke powerful emotions. Some parents believe they don't know sufficient facts and therefore don't know what to say. Others fear that discussing issues of alcohol and drugs will create a problem where none currently exists.

Mothers can help their children with these issues in a variety of ways. Role-modeling and encouraging a healthy lifestyle are important starting points. This may entail preparing and eating nutritious foods, making time for and enjoying exercise and other leisure time activities, and having a network of friends and family who are part of everyday life. Mothers can also help their children by encouraging them to develop areas of interest they enjoy, such as reading, sports or music, and encouraging the relief of stress and mild physical complaints like headaches or backaches without the use of drugs. Children need to learn at a young age that medicine is not food or candy—even though it often is sweet enough to be a tasty dessert—and is to be taken only under adult supervision and for a particular health need. The general message to convey about prescription and over-the-counter drugs is that drug taking is a solution of last resort when other remedies have failed.

Supporting a child's self-esteem and helping her to feel appreciated has a significant impact on the likelihood of developing a drug or alcohol problem. Research indicates that building self-esteem and decision-making skill is particularly important for girls and women who are strongly influenced by the drug use patterns of important people in their lives, such as siblings, parents, friends and husbands. Girls, therefore, need to believe that they can rely on themselves for decision-making, problem-solving and defining likes and dislikes. With a positive and solid sense of self girls will not need to look to others, usually boys and men, to feel powerful and complete.

Some suggestions for helping children build self-esteem are to praise them, treat them with respect, support them in making choices to help develop a sense of control over their lives and encourage them to take on challenges. Mothers can help girls learn to believe that being female does not have to limit opportunities.

The parent must learn as much as she can about alcohol and drug use and abuse through reading, television and radio programs, attending community lectures and through talking with knowledgeable friends. She can then be better prepared to help educate her children. Daily activities such as taking a walk or watching television together provide opportunities for parents to talk to their children. Discussions about alcohol and drug use can come up naturally in response to watching a television program together or seeing an advertisement. Children can learn to critically view media that push pills to lose weight or encourage alcohol use and smoking by portraying these activities as glamorous, sexy and adventurous. Other possibilities for discussion might arise from seeing someone drunk on the street. Children need to know basic facts about alcohol and drugs, and to learn that being drunk or "high" on drugs is not funny. Alcoholics and drug addicts are ill and do not behave the way they do out of free choice.

Parents and children can acknowledge and discuss together the pressures children face to experiment with alcohol and drugs. These pressures can be powerful, coming both from the media messages previously mentioned and from peers. The need to feel a sense of group belonging may lead a young person to drink or use drugs even when his or her preference is not to use.

Research shows pre-teen and teenage girls often feel more pressure to be part of a group than do boys. An area in which girls are particularly vulnerable, and therefore need to be armed with information and a solid sense of self, concerns the connections between sex and drugs. Many people do things under the influence they would not ordinarily do, but for girls and women the stakes are high. There are risks of unwanted pregnancies, rape and AIDS. All children need discussion and clear guidelines about driving and alcohol and other drug use.

In general, children need to know that mother is approachable and open to discussing these topics. She should try to listen carefully to what is being said and give facts and information in a non-judgmental, neutral way. It is also helpful for families to discuss beforehand situations that might arise, thinking through possible responses and solutions. For example, going to a party where drugs are being taken or discovering that the person who is giving you a ride home has had too much to drink.

All of the above areas are important, but parental alcohol and drug use is perhaps the major determining factor in whether and how children will use these substances themselves. For better or worse, parents are children's most influential teachers. Ideally, the parent will be a role model for positive behaviors and set a consistent example of moderate drinking or a sober lifestyle and use of healthy coping techniques in relieving stress, such as talking with friends, exercise, meditating or watching a movie. For a mother who does not drink at all, it is helpful for her children to understand why she has made this choice. For a parent who abuses alcohol or other drugs, she can acknowledge her over-use and her desire to stop and seek help for herself. This sets a positive example of how to handle having a substance-abuse problem.

When A Child Abuses Alcohol or Other Drugs

Single mothers have responsibilities for so many areas of life that it is often hard to attend fully to everything. It is tempting, at times, to overlook problems in the hope they will disappear. A problem that generally gets worse with time and does need serious and thoughtful attention is a child's abuse of alcohol or other drugs. Signs of a chemical dependency problem include:

- Unexplained changes in mood and in behavior, for example, becoming more easily upset, angry or argumentative; sleeping more or less; losing interest in school, friends or recreational activities
- Switching friends to those who drink and use drugs
- Strongly defending the right to drink or use drugs or adamantly denying usage or a problem
- Increase in fights and disagreements at home
- Lack of honesty
- Trouble with the law
- Missing cash or items that can easily be turned into cash
- Irresponsible driving
- Changes in eating patterns, such as bingeing or loss of appetite
- Medical problems, such as ulcers, high blood pressure, gastritis, liver or kidney problems, unexplained accidents
- Emotional problems, such as anxiety, fears, depression, mood swings, suicidal thoughts or actions
- Deterioration of relationships in the family
- Child smells of alcohol or marijuana, eyes red and blurry or slurred speech

After noticing signs of an alcohol or drug problem, the question arises as to how to help the child who is in trouble. Intervening early when the abuse is not entrenched can be an easier time to address the problem. It is never too late, however, with children or adults, to help change alcohol- and drug-abusing behavior. Frank conversations between mother and child about the problem are needed when the child is clear-headed and not under the influence of a substance and when the mother is not feeling furious and desperate. The issue is volatile, but needs to be approached in a factual and non-judgmental manner to minimize defensiveness. Concrete examples of why there is concern and what problems alcohol or drug

abuse cause are very helpful. For example, "I have noticed that we have more fighting in the family after you have been to a party. I am concerned that you are smoking marijuana or drinking because you seem different after these parties," or "We both know that your grades are not what they used to be. It seems to me that your grades began to drop when you began to drink."

When there is a child abusing alcohol or drugs, it is particularly important that ground rules relating to unacceptable behavior at home are clearly understood. For example, a mother might decide that her children coming home under the influence or drinking or using drugs at home will not be tolerated. Rules made must be enforceable and consistently enforced or, obviously, they will be disregarded.

It is not easy, particularly for a single parent without support from a partner, to help a chemically dependent child. The toll on the mother and other family members can be enormous. Information, counseling and support can be invaluable in minimizing the sense of isolation and feelings of guilt, anger, and powerlessness. Counseling and support for the parent can help maximize an effective strategy for intervention for her child. Adults can seek help from professional treatment programs, Al-Anon and friends who have experienced similar problems. Women's centers, if knowledgeable about substance abuse, can also be a valuable resource. They could serve as natural meeting places for women to connect with other women concerned with their children's alcohol and drug use. The child should also be encouraged to get professional help. With the parent's assistance and approval, she or he can select who to see so that the child feels a sense of control over who the counselor will be.

Throughout the process of recognizing and accepting that a child is in trouble with alcohol or other drugs, it is important to know, and to be repeatedly reminded, that chemical dependency is treatable. There is hope for recovery and help is available. Many families are experiencing the consequences of substance abuse and there are many people and places to turn to for support and guidance.

Special Issues When the Parent Is in Recovery

Helping children with the complex issues of alcohol and drug use becomes even more difficult if the mother herself is in recovery from chemical dependency. In this situation, alcohol and drug use becomes an emotionally charged topic and therefore is not easy to approach in a neutral style.

Substance abuse problems tend to run in families for a combination of genetic and environmental reasons. If a mother is alcoholic or drug-addicted then there is a greater likelihood that her children will become substance abusers as well. It is therefore particularly important that children from these homes are assisted in developing a healthy sense of self-esteem so they can more easily resist pressures to drink and use drugs. Providing factual information about alcohol and drug use and abuse is also very helpful. These children will benefit from seeing non-drinking behavior and a mother who now responds to stress and disappointment with positive coping skills such as calling a friend, taking a walk or listening to music rather than medicating her feelings with a drink or a pill. A recovering mother demonstrates very powerfully that alcoholics and drug addicts can dramatically improve their lives through abstaining from chemicals and joining self-help groups.

Single mothers have very little, if any, "free" time, but when deciding how time should be spent, a mother's needs must also be taken into account. A mother needs time for herself, including attending self-help meetings, to sustain her own recovery. It is also valuable for the children to have as a role model a mother who pays attention to her health and her own interests.

Families are often surprised that life does not automatically improve when the chemically dependent person becomes sober or drug-free. For children accustomed to being on their own with few limits, it can be hard to have Mom back in charge and making the rules. Some children enjoy the responsibilities and decision-making they assume in the absence of a clear-headed parent. Resistance to a change in the status quo, even with all the problems substance abuse brings, is not uncommon. The entire family can benefit from counseling or self-help support to ease the transition. Suggesting children attend an Alcoholics Anonymous or Narcotics Anonymous meeting with their mother can help further an understanding of addictions and recovery.

When a mother has been sober for some time and feels emotionally ready, she might begin to help her children express feelings about her drinking and drug use. This can be a painful process made somewhat easier by having the support of a treatment program, a self-help group or other recovering mothers to help prepare her for what might be said. Before attempting this, a mother should have worked through some of her guilt. It can be helpful to anticipate what might be said and to perhaps act out a role play of the discussion between mother and child with a friend or counselor.

Women's centers can play an important role by first becoming knowledgeable about alcohol and other drugs and second, by providing a variety of services, including information and referral to substance-abuse treatment resources, support groups for single mothers that incorporate education about alcohol and drug use

and abuse, groups for young children and adolescents that provide alcohol and drug education, and support for children growing up in substance abusing families.

References

1. U.S. Bureau of the Census, "Money Income and Poverty Status of Families and Persons in the U.S.: 1985 (Advanced Data from the March 1986 Current Population Survey)," *Current Population Reports*, (1986), Series P-60, No. 154.
2. D.S. Burden, "Single Parents and the Work Setting: The Impact of Multiple Job and Homelife Responsibilities," *Family Relations*, 35 (January, 1986), 37-43.
3. D. Pearce and H. McAdoo, *Women and Children: Alone and in Poverty* (Washington. D.C.: National Advisory Council on Economic Opportunity, September, 1981).
4. D.S. Burden and N. Gottleib, *The Woman Client: Providing Human Services in a Changing World.* New York and London: Tavistock Publications, 1987.
5. U.S. Bureau of the Census, Current Population Reports, 1986.
6. R.A. Brandywein, "The Single Parent Family Revisited," paper prepared for the annual meeting of the Society for the Study of Social Problems, Family Division, New York City, August, 1973.
7. U.S. Bureau of the Census, op. cit.
8. U.S. Bureau of the Census, op. cit.
9. D.S. Burden and N. Gottleib, op. cit.
10. D.S. Burden and B. Googins, "Managing Work and Family Stress in Corporations," *Boston University Balancing Job and Homelife Study*, Boston University: 1987.
11. R.C. Barnett and G.K. Baruch, "Women's Involvement in Multiple Roles and Psychological Distress," *Journal of Personality and Social Psychology*, 49 (1985) 135-145.
12. S.C. Wilsnack, R.W. Wilsnack and A.D. Klassen, "Women and Alcohol: Health Related Issues. Research Monograph no. 19," *Epidemiological Research on Women's Drinking*, 1987-1984 DHHS Publication No. (ADM) 86-1139, 1-68.
13. B. Reed and R. Moise, "Implications for Treatment and Future Research," in *Addicted Women: Family Dynamics, Self-Perceptions and Support Systems* (Rockville, MD: The Institute, 1980), NIDA, DHEW Pub. No. (ADM) 80-762.
14. E. Gomberg, "Women and Alcohol: Health Related Issues. Research Monograph No. 16," *Women and Alcoholism: Psychosocial Issues*, DHHS Publication No. (ADM) 86-1139, (Wash-

ington, D.C.: U.S. Gov't Printing Office, 1986),
78-120.

15. D.S. Burden and B. Googins, op. cit.
16. D. Belle, "Depression and Low-Income Female
     Headed Families," *Families Today*, 1 (1979),
     323-345.
17. E. Gomberg, op. cit.

18. S.C. Wilsnack, R.W. Wilsnack and A.D. Klassen,
     op. cit.
19. N. Finkelstein, K. Brown and C. Latham,
     "Alcoholic Mothers and Guilt: Issues for Car-
     egivers," *Alcohol Health and Research World*, 6
     (1) (1981), 45-49.

11 Sororities of Helping and Healing: Women and Mutual Help Groups

Stephanie S. Covington, Ph.D.

"It is impossible to describe the variety of A.A. meetings and members that exist at this time. There are specialized meetings for women, lesbians, Native Americans, nurses, non-smokers, people who are HIV-positive and scores of others who may share some other characteristic in addition to their desire to stop drinking."

Introduction

For centuries women have sought to teach and support themselves and each other by meeting in groups and pooling information and experiences. In traditional and modern societies alike, women continue to meet to wash clothes and sew quilts together, share stories around a coffee pot, play cards and watch children. These activities have always and will always involve offers of solace and support that come in casual conversation with dependable and cherished sisters.

Today, women who meet in mutual help groups do so for many of the same reasons that their forebears gathered together. They may feel that professionals have not been able to help. They may be unable to afford ongoing therapy. Many are disgusted with condescending males who profess to know it all.

With growing consciousness of the social forces that shape people's lives, women have begun to question their traditionally designated roles and have become angry at their sense of helplessness in the "scheme of things." By meeting in groups and sharing these feelings and questions, women have sought information, knowing that knowledge is power.

Few developments of recent years have become so widespread as the use of mutual help groups to recover from drug and alcohol addiction. The phenomenon is most obviously measured by the growth in the sheer number of such groups. These include Alcoholics Anonymous (A.A.), Women For Sobriety and Narcotics Anonymous, which are the predominant examples of mutual help groups concerned with addiction. More-

The Author wishes to thank Mary Dana Phillips for her assistance in the preparation of this chapter.

over, the so called "Twelve Step Model," which originated in A.A., is now used by over 126 "anonymous" groups to deal with a host of other problems.[1] Overeating, gambling, workaholism, sexual and incest issues, and other relationship topics are now addressed by people meeting in mutual self-help groups modeled after A.A.

Mutual help groups and the Twelve Step Model have a tremendous appeal to a wide variety of people. They use them to cope with a spectrum of substances, behaviors and processes. Quite clearly these are people with problems to which complete solutions have not been found in traditional places offered by established helpers.

Self-help or mutual help groups are comprised of people who voluntarily come together to discuss a common problem, often to share solutions and coping techniques. The key feature of any mutual help group is that there is no involvement by professionals or experts who yield either authority or knowledge. Face-to-face interactions are stressed and members are encouraged to accept personal responsibility for themselves. Self-help or mutual aid groups offer their members social support through the creation of a caring community. They increase members' coping skills through the provision of information and sharing of feelings, experiences and solutions. This is accomplished without the use of professionally trained staff or the reliance upon outsiders for financial support or legitimacy.

This chapter presents a broad overview of mutual help groups for people recovering from alcohol and drug problems while focusing on issues specific to women. Traditionally, women have not been provided with specific services to help them into treatment and recovery. The problems women experience with drugs and alcohol have only recently been identified as requiring specialized solutions because their patterns of use and consequences are so different from men's. During the last decade, advances have been made to design therapeutic programs that address women's issues, both in the development of and recovery from substance abuse.

There has also been a delay in the development of women's mutual aid groups to help each other to recover from drug and alcohol problems. Some feminists claim that this is because of the inherent sexist and hierarchical nature of the predominant Twelve Step Model. Others maintain that it is more a reflection of the slow evolution of all kinds of alcohol treatment services for women that exists more generally.

Women have been a part of A.A. since its beginnings, although in the early years they were relegated to making coffee, cookies and curtains for the clubhouse. As women, they were rarely acknowledged as alcoholics, and were most commonly a part of the early groups as the wife, mother, sister or daughter of a male alcoholic. A.A. reflects the dominant culture in many ways and this is one of the more obvious examples of it. Women have had some difficulty in A.A. over the years establishing themselves—both as drinkers and as recovering alcoholics.

More recent feminist critiques of A.A. have suggested that it espouses a primarily male model of alcoholism. It follows, then, that neither the understanding of alcoholism in a person's life nor the meaning of recovery have been completely relevant for women. Nonetheless, until other models are developed, A.A. is a viable resource for women. It is certainly better than untreated alcoholism or women struggling on their own to achieve sobriety.

With some caveats, then, A.A. is a place for women to go and to find help for their alcohol problems. Women seem to be increasingly turning to drugs and alcohol. Maybe they are simply showing up in mutual help groups and other treatment centers sooner and in greater numbers than ever before. In any case, the presence of women has become progressively more common and accepted over the last twenty years in A.A. As their presence grows, so might their experiences have an impact on the way we think about recovery from alcoholism. Women continue to benefit from A.A. whether they attend mixed-sex or women-only meetings.

The use of mutual help groups by women to help themselves and each other to recover from addiction is an important phenomenon for women's lives more generally. Women conceived of and started Al-Anon to help each other and their families deal with their husbands' drinking. It was the second Twelve Step program and was begun in the late 1940s.[2] More recently, women have participated in Adult Children of Alcoholics groups that have developed out of the Al-Anon tradition. A full consideration of the issues for women in mutual self-help groups is beyond the scope of this chapter. It will address the key issues involved in understanding A.A.'s Twelve Step Model as it continues to have an impact on women seeking solutions to their alcohol problems.

History of Mutual Help Groups: The Twelve Step Model

Mutual help groups have been used by people to provide support for one another since prehistoric times. The first groups to discuss alcohol issues were formed at least two hundred years ago. Alcoholics Anonymous is nearly fifty-five years old. It is easily the most famous of all mutual support groups. A.A. marks its beginning in 1935 when one hopelessly alcoholic but dry drunk contacted another still drinking and equally desperate alcoholic. The power that they found in sharing their experience, strength and hope with one another got and kept them both sober.[2]

Sharing their message with other alcoholics kept them from returning to drinking and to the old ideas that accompany it. What's more, the message proved to be transmissible and many of those they contacted were also able to stop drinking. By 1939 the one hundred sober "alcoholics anonymous" published a book by that same name describing their program. By the end of 1941, membership had ballooned to over 8,000.[2] Currently 1.7 million members are estimated to meet in nearly 80,000 groups around the world.[1]

The A.A. program teaches its participants to transform negative self-images into positive self-images. As people accumulate sober time they acquire a totally different set of values. These include developing honesty, humility and personal responsibility. The A.A. program is comprised of many beliefs and principles that encourage its members to take life one day at a time. Members are convinced to abandon the rigidity and omnipotence that characterized them in their drinking days. The program's main tenet is that an alcoholic's problems are due to the debilitating effects and consequences of alcoholic drinking and not because of some underlying mental or emotional problem. The desire to drink is a compulsion and becomes a habit because it gradually or quickly becomes the only solution to life's problems.

Periods of alcoholic drinking often span years in women's lives and may begin in childhood or adolescence. Women may begin to drink for a variety of reasons. For some, drinking is a reaction to otherwise untenable situations to which there do not seem to be any other responses. But for any woman, drinking alcoholically does not allow her to develop reasonable responses to life's challenges, much less a coherent and comfortable inner or emotional life.

Recovery from alcoholism in A.A. entails admitting the limits of one's self and accepting that alcoholism is much more than simply drinking too much. What the A.A. program offers exists in sharp contrast to the fundamental limitations and isolation suffered during active alcoholism. It emphasizes the limitless potential for growth and well-being. This becomes available to anyone who possesses a desire to stop drinking, which is the only requirement for membership. Membership in A.A. is measured solely by how active a person is in the program and not by how long one has been sober.

Many people use the A.A. program to stop drinking and many more seem to also use it as a way of life. Part of the therapeutic action of the program rests on the individual's concession to the existence of a power greater than the self (ego). This may be conceived of as a Higher Self or a Deeper Self that may exist in one's mind and heart. It may also be reflected by a loving and supporting group or by other individuals striving for a better life. In A.A. you can stop drinking and stop there or go on to actively join a community of recovering people who support one another.

The program is "practiced" in a variety of ways that includes reading A.A. literature, talking to others—especially to a person chosen by you to be your "sponsor"—and attending meetings. The latter is the main activity of A.A. members. This is the central therapeutic component of the program and the one in which primary social relationships are reconstructed without the use of alcohol or other mind-altering chemicals. A.A. meetings may be found nearly everywhere but are often quite different from one another because of the characteristics of a particular group's members and the meeting format itself. The three main types of meetings are: 1) speaker-only meetings; 2) speaker-discussion meetings; or 3) discussion meetings. Any of these types may be "open" or "closed." Open meetings welcome anyone who is interested in A.A., including non-alcoholics. Closed meetings are restricted to those people who think they are alcoholics or who think of themselves as members of A.A.

Participation in any meeting is wholly voluntary although some discussion meetings routinely call on people to speak. You can decline, but there is undeniably pressure in A.A. to talk because talking is the primary mechanism of healing. Talking allows unburdening to occur. Worries, fears and concerns that were once powerful secrets become avenues of mutual sharing. Talking allows others to identify, thereby reducing shame while engaging others to work on solutions to common problems. "Cross-talk," or the

practice of responding to a previous person's remarks with advice or comment, is strongly avoided. A.A. is not about judgment or having oneself measured against some standard. People are encouraged to come to meetings and benefit from what is heard rather than interfere with it by attempting to change someone else's reality. Members are reminded in a variety of ways to stick to their own experiences and understanding, and not to stray from the discussion of their own situation and progress.

Standard materials taken from the A.A. book are read by way of opening and closing every meeting. Other rituals commonly observed include asking new people to identify themselves so that they may be individually welcomed, passing the basket for voluntary contributions to pay for rent and coffee, asking members to announce their sober-time anniversaries, making announcements about events in the local A.A. community and indicating that there is literature available free to newcomers and for a nominal fee to others.

Groups are technically autonomous, but are guided in their dealings with one another and with the outside world by the Twelve Traditions of A.A.:

1. Our common welfare should come first; personal recovery depends upon A.A. unity.
2. For our group purpose there is but one ultimate authority—a loving God as He may express Himself in our group conscience.
3. The only requirement for A.A. membership is a desire to stop drinking.
4. Each group should be autonomous except in matters affecting other groups or A.A. as a whole.
5. Each group has but one primary purpose—to carry its message to the alcoholic who still suffers.
6. An A.A. group ought never endorse, finance or lend the A.A. name to any related facility or outside enterprise, lest problems of money, property and prestige divert us from our primary purpose.
7. Every A.A. group ought to be fully self-supporting, declining outside contributions.
8. Alcoholics Anonymous should remain forever non-professional, but our service centers may employ special workers.
9. A.A., as such, ought never be organized; but we may create service boards or committees directly responsible to those they serve.
10. Alcoholics Anonymous has no opinion on outside issues; hence the A.A. name ought never be drawn into public controversy.
11. Our public relations policy is based on attraction rather than promotion; we need always maintain personal anonymity at the level of press, radio and films.
12. Anonymity is the spiritual foundation of all our

traditions, ever reminding us to place principles before personalities.

[Reprinted with permission from the *A.A. Grapevine*]

These are basic principles for conduct that, among other things, disallow any A.A. group or member from affiliation with an outside organization. They encourage members to place principles before personalities and to value the group over any individual, especially the self. Related to this is the emphasis placed upon personal anonymity, which discourages prideful acts and encourages members to think of themselves as common drunks who are only special because they have been given the opportunity to get sober. The power and wisdom of the Traditions are rarely discussed. Perhaps it is sufficient that A.A. is the only mutual help organization of its kind that has avoided professionalization or co-optation by outsiders, especially where money is involved.

It is impossible to describe the enormous variety of A.A. meetings and members that exist at this time. There are specialized meetings for women, lesbians, Native Americans, nurses, non-smokers, people who are HIV-positive and scores of others who may share some other characteristic in addition to their desire to stop drinking. Research from A.A.'s own membership surveys reveals that over the past twenty-two years, the percentage of female members found in a sample of North American meetings has climbed from 22 percent to 34 percent. The number of people under the age of thirty-one has jumped from 7 percent in 1968 to 21 percent in 1986.[1]

There is very little research that points to the diversity and variability of A.A., but it is certainly safe to say that it is no longer a "fellow"-ship of middle-class, middle-aged, White Protestant males. Finding a meeting is easy though it may be harder to find one where you feel comfortable. In some respects, A.A. meetings are only places to find out about alcoholism and recovery from it and do not have to be politically correct. But it is also true that for people to "hear" things they must be said in appropriate ways using non-offensive language. Identifying meetings where you can feel safe and comfortable and open to ideas is something everyone does in A.A.

In A.A. there is the idea of the "home group" which is most often a meeting you choose to attend every week without fail. It is where everyone learns to take on the first responsibilities of staying sober the A.A. way—helping to set up the chairs, acting as the treasurer, greeting newcomers at the door—so that, in time, responsibility may be assumed for the life outside of A.A. It becomes a place where a great deal of time will be spent in recovery from alcoholism and as such it may be a recreation or creation of a family. Finding a home group along with other meetings where you feel safe and comfortable and encouraged to interact with others is an essential part of recovery.

Some women will be fortunate enough to attend women-only meetings where they can appreciate the depth and detail of discussions that do not occur in mixed-sex groups. In same-sex groups women are not under pressure to remain attractive to males while revealing feelings of shame or remorse about some previous or current behavior or thought. Women are able to talk about childhood experiences of oppression or abuse by males when with other women. They are also able to discuss their current lives more openly, talking about their lovers and husbands and families to other women who will not find fault with their interpretations of reality.

Women who do go to mixed-sex groups will also be able to achieve sobriety and may discover a level of communication occurring between men and women that is very different from what they are used to. Participating in A.A. means partaking of a unique and supportive group that may well include men who are also aspiring to leave their old selves behind. In some cases, women are able to enjoy their first healthy social relationships with men inside A.A. This is because meetings are a part of a structured environment that is qualitatively different from the culture at large.

The Twelve Steps

The most distinctive feature of the A.A. program is its Twelve Suggested Steps of Recovery:

1. We admitted we were powerless over alcohol—that our lives had become unmanageable.
2. Came to believe that a Power greater than ourselves could restore us to sanity.
3. Made a decision to turn our will and our lives over to the care of God *as we understood Him*.
4. Made a searching and fearless moral inventory of ourselves.
5. Admitted to God, to ourselves and to another human being the exact nature of our wrongs.
6. Were entirely ready to have God remove all these defects of character.
7. Humbly asked Him to remove our shortcomings.
8. Made a list of all persons we had harmed, and became willing to make amends to them all.
9. Made direct amends to such people wherever possible, except when to do so would injure them or others.
10. Continued to take personal inventory and when we were wrong, promptly admitted it.
11. Sought through prayer and meditation to improve our conscious contact with God *as we understand Him,* praying only for knowledge of His will for us and the power to carry that out.

12. Having had a spiritual awakening as a result of these steps, we tried to carry this message to alcoholics, and to practice these principles in all our affairs.

[Reprinted with permission from the *A.A. Grapevine*]

The Steps rely on help that is believed to come from a power outside of the self. It may be understood however one wishes. The Steps may be viewed as a series of progressive shifts in attitude that allow constructive action to be taken in one's life. Attitudes are further refined by the results of lasting behavioral changes. The goal of the Steps is not merely one of remaining abstinent from alcohol and drugs. They are first used to move beyond obsession about drinking and to establish sobriety. The Steps may also be used in all aspects of one's life to perpetuate the fundamental and lasting shifts that have occurred. Staying in A.A. and living life according to the Steps allows one to remain comfortably sober while developing a philosophy of life and way of living that is productive and feels okay.

The Twelve Steps are the core of the A.A. program of action. The program is not about having something done to you or taught to you while you sit passively on a chair. Working the program necessarily involves recreating for yourself the meaning and relevance of ongoing sobriety. Choosing not to drink day after day and not to indulge in dishonesty or other destructive behaviors are actions one does for oneself. Recovery is an ongoing process in which one is engaged and heavily invested.

The Twelve Steps may also be the most misunderstood part of the program for two main reasons. The first is their repeated mention of "God" which conveys very strong traditional images shared with institutionalized Judeo-Christian religions. It must be understood that at the time of their writing, the Twelve Steps and their use of the term "Higher Power" were considered to be progressive and more secular than religious. One of the original members who was involved in drafting the Steps was an atheist who insisted that the idea of Higher Power be flexible, individualized and inclusionary and not be rigidly prescribed or insisted upon.

A.A. was not and is not now about religion in a formal institutionalized sense. Spiritual progress is the goal of its members who are encouraged to define their own Higher Powers for themselves. Membership in A.A. may expose one to ideas and philosophies that are found in Christianity as it is practiced both inside and outside of the Church, but it must not be mistaken for joining a religious sect or cult. Over the years the A.A. program and its members have shown their capacity for adaptive change so that today, Higher Power is a tremendously personalized idea. Everyone's Higher Power is allowed to coexist because yours need not work for anyone but you. Forcing one's own understanding of God onto someone in A.A. is not condoned behavior. As a result, people in some A.A. groups may choose to call their Higher Power "Goddess" or "Buddha" or refer to it as a "Deeper Self" and it is not against any rules. Simply put, there are no regulations in A.A. for how one chooses to think about this subject. We do not have to be misled by archaic language and presume that the ideas it conveys are equally old-fashioned.

The second most misunderstood part of the A.A. program that finds expression in the first of its Twelve Steps is the concept of powerlessness. Critics of A.A. say that to urge women to admit their powerlessness over alcohol—and by elaboration in the Program, over people, places and things—is to set them up as victims who are discouraged from taking control over their lives. These critics are missing one of the enduring paradoxes of A.A. that perhaps contributes to its success in many people's lives. When people get to A.A. it is because they are in fact powerless to bring about desired feelings or to accomplish their goals without using alcohol. Admitting powerlessness can be a comforting and empowering act and it is a premise of A.A. that deserves elaboration. The paradox is that admitting where you are powerless in life actually empowers you. It allows you to be in touch with personal power, areas of your life where you do have power and control.

Admission to powerlessness over alcohol permits the identification of times when choices can be made and things can be changed. For example, a woman involved in an abusive relationship may admit to her powerlessness over drinking and, once sober, be able to identify areas in her life where she can make choices about how to think and how to behave with regard to her relationship. Yet she remains fundamentally powerless over changing others; instead, she directs her energy into changing herself.

Taking the alcohol away with an admission of powerlessness over it is not about the passivity and immobilization that typically characterize victims. It is about taking a positive action to realistically assess one's own capacity for change and potential for growth. One of the primary tasks in recovery is to identify desired boundaries and limits. Learning to distinguish which situations and relationships with people may be accepted, avoided or changed without feeling threatened or fearful is hard work. It depends on self-awareness, persistence, hope and trial-and-error. Learning to make these distinctions, going on to construct boundaries and, once constructed, to respect them is an achievement of sobriety. Developing goals for oneself and strategies to attain them is also a major component of ongoing recovery. It is comprised of incremental processes that begin with an understanding of the paradox of powerlessness.

Other "Anonymous" Groups : The Extension of the Twelve Step Model

Twelve Step recovery groups are appropriate for many problems that have escaped the attention or expertise of conventional problem-solving professionals. There are many groups using the Twelve Steps with the permission of A.A. to deal with one's own drug or alcohol problems as well as with the drug or alcohol problems of one's family, spouse, lover or friends. Most well-known of these groups designed to help people deal with other people's alcohol- and drug-related problems are Al-Anon, Alateen, Nar-Anon, Adult Children of Alcoholics and Codependents Anonymous. All of these have groups and activities that are organized very similarly to A.A. They use the Twelve Steps, have specific program literature and conduct meetings. To find out which groups are represented in your community, look in the Yellow Pages of the telephone book or write to the addresses listed at the end of this chapter.

Another group that women use to recover from addiction is Women For Sobriety (W.F.S.). Founded in 1972, it is less like A.A. and more like a traditional feminist consciousness-raising group where women share their lives with each other from a distinctly female perspective. In place of the Twelve Step are the Thirteen Statements of Affirmation or Acceptance:

1. I have a drinking problem that once had me.
2. Negative emotions destroy only myself.
3. Happiness is a habit I will develop.
4. Problems bother me only to the degree I permit them to.
5. I am what I think.
6. Life can be ordinary or it can be great.
7. Love can change the course of my world.
8. The fundamental object of life is emotional and spiritual growth.
9. The past is gone forever.
10. All love given returns two-fold.
11. Enthusiasm is my daily exercise.
12. I am a competent woman and have much to give others.
13. I am responsible for myself and my sisters.

The Women For Sobriety program is an affirmation of the value and worth of each woman, focusing on her as, in the words of its founder, "the A.A. program cannot (focus on women) because it was not designed to."[3] W.F.S. meetings may be located by looking in the telephone book or by writing to the address that appears in the back of this chapter.

Women today also have the choice of attending a new program called Save Our Selves (S.O.S.) which was begun in 1984 to address the needs of agnostic, atheistic and humanist alcoholics who were dissatisfied with A.A. Much of the program and format is similar to A.A. but its tenets and philosophy are decidedly secular and may appeal to women who are unprepared to reckon with a Higher Power in any form. S.O.S. meetings may be located by looking in the telephone book or by writing to the address that appears in the back of this chapter.

Limitations of Twelve Step Groups

There has been some discussion of the limitations of the Twelve Step Model throughout this chapter and several more points may be added. Part of the current wave of criticism of A.A. and its model stems from its insistence on individual pathology and individual change as the solution to life's problems. Alcoholism and other problems that cripple women and may be related to their drinking are not viewed from a social context. A.A. ideology does not encourage discussions of the social and political causative factors of alcoholism. For women, it may be that the environment contributed to the drinking and the environment prevents the recovery from occurring.

Many of the problems women have with alcohol exist through systems of domination. Women exist in a culture dominated by males. Women are routinely subordinated to roles that are primarily supportive to men and not to themselves. Problems women have in getting sober may also be contingent on their compliance to cultural values that do not encourage women to be assertive, independent and political. Sometimes getting sober in A.A. seems to mean accepting the inequalities, frustrations and limitations of being female in the culture. A.A. does not provide a forum for discussion of structural and political issues that contribute to a woman's alcoholic drinking and may prohibit her recovery.

It is also true that much of the A.A. literature was written twenty to fifty years ago and is overtly sexist in its content and connotations. The same cannot be said for W.F.S. or S.O.S., groups that are newer and much more sensitive to this issue. It is also true that some groups have taken it upon themselves to read the Twelve Steps and other parts of the A.A. literature substituting gender-neutral pronouns. There is also a movement to request that the Big Book of A.A. be rewritten in its entirety to become non-sexist. The possibility of this occurring anytime soon is somewhat remote, but there is certainly evidence of a recognition that some of the program's materials are limited in their appeal.

Although self-help has tremendous potential, it can also be quite easily misunderstood by service providers who have never gone to a meeting or talked with women for whom A.A. has worked. Perhaps the gravest limitation of self-help is for women who may be in need of professional counseling. A woman may need a clinically trained therapist when there has been rape, incest and/or severe battering in the past or in the present. Often it is an issue like this that prevents a woman from achieving comfortable or long-lasting sobriety. Repeated relapse can be the signal that there has been extreme abuse that requires the help and care of a trained professional who will work with the woman—with or without the use of self-help—to prevent repeated returns to drinking.

Despite all of these shortcomings and potentials for pitfalls, women should be encouraged to seek out groups and to start new ones. They are not just a personal solution to individual women's needs; they are a tool for inducing collective thought, action and social change.

Women do not have to feel alone, isolated or victimized in sobriety. A.A., N.A. and other mutual help groups have saved the lives of millions of men and women and offer attractive alternatives to active alcoholism and drug addiction.

Advantages of Mutual Help Groups for Women in Recovery

The first major advantage of mutual help groups to women in recovery is that they are free and, in most urban communities, readily available throughout most of every day. It is in this respect that they are most unlike conventional problem-solving techniques where help is provided only on occasion, almost exclusively as a response to a specific request from a particular individual. Mutual help recovery groups are often found in women's centers or other places in communities that provide other types of help to women. There are no dues or fees for membership and people are permitted to come and go freely without records being kept or contracts drawn. Meetings occur as scheduled through cooperative efforts; they are dependable and consistent in their format.

Also, women in all stages of recovery can find something useful in A.A., whether in same-sex or mixed-sex groups. You can use meetings for a variety of reasons that may be related to the development of different values as well as to staying sober. A woman's needs shift in sobriety and the meetings she attends may change to reflect this. Different groups can offer different things depending on the people who attend them and the focus of the discussions. A.A. is a highly differentiated program that is suitable for a variety of women.

Secondly, every woman is made to feel worthwhile. There are no bosses in A.A. and the only experts are the members. If you have made it to A.A. or N.A. you are

surely an expert in drinking and using drugs. Experiencing quality time in the program makes you an expert on staying sober, too. Even the woman with very little in terms of material resources or accumulated sober time can hold out her hand to offer support to a woman who is at her first meeting. The sharing that occurs in mutual help meetings is not dependent on hierarchy or status; in this way it is very different from the dominant culture. The value of participation in a program like A.A. is twofold: one benefits by giving as well as by getting. One is valued both for what she shares of herself and for what she offers of herself to others. A.A. offers a program for living that may be shared by newcomers and oldtimers alike where both benefit from the other. Related to this is that no one is made to feel "less than" if she asks for help. Asking for help is a major part of the prescription for recovery. Asking for and offering help become mutually reinforcing.

Thirdly, participation in A.A. and other mutual help groups is a wonderful opportunity for social activities that are alcohol- and drug-free. Meetings and the stories that are told during them can be tremendously entertaining and fun, in addition to being legitimately therapeutic. People are, for the most part, kind. The format is typically active listening where personal attacks or judgments are not tolerated. It is possible to find in A.A. a safe place where you can learn who you are and how to become that person before going out into the world where it may not be so safe. A.A. is also a place for women to find and make friends. Part of the program is sharing with other members outside of the meeting time; contacting people on the telephone during the times between meetings yields friends as well as supportive contacts. Many in A.A. talk about the "meeting after the meeting" where people go out together for coffee and continue the discussion in a less formal way or simply talk about other things.

Many meetings that are being run by women reflect their concerns and the realities of their lives. Child care may be offered during meeting time; exchanging information about ride-sharing may be a part of the actual format of the meeting. Temporary sponsorship programs may be in place to encourage women to reach out to their sisters.

Because of the culture, women have often been excluded from the mainstream of life, including receiving quality treatment for their alcohol and drug problems. One could argue that this is a reason why it is important that women may need to develop their own mutual help groups. As oppressed people, women have an additional need to find a place to be heard and to feel useful. Recovery from active alcoholism or drug addiction is accomplished through a renewal of consciousness, by restoring a sense of the self and its worth. This kind of work is able to be accomplished in both same-sex and mixed-sex A.A. or N.A. meetings, though different issues may require different groups. If there is not a women-only group in the community, start one. If it is not possible to start one, take advantage of the quality sobriety among both men and women in the local A.A. or N.A. community. Self-help groups are a place to begin and to continue recovery from drug and alcohol addiction.

References
1. Alcoholics Anonymous World Services, 1989. Analysis of the 1986 A.A. Membership Survey. New York.
2. Wilson, Bill. *Alcoholics Anonymous Comes of Age.* New York: A.A. World Services, 1965.
3. Kirkpatrick, Jean. *Turnabout: Help for a New Life.* New York: Doubleday, 1978.

Where to Get Information About Groups

National Clearinghouse for Alcohol
and Drug Information
P.O. Box 2345
Rockville, MD 20852
(301) 468-2600

Alcoholics Anonymous
P.O. Box 459 Grand Central Station
New York, NY 10163-1100
(212) 686-1100

Al-Anon/Alateen Family Group Headquarters, Inc.
P.O. Box 862 Midtown Station
New York, NY 10018-0862
(212) 302-7240

Adult Children of Alcoholics
6381 Hollywood Blvd., Suite 685
Hollywood, CA 90028
(213) 464-4423

National Association for Children of Alcoholics
31706 Coast Highway, Suite 201
Laguna, CA 92667
(714) 499-3889

The Augustine Fellowship,
Sex and Love Addicts Anonymous
P.O. Box 88 New Town Branch
Boston, MA 02258

Save Our Selves (National Organization for Secular Sobriety)
P.O. Box 15781
North Hollywood, CA 91615-5781

Overeaters Anonymous
2190 190th Street
Torrance, CA 90504

Women for Sobriety, Inc.
P.O. Box 618
Quakertown, PA 18951
1 (800) 333-1606

Narcotics Anonymous
P.O. Box 9999
Van Nuys, CA 91409

12 Issues for Latinas: Puerto Rican Women

Marilyn Aguirre-Molina, Ed.D.

"Special recognition must be given to the fact that Puerto Rican women who are problem drinkers are solitary drinkers who drink in the privacy of their homes. Cultural factors still appear to play a role in the way these women behave toward alcohol. If women's centers and other women's service organizations are to reach these women, efforts must be made to recognize their unique warning signs. Culturally appropriate methods to encourage participation in treatment programs are critical."

It is probably safe to conclude that public attitudes/mores about alcohol- and other drug-related problems among women of all classes and ethnic groups are at best, ambivalent, and at worst, driven by double standards and stigma. Unfortunately, this is particularly true among people in cultural and ethnic groups that value traditional female sex roles, especially Puerto Ricans and other Latinos.

This chapter deals with Puerto Rican women living in the United States and their issues related to alcohol and other drug use among them. A sociodemographic profile of the Puerto Rican woman is provided to help professionals working with these women develop a comprehensive understanding of their current status and condition. Attention is given to the elements that contribute to risks among these women, the cultural and social factors that effect their access to intervention and treatment, and recommendations for alcohol and drug abuse prevention.

There is always the danger of oversimplification in overviews of this nature. Efforts have been made to prevent or at least minimize this risk, as the literature is already replete with stereotyped interpretations that misrepresent Puerto Rican women's realities.

A Profile of the Puerto Rican Woman in the United States

Latinos, numbering 19.4 million, make up 8.1 percent of the U.S. population. From 1980 to 1988, the entire Latino population living in the United States increased by 34 percent (about 5 million people) as compared to 7 percent for the rest of the population.[1] Projections are that the Latino population will increase at a rate of more than three times the growth rate of the total U.S. population. By the year 2000, the Bureau of the Census estimates that there will be 25 million Latinos in the United States, making them the largest ethnic-racial group in the country. They are also one of the youngest of the ethnic-racial minority groups.[2] Puerto Rican women, who represent 13.1 percent of Latino women in the U.S., confront a set of unique economic and social conditions and experiences.

The 1980s were to have been the "Decade of the Hispanic." But this has become a meaningless slogan for the more than 1.3 million Puerto Rican women living in the United States. Puerto Rican women make up more than half of the Puerto Rican population (53.3%). It is interesting to note that in no other population group—Mexicans, Cubans, other Latinos, Whites or Blacks—is there a higher percentage of females.[2] Puerto Rican women are distinguished from other groups in terms of their age (half of the population is below 25) and their high fertility rates. Puerto Rican females, like Mexican American women, tend to have their children at an earlier age than non-Latinos, and have larger families (an average of 3.62 children), second only to Mexican Americans.[1]

After Cubans, Puerto Rican women are the most highly urbanized of all female minority group populations. Over seventy-five percent (75.6%) of these women live in the Northeast, primarily in New York City (50.5%) and urban New Jersey (12.1%). Sixty-five percent of all Latinos living in the tri-state region of New York, New Jersey and Connecticut are Puerto Rican.[2]

Economic Status and Poverty

While some of the Latino subgroups in the United

States have made small economic gains during the 1980s, the problems faced by Puerto Ricans far outweigh the other groups' successes. Puerto Ricans have the lowest income level of any Latinos (median family income is $12,371), their poverty rates (41.9%) exceed those of the Black community and they have the lowest labor force participation rates for males (66.9%) and females (39.0%). Between 1959 and 1984, the Puerto Rican mean family income decreased by approximately 25 percent (in constant dollars), a decrease twice that of Blacks and more than any other Latino group.[3]

Forty-four percent of Puerto Rican households are headed by single females, and Puerto Ricans represent by far the highest percentage of female-headed households of all groups living in the United States. Seventy-four percent of these women are living below the poverty level.[2] Yet, according to several researchers, female headship in and of itself does not explain the depressed economic status of these women. They argue that female-headed households are a symptom, not a cause, of broader social and economic problems.[4]

Labor Force Participation

A number of explanations have been offered for the low economic status of Puerto Rican women: for example, Puerto Rican women have language barriers, newly arrived status and cultural norms which relegate them solely to the roles of mothers and homemakers. But these explanations ignore the fact that the condition of Puerto Rican women has become gradually worse over the last two decades and that their depressed economic status is related to various economic factors and shifts in the economy.[5] The Santana, Cooney and Colon study of Puerto Rican women in the labor force states that "in 1950, the participation rate of Puerto Rican females was higher than both Whites and Blacks. In fact, only the Japanese female had a higher (labor force participation) rate than the Puerto Rican in 1950."[6] But since that time, of the eight groups studied by Santana, Cooney and Colon, "only the Puerto Rican females have experienced a decline in participation, from 38.9 percent in 1950 to 36.3 percent in 1960 to a low of 29.8 percent in 1970."[6]

Why are Puerto Rican women so under-represented in the labor force and why do they suffer such high rates of unemployment? Santana, Cooney and Colon explain that the decreased labor force participation and subsequent diminished economic status of Puerto Rican women is largely due to structural factors beyond their control.[6] Specifically, New York City has suffered the greatest decline in those industries where Puerto Rican women are heavily employed.

In the course of the last three decades, many factories that traditionally employed Puerto Rican women moved out of the country or to the suburbs. Some reduced their workforce through automation. This pattern of job decline in the manufacturing sector has continued into the 1980s.

Educational Attainment

Another factor related to the ability to obtain employment is educational attainment. Potential income is greatly affected by educational level, which enhances or diminishes one's ability to compete in the labor market. Examination of the educational profile of Latin women, and Puerto Rican women in particular, provides a partial explanation for why they tend to be concentrated in the lowest-paying and the least stable sectors of the economy.

The two groups with the lowest levels of schooling in the United States are foreign-born Mexicans, who average approximately 11 years of schooling, and Puerto Ricans, who average approximately 8 years.[7] Puerto Ricans have relatively low high-school graduation rates—only 54.3 percent for men and 52.7 percent for women. These rates are well below the average for American Indian women (71.1%), Black women (74.7%) and White women (87.6%).[7]

The low educational attainment of Puerto Rican women is largely due to the institutional racism they encounter in school. Increasingly, Puerto Ricans attend segregated schools. The New York, New Jersey and Connecticut region schools where Puerto Ricans are enrolled have 90-100 percent minority student populations. In 1984, the schools in this region educated 12 percent of the nation's Latino children but accounted for only 9 percent of the graduates.[8]

The declining rates of labor force participation are also attributable to the increasing educational requirements of the labor market, which limit the Puerto Rican woman's access to jobs. But even when Puerto Rican women have the same educational level as non-Puerto Ricans, they still do not get jobs at the same level as their White counterparts.[9]

Impact of Race

These factors do not fully explain the status of Puerto Ricans. Racial prejudice also contributes strongly to economic stratification. Many Puerto Ricans are of mixed ancestry—Indian, White and Black—a result of the colonial and racial history of the island which was inhabited by Indians, colonized by White Europeans (primarily Spaniards), and later inhabited by African slaves who were brought by the Europeans to work the mines and replace many of the indigenous population that were brutalized by the colonizers.

Because of this racial and cultural history Puerto Ricans, who are racially diverse, identify along ethnic lines, not racial lines. Much of the conflict Puerto Rican women encounter is a direct consequence of the social system in the United States, which is fixed on categorizing individuals along racial lines. This is compounded by what has been described as "double jeopardy" for Puerto Rican women: gender and color.

For these reasons, women's centers that are informed about and sensitive to the needs of women of color can play a very important role by demonstrating respect for diversity and conducting programs that reflect multicultural understanding. A sensitive environment can help reaffirm the identity of Puerto Rican women by validating their culture.

Puerto Rican Women: Alcohol and Other Drugs

Few studies have been done on the prevalence and patterns of alcohol and other drug use among Puerto Rican women. When studies refer to them, it is often in the context of the male's alcohol or drug use. For these reasons, much of what is known is often spotty and must be used with discretion.

Drug Use and Related Problems

Researchers are just beginning to examine drug problems among Puerto Rican women, and they limit the focus to those in state or local drug agencies. This makes it difficult to obtain accurate figures describing the extent of the problem among Puerto Rican women. State and local drug agencies often collect and report data using the single category of "Hispanic," thereby limiting knowledge specific to Puerto Ricans. The use of this aggregate unfortunately obscures the differences among the various sub-groups that comprise the Hispanic population.

What little is known about Puerto Rican female drug use derives from the recent Hispanic Health and Nutrition Examination Survey conducted by the National Center for Health Statistics between 1982 and 1984.[10] In this survey, the overwhelming majority of Puerto Rican females reported they had never used marijuana (64%), cocaine (83.2%), or sedatives (96.3%). They also reported substantially lower rates of current or ever use of marijuana, cocaine and sedatives than Puerto Rican males. However, their use of these drugs appeared to be higher than their female Mexican counterparts.[10] Before any conclusions can be drawn, however, it needs to be determined if these self-reports are accurate or if they reflect an underreporting of use due to cultural norms that greatly circumscribe women's behavior. If these reports are accurate, these patterns must be monitored to assure the rates remain low and prevention efforts are initiated.

No matter what their age, race or ethnicity, women who use drugs encounter numerous problems. One of the few studies of female Puerto Rican drug abusers found they encounter several difficulties that may have

actually contributed to their drug use.[11] First, they face the problem of adjusting to a Puerto Rican value system within the United States culture. Then they must meet the role expectations placed on women by Puerto Rican culture. Compounding these pressures is the problem encountered by all women who are drug abusers—the stigma of being on the margin. Drug-abusing women experience low status and devaluation by society because they fall outside the norm of expectations for women. For these reasons, Puerto Rican women are in special need of intervention and treatment sensitive to their culture, which helps resolve the cultural, sex-role, and race conflict they experience. Women's centers are in an excellent position to be advocates for these women and promote services responsive to their unique cultural needs.

Prescription Drugs

A common occurrence yet to be reported in the research literature, but well known among those who work with the community, is the sharing of psychotropic prescription drugs among Puerto Rican women. Puerto Rican women customarily share these drugs among themselves to combat *mal de los nervios*—a state of nervousness or anxiousness that is often described among Puerto Ricans and other Latinos. Problems develop because women take drugs not prescribed for them in an unsupervised manner that can result in dependence.

Another consideration must be raised concerning prescription drugs. It has been reported that Latinos entering medical care settings are often misdiagnosed by majority culture physicians and other mental health professionals.[12] This occurs when a Spanish-speaking patient with a limited mastery of the English language is interviewed in English. The slow, affect-free speech of a Latino who is struggling with the language has been interpreted as symptomatic of depression or other forms of "flat affect." According to the study, many a Latino has received an unwarranted psychiatric diagnosis and a prescription for a psychotropic drug. When patients fail—for whatever reasons—to inquire about the drugs they are prescribed, they run a greater risk of unnecessary drug use.

For these reasons, it is important that women's centers provide their Latino clients with consumer health education regarding the use of prescription drugs. Training in how to question health care professionals about their prescriptions and treatment is also important. Both are essential for the prevention of drug abuse and drug-related problems among Puerto Rican women.

Alcohol Use and Alcohol-related Problems

Little data exists describing alcohol use among Puerto Rican women. A New York City study conducted in 1970 by Haberman found that Puerto Rican women reported the highest rates of abstinence for all women, with over 80 percent reporting themselves to be abstainers.[13] Since that study, the common perception has been that Puerto Rican women are strongly influenced by cultural norms which inhibit women from drinking. Caetano found that Latinas with higher levels of education and acculturation tend to be heavy frequent drinkers,[14] and that Puerto Rican women in particular tend to have more liberal attitudes than Mexican American and Cuban women regarding drinking by women of all ages.[15] But the number of Puerto Ricans in this sample was so small that it is difficult to generalize from these results.

The only study to date on Puerto Rican women who are problem drinkers was conducted in 1986 by Fernandez-Pol, et al.[16] Although the sample included only 18 women in an inner-city alcoholism treatment program in New York City, the study provides a preliminary picture of Puerto Rican women alcoholics. The study found that Puerto Rican women alcoholics first experienced drunkenness at a significantly later age than women in other groups. Although they started later, they reported frequent daily drinking, with distilled spirits as their preferred alcoholic beverage.

These women said they drank because it helped them to be mentally alert. This alertness was associated with the feeling that alcohol helped them relax. We can speculate that alcohol may have served to calm a case of *mal de los nervios* (anxiety or depression).

Interestingly, the study found that unlike any other group, Puerto Rican women (87%) reported they drank most often in their homes, not in bars, clubs or other public places. This is in keeping with the cultural norm that discourages women from drinking in public.

Although these findings are very preliminary, they do offer some insights for those who will be working with Puerto Rican women. Puerto Rican women who are not yet heavy or problem drinkers appear to have more liberal attitudes towards alcohol use than Mexican American or Cuban women. This attitude may place them at a greater risk for alcohol abuse and related problems. Thus, it would be beneficial to offer education and prevention programs to offset this possibility.

In addition, special recognition must be given to the fact that Puerto Rican women who are problem drinkers are solitary drinkers who drink in the privacy of their homes. Cultural factors still appear to play a role in the way these women behave toward alcohol. If women's centers and other women's service organizations are to reach these women, efforts must be made to recognize their unique warning signs. Culturally appropriate methods to encourage participation in treatment programs are critical.

Tobacco

Puerto Rican women use tobacco at higher rates than women in any other Latino group.[17] Although there are indications that smoking is decreasing among Latino men, smoking actually increased among Puerto Rican women over the last decade. This is also true of Puerto Rican adolescent females. Although the gender gap that existed between adolescent males and females is closing for all groups, Puerto Rican girls are catching up with boys at a greater rate than girls of other ethnic groups. These young women will probably continue to smoke as adults and face the increased health risk of using alcohol in combination with tobacco. Therefore, prevention and intervention is essential for both adolescent and adult Puerto Rican women. Smoke cessation and related health promotion programs are an important program ingredient for women's centers that serve Puerto Rican women.

Puerto Rican Women as Partners of Alcoholics/Drug Abusers

While high rates of alcohol and drug use and their subsequent problems among Puerto Rican women have not yet appeared, there is little question many of these women are affected by the alcohol and drug problems prevalent among their husbands, partners, sons, fathers and brothers. There is strong evidence that Puerto Rican men exceed the general population in rates of alcoholism and drug abuse.[13, 18, 19]

The Puerto Rican adult male population tends to include relatively high proportions of heavy drinkers who suffer from many alcohol-related problems.[13] These include such medical conditions as liver cirrhosis and cancer of the mouth and throat. Family disruptions, including work problems, family neglect or violence, are also factors related to heavy drinking by Puerto Rican males. In New York City, where more than 50 percent of the Latino population is Puerto Rican, Hispanics have higher rates of marijuana, cocaine, heroin and illicit methadone use than non-Latinos.[18] Of the three major Latino groups (Cubans, Mexicans and Puerto Ricans), Puerto Ricans exhibit higher rates of lifetime and current use of cocaine.[19] The National Drug and Alcoholism Utilization Survey suggested in 1982 that "Hispanics are almost three times more likely to be in treatment for a drug abuse-related problem than are Whites."[18]

Acculturation-related stresses, induced by cultural changes, language barriers and discrimination, often lead to heavy drinking and alcoholism.[20] The impact on the family can be severe. Nine percent of Latino men report that drinking has had harmful effects on homelife, whereas only six percent of Black men and four percent of White men report this problem.[21]

These reports document the fact that a substantial

number of Puerto Rican women are living with alcohol and drug problems, and are facing the many difficulties the "significant other" of an alcoholic or addict experiences. For this reason alone, providing relevant and appropriate services to the Puerto Rican woman requires exploring the possibility that she is struggling with the alcohol or drug problems of another person. Because of this, she may well be in need of intervention herself.

The problems of Puerto Rican women who are partners of IV drug users are further compounded by the AIDS epidemic. In the United States, 20 percent of all women who are HIV-positive for AIDS are Latino. Most of these women are concentrated in New York, New Jersey, Florida and Puerto Rico where, with the exception of Florida, the majority of the Latino population is Puerto Rican. Eighty-eight percent of Latinas with AIDS are the sex partners of intravenous-drug-using, bisexual or HIV-infected men.[22] The risk to the future generation of Puerto Rican children is great, since there is a 30-50 percent probability of perinatal transmission of HIV infection.[22] Urban centers must deal with large numbers of HIV-positive Latinas and their babies, with limited resources to treat them adequately.

If women's centers and other women's service organizations are to help Puerto Rican women, they must be prepared to engage aggressively in AIDS education and prevention programs, and to become advocates for more treatment services for these women and their children.

Impact of Culture and Acculturation

A discussion of Puerto Rican women would be incomplete without reference to the influence of cultural norms. The work done by Soto offers important insight into Puerto Rican women.[23] Soto found that Puerto Rican women receive more traditional sex-role socialization than do non-Puerto Rican women. This socialization discourages assertiveness which in turn contributes to psychological problems such as depression and psychosomatic symptoms. Though the woman's generation and educational attainment had a significant effect on how she was tied to traditional sex roles, even controlling for age, Puerto Rican women were still more traditional than non-Puerto Ricans.

Puerto Rican women who are more involved in religion tend to be more sex-role traditional and less assertive than their non-religious counterparts. Those who are involved in folk religious beliefs such as *Espiritismo* are even more traditional and display more symptoms.[23]

These socialization patterns include a set of beliefs about the attributes of a "good" woman. Most important is that the woman be a pillar of virtue—a good wife,

mother and daughter. The traditional culture frowns upon women who deviate from this norm and a woman who has problems with alcohol or other drugs is perceived as *una mujer caida* (a fallen women). Thus, it may take a long time before a Puerto Rican woman seeks treatment or her family brings her into treatment. The latter may occur only because men in the family feel a sense of embarrassment when alcohol or drug problems affecting female family members occur and may not know what to do.

The family's delay in getting the woman to treatment may also be a result of Puerto Ricans' general lack of knowledge of alcohol- and other drug-education programs or outreach services. This is partly due to the lack of special attention this population receives, as well as to the ineffectiveness of education and outreach approaches. Women's centers with culturally relevant and effective education and outreach programs are in a unique position to provide much-needed services to Puerto Rican women.

Providing education appears to be a critical intervention in helping women liberate themselves from traditional expectations and patterns of behavior. Education can help free them from the depression and psychosomatic symptoms they may experience. Assertiveness training that is culturally appropriate and sensitive to the Puerto Rican woman can be very effective. Thus, women's centers have a great deal to offer. Facilitating women's access to education and training, in addition to offering assertiveness training, can contribute substantially to the prevention of alcohol and drug problems.

Risks and Barriers to Care

It is well established that a relationship exists between low income and poor health status. Income and standard of living are the most important determinants of health and the quality of life.[24] This reality is unfortunately reflected in statistics that show Puerto Ricans have the highest death rate of all Latino groups in the United States.[25] The health of Puerto Rican women and their children is affected by the poor social and economic conditions in which they live, putting them at high risk for a number of health problems.

Financial Barriers to Treatment and Care

Access to care and the ability to pay for services—either out of pocket or via health insurance coverage—is very low among Puerto Ricans. The Hispanic Health and Nutrition Survey found that most Puerto Ricans do not receive any form of support through available payment assistance programs.[26] This financial barrier to care severely limites access to medical care and further impedes access to services if a woman should need treatment for alcoholism or other drug addiction.

Helping Puerto Rican women through the maze-like process of applying for Medicaid or some other form of coverage is another service women's centers can provide.

Housing Conditions As a Risk

Many Puerto Rican females suffer the difficulties of poor and inadequate housing in decaying sections of the city. Some are forced to live in public shelters.[27] Needless to say, poor living conditions greatly influence the health status of a population.

Street drugs are commonplace in major urban centers where Puerto Rican women live with their children. The availability of cocaine and crack are not only risks for the women themselves, but a concern for them as mothers with children who are exposed daily to the threat of drug use. Although some women's centers may not see housing advocacy and organizing women tenants as activities that fall within their domain of service or mission, these activities are critical prevention interventions for women and their children.

Alcohol and Tobacco Industries
Targeting Latino Women

As if things weren't bad enough, the environments in which Puerto Ricans live are saturated with alcohol and cigarette advertisements, which bombard the community. Black and Latino communities are permeated with billboards and signs trying to appeal to the population. Spanish-language radio and television stations advertise alcohol in a way that has not been seen in the English-language media since the 1950s.

A recent report published by the Center for Science in the Public Interest (CSPI), *Marketing Disease to Hispanics—The Selling of Alcohol, Tobacco and Junk Foods,* clearly demonstrates the excessive amount of marketing and advertising directed at Puerto Ricans and other Latinos.[28] The sexual messages and degrading images of scantily clad women that are used to attract smokers and drinkers are a major disservice to a community already suffering the health and social consequences of alcohol and tobacco use. The CSPI report is important reading for those who work with Latino women.

This unfortunate situation nevertheless provides women's centers with the opportunity to raise Latino women's awareness of subtle but pervasive marketing strategies and to organize community action to rid the neighborhood of these messages. An excellent resource for doing just that is the recently published handbook, *Citizen's Action Handbook on Alcohol and Tobacco Billboard Advertising,* by Ed McMahon and Pat Taylor.[29]

Summary and Conclusions

From the profile of the Puerto Rican woman presented, it becomes apparent the prevention of alcohol- and other drug-related problems requires a comprehensive approach that goes beyond the provision of alcohol and drug education. Puerto Rican women are at risk because of their economic status, because of the environment in which they live and because little has been known or understood about their culture by health and human service providers.

If women's centers are to achieve a measure of success in their work with these women, they must address the multiple risk factors Puerto Rican women face. In program terms, it means the delivery of comprehensive and coordinated services and programs in a number of areas. All centers may not be equipped to deliver diverse services. A critical role these centers can play is that of advocate, to work with those in the community who can provide the needed services.

Below are some program examples to address the needs of Puerto Rican women.

Education, Training and Child Care

If Puerto Rican women are to overcome the poverty and deprivation that put them at risk for alcohol and drug problems, access to education and training programs is an essential first step. But affordable and safe child care must be integral to these programs if single-parent women are to participate to the fullest degree. If women's centers cannot provide these services, they could help to establish a community network that can.

Access to Health and Human Services

A directory of culturally sensitive referral services would assist women's centers in addressing the health and social service needs of Puerto Rican women. Establishing linkages and communicating with these services before they are needed is very useful and prevents last-minute "frantic scouting around." This can happen easily and often for those women who are in need of alcohol and other drug treatment services.

Addressing the women's health and human service needs not only requires appropriate referral, but must include a process by which women are helped to negotiate the maze of services. Puerto Rican women would benefit from the consumer health education and assertiveness training programs previously discussed. These programs should be designed to help Puerto Rican women cope with these environments. This is a very important first step toward empowerment.

Alcohol and Drug Health Promotion

Health promotion does not refer exclusively to jogging and health foods, even though this narrow interpretation is sometimes used to describe the concept. Health promotion is any combination of educational, organizational, environmental, political and social action or activities that support the health and well-being of individuals and communities. It includes strategies designed for women to improve their health and prevent health-related problems. It also entails collective action and advocacy to facilitate the achievement of positive health status and social well-being.

Puerto Rican women are in need of health promotion programs in the fullest sense. These programs should include alcohol and drug health education, AIDS education, stress management and assertiveness training. Community education about alcohol and drug problems is also greatly needed in Puerto Rican communities.

The concept of health promotion for Puerto Rican women includes collective actions such as advocacy for decent, affordable housing; community action to confront drug availability in the form of both illicit drug distribution and excessive advertisements and promotions of alcohol and tobacco; and advocacy that facilitates access to health and human services. Women's centers can address these needs by starting or joining coalitions, by becoming involved in social action, and by confronting the risk-inducing circumstances in the environment.

References

1. U.S. Bureau of the Census (1989). *Current Population Reports*, Series P-20, No. 438, The Hispanic Population in the United States: March 1988, US Government Printing Office, Washington, DC, 1989.
2. U.S. Bureau of the Census (1989). *Statistical Abstract of the United States: 1989*, (109th edition) Washington, DC.
3. Tienda, Martha, and Jensen, Leif (1988). Poverty and Minorities: A Quarter-Century Profile of Color and Socioeconomic Disadvantage (pp. 23-61). In: Sandefur, G., and Tienda, M, (eds.), *Divided Opportunities—Minorities, Poverty and Social Policy.* New York: Plenum Press.
4. Melendez, Edwin, and Rodriguez, Clara (1988). Puerto Ricans in the Northeast and the Changing Economy: A Summary of Research Issues. *Dialogo*—Newsletter of the National Puerto Rican Policy Network, No. 5, Fall 1988.
5. Moore, J. and Pachon, H. *Hispanics in the United States*. Englewood Cliffs, N.J.: Prentice Hall.
6. Santana, Cooney and Colon (1980). Work and Family: The Recent Struggle of Puerto Rican Females, in Rodriguez, C., Sanchez Korrol, V., Alers, J. (eds) *The Puerto Rican Struggle: Essays on Survival in the U.S.* Maplewood, N.J.:Waterfront Press.
7. Mare, Robert, and Winship, Christopher (1988). Ethnic and Racial Patterns of Educational Attainment and School Enrollment. In: Jensen, G., and Tienda, M. (Eds.) *Divided Opportunities: Minorities, Poverty and Social Policy.* New York: Plenum Press.
8. Latino Commission of Tri-State (1988). *Outlook—The Growing Latino Presence in the Tri-State Region.* United Way of Tri-State, New York, NY.
9. Almquist, Elizabeth McTaggart (1979). *Minorities, Gender and Work.* Lexington, MA: Lexington Books.
10. National Institute on Drug Abuse (1987). *Use of Selected Drugs Among Hispanics: Mexican Americans, Puerto Ricans, Cuban Americans.* Rockville, MD.
11. Obeso, P. and Bordatto, O. (1979). Cultural Implications in Treating the Puerto Rican Female." *American Journal of Drug and Alcohol Abuse*, 6(3):337-344.
12. Marcos, Luis (1973). The Effects of Interview Language on the Evaluation of Psychopathology in Spanish American Patients. *American Journal of Psychiatry*, 130:549.
13. Haberman, P. (1970). Denial of Drinking in a Household Survey. *Quarterly Journal of Studies on Alcohol*, 31:710-717.
14. Caetano, Raul (1986). Patterns and Problems of Drinking Among U.S. Hispanics. In: *DHHS Report of the Secretary on Black and Minority Health*. Volume VII: Chemical Dependency, 143-186. Washington, DC: Government Printing Office.
15. Caetano, Raul (1988). Alcohol Use Among Hispanic Groups in the United States. *Am. J. Drug and Alcohol Abuse*, (14):293-308.
16. Fernandez-Pol, B., Bluestone, H., Missouri, C., Morales, G., and Mizruchi, M., (1986). Drinking Patterns of Inner-City Black Americans and Puerto Ricans. *Journal of Studies on Alcohol*, 47(2):156-160.
17. Escobar, L.G., and Remington, P.L. (1989). Birth Cohort Analysis of Prevalence of Cigarette Smoking Among Hispanics in the United States. *JAMA* 261(1):66-71.
18. DHHS—*Report of the Secretary on Black and Minority Health (1986)*. Volume VII: Chemical Dependency. Washington, DC: Government Printing Office.
19. Trimble, E., Padilla, A., and Bell, C., (Eds.) (1987). *Drug Abuse Among Ethnic Minorities*. USDHHS—National Institute on Drug Abuse. Rockville, MD.
20. Alcocer, A. (1982). Alcohol Use and Abuse Among the Hispanic American Population. In: *Special Population Issues: Alcohol and Health*

Monograph No. 4. National Institute on Alcohol Abuse and Alcoholism. Rockville, MD.

21. Caetano, Raul (1987). Drinking and the Hispanic American Family Life. *Alcohol Health and Research World,* Winter 1986/87, pp. 26-23.

22. Centers for Disease Control (1988). Leading major congenital malformations among minority groups in the United States, 1981-1986. In: *CDC Surveillance Summaries.* MMWR 37(355):1755-2455.

23. Soto, Elaine (1983). Sex Role Traditionalism and Assertiveness in Puerto Rican Women Living in the United States. *Journal of Community Psychology,* (11):346-354.

24. Terris, Milton (1987). Redefining the Public Health Agenda. *Journal of Public Health Policy,* Summer 1987.

25. Rosenwaike, I. (1987). Mortality differentials among persons born in Cuba, Mexico, and Puerto Rico residing in the United States, 1979-81.

American Journal of Public Health, 77(5):603-606.

26. Hispanic HANES (1987). *Adolescent and Adult History Questionnaire: Public Use Tape Documentation* (Version 2, March 1987). National Center for Health Statistics. Hyattsville, MD.

27. Falcon, A., Delgado, M., and Borrero, Gerson (Eds.) (1989). *Towards a Puerto Rican-Latino Agenda for New York City.* Institute for Puerto Rican Policy, New York, NY.

28. Maxwell, Bruce, and Jacobson, Michael (1989). *Marketing Disease to Hispanics—The Selling of Alcohol, Tobacco, and Junk Foods.* Washington, DC: The Center for Science in the Public Interest.

29. McMahon, Edward, and Taylor, Pat (1990). *Citizen's Action Handbook on Alcohol and Tobacco Billboard Advertising.* Washington, DC: The Center for Science in the Public Interest.

13 The Effects of Drug Use During Pregnancy

Anne Geller, M.D.

"Concern for the developing fetus has led us to single out the pregnant woman as an important target for drug education. However, the drugs that are hazardous to the fetus are also hazardous to the woman. The difference is one of degree and dose."

Any non-food substance taken into the body presents risks as well as possible benefits. This applies to preparations in health food stores, over-the-counter medications and prescription drugs, as well as legal and illegal intoxicants. For the pregnant woman, the risk side of the equation is markedly increased because of the greater sensitivity of the developing fetus to these substances. In pregnancy, as in life, the safest course is to "above all do no harm" and to avoid all foreign substances, except those absolutely essential to the maintenance of health. This simple and obvious recommendation is followed by few people, male or female. The emphasis on the hazards of intoxicant use, which are well documented, should not detract from concern about potential risks of using any foreign substance during pregnancy.

Pregnant women, though a very appropriate target for education in this area and for intervention when addicted to intoxicant drugs, are not an appropriate target for social persecution or criminal prosecution. Women who continue to use foreign substances during pregnancy may be unaware or unconvinced of the risks and require education. Or they may be addicted. Those who are addicted may be aware of the risks to themselves and to the fetus, but cannot stop using substances. Addiction is not effectively treated by societal censure or by jail sentences. Pregnant women are no different from others in this respect.

The following position statement from the American Society of Addiction Medicine summarizes the ways in which the use of mood altering drugs can result in harm to the developing fetus.

The human fetus is entirely dependent on the maternal environment for its safety, health, growth and development. Alcohol and other mood altering drugs taken by a pregnant woman may damage the developing fetus in a variety of ways. Drugs cross the placenta and enter the bloodstream of the fetus interfering with growth and development both physical and mental, causing reduced birth weight, birth defects, learning and behavior disorders and distress during the newborn period. The developing fetus cannot get rid of these drugs because it does not yet possess the biochemical systems to do so. Drugs may interfere with the normal physiological processes of pregnancy. This may result in spontaneous abortion, prematurity and obstetrical complications threatening to both maternal and infant health. Intoxication due to alcohol or drug use during pregnancy is associated with motor vehicle accidents, falls, or trauma to mother and child.

Women who are dependent on alcohol or other drugs during pregnancy may not obtain adequate nutrition or take care of their health generally. They may not obtain adequate antenatal care. When the mother is physically dependent on alcohol or drugs at the time of delivery, the newborn may go through an alcohol or drug withdrawal which will cause psychological and physical distress in the infant and may be life threatening. Excessive alcohol and drug use during pregnancy may interfere with interpersonal, occupational and social functioning and damage the adequacy of the family unit to nurture the resulting infant. Child neglect or abuse may accompany family dysfunction. Alcoholism and other drug dependence may interfere with parent-infant bonding.

Although different drugs can produce very specific kinds of damage to the fetus, it is often difficult to separate out the effects, since in practice women who use any drugs at all during pregnancy are frequently using more than one. Heavy use of one drug is very often associated with heavy use of another. For example, heavy drinkers are very often also heavy smokers (alcohol and nicotine are, of course, considered drugs). With any drug, the effects are related to the dose. The more one uses, the greater the effects. This is true for both mother and fetus. The more the mother drinks, the more intoxicated she will become, and the more intoxicated the fetus will become. There are, however, important differences. The fetal tissues,

101

particularly the developing brain, are much more sensitive than maternal tissues to drugs, and the fetus lacks the enzyme systems that are present in adults to break down drugs.

The use of prescription drugs is more complex, since there is a balancing of need and risk which requires an individual medical assessment in each case. Every drug has to be considered as potentially teratogenic (capable of causing malformations) until proved otherwise.

The effects of a variety of drugs on the fetus can take many forms. Generally, there may be a reduction in birth weight. More specifically, there may be effects on the developing nervous system resulting in a wide variety of disturbances from poor sucking to profound retardation. The milder effects may only become apparent when groups of children born to drug-using women are compared with those born to non-drug-using women. Development anomalies of all kinds, from extra fingers to anencephaly (absence of the brain), appear to be more common in babies of drug-using mothers. Of course, babies born to women who have used no drugs at all may have low birth weight, be retarded or have a congenital anomaly. Using drugs increases the chances of these events occurring. It is very important that women be aware of the chance occurrence of fetal abnormalities. Pediatricians have reported cases in which women have berated themselves and have sunk into serious depression worrying whether the single marijuana cigarette or the party at which they had six drinks before they knew they were pregnant could have been the cause of their infant being retarded or otherwise abnormal.

There are few cases in which a specific fetal abnormality can be directly related to a particular drug, other than the fetal alcohol syndrome. However, it can be said with assurance that the more frequently a drug is used, the greater the average amount used at a time and the longer during the period of gestation it is used, the greater the chance that an abnormality in the fetus is related to that drug use.

Besides direct damage to the fetus, the use of drugs during pregnancy can have indirect effects as well. Spontaneous abortions are more common in drug-using women and may be due to a number of causes such as severe abnormalities, inadequate placental blood supply and a hyper-reactive uterus. Drugs like cocaine, which cause a sudden increase in blood pressure and narrowing of the blood vessels, may cause an inadequate blood supply for the fetus, a hemorrhage in the fetal tissues or premature separation of the placenta.

Women may continue to use drugs during pregnancy because they are unaware of the hazards to the fetus or because they believe that occasional use is not harmful. Perhaps the particular drug they are using is not included among those which have been found to cause fetal effects. However, there is another group of women who continue to use drugs during pregnancy, those who are unable to stop. These women are dependent on a particular drug, and no matter how concerned they are about the health of their baby, they are unable to stop or even reliably cut down. This group of women is in need of help to stop using drugs. It is among infants born to drug-dependent women that we see the most severe fetal effects. Not only is the fetus exposed to high and frequent dosing throughout pregnancy, but it too becomes physically dependent on the drug, so that when removed from the maternal drug supply at birth the infant goes through a physical withdrawal. The exact picture of this varies with each drug, but generally the newborn is jittery, sleeps and eats poorly, startles easily and in some cases may have seizures. Dependent women represent 2 to 5 percent of all mothers, and are the group where intervention can produce the most dramatic results. The earlier in pregnancy that drug use stops the better, but even intervention as late as the third trimester can improve the outcome for the fetus.

Specific Drugs

Alcohol

Alcohol has been the most studied of all drugs during pregnancy.[1,2,3] The Victorians were well aware of the association between heavy-drinking women and puny, poorly developed children. There was even quite a bit of research between 1890 and 1910, both with humans and animals, showing a relationship between the amount of alcohol during pregnancy and damage to the fetus. Somehow this research was forgotten, and for many decades the conventional medical wisdom was that alcohol was harmless to the fetus unless the mother ate poorly as a consequence of drinking. It was not until the 1960s when Lemoine in France and Jones in the United States described a distinct pattern of physical and behavioral abnormalities in the children of women who were drinking alcoholically during pregnancy. The most dramatic effect of alcohol, the fetal alcohol syndrome, occurs in 1-2 per 1,000 births. These infants, in addition to being mentally retarded, have a set of facial abnormalities which gives them a quite distinctive appearance. Their eyes are widely spaced, their nose is short, their lips are thin and the groove between the nose and upper lip is missing. Infants with fetal alcohol syndrome are born to women who are heavily alcohol-dependent. More pervasive, and therefore of more general concern to women, are a lesser range of effects known as fetal alcohol effects. These include intrauterine growth retardation (the infants are small), smaller head circumference, increase in anomalies and, of great concern, impaired mental abilities. Taken in groups, children born to mothers who drink during pregnancy develop less well mentally than those born to nondrinking mothers. This effect is dose-related. The more the mother drinks, the greater the chance of a baby having lower than expected mental abilities. Of course, this is a statistical analysis. Just as there are people smoking three packs of cigarettes a day who live to be 95, so there are women drinking a quart of whiskey a day who have infants who develop into highly intelligent adults. It is not advised that women do this, however. The risks are too great.

Social Drinking

The National Institute on Alcohol Abuse and Alcoholism defines "heavier" drinking as more than 60 drinks per month (2 standard drinks a day or 14 standard drinks a week). While most women are aware that consuming as high a dose as 6 drinks a day on average (used in many studies as an indicator of alcoholism), or drinking to intoxication is hazardous to the fetus, what about moderate or light social drinking (2 standard drinks a day or less)? In a 1988 report, Marcia Russell looked at the amounts of alcohol women had been drinking prior to realizing they were pregnant. She found that the risk of spontaneous abortion increased with increasing levels of reported alcohol consumption, and that there was no threshold for this effect. This means that there is *no absolutely safe level of alcohol consumption* and that the risk increases with every drink above zero. Kline also reported an increased rate of miscarriage in women drinking more than two drinks twice a week, and a large study of 32,000 women in the Kaiser Health Plan in California found an increase in miscarriage in women drinking 1-2 drinks a day compared with those who drank less than one.

Studies published over several years by Ann Streissguth and Ruth Little in Seattle have shown that women who drink an average of 2 drinks per day give birth to smaller infants. The infants show more body tremors, less motor activity and less habituation if the mothers drank socially during pregnancy, and this is proportional to the average daily amount consumed. When tested at four years of age, children born to women who drank an average of 1 drink per day showed less ability to sustain attention and were more fidgety than children born to nondrinking mothers. These observations with humans are supported by research with a wide variety of animal species showing a dose-related effect of alcohol on spontaneous abortion, stillbirth, malformations, birth weight and behavior at birth.

It is impossible from the evidence, therefore, to construct a safe level of drinking during pregnancy. It may be that there is a threshold for some effects, whereas others might be strictly dose-related. It is important that women understand that, in a risk-benefit analysis, the risk of any alcohol intake outweighs the benefits during pregnancy.

Educating Women

Women of childbearing age should be advised to abstain from alcohol if they intend to become pregnant or as soon as they learn that they are pregnant. Women, however, should also know that an occasional drink during pregnancy or a pattern of having consumed 1-2 drinks a day prior to becoming aware of pregnancy is unlikely to be associated with a severe fetal outcome. Some women may need to be reassured about this. Every effort should be extended to reach those women who are problem drinkers or alcohol dependent—those who are unable to stop in spite of being aware of and concerned about the hazards to the fetus of their drinking. Efforts should include routine screening for alcohol use at antenatal clinics and obstetricians' offices and referrals to treatment, where possible, for women whose alcohol use patterns are cause for concern.

Cocaine

It is becoming increasingly clear that any cocaine use during pregnancy is hazardous to the fetus.[4,5] Cocaine easily crosses the placenta and the fetal enzyme systems are immature and unable to destroy it. Cocaine is a drug that produces effects similar to stimulation of the sympathetic nervous system, the "fight or flight" reaction. Following cocaine use, there is an abrupt rise in blood pressure, heart rate, breathing rate and temperature. The sudden rise in blood pressure may cause bleeding into the placenta, premature separation of the placenta from the wall of the uterus and bleeding in the tissues of the fetus, particularly the brain. The fetus can thus suffer a cerebral hemorrhage or stroke and be paralyzed prior to birth. Cocaine is an excitatory drug and can cause convulsions, irregular heart beat and excessive contraction of the uterus.

Studies of the specific effects of cocaine on pregnant women are complicated by the fact that people seldom use just one drug. For example, in one study in Boston among a low socioeconomic group of women, 18 percent of the women used cocaine during pregnancy. Of these women, 90 percent also smoked cigarettes and 80 percent also used alcohol. Half of the cocaine-using women used as frequently as once a week throughout pregnancy. Cocaine has an effect on birth weight. Infants born to cocaine-using mothers are smaller for gestational age and also shorter. More significantly for brain development, the head circumference of these infants is also reduced. Cocaine use during pregnancy is also associated with behavioral abnormalities during the newborn period. The infants are jittery and have a high-pitched cry and abnormal sleep patterns. They also have difficulty modulating responses, that is, they tend to over-react to stimuli and continue to react beyond the time when normal babies have quieted down. This may possibly have long-term implications for development and may interfere with mother-infant bonding, since the infant is difficult to handle. Congenital anomalies of the genito-urinary tract, with underdeveloped sex organs and absence of some abdominal muscle, have been reported in infants born to cocaine-using women. An increase in sudden infant death has also been reported.

Educating Women

Use of cocaine during pregnancy increases the risk of spontaneous abortion, increases complications during delivery and damages the fetus. Although the risk is dose-related, *a single use of cocaine* can cause serious harm to the fetus through cerebral hemorrhage, seizure or premature separation of the placenta. No use of cocaine whatsoever during pregnancy is advised.

Marijuana

As with cocaine, it has been difficult to separate the effects of the use of marijuana during pregnancy from those of the other drugs, including alcohol and nicotine.[5] It now seems clear that there is an independent effect of marijuana itself. Weekly use of marijuana during pregnancy results in a lower birth weight for gestational age. Marijuana affects uterine contractility, and there have been reports of precipitate delivery in marijuana-using mothers. Fried has reported abnormalities in behavior in infants born to heavy marijuana users. The abnormalities reported were tremulousness and a high-pitched cry. This has not been confirmed in other studies, however. It is also not clear whether marijuana use during pregnancy increases the risk of congenital anomalies. The long-term effects of marijuana on the development of both the fetus and the infant require further study.

Tobacco

Tobacco use during pregnancy has been shown to have significant effects. There is a clear dose effect on infant birth weight, with an average reduction of 150 grams in weight in infants born to women who smoke. On the basis of these studies, it has been estimated that the daily use of 20 cigarettes will reduce the infant's birth weight by 220 grams or *11 grams per cigarette*. Tobacco use also shortens the period of gestation. Twenty percent of infants born to women who smoke are born prematurely. There is also an increase in spontaneous abortions. In terms of behavior at birth, newborns cry more, are less alert and have less ability

to orient themselves. The effects of this behavior on later functioning are not known. So far, no increase in congenital abnormalities has been reported with tobacco use during pregnancy.

Other Mood-altering Drugs

Phencyclidine (PCP), heroin, methadone, barbiturates, benzodiazepines (e.g., Valium, Librium, Ativan), amphetamines, LSD and many other abused drugs have been studied during pregnancy. These studies require large numbers in order to separate out the effect of one drug from the others which may be used at the same time, as well as the more general effects of nutrition, age and antenatal care. The use of any mood-altering drug during pregnancy tends to be associated with a higher risk of adverse outcome. At the present time, it is reasonable to say that the use of any drug during pregnancy requires medical justification that the benefits outweigh the possible risk to the fetus.

Prescription Medication

The teratogenicity (fetal damage potential) of many medications is unknown. Package inserts usually contain warnings that the drug has not been tested for safety in pregnant women. The risks and benefits of a specific medication obviously need to be discussed with the physician who is prescribing. Caution and a common sense approach will help women avoid, on the one hand, the use of medication for relatively minor conditions such as muscle aches and pains, poor sleep patterns or headaches, for example, but will allay worry about the use of essential medications for conditions such as diabetes, heart disease or hypertension, to name only a few. Damage to the fetus, miscarriage or damage to the placenta can occur if a serious medical condition is untreated. The final decision about the use of prescription medication should be made following an analysis of the risks and benefits of medicating or not medicating for both mother and fetus. A pregnant woman needs, above all, to be convinced that the medication decisions she makes have been carefully thought through and that her decisions are the best under the circumstances so that she herself is healthy, and she can enjoy a worry-free pregnancy.

Over-the-Counter Medications

Most over-the-counter medications are for symptoms relief in disorders which are usually time limited, such as coughs and colds, headaches, muscle pain and gastro-intestinal upset. Since these conditions will for the most part run the same time course with or without medication, they do not attack the cause of the illness but do provide relief from discomfort. Women should weigh this relief against the possibility, however remote, of fetal effects. There is no evidence thus far that the occasional use of aspirin for headache relief or of antihistamines for relief of seasonal allergies is associated with fetal abnormalities or even more subtle behavioral effects. However, unless there is a compelling reason to use medication during pregnancy, it is better for women not to do so.

Socioeconomic Status

The consequences of drug use during pregnancy are compounded by poor nutrition, poor health and lack of antenatal care, which are frequently, though not exclusively, related to lower socioeconomic status. This group of pregnant women is frequently not exposed to the usual information about drug and alcohol use during pregnancy, nor is intervention to promote abstinence possible if the women are not in contact with health care providers. *Special outreach programs are urgently needed,* since many women of lower socioeconomic status have infants who demonstrate the most devastating consequences as a result of a combination of adverse factors, of which alcohol and drug abuse are only a part.

Ethnicity

Little research data is available on drug abuse during pregnancy among varied ethnic groups. Native American women, however, have an especially high prevalence of fetal alcohol syndrome, ranging up to 98 per 1,000 live births in one study.[6] Other factors such as lifestyle, smoking, other drug use, poor diet or poor general health are also prevalent among Native American women and may be interacting with alcohol to produce this result.

Significance of Neuro-behavioral Effects

When newborns go through drug withdrawal or show signs of central nervous system irritability, immaturity or abnormal functioning, the significance of this to their subsequent development is not known. In some cases, after a "catch up" period, the infants may develop normally. In others, signs of hyper-reactivity, short attention span and poor adaptation may persist into childhood. An irritable, "crotchety" child may respond poorly to the mother's attempts to comfort and cuddle because of an excessive and prolonged reaction to any stimulus. This in turn can result in frustration and hopelessness on the part of the mother, with a failure to bond to the irritable infant. Thus a vicious cycle may be created. Mothers may need help in learning how to respond to these difficult children so that ongoing difficulties are minimized or avoided.

Breast-feeding

Most drugs which cross the placenta also appear in breast milk, although usually in lower concentrations than in maternal blood. Cases have been reported in which infants have had seizures following a breast-feeding after the mother had used cocaine. Mothers who are on methadone maintenance will pass some to the infant in the milk. Although the breast-feeding infant is not as sensitive to drugs as the developing fetus and concentration is less in milk, nevertheless the infant still has immature enzyme systems and may not detoxify drugs as readily as the adult. Therefore, breast-feeding mothers should be advised to abstain from drug use other than an occasional drink. Overall, there is much less research available on breast-feeding than on drug and alcohol effects during pregnancy.

Paternal Drug Use

Many abused drugs have been shown to produce chromosome changes, and there have been studies suggesting that drug use by the father may have adverse fetal effects. Alcohol, in addition to decreasing the sperm count, is also associated with abnormal spermatozoa. Paternal alcoholism may be a cause of fetal abnormalities but this evidence has been much more difficult to obtain and is not yet definite.

Summary

Concern for the developing fetus has led us to single out the pregnant woman as an important target for drug education. However, the drugs that are hazardous to the fetus are also hazardous to the woman. The difference is one of degree and dose. The developing brain is sensitive to doses of drugs which may have little or no effect on the mature brain, and changes in blood flow which may have little effect on the woman may be highly significant in delivery of blood to the fetus through the placenta. The health message of the benefits of abstaining from mood altering drugs applies equally to males and females of all ages. While drinking two or less standard drinks of an alcoholic beverage a day has not been shown to have deleterious health effects—with the possible exception of breast cancer in women—use of tobacco and illicit drugs in all dosages is associated with adverse consequences. Pregnant women should be advised to abstain from the use of all mood-altering drugs and to exercise caution in the use of medications generally—so, perhaps, should we all.

References

1. Streissguth, A.P., Sampson, P.D., Barr, H.M., Darby, B.L., Martin, D.C., "IQ at age 4 in relation to maternal alcohol use and smoking during pregnancy." *Developmental Psychology* 25: 3-1, 1989
2. Gusella, J.L., Fried, P.A., "Effects of maternal social drinking and smoking on offspring at 13

months." *Neurobehavioral Toxicology and Teratology* 6: 13-17, 1984

3. Abel, E.L., *Fetal Alcohol Syndrome and Fetal Alcohol Effects.* Plenum Press, New York, 1984

4. Chasnoff, I.J., Burns, W.J., Schnoll, S.H. et al., "Cocaine use in pregnancy." *New England Journal of Medicine* 313: 666-69, 1985

5. Zuckerman, B., Frank, D.A., Hingson, R. et al, "Effects of maternal marijuana and cocaine use on fetal growth." *New England Journal of Medicine* 320: 762-68, 1989

6. May, P.A., Hymbaugh, K.J., Aase, J.M., Samet, J.M., "Epidemiology of fetal alcohol syndrome among American Indians of the South West." *Social Biology* 30: 374-387, 1983

14 Punishing Pregnant Addicts

Kary L. Moss, J.D.

"*Women who use drugs during pregnancy are being singled out and punished for their behavior in ways that are unprecedented. The phenomenon of punishing pregnant women for being 'bad mommies' because they did not behave 'properly' while pregnant is not new. In the past, courts have authorized cesarean sections against the mother's wishes or have taken guardianship of a fetus away from the mother, but these cases were rare. Today's drug problem, however, has provided a new context in which state intervention over the lives of pregnant women becomes more acceptable because of the danger that excessive drug use poses to the fetus.*"

Introduction

The incidence of infants exposed to drugs *in utero* has generated increasing nationwide attention from the media,[1] social service agencies,[2] state prosecutors, state legislatures and Congress. One dominant theme which has emerged from all this attention is that women who use drugs during pregnancy are being singled out and punished for their behavior in ways that are unprecedented. The phenomenon of punishing pregnant women for being "bad mommies" because they did not behave "properly" while pregnant is not new. In the past, courts have authorized cesarean sections against the mother's wishes[3] or have taken guardianship of a fetus away from the mother,[4] but these cases were rare. Today's drug problem, however, has provided a new context in which state intervention over the lives of pregnant women becomes more acceptable because of the danger that excessive drug use poses to the fetus.[5] Some prosecutors, courts and legislatures seem to believe that women who are pregnant may be punished and their rights curtailed because of "fetal rights." It is not difficult to see that if upheld in this context, a precedent will be created for state intrusion that will affect the right of all women to bodily integrity and equality, even when they do not engage in illegal behavior.[6]

This chapter will review some of the most recent developments in this area, including the most major criminal cases and state legislative efforts undertaken in

1989. The legal problems and implications of these developments will be explored and several alternative responses will be proposed.

Penalizing Pregnant Women for Drug Use

In 1985, Pamela Rae Stewart was criminally charged in California under a child support statute for failing to follow her doctor's instructions while pregnant.[7] Stewart had given birth to a severely brain-damaged son who died approximately six weeks after birth. The national media focused on the allegation that she had used illegal drugs during her pregnancy, but the prosecution emphasized other aspects of her prenatal behavior. Although the San Diego Municipal Court dismissed the case in 1987 on the grounds that the statute did not cover the conduct alleged, the case represents one of the first times that prosecutors had applied a statute designed to protect children against a woman because of her behavior during pregnancy.[8] With the burgeoning crack epidemic, prosecutors around the country have followed this example by applying novel theories to existing state statutes in an effort to prevent pregnant women from engaging in harmful behavior.

Jennifer Johnson: Violation of Women's Rights

On July 13, 1989, Jennifer Johnson became the first woman criminally convicted for giving birth to a drug-exposed infant, after she had given birth to two such infants over a 14-month period.[9] Johnson, who had used cocaine during her pregnancies, was charged under a Florida statute which makes delivery of drugs to a minor illegal. The prosecutor successfully argued to the court that Jennifer Johnson had delivered a

This article is excerpted from a larger article which appeared in the Spring 1990 edition of the Harvard Women's Law Journal, *(forthcoming). This excerpt is reprinted with the* Journal's *permission.*

derivative of cocaine through the umbilical cord to her child after "birth," during the sixty to ninety seconds before the cord was clamped.

The court sentenced Ms. Johnson to 15 years, one year to be served on "community control," which is a form of intensive, supervised custody in the community, home or noninstitutional residential placement which, if violated, will render the defendant subject to specific sanctions. She was also sentenced to 14 years of probation and ordered to participate in a drug rehabilitation program, obtain a high school equivalency diploma, and not possess controlled substances, associate with those who possess drugs, consume alcohol or enter a bar without the permission of her probation officer. She must perform 200 hours of community service and remain employed. If she becomes pregnant, she must enter a judicially approved prenatal care program. Ms. Johnson has appealed this verdict and the order denying her motion to dismiss.[10]

Defense attorneys have attacked this novel application of the delivery statute as violating Ms. Johnson's constitutional right to receive notice of the acts considered to be crimes. For example, the delivery statute had never before been applied to a woman who used drugs during pregnancy. Consequently, the prosecutors had to apply novel definitions of the term "delivery" that Ms. Johnson could not have known would become a basis for her conviction. Also, because the evidence used against her was the positive toxicology of her newborn, a question existed as to whether it was cocaine that had been "delivered." Metabolized, cocaine is not the same substance that the statute contemplates should not be delivered.

In addition, the defense argued that the conviction violates Ms. Johnson's right to procreate and her right to autonomy in reproductive decision-making, as the court's rationale required that a pregnant addict who is unable to overcome her addiction either have an abortion or face criminal prosecution.[11] They argued that Ms. Johnson was punished for merely continuing the pregnancy and giving birth. Moreover, the defense maintained that Johnson's right to medical privacy was violated when her statements to health care providers and her medical records became part of the prosecution's record.

Since her conviction, there have been at least a dozen more prosecutions of women who have given birth to drug-exposed infants. In most of these cases, states are applying criminal statutes without any regard for the right to due process of the law, privacy and bodily integrity, equal protection of the laws or to the availability of adequate and appropriate drug or alcohol treatment programs.

Other cases

The resolution of the Johnson case may have national impact, as the Florida District Court of Appeals' decision could significantly affect the willingness of other states to use their own criminal laws to prosecute pregnant women. Already, prosecutors in several states have used similarly novel interpretations of statutes to prosecute women who used drugs while pregnant. In Michigan, for example, K.H., a 22-year-old single mother of three, was prosecuted for giving birth to a baby born with traces of cocaine in his urine.[12] The prosecutor alleged, as in Florida, that K.H. "delivered" drugs to her fetus, a felony punishable by up to 20 years in prison and a $25,000 fine, between the time the baby passed through the birth canal and before the umbilical cord was cut. The prosecutor also alleged that she committed second degree child abuse, punishable by up to four years in prison, "by using cocaine prior to delivery of the child." The primary evidence relied upon by the prosecution was the positive toxicology of the newborn at birth. The action is still pending. Another woman has just been indicted under a similar statute in Jackson County, Michigan.[13]

In South Carolina prosecutors have arrested at least 18 women, charging them with criminal neglect or distribution of drugs to a minor.[14] In August 1989, for example, Candace Woolery was charged with criminal neglect after giving birth to a baby with heroin in her blood. She spent four days in jail and faces up to 10 years in prison. Another woman was arrested in her seventh month of pregnancy and charged with possession and distribution based upon a positive drug test. She was placed under house arrest for the duration of her pregnancy.[15] Women have also been prosecuted in Alaska,[16] Connecticut,[17] the District of Columbia,[18] Georgia,[19] Illinois,[20] Indiana,[21] Massachusetts,[22] Ohio[23] and Texas.[24]

Illegal drug use is not the only behavior targeted. In January 1990, Diane Pfannensteilm, a battered woman who was pregnant and also an alcoholic, went to a hospital from her local shelter to obtain treatment.[25] Hospital personnel tested her and gave the positive results to a local district attorney who arrested her and charged her with criminal child abuse. The case has been dismissed but it will probably not be long before another prosecutor tries a similar theory.

Faulty Assumptions Behind the Prosecution of Pregnant Drug Users

Each of these prosecutions is premised on erroneous assumptions that may have disastrous effects on these women's lives. One assumption of these prosecutorial theories is that pregnant addicts are indifferent to the health of their fetuses, or that they willfully seek to cause them harm.[26] For example, South Carolina Circuit Solicitor Joe Watson has defended the prosecutions in that state: "It sort of came to a focus when we had three or four in a row. . . . We decided to sit down and see if we could . . . force these women to do something."[27] U.S. Senator Pete Wilson stated in a Congressional discussion on the topic: "I recall a woman named Cheryl. . . . It wasn't until Cheryl's seventh drug-addicted child that she realized what she was doing to her children was bad."[28]

However, it is not true that the majority of these women are insensitive to their children's needs and simply need reminders of the dangers of drug use. Real resource constraints often prevent women from securing treatment or proper care during their pregnancies.[29] Even when women can secure treatment, they may still be constrained by the nature of the addiction process itself. Addiction typically involves loss of control over use of a drug and continued involvement *even when* there are serious consequences.[30] Furthermore, addiction may be caused by genetic predispositions and environmental factors. Drug dependency and alcoholism also include the development of tolerance.[31] Thus, to treat pregnant addicts as indifferent is to misunderstand the addiction process.

A second erroneous assumption is that drug treatment is available and pregnant women willfully seek to avoid it. For example, in *In re Troy D.*,[32] a case in which a California woman lost custody of her newborn after the newborn tested positive at birth for drugs, the court reasoned in part: "To enable juvenile courts to protect drug-exposed infants and to compel parents to undergo drug rehabilitation therapy . . . courts must be able to assert jurisdiction over infants . . . because of prenatal exposure to dangerous drugs."[33] The court did not examine the availability of drug or alcohol treatment open to the defendant. Had it done so, it would have found that many treatment programs will not admit pregnant women because they fear liability or do not have services, such as child or obstetrical care.[34]

In New York, for example, according to Dr. Wendy Chavkin, a former Rockefeller Fellow at the Columbia University School of Public Health and former Director of Maternity Services for the City of New York, 54 percent of the 78 drug treatment programs refuse to treat pregnant women, 67 percent refuse to treat pregnant women on Medicaid, and 87 percent have no services available to pregnant women on Medicaid, or who are Medicaid eligible and addicted to crack.[35] Less than half of those programs that accept pregnant women provide or arrange for prenatal care. Although lack of child care is a major obstacle to participation in drug treatment for many women, only two programs make provisions available for clients' children. It is thus premature at best to talk about prosecuting a population when there are no treatment programs available.

A third assumption is that prosecution will deter women from alcohol and drug use. For example, one reporter has observed: "Prosecutors, judges and state child protection officials say they feel an obligation to protect fetuses and newborns from the ravages of drug abuse."[36] Yet punitive measures will, in our experience, deter women from using the health-related services that will most benefit themselves and their children. Punitive actions will drive these women away from the health care community as soon as they believe that their doctors also function as police.[37] As the California American Medical Association has stated: "Prosecution is counterproductive to the public interest as it may discourage a woman from seeking prenatal care or dissuade her from providing accurate information to health care providers out of fear of self-incrimination."[38]

Implications and Impact of These Prosecutions

The problems posed by the institution of these cases have far-reaching implications for all women. First, when society chooses to punish pregnant women for their drug use, it opens the door to the placement of additional restrictions on women's behavior during pregnancy. Preventing pregnant women from smoking cigarettes or drinking alcohol is the most obvious such restriction. However, restrictions could go as far as to require women to obey all of their doctor's orders while pregnant, including instructions to quit their job or to stay in bed for a period of months.

In addition, there would be rational arguments to extend such restrictions to all fertile women of childbearing age, since it has been shown that alcohol consumption can harm a fetus even before a woman may realize she is pregnant. To criminalize non-obedience of doctor's instructions merely to prevent possible harm to a fetus would severely impinge on a woman's right to bodily integrity.

Second, the control over prenatal behavior and concern for the fetus may extend to other areas of women's lives. One vivid example that exists already is the recent Seventh Circuit case, *UAW v. Johnson Controls*,[39] which upheld an employer policy that excluded all fertile women, regardless of their sexual preference, from jobs in which exposure to lead could *potentially* harm a fetus. In its decision, the court repeatedly portrayed women as fetal vessels, for whom employment and personal autonomy are secondary concerns.[40] The dissent estimated that the decision would affect 15 to 20 million industrial jobs for working women.

In each of these cases, prosecutors attempt novel application of their own state laws. While each state law may be different, most prosecutors are attempting to apply state laws to protect fetuses that were established to protect children. If courts adopt these theories, they will, despite legislative intent to the contrary, afford greater rights to fetuses than those afforded to women.[41] This is bound to affect women's right to choose to have an abortion or to refuse medical treatment that, while not in her best interest, may or may not be in the best interest of the fetus. Precedent-setting decisions such as these will open the door even wider to limiting the right to privacy in other areas.

Of concern in all of these cases is the fact that pregnancy is being singled out for criminal liability, while similar behavior engaged in by men or non-pregnant women remains immune. For example, men and non-pregnant women who arrive at a hospital are not asked if they have children, they are not tested for drug use, and their medical records are not turned over to police or child welfare authorities. Men are not required to avoid alcohol, a substance which has been shown to contribute to decreased infant birth weight.[42] Men who are abusing drugs and enter hospitals are not asked if they have children and, if they are, they are not subjected to termination proceedings of their parental rights. Men are not required to subordinate their own interest for the sake of another. A father, for example, would not be required to donate a kidney to his dying daughter,[43] nor would he be charged with manslaughter for not running into a burning building to save his child.

The importance, therefore, of these cases cannot be underestimated. They raise vital civil liberties issues that affect maternal and child health, particularly for low-income women, and that importance extends into women's very right to equality.

State Legislative Responses

In a predictable move, state legislatures have begun to modify child abuse and neglect statutes to allow for the punishment of women who use drugs during pregnancy. For example, Illinois has amended the Juvenile Court Act definition of "neglected minor" to include infants born with controlled substances in their systems,[44] as has Indiana,[45] Minnesota,[46] Nevada,[47] Florida,[48] and Oklahoma.[49] These laws raise similar maternal-fetal rights conflict issues that arise in the criminal prosecution context.

Other states are enacting laws which require health officials to report women who use drugs during pregnancy to child welfare authorities. For example, Minnesota amended its Reporting of Maltreatment of Minors Act to mandate the reporting of drug use by pregnant women.[50] Minnesota requires, under certain circumstances, that doctors test pregnant women and newborns for the presence of drugs and report the

results to the Department of Health. Oklahoma also requires mandatory reporting to social services.[51] If social service agents find evidence of abuse, they are authorized to provide that information to district attorneys. Failure to report may be a misdemeanor. Utah now requires medical personnel to report a child's mother whenever they discover a child born with fetal alcohol syndrome or drug dependency.[52]

Unfortunately, reporting is often the impetus to criminal prosecution and penalizes poor women and women of color more than any other group. In a number of jurisdictions, women in government-subsidized facilities are routinely tested for drug use when women who can afford private health care are not tested. One recent study of Pinellas County, Florida, conducted by the National Association for Perinatal Addiction Research and Education, found that African American women were 10 times more likely to be reported to child abuse authorities than were White women.[53] Researchers surveyed five public health clinics from January 1 through June 30, 1989, testing a total of 715 women, 335 who were in private care. The researchers found that 14.6 percent of all the women tested positive for alcohol, marijuana, cocaine and/or opiates. White women were 1.09 times more likely to have used alcohol or drugs prior to their first visit to the doctor. Yet, of the 133 pregnant women reported to county health authorities, 85 were African American and 45 were White. The study concluded that African American women were 9.58 times as likely to be reported for substance abuse in pregnancy as compared to White women, even though White women were more likely to have used drugs prior to their first visit to the doctor.

Reporting requirements also violate women's right to confidential medical information. This privacy requirement should prevent hospitals from revealing patients' medical histories to county prosecutors or social service agencies. It interferes with the physicians' ethical and legal obligation to protect confidences told to them by a patient. Obviously, a duty of care is owed the infant by the pediatrician. However, reporting to social service agencies is ultimately premised on the notion that the woman will again engage in conduct which will harm the infant, a premise which is problematic.

Mandatory reporting laws can also scare pregnant women away from prenatal services as well as drug treatment programs.[54] In Minnesota, the reporting statute imposes no criminal sanction and is designed only to get more women into drug treatment programs. Yet many doctors in Minnesota fear that the law is having the opposite effect, as pregnant drug users avoid treatment and withhold information from their doctors in order to avoid being reported.[55]

Finally, reporting may not be in the best interests of

the child given the current state of foster care in the United States. The acute shortage of foster care, particularly in major urban areas, must be accounted for when children are threatened with separation from parents especially when the parents may be fit. A program in Los Angeles found, for example, that the 13 children in the program who had been exposed to drugs in utero had been placed in a total of 35 foster homes before reaching the age of three.[56] When foster care resources are scarce, removing a child from the parent's custody may not best serve the interests of the child. Accordingly, positive test results should not trigger presumptions of neglect without a more proving review of parental fitness and the best interests of the child.

Alternative Responses to Infant Illness and Mortality

There are better ways to address the problems facing children who were exposed to drugs in utero than by punishing their mothers and by abrogating their rights. The mothers' and children's rights need not be adversarial. Drug and alcohol treatment programs should not be allowed to exclude pregnant women. In pursuit of this goal, the American Civil Liberties Union Women's Rights Project filed, in December 1989, the first in a series of cases on behalf of pregnant crack addicts and alcoholics who had been turned away from four private alcohol and drug treatment programs in New York City.[57]

States can engage in measures which account for the health care needs of pregnant women who use drugs, and yet not drive pregnant women away from the health care system. Laws may provide for early treatment intervention and child care services for parents in need of alcohol or drug treatment, or prohibit use of positive test results as the basis upon which to prosecute women. Florida, for example, has passed a law providing that "no parent of such a newborn infant shall be subject to criminal investigation solely on the basis of such infant's drug dependency."[58] In New York, Assemblywoman Gloria Davis has introduced a bill in the state legislature which would prohibit the preventive detention of pregnant women and the use of any evidence obtained from a fetus in utero or from a newly born infant obtained within one week after the birth of such an infant to demonstrate either parental unfitness or child abuse.[59] States can allocate more funds to treatment programs. Washington has passed a law, for example, mandating an increase in funds to alcohol and drug treatment programs.[60] States can also pass laws prohibiting the exclusion of pregnant women from alcohol and drug treatment programs.

Conclusion

The maternal-fetal rights issue is inseparable from the issue of women's right to bodily integrity, liberty and equality. Some women who recognize that they will not be able to get adequate prenatal care or drug treatment as a result of addiction may not be able to get an abortion because of restrictive abortion laws. Others may not want to have an abortion but will do so to avoid prosecution. The highly charged nature of the context—drug-addicted women giving birth to drug-exposed babies—makes it painful to defend these women. The specter of a newborn going through withdrawal is horrible. Yet allowing this scene to feed our punitive impulses is at a cost to the health of pregnant drug addicts, to their newborns and to ourselves. All of these cases are indicative of a burgeoning health crisis that requires the attention of the health care community. It should not require the involvement of lawyers. Unfortunately, it does.

References
1. See, e.g., Diesenhouse, S., Ideas and Trends, *The New York Times*, Sept. 10, 1989, at E5, col. l; Mother Charged After Her Baby Dies of Cocaine, *The New York Times*, May 10, 1989; LaCroix, S., "Jailing Mothers for Drug Abuse," *The Nation*, May l, 1989 (hereafter LaCroix); Lewin, T., "When Courts Take Charge of the Unborn, *The New York Times*, Jan. 9, 1989.
2. E.g., Topping, R., "Drug Use as Child Abuse," *Newsday*, Sept. 12, 1988; Whitaker, B., "Tot Welfare at Issue in Drug Cases," *Newsday*, Nov. 6, 1989.
3. See Kolder, A. "Court Ordered Obstetrical Interventions," 316 *New Eng. J. Med.* 1192 (l987); Nelson, L., "Forced Medical Treatment of Pregnant Women: Compelling Each to Live as Seems Good to the Rest," 37 *Hastings Law Journal* 703 (1986); Rhoden, N., "The Judge in the Delivery Room: The Emergence of Court-Ordered Cesarean," 74 *Calif. L. Rev.* 1951 (1986).
4. E.g., In re A.C., 533 A.2d 611 (D.C. l987), reh'g granted, 539 A.2d 203 (D.C. 1988) (D.C. Court of Appeals originally affirmed a trial judge's order to force a cesarean section on a terminally ill pregnant woman over her objections, in spite of the danger to the woman's life.) On appeal, this decision was overturned April 26, 1990.
5. Chasnoff, I., "Temporal Patterns of Cocaine Use in Pregnancy: Perinatal Outcome," 261 *J.A.M.A.*, (March 24/31, 1989); Cherukuri, et al., "A Cohort Study of Alkaloid Cocaine (Crack) in Pregnancy, 2 *ACOG Current J. Rev.*, No. l, (1989); "Mothers, Babies and Crack," *The New York Times*, May ll, 1989; Edelin, et al., "Methadone Maintenance in

Pregnancy: Consequences to Care and Outcome,
71 *Obstetrics and Gynecology* 399 (March 1988);
Goleman, D., "Lasting Costs for Child Found
from a Mother's Early Drinks," *The New York
Times,* Feb. 16, 1989; But see Rosett, et al.,
"Patterns of Alcohol Consumption and Fetal
Development, 61 *Obstetrics and Gynecology,*
545, No. 5 (May 1983)("No associations between
alcohol use and fetal development were observed
in the newborn nursery among offspring of
moderate or rare drinkers."); Koren, G., "Bias
Against the Null Hypothesis: The Reproductive
Hazards of Cocaine," *The Lancet,* Dec. 16, 1989.
("The bias against the null hypothesis may lead to
distorted estimation of the teratogenic risk of
cocaine and thus cause women to terminate their
pregnancy unjustifiably.")

6. As one commentator observed: "It doesn't take a
great intuitive leap once you start locking up
people to protect the fetus to imagine getting to
the point where a representative for the fetus has
to be appointed every time a woman wants an
abortion." Lewin, supra, at note 3.

7. *People v. Pamela Rae Stewart,* No. M 508197 (San
Diego Mun. Ct. 1987). See Defendant's Memo-
randum of Points and Authorities in Support of
Motion to Dismiss. Briefs are available from the
ACLU Reproductive Freedom Project. See also
Jennifer Warren, Infant Death Case: Mother
Innocent of Prenatal Crime, *L.A. Times,* Feb. 27,
1987, at 3; Martha Field, "Controlling the
Woman to Protect the Fetus," 17 *L. Med. &
Health Care* 114, 118 (1989).

8. Stewart, at 9-11 (The child support statute was
designed to assure financial support for children,
not to control a mother's behavior during pregnancy).

9. Salamone, D., "Cocaine Mom Gets 14 Years of
Probation," *The Sentinel,* Aug. 26, 1989; Appellant's Initial Brief, *Jennifer Johnson v. State No.
89-1765* (Fla. Dist. Ct. App. brief filed Dec. 28,
1989) [hereinafter Johnson Appellant's Brief].

10. Ms. Johnson is represented on appeal by Lynn
Paltrow, Esq., and Louise Melling, Esq., of the
ACLU's Reproductive Freedom Project and ap-
pointed counsel James Sweeting.

11. Procreative rights and rights to reproductive
decision-making have been recognized by the
U.S. Supreme Court under the doctrine of right
to privacy. See *Skinner v. Oklahoma,* 316 U.S.
535 (1942) (overturning Oklahoma law which
authorized involuntary sterilizations of felons
convicted of crimes of moral turpitude); *Griswold
v. Connecticut,* 381 U.S. 479 (1965) (recognized
right of privacy in overturning law which prohib-

its use of birth control); *Roe v. Wade,* 410 U.S.
113 (1973) (right of privacy extends to women's
right to have an abortion).

12. *People v. K.H.,* File No. 89-2931-FY (60th
District Court, County of Muskegon, arraign-
ment on Nov. 13, 1989); Simon, H., "Policing
Pregnancy in the Drug War," *The Detroit News,*
Dec. 8, 1989.

13. Conversation with Paul Dennenfeld, 1/3/90,
Legal Director of American Civil Liberties
Union, Counsel representing K.H..

14. Henderson, B., "Mothers of Infant Addicts: Does
Prosecution Help?"; *The Charlotte Observer,*
Aug. 26, 1989 (hereinafter Henderson); Groat,
E., "Mothers on Drugs Face Prosecution,"
Journal-Scene, Aug. 30, 1989.

15. Plazza, B., "Addicted baby's mother charged,"
Piedmont News, Aug. 16, 1989; Zogg, J., "Three
charged with neglect of drug-addicted infants,"
Piedmont News, Aug. 17, 1989.

16. "Debate raised over 'prenatal police patrols,' "
The Alaska Republic, Dec. 7, 1989.

17. Singleton, D., "Mom to be is held," *Daily News,*
Aug. ll, 1989.

18. *United States v. Vaughn,* No. F-2172-88B (Super.
Ct. of D.C., Aug. 23, 1988).

19. *State of Georgia v. Coney,* No. 14/403-04 (Super.
Ct. of Crisp Cty., filed Nov. 6, 1989).

20. "Grand jury won't indict mother in baby's drug
death," *Chicago Tribune,* May 27, 1989.

21. "Woman charged after giving birth to addict,"
The Indianapolis Star, Oct. 7, 1989.

22. *Commonwealth v. Levy,* No. 89-2725-2729
(Super Ct. of Mass), motion to dismiss filed Nov.
10, 1989; *Commonwealth of Mass. v. Pellegrini,*
No. 87970 (Super. Ct. of Mass.).

23. *Cox v. Court of Common Pleas,* Franklin City,
No. 88AP 856 (Oh. Ct. App. Dec. 13, 1988); *State
of Ohio v. Andrews,* No. JU 68459 (Ct. C.P. of
Stark County, Ohio, June 19, 1989); *State of Ohio
v. Gray,* No. CR88-7406 (Ct. C.P. of Lucas
County, Ohio, July 13, 1989).

24. *State of Texas v. Rodden,* No. 0373625R (Dist.
Ct. for Tarrant Cty, filed June l, 1989); Crawford,
S., "Legal system grapples with newborn ad-
dicts," *The Dallas Morning News,* July 19, 1989.

25. "Pregnant Woman is Charged with Child Abuse
for Drinking," *The New York Times,* January 22,
1990.

26. See, e.g., S. Boyer, "Time to Sterilize Addicted
Mothers," *Blue Bell, Pa. Observer,* Sept. 6, 1989.

27. Henderson at note 20.

28. 135 Cong. Record 9319, 9320 (1989)(Introduction
of Drug Abuse During Pregnancy Prevention Act

of 1989, introduced on August 1, 1989 by Senator Pete Wilson).

29. For example, although Pamela Rae Stewart was ordered by her doctor to stay off her feet, she simply could not do so because she was the primary caretaker of her two children. Similarly, Jennifer Johnson had sought drug treatment during her pregnancy but was unable to obtain it in her area. There is no evidence that the court considered this relevant.

30. Cohen, S., M.D., *The Chemistry of Addiction*, 59.

31. Id. at 87-98.

32. 215 Cal. App. 3d 889, 263 Cal. Rptr. 869 (Cal. Ct. App. 1989).

33. 215 Cal. App. 3d, 263 Cal. Rptr. at 872-873.

34. Polsky, C., "Crack in Family Portrait," *Newsday*, Nov. 5, 1989 (hereinafter Polsky); *Elaine W., et al. v. North General Hospital, et al.*, (N.Y. Sup. Ct.), Complaint filed by the Women's Rights Project of the American Civil Liberties Union.

35. Chavkin, W., "Help, Don't Punish Pregnant Addicts," *The New York Times*, July 17, 1989; A facility's ability to provide care for a woman's other children can also be the determining factor as to whether she undergoes treatment. Virtually no programs provide such care. See Polsky 60.

36. Lewin, J., "Drug Abuse in Pregnancy: A Conflict Over Rights," *The New York Times*, Jan. 9, 1989 (hereinafter Lewin).

37. See LaCroix at 586 at note 1.

38. See note 12, *Stewart* brief

39. 886 F.2d 871 (7th Cir. 1989).

40. Id. (The majority went into great detail on the harm that might be done to a fetus exposed to lead on the job site, but the effect that its decision would have on the lives of women excluded from these positions was not discussed).

41. Presumably, in the absence of legislative action to the contrary, defendants will win on appeal when they challenge the application of these laws to the fetus. However, while the appeals are pending, many women may have to face jail, prolonged public exposure, the institution of neglect proceedings against them, or any other variety of harms.

42. Little, R. and Sing, C., "Father's Drinking and Infant Birth Weight," *Teratology* 36:59-65 (1987).

43. For example, in *McFall v. Shrimp*, 127 Pitts. Leg. J. 14 (Allegheny Cty., July 26, 1978) Judge John Flaherty refused to order a man to donate bone marrow that might have doubled his cousin's chances of survival from aplastic anemia.

44. Ill. Juvenile Ct. Act, Ill. Rev. Stat. ch. 37, para. 802-3, s. 2-3(l)(c).

45. Ind. Code. Ann. 3l-6-4-3.1 (Burns l987) (expanded definition of a "child in need of services" to include a child born with fetal alcohol syndrome or an addiction to a controlled substance. A child "at substantial risk of a life threatening condition" that arises or is aggravated by a mother's addiction to a controlled substance or alcohol during pregnancy will also be considered in need of services).

46. 1989 Miss. Sess. Law Serv. Ch. 290, Art. 5 (West).

47. Nev. Rev. Stat. Ann 432B.330 (Michie 1989) (expanded definition of "child in need of protection" to include any child suffering from congenital drug addiction or fetal alcohol syndrome).

48. Fla. Stat. Ann. 415.503(8) (West 1989) (expanded definition of "harm" to child's health to include physical dependency of a newborn infant upon a controlled drug).

49. Okla. Stat. Ann. tit. 10, 1101 (West 1989) (expanded definition of a "deprived child" to include a child in need of special care or treatment as a result of being born in a condition of dependence on a controlled dangerous substance).

50. Minn. Stat. 626.556 (1988).

51. Okla. Stat. Ann. tit. 21 at 846 (West 1989).

52. Utah Code Ann. 62A-4-504 (1989).

53. See National Association for Perinatal Addiction Research and Education (NAPARE) press release, 9/18/89.

54. Lerner, M. "Law Requiring Reporting of Pregnant Drug Users is Backfiring, Critics Say," *StarTribune*, Jan. 15, 1990.

55. Id.

56. Interim Hearings on Parental Substance Abuse and its Effects on the Fetus and Children Before the Senate Select Committee on Substance Abuse, California Legislature, at 30 (1988) (statement of Carol Cole, child development specialist/teacher in the Preschool Educational Development Program at the Salvin Special Education Center, Los Angeles Unified School District).

57. *Elaine W., et al v. North General Hospital, et. al.* (no index number). Copies of the complaint and briefs may be obtained from the Women's Rights Project.

58. Fla. Stat. Ann. 415.503(8)(a)(2).

59. Legislative Bill Drafting Commission 12099-03-0.

60. 1989 Wash. Laws, Chp. 271.

15 Women and AIDS

Lynne C. McArthur

"When diagnosed, AIDS has had a disproportionate impact on women and children of color; and because so many of these women and children are poor, they have had the fewest medical, social and economic resources available to them."

Overview

AIDS—Acquired Immune Deficiency Syndrome—is readily acknowledged as a major public health issue, one that affects us all. Originally portrayed as a disease found in gay men, and more recently intravenous drug users, AIDS is now also recognized as having an increasingly devastating impact on women and their families. In fact, women are currently the fastest-growing group of people with AIDS.

Nationally, women constitute 9 percent of the people diagnosed with AIDS, as defined by the Centers for Disease Control (CDC), up from 7 percent just a short time ago.[1] These figures, however, vary with geographic location. In New York, women make up 15 percent of the cumulative total of those with AIDS[2] and 18 percent of those diagnosed in 1989[3]; while in California the percentages are much lower.

Furthermore, the number of women with AIDS or who die from HIV-related diseases may be higher than we know. AIDS in some women may go unrecognized by physicians who often do not expect women to have it. Other women may not survive long enough to develop or be diagnosed as having the "full-blown" AIDS that is used by the CDC to count cases. Most worrying is the possibility that the spectrum of HIV-related diseases in women may be different than that seen in men and may therefore go unrecognized. Gynecological diseases or infections are frequently found in HIV-infected women and do not respond readily to conventional treatment; HIV-infected women also have a higher incidence of cervical cancer, a disease which has been strongly associated with specific strains of the human papillomavirus, than do non-infected women.[4]

When diagnosed, AIDS has had a disproportionate impact on women and children of color. Because so many of these women and children are poor, they have had the fewest medical, social and economic resources available to them. Nationally, 52 percent of the women with AIDS are Black, 20 percent are Hispanic, and 27 percent are White.[5] The proportions of children of color with AIDS reflect those of their mothers: 57 percent are Black and 33 percent are Hispanic.[6]

It is important to remember, however, that as devastating as the AIDS epidemic has been for women, in many respects it has presented us with no new issues. AIDS has served to highlight the intransigent social and economic problems that have had increasing impact on women, particularly in the past few decades—poverty, racism, sexism, poor health care, inadequate housing, lack of emotional support, inappropriate and inadequate drug and alcoholism treatment services, homelessness, insufficient child care and unavailable legal services. Our ability to truly help women affected by AIDS will be directly related to our ability to solve these fundamental problems.

Transmission

AIDS, or more accurately, the human immune deficiency virus that causes AIDS, is not easy to transmit. In fact, all of the research to date indicates that HIV is found in just a few body fluids in high enough proportions to cause infection, namely, blood and blood products, semen and vaginal secretions and breast milk. This means that to become infected, a person generally must: 1) share needles or other drug paraphernalia with an infected person: 2) have sex with an infected person; or 3) be the newborn or nursing infant of an infected mother. Until June 1985, one could also become infected by receiving infected blood in a transfusion. Now, however, the blood supply is tested for HIV antibody and the risk of receiving infected blood is extremely low.

Drug Use and AIDS

As noted, HIV infection may occur through the sharing of a needle or other paraphernalia with an infected person. Most often this sharing occurs among intravenous drug users (IVDUs), but we should remember that intravenous drug users include athletes using needles to inject steroids; first-time IV drug "experimenters," who virtually always share needles; occasional injectors of cocaine, who may share needles at a weekend party; and anyone else who shares a needle for any purpose.

Although women are less likely than men to use drugs intravenously, women nevertheless constitute 20 to 25 percent of all IVDUs in this country.[7] These women are at risk for infection, as evidenced by the fact that nationally 52 percent of the women with AIDS are classified as IVDUs.[8]

Many more women, however, are the regular, non-drug-injecting sex partners of men who are IV-drug-users. In New York State it is estimated that 100,000 women are at risk for infection because of their relationships with IV-drug-using men;[9] their risk is especially high because the HIV infection rate among IVDUs in New York is 55 to 63 percent.[10] In fact, more than 81 percent of the heterosexual transmission cases of AIDS in New York involve transmission from a male IVDU to a non-drug-injecting female partner.[11] In other areas, where the infection rate among IVDUs is lower, sex partners of IVDUs may have a lower risk; even so, the risk is much higher than in the general population. Intravenous drug use is also closely linked to cases of pediatric AIDS. Approximately 77 percent of the children with AIDS have infected mothers who are IV drug users themselves, or are the sex partners of IVDUs.[12]

Experts have also become increasingly concerned about the relationship between HIV infection and the use of crack, a smokeable form of cocaine. Some crack users are former or current IVDUs; others, both male and female, trade sexual favors in order to obtain the drug or engage in prostitution in order to purchase their drug supplies. Since the crack "high" is extremely short-lived, users may engage in a higher frequency of sexual encounters to finance their habits. This, in turn, increases the possibility of developing sexually trans-mitted diseases which have been linked to high HIV infection rates. These issues are of particular concern for women, since women often work in the sex industry in order to purchase drugs for both themselves and their partners, or will exchange sexual favors in order to obtain drugs. The rapid increase in crack use by women underscores our concern. Adolescent women, particu-larly those who are runaways or homeless, are especially at risk for HIV infection through prostitution or the exchange of sex for drugs. These young women often have no other means of support and the drugs help them cope with the pain that permeates their daily lives.

The Alcohol Connection

Many experts hypothesize that alcohol plays a role in the development of HIV infection and the progression from seropositivity to full-blown AIDS. Research is currently underway to explore the validity of this hypothesis, and, given the adverse effects of chronic alcohol use on the immune system, it may well prove to be true.

Specifically, alcohol abuse: 1) decreases the number of white blood cells, which make up a significant portion of the immune system; 2) causes liver disease, which inhibits the body's ability to form T-cells, the white blood cells targeted by the human immune-deficiency virus; 3) often leads to a decrease in the number of T-cells and to poor health; and 4) results in stress, which harms immune functioning. In addition to the obvious implications for seropositive people or those with HIV illness, there is an additional and serious consequence: chronic alcohol use causes liver damage, and AZT, one of the few drugs available for treating AIDS, is contraindicated for people with liver damage.

The use of alcohol is also implicated as a factor in behavior that results in infection, either through the increased likelihood of IV drug use or the decreased likelihood that individuals will practice safer sex. Because of alcohol's disinhibiting effects, people may engage in behavior they would have avoided if sober. Studies show, for example, that alcohol use by one or more partners is found in over half of the cases of other sexually transmitted diseases. The role that alcohol may play in subverting intended behavior is not, however, generally recognized, even by those who are actively trying to avoid HIV infection.

In addition, alcohol is often used in conjunction with other drugs. In a recent study by the National Institute of Drug Abuse, researchers found that 73 percent of the IVDU women and 71 percent of the *non*-IVDU women reported alcohol use in the six months prior to the interview. Twenty-nine percent and 20 percent of the women in the respective groups reported daily use.[13] This and other forms of polydrug use may well compromise immune functioning as well as judgment, making other risk-taking behaviors more likely.

Furthermore, we must remember that many people who are now entering alcoholism treatment have used drugs intravenously within the last ten years. This IV drug use often involved cocaine as well as heroin and various combinations of heroin, cocaine, and ampheta-mines. Their sex partners, who are often also treated within the alcoholism service system and who generally are women, are additionally at risk, as are their unborn children. The risk may be exacerbated by the fact that HIV infection and alcoholism are not viewed by most people as being connected. Thus, a woman whose partner is alcoholic may erroneously believe she has no cause for concern about his or her HIV status.

Sexual Transmission

As noted throughout, the human immune deficiency virus can be transmitted through sexual intercourse with an infected partner. The transmission may occur male-to-male, female-to-female, male-to-female, or female-to-male.

At this point in the United States epidemic, women appear to be the group at greatest risk for sexual transmission of infection. Education and consequent behavior change have resulted in decreasing risk for non-IV-drug-using gay men; and although it has not yet been proven, female-to-male sexual transmission does not appear to be as efficient as male-to-female transmission in the United States. (For a variety of reasons, not all of which are known, men and women in Africa appear to be equally at risk.) In fact, women account for 96 percent of the diagnosed AIDS cases occurring among non-IV-drug-using heterosexuals who were not born in countries where heterosexual transmission is a major factor (e.g. Africa and Haiti).[14] Thus, for women who do not use drugs intravenously, intercourse with an infected partner is a major risk factor.

The risk to women of sexual transmission is of particular interest when we examine women who work as prostitutes. Much has been written about them as carriers of disease, and the media has been quick to portray prostitutes as the vectors through which HIV infection will enter the so-called "general population." In fact, the rate of HIV infection among prostitutes varies enormously—from zero percent in Nevada, where prostitution is legal and prostitutes are regularly tested for disease, to 60-70 percent in parts of Newark, New Jersey, where the rate of IV drug use in prostitutes is very high.[15]

A study in the April 17, 1987, *Journal of the American Medical Association* entitled "Antibody to Human Immunodeficiency Virus in Female Prostitutes" concludes that "the prevalence of HIV antibody in prostitutes so far tends to parallel the cumulative incidence of AIDS in women in the seven research sites, suggesting that risk factors for AIDS in female prostitutes may be similar to those in other women living in these geographic areas."[16] A CDC study further suggests that prostitutes are probably at the same risk for AIDS as other women with multiple sex partners.[17] Thus, the risk factors for prostitutes are needle-sharing and sexual intercourse with an infected partner. They do not, however, represent a major vehicle for transmission of infection to others.

Perinatal Transmission

Among children with HIV infection, the major risk factor is maternal transmission associated with intravenous drug use. In the majority of cases (60%) the mother is or was an IV drug user, and an additional 15 percent had mothers whose sex partners were IV drug users.[18] Transmission through infected blood has occurred in only 25 percent of the children with AIDS, a percentage that is decreasing because of testing of transfused blood.[19]

It appears (in this country) that 30-50 percent of the children born to infected mothers will develop infection themselves, although the rate may be higher if an infected woman has a second child.[20] At birth, the child of an infected mother will carry the mother's antibodies to HIV; when the child is about 15 months of age, testing will determine if the child has developed its own antibodies and is infected.

The overwhelming majority (over 90%) of these children are Black or Hispanic and their cumulative mortality is high. Those with perinatally acquired HIV infection have a very poor prognosis and most become symptomatic before one year of age.[21] Male and female children appear to be equally at risk.

It appears that infected breast milk may transmit HIV to a nursing infant. A few such cases of transmission have, in fact, been documented. Hence, at this point, infected women are advised to avoid breast-feeding their infants.

Media Portrayal of Women

The media has failed to accurately, adequately, or compassionately portray the impact of the HIV epidemic on women. When women *are* discussed, it is generally as mere vectors of disease; that is, as vessels that transmit infection to "innocent victims" or as prostitutes that transmit infection to men. In neither instance are women viewed as anything other than objects; and as noted earlier, the portrayal of prostitutes as disease carriers is not particularly accurate.

It must be noted, however, that the media merely reflects and transmits a message that our society in general communicates to women: we are stigmatized, isolated and ignored if we do not live up to society's expectations of what a woman should be. Since women become infected by engaging in stigmatized behaviors or through involvement with partners who have engaged in these behaviors, we should not be surprised when the media's portrayal of women's risk is less than compassionate or accurate. We should be even less surprised when the media messages that *are* sent are not viewed by women as being relevant. To admit the relevance of the message is to admit to behavior (or to having a partner) that society views as deviant.

During the past few years the print media have published numerous articles, reports, and books sympathetic to the plight of White gay males with AIDS. Several compassionate and accurate television programs have also been produced about the same topic, some to wide acclaim. HIV-infected women, however, have yet to be portrayed in this manner, a fact which is not likely to change in the near future. It is critical, therefore, for those of us who are concerned and who care about women to develop compassionate, nonjudgmental messages that women can truly hear.

Education and Prevention Issues for Women

HIV education and prevention appears at first blush to be a relatively simple matter. Women need to learn how the virus is transmitted and how transmission can be prevented. We tell women very simply:

- Don't use IV drugs; get into treatment.
- If you do use IV drugs, don't share. If you must share, sterilize your needles.
- Don't have sex with an infected partner. If you're not sure about your partner's sexual or drug-using history, use protection (condoms, oral dams, and spermicides).

This information is accurate and women are not likely to become infected if they follow these instructions. Unfortunately, the instructions are easier to read than to follow.

First, women who are IV drug users will usually experience great difficulty in obtaining treatment, since long waiting lists exist in areas where IV drug use is most widespread. Even if treatment is available, however, it may not meet the special needs of women, particularly those women with children. Child care is rarely available at drug treatment programs, and residential programs for women and their children are almost nonexistent. Furthermore, in many instances, drug treatment programs are developed and directed by men. Program components and treatment approaches may not be relevant to or appropriate for women. Women from non-dominant cultures face even greater difficulties since programs may not be culturally sensitive or appropriate.

The sharing of IV needles is an integral component of the drug culture in many parts of the United States. This sharing is often made necessary in states where syringes can only be purchased by prescription. For women, the sharing of needles may also be a component of a sexual relationship. In some cities, packets of bleach and instructions on how to clean needles are handed out in areas of high drug use, and the research data indicate that many addicts are attempting to clean their "works" at least some of the time.

Unfortunately, bleach and information on sterilization may be reaching proportionately more men than women. Women tend to shoot up at home rather than in the "shooting galleries" where male addicts tend to congregate when they need to get high and where street outreach workers consequently go to hand out bleach and information. Thus, women may be less

likely to obtain the information and products they need to reduce their risk.

Despite these problems, the most difficult prevention issues for women probably revolve around sexual concerns. First, it is clear that women often do not know that their partners are at risk. In a 1987 study of women who had just given birth in a New York City-based hospital, 42 percent of the HIV-positive women did not acknowledge or could not identify any risk factor for HIV infection during an extensive pre-test interview conducted by skilled and experienced interviewers.[22] Women may not know that their partners are current or former IV drug users, have had homosexual encounters, have had sex with numerous other partners, have a history of sexually transmitted disease, and so forth.

Even when women try to elicit this information, they are unlikely to learn the truth. Vickie Mays and Susan Cochrane, California psychologists, recently published the findings of a study that indicated that the ordinary lies that people tell in order to make a good impression with a potential sex partner may, in fact, be a contributing factor in the spread of HIV infection, particularly among women. The majority of women in the study said they relied on asking about sexual and drug-taking histories to assess their risk for HIV transmission. Thirty-five percent of the men admitted to having lied to a woman in order to have sex with her. Sixty percent of the women believed they had been lied to. The researchers considered the men's estimates to be low. Twenty percent of the men said they would lie to a woman who asked if they had had an AIDS test. Two-thirds of the men considered at high risk (because of sexual and drug-using histories) said they considered condoms unnecessary.[23]

Heterosexual women who try to protect themselves have been given only one sexual option: condoms. Condom use, however, clearly depends on the cooperation of the male. Zena Stein, co-director of the HIV Center for Clinical and Behavioral Studies in New York City, writes, "Even family planning professionals who have written on the HIV problem have seemed insufficiently aware that the HIV epidemic restored to men the locus of control over the consequences of sexual behavior."[24]

In response to this concern, Dr. Stein and Dr. Anke Ehrhardt (also a co-director of the HIV Center) are advocating for the development of a topical viricide and other vaginal barriers that women could use before or after intercourse to prevent or at least reduce the risk of HIV infection. At this point, however, more than a decade into this epidemic, preventive methods that *women* could control have claimed very little attention and even less financial backing.

For many women condom use is not viewed as a

viable consideration. Ruth Rodriquez, former director of the Hispanic AIDS Forum in New York City, notes, "A good Hispanic woman does not use a condom, and she *certainly* would not consider making any kind of demands in regard to sex. Although it may seem impossible, we have to convince some women that their lives are worth saving."[25] In fact, women in general, and particularly Black and Hispanic women, face a host of cultural barriers that severely limit their ability to insist on low-risk sexual behaviors.

Furthermore, some women may place themselves in physical jeopardy should they insist that a partner use a condom, while others would place themselves and their children at economic risk if they were to tell their partners to either use a condom or have no sex. For other women, condom use means they are unlikely to get pregnant, and this is unacceptable, regardless of the risk. Many women grow up in a culture that honors and respects them *because* they give birth; and for drug-using women, pregnancy may be the only time in their lives that they are considered special or are attended to by their families.

In short, the prevention of HIV transmission in women is neither simple nor easy. We are asking women to change intimate, deeply personal behavior in the face of enormous social, cultural, ethnic, racial and religious barriers. Clearly, pamphlets, subway posters, and PSAs will not suffice. Prevention of HIV infection is, instead, a long-term, labor-intensive process, which is best handled by those who live in a particular community and who are trusted by community members. The success of our prevention efforts will depend on our ability to develop messages that women can hear and strategies that will empower them to act in ways that reduce the risk of HIV transmission.

A Word About Caregivers

Most discussions of AIDS and its impact on women completely ignore the fact that women constitute the primary group of people who provide care to individuals with AIDS. Family members, who are most often women, not only face the problems of caring for a loved one with a chronic, debilitating illness, but must also frequently deal with poverty, inadequate housing, poor access to health care, inadequate social services, discrimination, racism and a lack of support services for themselves. Because of the stigma of AIDS, these caregivers almost always face these problems in near-total isolation. Paid caregivers—physicians, nurses, social workers, alcoholism and substance-abuse counselors, home care and home health aides, and others—the majority of whom are women, are overworked, underpaid, rarely recognized for the emotionally draining work they do, and are also lacking in support services. Under such conditions, both groups

of caregivers are at increased risk for alcohol and other drug abuse. Unless we make a concerted effort to provide these caregivers with the honor, respect, recognition, and support they deserve, we can expect to see increasing levels of chemical abuse, emotional problems, physical illness and job turnover among those on whom our HIV-infected brothers and sisters depend.

References

1. "HIV/AIDS Surveillance Report—United States." Centers for Disease Control, December 1989.
2. NYS Department of Health, Bureau of Communicable Disease Control, "AIDS Surveillance Monthly Update for Cases Reported Through November 1989."
3. Pauline Thomas, M.D., NYC Department of Health. From a presentation before the Committee on the Care of Women and Children with HIV Infection, Jan. 10-12, 1990.
4. Robert Klein, M.D., Montefiore Medical Center. From a presentation before the Committee on the Care of Women and Children with HIV Infection, Jan. 10-12, 1990.
5. "HIV/AIDS Surveillance Report—United States," *op. cit.*
6. *Ibid.*
7. "Women's Health," Report of the Public Health Service Task Force on Women's Health Service Task Force on Women's Health Issues, Vol. II, U.S. DHHS, 1984.
8. "HIV/AIDS Surveillance Report—United States," op. cit.
9. "AIDS: New York's Response." A Five-Year Interagency Plan, January 1989, p.41.
10. *Ibid*, p. 41.
11. *Ibid*, p. 41.
12. *Ibid*, p. 41.
13. "NADR Project Revealing New Data on High-Risk Behaviors among Women." *Network*, Summer 1989, Vol. 1, Issue 2, p. 5.
14. NYS, Department of Health, Bureau of Communicable Disease Control, *op. cit.*
15. Barbara Santee, "Women and AIDS: The Silent Epidemic." Published by the Women and AIDS Resource Network, Brooklyn, NY, April, 1989, p. 15.
16. Priscilla Alexander, "Prostitutes Are Being Scapegoated for Heterosexual AIDS," in *Sex Work.*, F. Delacoste and P. Alexander (eds). Pittsburgh, Cleis Press, 1987. pp. 248-262.
17. "Antibody to Human Immunodeficiency Virus in Female Prostitutes," *Morbidity and Mortality Weekly*, Vol. 36:11, 1987. Centers for Disease Control.

18. "HIV/AIDS Surveillance Report—United States," *op.cit.*

19. *Ibid.*

20. "Perinatal AIDS: Care for Our Children, Care for Our Future." National Commission to Prevent Infant Mortality. Washington, D.C., 1987. p. 1.

21. G.B. Scott, C. Hutto, R.W. Makuch, et al. "Survival in children with perinatally acquired human immunodeficiency virus type 1 infection." *New England Journal of Medicine*, 1989. Vol. 332:1, 1791-96.

22. S. Landesman, H. Minkoff, S. Holman, et al. "Serosurvey of human immunodeficiency virus infection in parturients: Implications for human immunodeficiency virus testing programs of pregnant women." *JAMA*, 1987. 258: 2701-2703.

23. "Many People Lie About their Risk for AIDS, According to Report," *Common Sense About AIDS*, October 1988.

24. Zena Stein, "HIV Prevention: Methods Women Can Use." HIV Center for Clinical and Behavioral Studies, New York State Psychiatric Institute, the School of Public Health, and G.H. Sergievsky Center, Columbia University, New York, (n.d.), p. 2.

25. Ruth Rodriquez, personal communication, 1987.

16 Issues for Women at the Workplace

Miriam Aaron

"In addressing issues of women and alcoholism at the workplace, the tendency to view women as a single group, combined with an increasingly false perception that women in most jobs are easily replaceable, presents major problems for women."

The needs of women at the workplace are generally assessed from the perspective of job opportunities, salary levels and access to higher-level positions. Although women may have differing needs based on various factors such as educational level, socioeconomic and ethnic and cultural background, they frequently tend to be viewed as a single group with a single set of problems and needs.

In the past two decades, since the passage of civil rights legislation with guarantees for affirmative action and equal opportunity for women,[1] the types of jobs held by women have changed and the number of women in the workplace has increased substantially. The participation of women in occupations or professions that were considered outside their reach prior to the 1960s has also increased. For example, as reported in numerous publications and newspapers, the number of women who seek nursing and teaching as professions has decreased and the number of women who become lawyers and physicians has increased.

However, some believe access to powerful positions is still limited for women, despite their increasing numbers in the professional and corporate worlds. In 1989, women earned only an average of 70 cents for every dollar earned by men. More than 50 percent of working women are still employed in low-status, low-level positions.[2] Many women hold jobs that do not require the use of the full extent of their knowledge or ability. In many instances, issues such as child care considerations and the need to work close to home limit women's access to well-paying positions. In addition, the type of organization or business in which some women work reflects their need to work close to home. This need may contribute to poverty and an inability to obtain appropriate health care for the woman and her children. Employed Black and Latino women are more likely than their White counterparts to work as domestics—cleaning houses or babysitting—or in small, neighborhood worksites, where salaries and benefits are low and job stability is poor.

In addressing issues of women and alcoholism and other drug problems at the workplace, the tendency to view them as a single group and as easily replaceable presents major problems for women.[3,4] This view results in a failure to recognize workplace structures and hierarchies that create barriers to identifying women with alcohol and drug problems. Many work-based programs, such as employee assistance programs and employee counseling programs, report equal participation by men and women. But a close look at program participation data reveals that women seek program services for different reasons and often under different circumstances than men.[5] In addition, the diagnoses of women and men who participate in work-based programs are different, with women representing a small percentage of those diagnosed with alcoholism and other substance-abuse problems.

To understand the role of work-based programs in helping women with alcoholism and other substance-abuse problems, it is necessary to examine the programs' basic theoretical concepts as well as issues that may create barriers to participation by women.

Work-based Programs

During the past two decades, the role of the workplace in identifying people with alcoholism and other substance-abuse problems has increased in importance. The number of worksites with such programs has grown from less than 50 in the early 1970s to more than 5,000 in the late 1980s. The goal of the programs is to address addiction problems at the workplace and restore employees to useful productivity through work-based strategies. Some programs were initiated in response to federal legislation, such as the

Anti-Drug Abuse Act of 1988, which contained the Drug-Free Workplace Initiatives. Others were developed out of concern by employers and unions. In 1989, according to the United States Department of Labor's Bureau of Statistics, 57.3 percent of the labor force was composed of women. However, while the number of women in the workforce continues to increase, women are under-represented in programs designed to provide early intervention, assessment, referral and follow-up for alcohol and other drug-related issues. Research reported in the *New England Journal of Medicine* in January, 1990[6] supports earlier beliefs that women's ability to metabolize alcohol is different from that of men and that women generally tend to be in poorer health than men when seeking treatment for alcoholism.[7,8] Women assisted through work-based programs tend to be in later stages of alcoholism than men. Staff seem to have difficulty identifying women with alcoholism and drug dependence (versus men), and have more difficulty referring women to appropriate services.

Actual and perceived roles of women at the workplace, society's ambivalent attitude towards women at work, social pressures and attitudes towards women addicted to alcohol and other legal or illegal drugs are factors that interfere with provision of adequate and appropriate services for women at the workplace. As mentioned earlier, a key consideration is the tendency to view all women as a single group. This view ignores the varied needs of women and the ways in which they are affected by alcoholism and other substance abuse.

History of Work-based Programs

Programs established by work organizations to handle employees' health issues, including alcoholism and other drug dependence, have taken many forms over time. These programs have undergone changes and modifications that reflect prevailing social attitudes as well as the incorporation of new knowledge. The evolution of workplace programs for employees reflects changing attitudes of employers towards their employees.

In the 18th and early 19th centuries, employees were expected to produce at a certain rate. Work environment and working conditions were of little concern. Employers did not perceive their role as providing for employee health, welfare or safety. Early programs for employees were largely based on the response of employers to legal claims resulting from severe accidents or illness, such as lung disease suffered by coal miners. Early programs focused only on job-related issues. In many industries, these early programs expanded to include home visits to ensure that an employee on sick leave was actually sick and not

"gold-bricking." The programs did not include concerns for any illness not deemed to be directly job-related, except when verifying the legitimacy of absences. Over time, occupational health programs reflected increased recognition by employers that improvement in the quality of life at work creates a more productive workforce. This recognition stemmed largely from experiments conducted during World War II on influences affecting productivity.

At the same time during the 1940s, Alcoholics Anonymous (A.A.) was recognized as having the ability to help alcoholics achieve and maintain sobriety. Some worksites established programs designed to identify alcoholic employees and to encourage them to go to A.A. in the hope they would be helped.[9] Many of these early programs relied on attempts to identify alcoholics through observation of physical signs such as staggering gait, bloodshot eyes and the smell of liquor on their breath. These programs were often viewed as "witch hunts," resulting in the identification of late-stage alcoholics who frequently quit their jobs or were placed on early disability rather than seek help. In the early 1970s, the National Institute on Alcohol Abuse and Alcoholism (NIAAA) was established. This federal agency promoted the development of work-based intervention programs for alcoholics and stimulated the proliferation of research and program development activities.

Through these efforts, employers recognized that they had a responsibility to help solve problems that interfere with employees' ability to function appropriately on the job. Combining theories of organizational dynamics with the need to provide early identification of alcoholics, a series of program procedures were developed. These included the formulation of a policy and procedure for program participation, training supervisors in monitoring employees' job performance, attendance and punctuality and teaching supervisors to document erratic patterns in job performance. Supervisors could then confront employees based on documented job performance criteria and refer them for assessment to determine their ability to perform their jobs adequately. As these programs were developed, experience quickly showed that problems other than alcoholism also manifested themselves in poor work performance patterns, and many programs expanded to include a focus on other problems. In recognition of this expanded role, these programs became known as Employee Assistance Programs (EAPs).

Women and EAPs Today

Today's Employee Assistance Program is defined by the New York State Division of Alcoholism and Alcohol Abuse as "a confidential service that acts as a resource for work organizations and their employees. This program operates as an integral part of an organization to assist employees with problems that can interfere with the ability to function on the job effectively, efficiently and safely. Such problems typically include but are not limited to: alcoholism, substance abuse, emotional, marital, family and other personal problems that affect job performance. These programs serve organizations and occupational groups by providing prevention, identification, intervention, assessment, motivation to treatment, referral and follow-up of employees."[10] This definition was developed in conjunction with academic and practitioner expertise in the EAP field.

Since EAPs began, program participation procedures have changed, and besides the supervisory referral process described, employees and (if covered) their family members may voluntarily seek assistance from the program's staff. Intervention provided through an EAP generally results in early identification and in prevention—before an employee loses a job and before an employer loses a valued worker. Benefits of early intervention include decreases in employee absenteeism, increases in morale, increases in productivity and cost-saving to unions, employers and employees.

Experience with Employee Assistance Programs and their predecessors—occupational alcoholism programs—has shown that while these programs succeeded in identifying employees in need of help and referring employees for assistance, they have not succeeded in reaching women. Several reasons have been identified for the underrepresentation of women.

Issues for Alcohol- and Drug-Dependent Women at the Workplace

Research about intervention with women at the workplace is scant and data to substantiate reasons for a low intervention rate with women are limited. Some theories, however, have been developed and some reflect a lack of awareness about women and their needs. They are as follows:

- A significant number of jobs held by women are low-level jobs, requiring little training and not requiring extensive skills. Women in these types of jobs who have alcohol or other drug problems may often continue to appear to be functioning at an acceptable level despite their problems. Supervisors are reluctant to engage in a lengthy process to document poor performance and confront the employee, especially when the employee is deemed expendable and easily replaceable. It is interesting to note that with the recent crisis created by a nursing shortage (raising the status of the nursing profession), many hospitals have begun to develop EAPs.

- Views of women in the workplace may compound the problem. Some supervisors (both male and female) may accept excuses for absences, lateness and erratic job performance more readily from women because of the belief that such behavior is "to be expected" in women and can be explained in terms of their "unpredictability." Thus, the needed intervention and referral is delayed or avoided.

- When women are identified or voluntarily seek help for what may be alcoholism or an addiction to another substance, they encounter several barriers to appropriate diagnosis and referral. Barriers include traditional attitudes about women with addictions as well as the belief that depression, mood swings and "hysteria" are to be expected during certain periods in a woman's life. There is also a tendency to assume that women who are articulate, well-dressed and employed are not addicted to alcohol or other substances. These attitudes interfere with the appropriate diagnosis until addiction problems escalate and can no longer be ignored. They also contribute to the avoidance of interventions for a significant portion of female employees.

- Adequate health insurance is a critical issue. Women in low-paying jobs frequently have inadequate insurance coverage and limited financial resources. Therefore, it is often difficult to locate appropriate, affordable referral resources. Some married women may resist using coverage provided by their husband's insurance for fear that their use of the coverage for treatment may jeopardize his job.

- Other theories postulate that the design and basic principle of work-based programs were established largely on motivational factors determined by the needs of male employees, and that a women's primary role as the caretaker of children creates barriers to her referral for residential treatment.

- Because of women's status in many areas of the workforce, they tend to be more reluctant than men to voluntarily seek assistance from work-based programs. Many women have stated that they fear for their job security if management discovers their need for assistance.

Recommendations for Action

Alcoholism and other substance-abuse prevention and intervention programs established at the workplace can only succeed if their design includes consideration for the multiple needs of their employees. The needs of women in the workforce must be included in program planning and implementation. When work-based programs were first developed, it was assumed that a single approach was appropriate for all employees. With experience, it was shown that some employees are more likely to have access to programs and to benefit from program activities than others. When it became apparent that women's needs were not served by work-based programs as fully as the needs of men, attempts to increase women's participation focused on increasing the awareness of supervisors that intervention with women should be based on the same criteria as intervention with men.

In the late 1970s, research sponsored by NIAAA produced additional recommendations, such as the development of workplace programs that encourage women to participate in a non-threatening context.[11] In his research, Dr. Reichman found that women seemed to respond well to group discussions around issues of mutual relevance, which led to the willingness of women to respond to recommendations made by the group, including problems related to alcohol and other substances.

Some programs have attempted to provide education for women undergoing periods of stress, such as divorce or separation. Education focuses on the risk of using alcohol as a means of stress reduction. This approach, however, tends to place the onus of seeking help on women. The problems the women are experiencing may make it difficult for them to seek help. Strategies established at the workplace to provide early identification and intervention with employees should apply to women as well as to men.

In addition to traditional strategies, effective interventions with employed women may require an element of peer identification and referral. To date, there are few such programs in operation. However, one setting where specific intervention strategies are employed with a measure of success is the program established by the Flight Attendants Union. Other examples can be found in peer intervention programs established by nurses in several states.

Researchers such as Gomberg have stated that "medical complications of alcoholism are a significant issue and that it would appear that women alcoholics are more vulnerable to several medical complications. Health concerns are important motivations for women to seek treatment."[12] On this basis, coordination between work-based intervention programs and corporate medical departments would appear to enhance the possibility of interventions with women who might be missed by traditional work-based intervention models. Statistical evidence indicates that women seek services from work-based programs for problems other than those associated with addictions. This suggests that incentives for program participation, other than those in current use, may be appropriate. Assurance of confidentiality and assistance for program participants, rather than punishment, is crucial for a program's success in any setting—but especially in one where employees may view themselves as more vulnerable because of their work status.

Finally, while it may be important to identify problems and strategies for prevention and intervention programming to address common issues of women at the workplace, and while it may be easier to address women's issues as a single category, it seems equally important to recognize that different women have different needs. Therefore, as we increase our awareness regarding workplace programming to meet needs dictated by specific environmental and worker conditions, we must continue to identify women's varying roles and motivational factors, and the implications of these factors to appropriate service delivery. Equal opportunity lies not only in the ability to obtain employment, but also in the expectations placed upon employees for efficient and effective functioning. The opportunity to receive needed assistance for problems that interfere with the ability to perform appropriately at work is part of equal employment. To do less is to limit opportunities for promotion, stability and respect at the workplace.

References

1. Civil Rights Act, 1964.
2. U.S. Department of Labor, Bureau of Labor Statistics, 1989.
3. In recent years, there have been several publications that address issues of women and alcoholism. Generally, a single chapter is devoted to women at the workplace, and women's needs in that setting are addressed as if all working women have the same needs.
4. The inaccuracy of these perceptions can be seen in current shortages that are creating crises in areas such as nursing.
5. This information is based on statistical data collected by the New York State Division of Alcoholism and Alcohol Abuse, Albany, N.Y.
6. Frezza et al.: High Blood Alcohol Levels in Women. *New England Journal of Medicine*; vol. 322, no. 2; January 11, 1990: pp. 95-99.
7. Wilsnack, Sharon C. & Beckman, Linda J., (Eds.) 1984. *Alcohol Problems in Women*. NY: The Guilford Press.
8. Gomberg, Edith Lisansky et al., (Eds.) 1982. *Alcohol, Science & Society Revisited*. Ann Arbor: The University of Michigan Press.
9. Several publications and articles include a discussion of the emergence of Employee Assistance

Programs. See for example: New Directions TASK FORCE, 7 Influencing Factors on EAP Function & Practice; The ALMACAN, vol. 19, no. 5, May 1989. The EAP Assoc. (formerly ALMACA)

10. *1990 Update to the Five Year Comprehensive Plan for Alcoholism Services in New York State.*

New York State Division of Alcoholism and Alcohol Abuse, Albany, N.Y., pp. 44-53.

11. Reichman, Walter. Affecting Attitudes and Assumptions About Women and Alcohol Problems; *Alcohol Health and Research World*; 1983: vol. 7, pp. 6-10.

12. Gomberg, Edith et al.; op. cit.

17 Issues for Asian American Women

An-Pyng Sun, Ph.D.

"It is well defined in traditional Asian society that a good woman should 'obey the father when unmarried, obey the husband when married, and obey the eldest son when widowed' and that women should not confront men in a formal or major way. Such rooted admonitions often put women in many difficult situations emotionally and physically. Some Asian wives of alcoholics may feel guilty or consider themselves as betrayers when seeking help from outside sources."

It is generally considered a fact that Asian Americans have lower levels of alcohol consumption and abuse than other ethnic groups,[1,2] yet it is by no means insignificant to explore the impact of alcohol and other drug use on this population. As manifested by Asian Americans, alcohol and drug problems have their own distinctive features and natures. These idiosyncratic cultural, sociological and psychological factors should be considered in the treatment of Asian Americans. It is also worth exploring why the prevalence of alcohol and drug use among Asian Americans is relatively low to better understand the epidemiology of these problems and to develop more effective prevention and treatment strategies.

Asian American women are often doubly invisible and doubly oppressed because of their minority status in their own race and inferior role in their own family and community.[3] Few studies have been done regarding this topic, so the pain that Asian American women suffer directly or indirectly from alcohol and drug problems is usually underestimated, if not ignored.

The purpose of this chapter is to discuss how Asian American women are affected by alcohol and other drugs, what their special needs and difficulties are and how they can be better helped. In this chapter, two separate categories of Asian American women are examined: those who have alcohol and drug problems themselves and those who suffer from their husband's or partner's alcohol and drug problems.

Asian American Women Who Have Alcohol and Drug Problems

Not many studies have been conducted on Asian Americans in general, and there are fewer still on Asian American women. Studies on topics as specific as Asian American women and alcohol and drug use are quite scarce. There are no formal statistics on the incidence of Asian American women's alcohol and drug use, but it is generally known that the rate is much lower than that of their male counterparts or of women of other ethnic groups. For example, a study done by Lubben et al. on the drinking behavior of 155 male and 125 female Koreans in Los Angeles concluded that all but one of the heavy drinkers were male and more than three quarters (75.2%) of the females were abstainers.[4]

In reviewing the literature and using the public health model as a frame of reference, three elements emerge to explain the possible reason for the low rates of alcohol and drug use among Asian American women. The first element is the traditional emphasis on family versus individualism and the more restrictive definition of the female role in Asia, which consequently affects and constrains the Asian woman's attitudes and behavior towards alcohol and drug use. The second element, which may be applied to both men and women, is the Asian's belief systems, Confucianism and Taoism, which stress and advocate the concept of moderation. The third element is that Asia is traditionally a non-drinking society, unlike American society.

It is well known that Westerners are individualistic and that traditional Asians are more family-oriented. An individual's own determination and well-being tend to be the first priority in the United States, while it is the family which has the utmost power in setting the guidelines for an individual's behavior in traditional Asian society. For Asian males, drinking is acceptable—yet drunkenness is considered deviant behavior for all and especially for females. Excessive drinking is highly discouraged and all drinking is regulated by the family.[5]

Moral standards are much higher for females than for males in Asia. Many studies show that traditional Asians do not constrain drinking behavior as long as it remains moderate. However, this only applies to males and there are many more restrictions placed on the use of alcohol by women, especially young and unmarried women.[6] Confucianism, which has dominated Asian culture for thousands of years, clearly defines the behavioral appropriateness and limitations of social intercourse and interactions at each age level, between elder and junior members of a family or community and between males and females. Alcohol consumption among females (and especially drunkenness) is not accepted by society. Chinese females usually drink less frequently and smaller amounts than Chinese males.[5,7]

Another internal value which may be related to the low rate of alcoholism among Asian women is the traditional culture's emphasis on moderation, which has been suggested by many researchers.[5,8,9] Heok states, "Drinking is permitted in the Chinese family but drunkenness is frowned upon . . . Excessive consumption or disorderly behavior contravene the social mores which have been influenced since ancient time by the teachings of Confucianism and Taoism. Both these philosophies emphasize moderation, order and harmony in the society, and invariably influence Chinese attitudes towards alcohol consumption."[10]

The external environment and lifestyle, along with internal values, may be another significant element which influences Asian drinking patterns. Many studies suggest there is no drinking-centered institution in the East compared with the West.[7,11,12] Drinking is a rather common and popular phenomenon in American society—people drink at parties, at home and at bars for a variety of reasons. There is a more pervasive drinking atmosphere and more access to alcohol in America than in Asia.

However, the documented low rate of alcohol and drug problems in Asian American women should not be misconstrued or perceived as an absence of alcohol or drug problems. This low rate could very well be due to the low reporting of alcohol and drug use or the low utilization of professional mental health and social services among Asian American women. Moreover, the incidence of alcohol and drug problems may be increasing among Asian American women following their acculturation into American society. As Asian American women become acculturated, many of the traditional protective measures mentioned above, such as the emphasis on moderation and family, may be diluted or fade altogether. Research studying both male and female drinking patterns among Asian and Caucasian Americans suggests that alcohol consumption is highly related to assimilation. It is found that those Chinese and Japanese who did not speak their

mother languages and who had more generations settled in the United States had greater rates of alcohol consumption.[13] Mizuno also pointed out that the majority of female Asian patients at a program on the West Coast are third-generation Americans from families with middle-class values and educations. Nearly 80 percent of them spoke only English. The drug of choice for the women in treatment has also switched from barbiturates and opiates to cocaine.[14]

Alcohol and drug problems among Asian Americans may share many similarities with those in other ethnic groups. For example, all may begin to experiment with a drug because of curiosity or peer pressure. All may use the drug attempting to escape from the unhappiness and pain of reality. What constitutes the distinctive features of alcohol and drug problems in Asian Americans are the ethnic identity crisis and racial identity struggle in society at large and the cultural conflicts in the home.[15,16,17] As Watanabe said in an article in *Rice* magazine, "The kinds of family, social and peer pressures found among Asian Pacific (groups) are, in most respects, very different from the kinds of conflicts that adolescent Blacks, Latinos or Whites grow up with."[16]

Asian Americans are usually perceived by American society as the "model minority." Less emphasized is the subtle and quiet way they cope with the racism they suffer, their ethnic identity crisis and "marginal man" phenomenon. Some Asian Americans may have difficulty identifying with their traditional culture on one hand, yet may also be unable to become fully accepted by American society on the other.[18] Although we cannot say such an ethnic identity crisis is the direct cause of the Asian American's drug problem, many Asian Americans' alcohol and drug problems, especially at the second and subsequent generation levels, are combined with ethnic identity crises and racial discrimination. In the *Rice* article, Watanabe stated, "Drug abuse is just one of the manifestations of growing up an ethnic minority in a racist society."[16]

Cultural conflicts at home are another major source of stress for the Asian American, particularly for second-generation children. It is not uncommon that first-generation parents have very different values from their children. The parents may emphasize academic achievement where the children may perceive such striving as materialistic. The parents may consider disobedience and assertiveness as disrespectful, where the children believe it to be their only way of gaining self-respect.[18]

Another issue is the Asian American parent's attitude toward drug use. In the *Rice* article, Watanabe stated that Japanese American parents have a dramatically different view of drug use from their children. "What is innocent fun for one, is the end of the family name to another, and reaches proportions of near hysteria."[16] In the same article, Inabe stated that "Asian American parents tend to feel that their children's struggles are a reflection on themselves and a reflection of the failure of the family system."

Asian American Women Whose Husbands Have Alcohol and Drug Problems

For some Asian American women, especially new immigrants with limited education, minimal working skills and low family income, the alcohol and drug problems they suffer usually do not originate with themselves but with their alcohol- and drug-using spouses. It is well recognized that alcoholism and drug dependencies are family diseases.[19,20,21] Not only does the drug-dependent individual suffer the consequences of his behavior, his non-drug-dependent family members will also be affected. Like the spouses of alcoholics and drug users in other ethnic groups, many Asian women experience emotional, verbal, physical and financial abuse resulting from their husbands' drinking and drug-using behaviors. "He scolds me without any reason," "He said that I'm crazy," "He threw a telephone at my head," "He told me to watch out because he will stab me with a knife someday," "He hasn't brought home any money for months"—these were just some of the experiences reported by Asian women with alcohol- and drug-using husbands. For the new immigrant, the pain and suffering resulting from a spouse's alcohol or drug dependency usually are exacerbated by having to cope with a new environment, new challenges, and the unique cultural legacy in which Asian Americans struggle between traditional moral restrictions and their desire for survival and individual well-being.

Since the Immigration Act of 1965, a large number of Asians have immigrated to the United States, with Asian women either arriving with their husbands or following at a later time. By 1980, at least half of the Asian American population in the United States was composed of new immigrants.[22] For example, 80 percent of the Korean Americans in the United States have immigrated in the last fifteen years.[4]

Much effort is demanded of the immigrant to adapt to the new host country. The new immigrant usually has to adjust to many challenges and to overcome many obstacles in order to survive, such as culture shock (different values and perspectives), language barriers, lack of marketable job skills, financial pressure, changing parent-child relationships (children may acculturate much faster than parents), unfamiliarity with school and other social systems, and the lack of network resources (fewer relatives and close friends available in the U.S.). On top of all these pressures, if the husband starts showing signs of alcohol or drug problems and

begins failing to perform his share of responsibilities, the emotional stress and financial pressure of trying to maintain the vitality of the family could be overwhelming to the Asian American woman. The stress is increased by the emotional, physical or legal intimidation of her by her alcohol- or drug-using husband.

Cultural legacy is another significant element in understanding the new immigrant Asian woman's stress resulting from her husband's alcohol or drug problem. Asian women are less likely than those in other ethnic groups to refer their husbands to treatment, and they often have very little power to openly urge their husbands to stop drinking or seek treatment. For some other ethnic groups of women with alcohol- or drug-dependent husbands, the act of seeking help for themselves or their husbands, even if this means separation or divorce, is more easily accepted as a means of self-protection. For the Asian American woman, however, it is much harder to make such a decision and to take such an action, because of both the cultural legacy and the complex immigration contexts.[23,24]

It is well defined in traditional Asian society that a good woman should "obey the father when unmarried, obey the husband when married, and obey the eldest son when widowed" and that women should not confront men in a formal or major way. Such rooted admonitions often put women in many difficult situations emotionally and physically. Some Asian wives of alcoholics may feel guilty or consider themselves as betrayers when seeking help from outside sources. Many Asian women, especially those with low incomes or minimal job skills, are insecure both financially and emotionally, and are afraid that they are going to lose everything—their home, their children, their financial support—if they ask for a divorce. The ethnic community may also tend to view the husband's abuse problems as his wife's fault. Therefore, when an Asian woman leaves her husband, she not only loses him, she loses the support of her community, including his and sometimes even her own family.

Intervening with Asian American Women

It is important to be knowledgeable about and sensitive to Asian American women's special needs and difficulties in relation to alcohol and drug problems when providing services to this population. Based on the information above, the following suggestions are offered in order to more effectively serve Asian American women.

At the service delivery level, it is critical to have bilingual and bicultural professionals available for newly arrived Asian women. As mentioned earlier, over half of the Asian American women currently in the United States are immigrants who came within the last

10 ⟨...⟩ gue is not English. F⟨...⟩ ⟨...⟩ian Americans ⟨...⟩ foreign born. Languag⟨...⟩ ⟨...⟩s often prevent the immigrant from seeking help.[25] Many studies have indicated that language and/or cultural barriers are prominent factors that result in the low utilization of mental health and social services among Asian Americans.[26]

The services need to be easily accessible. They should be offered in the immediate community and be delivered during flexible hours, since many immigrants' willingness to seek help decreases when they have to spend long hours in traveling to an agency or waiting for services, or have to take off from work frequently.

The setting should be designed in a personal rather than rigid way. When naming a new agency, it is helpful to think more in terms of "health" and less of "treatment." As mentioned earlier, Asians tend to be more sensitive to and fearful of the label of "mental illness" or "psychiatric dysfunction" than Westerners. Staff attitudes, including those of the administrative and clerical staff, must be sensitive to these issues, so that the stigma of coming for services can be reduced.

For professionals in the alcohol and drug field working with second or later generation Asian women, whether within the ethnic community or in a general setting with a mixed population, several areas are important. In order to be effective, professionals must be sensitized to the problems of racism from which their Asian clients may suffer. They need to help Asian American women re-establish self-confidence, self-acceptance, assertiveness and their ethnic and cultural identities. Service providers will also need to assist the woman's family in working through intergenerational cultural conflicts, as well as attitudes and feelings towards alcohol and drug problems and treatment, so that the women receiving services can communicate with and have the support of their families.

When working with the newly arrived Asian woman, professionals may need to be sensitive to a number of points. The needs of the woman should not be ignored or understated when the alcohol or drug abuser is the husband. Women with alcohol- or drug-dependent husbands who resist or reject services should still be considered in need of help. Asian women's strong feelings of guilt, shame and betrayal, which are embedded in their traditional role, need to be acknowledged and acted upon. A "system orientation" or "life model" approach may be most useful when working with newly immigrated Asian women. The problems and needs of these women must be viewed and assessed within the context of their cultural and immigrant status. Their problems and needs should not

be diagnosed as pathologies isolated from those contexts. Basic social services such as arranging child day care, helping to mediate between families and school authorities, providing training in job skills and language, and aiding in applying for medical assistance or legal advocacy may need to be provided in order to realistically help newly arrived Asian women. In addition, it is believed that Asians tend to value concrete or practical help more than abstract services like "counseling" or "talk therapy." Finally, extreme caution is needed when applying the concept of "co-dependence" to the newly arrived Asian woman with an alcoholic or drug using husband. The difficulties the women face in becoming individualized and independent may be rooted in their traditional roles and cultural legacy rather than because they are the wife of an alcohol- or drug-dependent man. The reality of the Asian American woman's cultural legacy must be acknowledged to ensure the most effective delivery of services.

References

1. Klatsky, A.L., Siegelaub, A., Landy, C. and Friedman, G. "Racial Patterns of Alcoholic Beverage Use," *Alcoholism: Clinical and Experimental Research*, Vol. 7, 1983, pp. 372-377.
2. Chi, I., Kitano, H.H.L. and Lubben, J.E. "Male Chinese Drinking Behavior in Los Angeles," *Journal of Studies on Alcohol*, Vol. 49, No. 1, 1988, pp. 21-25.
3. Fujitomi, I. and Wong, D. "The New Asian-American Woman," in S. Sue and N.N. Wagner (eds) *Asian-American Psychological Perspectives*, Palo Alto, California: Science & Behavior Books, Inc, 1973, pp. 252-263.
4. Lubben, James E., Chi., I., and Kitano, H. "The Relative Influence of Selected Social Factors on Korean Drinking Behavior in Los Angeles," *Advances in Alcohol & Substance Abuse*, Vol. 8, No. 1, 1989, pp. 1-17.
5. Barnett, M.L. "Alcoholism in the Cantonese of New York City: An Anthropological Study," in O. Diethelm and C.C. Thomas (eds) *Etiology of Chronic Alcoholism*, Springfield, Illinois: Charles C. Thomas Publisher, 1955, pp. 179-227.
6. Taylor, J. "Activities of the Scholar in Residence for Studies on Alcoholism," in W.T. Liu and P. Flattery (eds) *The Pacific/Asian American Mental Health Research Center, A Decade Review*, Chicago: The Pacific/Asian American Mental Health Research Center, the Univeristy of Illinois at Chicago, 1987, pp. 133-143.
7. Singer, K. "Drinking Patterns and Alcoholism in the Chinese," in M. Marshall (ed), *Beliefs, Behaviors, and Alcoholic Beverages*, Ann Arbor,

Michigan: The University of Michigan Press, 1979, pp. 313-326.

8. Chafetz, M.E. "Consumption of Alcohol in the Far and Middle East," *New England Journal of Medicine*, Vol. 271, 1964, pp. 297-301.

9. Singer, K. "The Choice of Intoxicant Among the Chinese," *British Journal of Addiction*, Vol. 69, 1974, pp. 257-268.

10. Heok, K.E. "Drinking in Chinese Culture: Old Stereotypes Re-examined," *British Journal of Addiction*, Vol. 82, 1987, pp. 224-225.

11. Wong, R.P. "A Study of Alcoholism in Chinatown," *International Journal of Social Psychiatry*, No. 14, 1968, pp. 260-265.

12. Yu, E.S.H., and Liu, W.T. "Alcohol Use and Abuse among Chinese-Americans, Epidemiologic Data," *Alcohol Health & Research World*, Vol 11, No. 2, Winter 1986/87, pp. 14-18.

13. Sue, S., Zane, N. and Ito, J. "Alcohol Drinking Patterns Among Asian and Caucasian Americans," Journal of Cross-Cultural Psychology, Vol. 10, No. 1, March 1979, pp. 41-56.

14. Mizuno, A., Residential Treatment Director, Asian American Drug Abuse Program, Los Angeles, CA, 1988. Interview with the author.

15. Mizuno, A., Residential Treatment Director, Asian American Drug Abuse Program, Los Angeles, CA, 1990. Interview with the author.

16. Marshall, B. "A War Against Drugs," *Rice*, August 1988, pp. 36-37.

17. Watanabe, M., Executive Director, Asian American Drug Abuse Program, Los Angeles, CA, 1990. Interview with the author.

18. Sue, S., and Sue, D.W. "Chinese-American Personality and Mental Health," in Sue, S. and Wagner, N.N. (eds) *Asian-American Psychological Perspectives*, Palo Alto, CA: Science & Behavior Books, Inc, 1973, pp. 111-124.

19. Cruse, S.W. *Another Chance*, CA: Science and Behavior Book, Inc. 1989.

20. Johnson, V.E. *Intervention*, MI: Johnson Institute, 1986.

21. Metzger, L. *From Denial to Recovery*, CA: Jossey-Bass Limited, 1988.

22. 1980 Federal Census.

23. Rubien, D. "For Asians in U.S., Hidden Family Strife," *The New York Times*, January 11, 1989.

24. Lum, J. "Battered Asian Women," *Rice*, March 1988, pp. 50-52.

25. Yu, E., and Liu, W. "The Underutilization of Mental Health Services by Asian Americans: Implications for Manpower Training," in Liu, W.T. (ed) *The Pacific/Asian American Mental Health Research Center, A Decade Review*, 1987, pp. 19-28.

26. Shon, S.P. and Ja, D.Y. "Asian Families," in M. McGoldrick, J.K. Pearce, and J. Giordano (eds) *Ethnicity and Family Therapy*, New York: The Guilford Press, 1982, pp. 208-228.

18 Linkages: Battering, Sexual Assault, Incest, Child Sexual Abuse, Teen Pregnancy, Dropping Out of School and the Alcohol and Drug Connection

Beth Glover Reed, Ph.D.

"Usually, we address the single problem of concern to the type of agency for which we work and perhaps explore another problem if its presence is obvious. . . . We tend to overlook problems we do not anticipate. Alcohol and other drug use is implicated often enough in other problems that its presence and effects must be assessed routinely."

Mary is a 32-year-old woman with four children: Jerry, 16; Sandra, 14; Teddy, 12 and Sonia, 6. Temporarily, they all live in a shelter for battered women and children—their third stay at the shelter in five years. Mary is working with shelter staff to find a steady job and affordable housing so she and the children can live separate from her husband and their father, Michael, who provided most of the family's financial support during the 16-year marriage.

Mary's story will illustrate how alcohol and other drugs interrelate with many other problems in women's lives. Her tale also shows how existing advocacy and service systems fail to effectively address these issues. This chapter combines an overview of issues and relevant research with a more detailed discussion of the problems Mary faces and the implications of her situation for other women and for women's centers. These implications are discussed using three categories of possible interventions women's centers could implement, depending on their goals:

Primary prevention: Programs that 1) strengthen the environment or the individual's ability to become healthy or resist developing problems; or 2) reduce environmental or individual risk factors that contribute to the problems. Environment is defined as both larger and smaller systems—countries, communities and families.

Secondary prevention: Programs that reduce the duration or severity of problem-causing circumstances.

This category usually includes 1) early identification of developing problems, thereby reducing contributing factors, and earlier intervention; or 2) crisis intervention, usually quick, intense intervention with early symptoms.

Tertiary prevention: Actions or programs that reduce the long-term negative consequences of a problem or disease. Treatment and rehabilitation programs usually fall into this category, since they are designed to arrest an existing problem.

An Overview

Mary's story illustrates a number of ways in which the use of psychoactive chemicals and other types of social problems can be intertwined. Each topic is complicated in itself and the links between each of them and the use of alcohol and other drugs cannot be fully covered in one chapter.

However, linking them in one chapter can help identify common questions, concerns and omissions in existing theory, literature, and research. Like Mary, many women experience several, sometimes all, of these life crises but must seek help from agencies that work with only one or two of the problems. To fully assist women and children to become survivors, agency personnel must recognize and be able to work with the ways various problems interconnect.

More information about ethnic, cultural or other

characteristics might change perceptions and conclusions about Mary's situation. What if Mary came from a devout Irish Catholic family, but Michael's family were Protestants who traced their lineage to the Mayflower? What if they lived in an inner-city *barrio?* What if they were Black, or one was Black and the other White? What if they were a lesbian couple?

Mary's situation shows the potential interrelationships of problems and how the current system often handles them. Important elements will be identified within several clusters of problems. Finally, aspects unique to each area will be indicated. Some major research and service questions will be found throughout the text.

MARY AND MICHAEL

Mary was very much in love with Michael during the early years of their marriage despite substantial stress in their lives. Michael was attending night school, they had three young children and very little money. She overlooked his periodic moodiness and withdrawal, and even the times he became so enraged he punched the wall or broke furniture. She saw these outbursts as stress reactions and assumed they would disappear when he finished school, when they were more financially stable, or when the children were older. Between these periods, he was considerate and appreciative of her efforts on behalf of the family.

Mary drank only occasionally when the couple socialized with their small circle of friends—some from high school and some from Michael's work. Michael drank more than Mary. He often stopped for a beer on the way home from work and regularly had a martini or scotch before dinner. He also used marijuana occasionally with friends. Mary saw several friends during the day—a neighbor and parents of her children's friends. Michael didn't like these friends, so they rarely saw them as a couple.

Over the past 10 years, Mary called the local women's center's 24-hour crisis line for several types of assistance. First, to inquire about how to apply for emergency financial aid when Michael was laid off. He was angry, depressed and drinking more heavily. Sometimes he disappeared for several days. Violent episodes increased and during this period he struck her for the first time.

Again, she worried about his enormous stress, made excuses to her family about her bruises and worked harder to provide comfort for Michael. She experienced great anxiety too, especially when there was no food for the children or her older son cried about wearing shoes that were too small. She kept this from Michael in order not to upset him further.

She told her doctor of this anxiety when he treated her for bronchitis. Mary was grateful he prescribed tranquilizers with six months of refills to help her through this period. Tranquilizers helped, but she only fully forgot her problems when she also had an afternoon drink or two with a friend. This made her feel quite giddy and enabled her to face yet another dinner of macaroni and cheese. The crisis center had helped her get extra government cheese following a call during which she alternately cried and giggled about the ridiculous state of her life.

The violence increased in frequency and duration. During one episode, Michael slapped and punched her several times, then lunged at Jerry who was begging him to stop. Mary again called the crisis center for assistance. The crisis worker called the police and told Mary about the domestic violence shelter. The police calmed Michael and advised Mary and the children to spend the night with relatives until he "sobered up."

Michael was remorseful and loving the next day when Mary called from her mother's house. He explained he'd had two difficult job interviews and was rejected for one job he'd wanted badly. He promised to work harder to control his drinking and said he would never hurt the children. Mary wanted to believe him and was relieved that he sounded more like the Michael she loved.

Staying at her mother's house made Mary uneasy. It was too small for four extra people; besides, Mary felt she and Michael should handle their own problems. Also, her relationship with her stepfather was strained.

Mary had never told her mother or sister about her stepfather's repeated attempts to fondle her after several beers, or about the two times he raped her while they were alone and she forgot to lock the bathroom door. She was deeply ashamed of these episodes and believed that, with more vigilance, she could have prevented his advances. Also, she did not want to upset her mother who was left emotionally devastated and broke after the death of her first husband. Mary recalled late night arguments between her mother and father before he was killed in an alcohol-related accident when she was eight. She also remembered her mother's nervousness and sometimes slurred speech after the arguments.

Her mother seemed happier in her new marriage and the adolescent Mary did not wish to threaten that happiness. Instead, she stayed home as little as possible, spending more time with Michael. She was pretty and he was thrilled when she agreed to go out with him (she was 14 and he, 15).

They had been together ever since. At first, he treated her almost with reverence and she adored him for his gentleness and concern. As he became more certain of her feelings, he pressured her to relieve his tension by having sex. She felt guilty denying him. One night, after consuming most of a bottle of wine while watching TV at his parents' house, she did not struggle as he tore at her clothes and penetrated her.

After that, they spent less time with their friends and had sex regularly. Mary enjoyed the physical contact with someone who loved her and felt more attractive and grown up, less shy and awkward, now that she had a steady boyfriend. She asked him several times about birth control but did not protest when he failed to use a condom. She was afraid to discuss this with her mother and did not feel close enough to a physician to seek assistance. After about six months she became pregnant.

As her suspicions grew, she alternated between terror about what would happen and pride in the new life growing within her. She finally told Michael. First, he was angry.

Her despair and shame increased when a friend said Michael bragged about his manhood to some friends. As the pregnancy progressed, she became more withdrawn and her mother began to suspect something. The family physician confirmed her pregnancy. After a conference between Mary's stepfather and Michael's father, Michael agreed to get married.

Mary attended a special school for a while, secretly proud of her changing body and the open envy of some of her old high school friends. Michael took a job after school and they lived with his parents until the baby came. Then they both dropped out of school, she to care for the baby and he to work full-time.

Mary was aware that Michael felt he had made many sacrifices for her in his life and she still was crazy about him when things were going well. Therefore, it took very little pleading to persuade her to return home when she first tried to flee his violence.

Several weeks later, they were both excited when Michael found another job that paid better than his last. They began paying off bills. Mary cut back on her tranquilizer use and made plans to take night classes. She wanted to earn her GED so she could seek employment when the children got older.

To her surprise, Michael was not enthusiatic about her return to school. He insisted he and the children needed her at home. He worried she would meet "man-hating" women and get crazy new ideas. She insisted on taking one course per term and he grudgingly agreed to pay so long as things ran smoothly at home. She persevered, although she had to withdraw during two semesters—once because she fell behind because of the children's repeated illnesses and another time when the family moved because Michael was promoted, with a significant increase in salary. When Mary made plans to find paid work, Michael grew increasingly agitated and talked of having another child.

The periods of moodiness and irritation that sometimes led to physical violence still occurred, but less frequently. Mary was therefore reluctant to risk confronting Michael about his lack of emotional support. She knew he resented the time her classes took away from the family, but she desperately wanted to finish her education. She felt guilty about this, and worked hard on meals, birthday parties and running the house well so her time away would be less difficult for the family. She did her school work late at night, drinking black coffee and sometimes taking a pill donated by a classmate to help her stay awake. Sometimes Michael would interrupt her studying, angrily demand sex and drag her into the bedroom. One of those nights, she became pregnant again.

The violence increased before and after Sonia was born. One night, after Michael kicked and shoved her down the stairs, Mary finally called the shelter and took the children there. The children cried to return to their father, their toys, their school and their friends. Mary gave in when Michael promised never to hit her again.

For a while, things were better. Then Michael began to stop at the local bar regularly with some friends. He gained weight, tried to diet and criticized Mary and the children for any disruption to his routine. Teddy's counselor at

school contacted Mary to express concern about the boy's falling grades and to say Teddy had gotten into several fights and had been surly with the teacher who broke them up. Mary promised to talk with him, so the counselor did not press her about what might be bothering Teddy.

Mary's concern for her children's safety grew, especially as Sandra approached adolescence. Mary overheard Michael telling a colleague how pretty Sandra was, although he refused to allow her to date, and he slapped both of them when Mary tried to convince him Sandra was old enough. Mary took more tranquilizers while she tried to keep peace.

Mary became depressed for several months, and on the advice of her physician, sought counseling. The counselor thought Michael might be alcoholic and suggested she attend Al-Anon. He worked with Mary to recognize and address her codependency. For a short period, he also put her on anti-depressant medication. Mary didn't like the way the medication made her feel, so she stopped taking it. She attended Al-Anon for several months and worked hard to identify her own needs and her contribution to the family problems.

One evening when Mary returned from class, she found Sandra crying in her bedroom—her clothing torn in several places. Mary knew Michael and several friends had planned to play cards in the kitchen. Gradually, she pieced together the story from the sobbing teen. Jerry had gone out with friends while Sandra kept Teddy and Sonia in their bedrooms. The card game grew louder and more boisterous as the players drank up a refrigerator full of beer. As the game broke up, Michael fell heavily asleep on the couch. Sandra thought everyone had gone, so she left her bedroom to clean the house before her mother got home. She was frightened when Fred, one of the players, came out of the bathroom. She was unable to wake her father and Fred saw her before she could disappear. He grabbed her, slapped her and told her he would hurt the other children if she made noise. He tore her clothes, pulled off her pants, and had wrestled her to the floor when he heard Jerry's car. He hurriedly got up, warned her again to keep quiet and ran out.

Mary comforted her daughter, who was especially upset because she had failed to carefully check that everyone had left. Mary didn't know what to do, so she called the on-call counselor at the shelter. The counselor asked if Sandra was physically hurt, told her about the local rape crisis service and suggested she call the police, file a report and collect evidence in case they decided to press charges. She said the rape program could send someone to help them talk with police. Sandra was mortified and didn't want to talk about it, especially since nothing "really" happened. Mary tried to talk with Michael about it. She was worried it might happen again unless he watched his friends carefully. He grew angry and accused her of inventing the whole thing, claiming she was jealous of his friends. He interrogated Sandra until she begged for everyone to forget it.

Mary moved the children to the shelter again two years after her first stay there, after Michael slashed the living room furniture and chased Jerry upstairs with a knife. Mary had drunk several beers on her way home from school, which infuriated Michael. The police treated Mary rudely when they arrived in response to a neighbor's call. They suggested Michael take a walk and muttered something about her sobering up. When they left, Mary collected the children's things quickly, fearing Michael would return. A shelter worker met them several blocks from their house and took them to the shelter.

Mary was determined not to return home out of concern for the children, but she still cared about her husband when he was the "old" Michael. Several discouraging weeks of searching failed to turn up housing she could afford on her welfare assistance and a meager part-time salary. When Michael agreed to seek counseling for his alcohol problems, she returned home again—despite shelter staff's worries about her safety.

For about two months, Michael saw a counselor in an out-patient alcoholism program and attended several AA meetings. He felt he learned a lot about alcoholism and that he could manage the consequences of his drinking. In counseling and at AA meetings, the violence was discussed only as a part of his drinking. As part of their intake process, alcoholism program staff interviewed Mary but did not ask her about violent behaviors or if she and the children needed assistance. She was required to attend educational sessions for family members where her understanding grew regarding ways that families can enable drinking behavior. She learned how she could provide support for Michael's recovery.

The night Mary left home for the shelter the third time, Michael had thrown her on the bed and raped her while Sandra ran to a neighbor's house for help. This time, the police took them all to the shelter after telling Michael to leave the house for a couple of hours. Jerry wanted to stay home and fight his father, but Mary convinced him to remain with his brother and sisters.

Mary is determined not to return to Michael this time. His behavior has become increasingly unpredictable and he rarely acts like the person she married. She suspects he now uses cocaine occasionally. A restraining order prohibits him from contact with her or the children. He has filed for child custody and she is terrified he might win since he is in a better position financially. Although she now has one year of college credit, Mary has little paid employment experience, cannot afford quality child care for her youngest child and feels even the older children still require substantial amounts of her time. She fears Michael will remove her and the children from his health care coverage.

Mary's own drinking and escalated use of tranquilizers concerns her. But the oblivion she sometimes reaches is the only time she can stop worrying if she and the children will survive. Since she arrived at the shelter, she has not had a drink. She's aware that another resident was asked to leave when she returned inebriated after an afternoon of searching for housing. Fearing the same fate, Mary has not mentioned her concerns about drugs to staff or in the support group. The shelter advocates do not believe Michael's use of chemicals helps cause his violence and Mary has not explored this topic with them.

Her advocate suggested Mary contact the displaced homemaker program on the other side of the county for assistance in finding a job. After lengthy travel by bus to the program, Mary filled out their initial assessment form. She would like to take their 8-week job-finding course, but worries about how long the children would be left alone. She noted that the assessment form asked about her use of alcohol and tranquilizers, if her former partner has substance-abuse problems, and even about alcohol and other drug consumption in her family while she was growing up. Answering the questions made her think about whether her parents had drug problems, the effects of Michael's alcoholism and her worries about her own use. She hoped she could discuss some of this when she saw a counselor or was able to take the course.

Gender Roles and Stereotypes

Understanding of the social problems, life events and criminal acts discussed in this chapter requires knowledge of gender roles, expectations, stereotypes and the societal value assigned to both sexes. Thorough coverage of these issues is beyond the scope of one chapter, but several useful examples are offered.

Role Expectations

Most people share strong societal stereotypes about gender roles and which characteristics are expected and accepted for each. These stereotypes affect how we perceive behaviors and evaluate ourselves and others. Typically, we have interpreted the use of alcohol and other drugs to fit and perpetuate these stereotypes. As a result, the use of alcohol often obscures the role that gender-related stereotypes and beliefs play—both in these problem areas and in maintaining women's lower status and men's power in relationships and society. Conversely, the presence of gender-related stereotypes about alcohol and other drugs can prevent recognition of and intervention in other problem behaviors.

For instance, Mary, Michael and their families strongly defined her role as taking care of Michael and the children. As a result, Mary feels responsible, guilty and even depressed when a family member is unhappy or in trouble, and others may even blame her. When she seeks help, she is "treated" for the depression with a drug, while her assumptions about responsibility for others' feelings go unchallenged. As the male "breadwinner," Michael was devastated about his job loss and is threatened by Mary's wish to augment their income. They and others excused his drinking and violence as a man's way of dealing with stress, rather than as an abusive way to maintain power and control in his life and in his relationship with Mary.

Also consistent with gender roles and status is that as an adolescent, Michael felt a great need to prove his manhood, first by acquiring a beautiful girl, then by

demonstrating his sexual prowess. He felt little responsibility for birth control, which he saw as the woman's
responsibility. His use of alcohol and other drugs is
expected masculine behavior, as is his belief that he
deserves sexual services. Mary's self-esteem was tied to
being desired by a man that she dared not risk losing.
Her self-worth is linked to pleasing her partner and
meeting his needs and the needs of family members
and friends. She is unable to refuse his sexual advances
or to insist they use birth control. Her alcohol use gives
her an excuse to violate society's "nice girl" expectations. Being pregnant and being a mother validates her
worth as a woman in a society that offers women very
few other unconflicted role options. Her teenage
pregnancy and the subsequent disruption of her
education makes attainment of economic self-suffi-
ciency less likely and increases her economic dependence on Michael. Homophobic attitudes help perpetuate rigid gender stereotypes, as Michael illustrates
when he worries that Mary will meet man-hating
women. Alcohol and other drug use lubricates all these
interactions and events.

The use of alcohol and illegal drugs is more
acceptable for men than women and the resulting
stigma may prevent women from seeking help for
problematic use. They and others may be less likely to
recognize problematic use until it becomes severe.
This stigma also causes others to feel a woman deserves
whatever happens to her while she is intoxicated, or
even if she has just "had a few," as the police showed in
Mary's case.

On the other hand, the acceptability of prescribing
drugs to women for anxiety and depression rather than
addressing the reasons for the anxiety and depression
means physicians often miss signs of drinking problems
in women. This perpetuates the use of chemicals to
"solve" or avoid problems rather than address them.
For a while, prescribed medications, alcohol or illegal
drugs may help a woman cope with reactions to trauma
and anxiety and give her a sense of control in her life.
Over a longer period, however, they are likely to
prevent her from recognizing she is not to blame for her
circumstances, and may interfere with her ability to
take actions to reduce her shame, increase her
self-esteem and improve her situation.

Gender-related Societal Status

Women's roles and women have less social worth
than men and men's roles. Some even argue women's
major societal value is to reproduce the human species
and be owned by men and provide them service—
through sex, through home-making and by bearing and
raising children. Violence by men against women (and
children) has long been tolerated by society—either
defined as men's right, or perceived as a private family

problem and no one else's business. Violence and other
socially disapproved behaviors are seen as a common
consequence of alcohol consumption. The courts often
fail to hold men accountable for illegal or destructive,
irresponsible behaviors that occur while they are
intoxicated. Feminists have worked hard to gain public
and legal acceptance of rape or assault as forms of
violence and not as sexual behavior or a man's right.
This process has been greatly complicated by the
accepted beliefs about alcohol.

Victims, especially women, are still often blamed
and stigmatized for criminal acts against them and
thought to secretly enjoy being violated. Societal
beliefs about women and alcohol strengthen this
stigmatization when a woman has an alcohol problem
and is also raped or beaten. Some feminist theorists
believe this acceptance of violence against women and
the link of violence to sexuality keeps women subservi-
ent and in their "proper" roles.[1] Gender-linked beliefs
about alcohol (and other drugs) also perpetuate status
differencess between women and men.

Mary and Michael both believe he has a right to
expect sex when he wants it and to be angry and
abusive if Mary's housekeeping doesn't meet his
standards. Mary believes she was responsible for her
stepfather's assaultive behavior. Both she and Sandra
feel deep shame and guilt about being sexually
assaulted. Such beliefs prevent women and others from
perceiving their victimization and from recognizing
that no one deserves to be beaten or sexually assaulted.
Drug use is one way to endure intolerable situations.
Since she does not believe she deserves better, Mary
does not take steps to remove herself from the situation
or to prosecute Michael, Michael's friend, Fred, or her
stepfather for sexual assault. Meanwhile, since Michael
can attribute his actions to chemical use, he is not
required to feel responsible for them or to experience
the guilt and disapproval of others.

Women's lower status also means society doesn't
value "women's work," therefore women have fewer
economic opportunities. If they have no male partner,
women often must live in poverty with their
children.[2,3] Less education makes this more likely.
Threat of severe economic disruption keeps women
from leaving their assailants and interferes with getting
the help they need such as transportation and health
care. Mary legitimately worries about the economic
consequences for her children if her marriage breaks
up. This contributes to her need to use chemicals to
cope. She also believes Michael's earning power may
influence the judge's determination of custody. Mary
fears any admission of a drug or alcohol problem would
jeopardize her chances of retaining custody, especially
if the judge shares societal stereotypes about women
who drink.

Women's centers and others concerned with prevention and intervention in these problems need to name, educate about and work to change the intertwined societal structures, beliefs and their consequences, which often go unrecognized in programs intended to prevent or treat chemical dependency. Similarly, feminist activists don't often perceive the "chemical connections" in the perpetuation of societal patterns and stereotypes. This two-sided lack of recognition means major contributors to developing problems and barriers to recovery and survival are not addressed by either women's centers or chemical dependency programs.

In primary prevention activities, information about these interrelationships should be included in community education efforts to influence goals and strategies for social change. Individual and smaller system skill training should include this information to promote self-help techniques such as assertiveness about contraception and self-defense skills. In secondary prevention activities, knowledge about interrelationships should help potential interveners recognize signs of trouble more quickly and help them intervene in ways that limit the negative effects of gender stereotypes. In tertiary prevention activities, gender information can be incorporated into treatment activities, support groups and other programming designed to help people reach optimal circumstances after experiencing one or more problems. This information will help people understand the societal contributors to these problems, resist their negative effects and revise the ways that they think about themselves and their relationships.

Research, Data, and Methodology

While research in each of these problem areas has developed exponentially over the past several years, earlier research was flawed by gender-biased assumptions and methods and other methodological problems. Questions were asked of women that were not asked of men, for instance about children, birth control, or "deviant" sexual behaviors such as incest, rape or promiscuity—or conversely—employability. Gender-biased researchers created designs and interpreted data in ways consistent with their assumptions. Therefore, the topics in this chapter were often labeled as forms of deviance in girls and women or as the result of moral lapses. In other cases, data on women were collapsed with data on men so gender differences could not be examined. Or women were assumed to be men's opposites, so little data was collected on women.

Our knowledge of the interrelationships between these problems is also limited by the assumption that alcoholism and drug abuse are primarily male problems, and the tendency to ignore prescription drug addiction as a problem. The first wave of gender-

sensitive research on alcohol and other drugs pointed out the omissions, limitations and biases in our existing knowledge and services. The second wave of research defined ways women with chemical dependency problems were similar to or differed from similarly afflicted men, and sometimes contrasted with women who had no alcohol and other drug problems. The interrelationships among these topics are only beginning to be addressed as the research moves to more complex studies of addiction.

Researchers of battering, rape, incest, adolescent pregnancy, or dropping out of school have tried to study the role(s) alcohol and other drugs play in other problems, but the imprecise and incomplete methods used to measure chemical use have limited understanding of the interrelationships and prevented its application to intervention planning. While many studies note the use of alcohol or other drugs, they rarely include information about the amount, frequency or types of use and less about use patterns or their relationship to other problems. However, when studies are designed by researchers knowledgeable about alcohol and other drugs, the measures of chemical use and dependency may be better. But researchers are likely to note only the presence of the other problems, rather than the interrelationship.

A reason is that researchers are rarely knowledgeable about more than one or two topics. They focus on a problem or event and not its connection to other problems and events. They often assume causality consistent with their particular theory or perspective, rather than creating designs with variables that can explore ways multiple characteristics, problems and events might interrelate.

The few existing studies that include multiple variables suggest complicated patterns of relationships among them and that interventions need to take multiple factors into account. We are better able now to identify the questions that must still be asked about the nature of these relationships than we are able to provide "answers."

The Interrelationships/Linkages

The literature presents some evidence for many types of relationships among life problems. The presence of a relationship is clear—the nature is not.

For instance, a high proportion of studies of battered women and their assailants report the presence of alcohol or other drugs—estimates range from 40 to 95 percent.[4] In one study, 41 percent of the children from violent homes report they believe their fathers had a drinking problem and were more abusive when drinking.[5]

In child sexual assault and incest cases, recent studies report 33 to 73 percent were associated with alcohol consumption and approximately 50 percent of the perpetrators had addiction problems.[6,7] In some studies, 60-70 percent of incest victims report their father was drinking the first time incest occurred.[8] Some studies of rape indicate about half of the offenders had been drinking and 24 percent of the victims were drugged, often to unconsciousness.[9] A high proportion of women seeking treatment for alcohol and drug problems have experienced incest or childhood sexual abuse.[10] Some all-women programs report as much as 90 percent.

Researchers also report the use of alcohol and other drugs is associated with premarital intercourse for unmarried male and female teenage parents.[11] Teen pregnancy and marriage are significant factors in dropping out of school.[12] Those who do not complete high school often use alcohol and other drugs both before and after they drop out.[13]

These figures represent only some that are available describing the concurrence of alcohol and other drug use with the other problem areas. What role does alcohol and other drug use play? Are alcohol and other drug problems and other problems "caused" by a third set of factors? To what degree is chemical dependency implicated in the incidence of these other events and crimes? To what degree is chemical dependency a condition resulting from other problems? How do the patterns for women differ from those of men?

Answers to all of these questions are important for the design of primary prevention programs, which usually aim to prevent problems by reducing factors that contribute to them. Knowledge of causes is also important in secondary and tertiary programs. If the causes are still present, they may need to be addressed before a person can resume a productive life.

The Contribution of Alcohol and Other Drug Use to Other Problems

At least three general types of theories and data stress the role of problems with alcohol and other drugs in the development of other problems. One type focuses on the effects of growing up with a chemically dependent parent (or parents). A second examines the effects of alcohol and other drug consumption on learning, role development and adaptive coping, especially if heavy use occurs at particular developmental periods. A third set seeks to explain why the presence of alcohol, in particular, seems to increase the likelihood of behaviors that are normally not considered acceptable.

Family-of-origin Theories

Research, descriptions of clinical experience, and popular publications appear every day describing characteristics of families and children of alcoholics or addicted persons.[14-20] Chemically dependent or otherwise dysfunctional parents or families that function according to behaviors, roles and norms learned by parents from chemically dependent families, leave children at risk for many types of other difficulties in childhood and in later life.

For instance, incest, child sexual assault, domestic violence and other forms of child abuse occur more frequently in homes with significant substance-abuse problems.[7,21,22] Adolescents who are children of chemically dependent families and/or victims of incest are more likely to run away, engage in prostitution, have difficulties with school, relationships or drugs, exhibit violent behavior, attempt suicide and experience difficulty with sexuality and intimacy.[23] They are also more likely to be sexually active and therefore more at risk of early pregnancy.[11]

These families often create unsafe environments in which children cannot develop self-esteem or learn coping behaviors that help them make good decisions and plan for a socially productive future. Family members organize to try to control the addiction or protect themselves from its effects, so attending to a child's needs may become secondary. The types of family dynamics listed in the references and cited earlier include imbalances in responsibility between the parents, unpredictable and inconsistent parenting, parents who are unable to protect or supervise children consistently because of drug use, children thrust into adult responsibilities, family secrets, rigid or blurred roles, distorted or muted affect, isolation and many other problem-producing dynamics and structures.

The effects of parental drug problems depend, among other things, on the severity of family disruption and the supports available to the children and partner. Children from dysfunctional families often have little basic trust or sense of themselves as separate, worthwhile people due to the family focus on controlling the addiction, not on child-nurturing. They may have little experience with a range of "normal" feelings and interpersonal interactions and therefore little confidence in their interpersonal skills and emotional reactions. Even having an emotional reaction may feel unsafe. The coping skills that help these children maintain some predictability, gain some satisfaction and reward and defuse unsafe situations within the family, may seem rigid, extreme, inappropriate and distorted to others. The child may be unable to meet the expectations of teachers and be preoccupied, self-blaming, ashamed and despairing of the family situation. School difficulties, self-medication, vulnerability to exploitation and various attempts to escape the situation are all likely results.

Very little work has been done on how gender influences experiences in a dysfunctional family of origin. Some speculate girls may be more strongly affected in ways often described as "codependency."[24] Female gender-role prescriptions assign more family responsibilities to girls and women and mandate more connectedness to the family of origin, while boys and men are "pushed" by societal norms into more autonomous identities with fewer and weaker emotional ties to the family. Although the data is sparse, the most dysfunctional parent's gender probably makes a difference, since women are still the primary caretakers of children.

Mary and Michael's story indicates that alcohol and other drug use may have been a problem in Mary's family of origin—her biological father was killed in an alcohol-related crash, her mother appeared to slur words after arguments and her stepfather may have an alcohol problem. During an assessment or early in treatment, these patterns need to be explored. Michael's background is not fully explored in the story, but anyone working with him should know about the consumption of alcohol or other drugs, and child abuse in his family of origin should be examined.

Those who design positive interventions for children from dysfunctional families need to recognize that skills and roles learned in such families can be useful elsewhere if the individual can understand them and develop flexibility in applying them. Acting to protect a child should be a first priority. Primary and secondary prevention efforts can provide alternatives to children from dysfunctional families to counteract negative family influences. Alternatives should include finding safe spaces and additional parenting sources to help the child recognize and practice flexible survival skills. Secondary prevention efforts should try to identify children who are already negatively affected and try to make beneficial changes. Children who exhibit destructive behaviors may also need treatment.

Primary prevention may be too late for adult children of alcoholics, although interventions might prevent more severe problems. Such interventions could help them identify the impact of their families and their own non-adaptive ways of interacting with others or with work and leisure activities. Support networks can be developed to reduce isolation. Education about alcohol and other drugs can help both young and adult children to stop blaming themselves and assuming responsibility for family problems.

Developmental Disruption

These theories say the use of addictive substances disrupts self-protective behaviors and positive, adaptive coping skills as well as development of self-esteem and the learning of interpersonal and emotional skills. The literature about this disruption has paid little attention to gender issues, although abundant data

show that women's lives, life tasks, coping styles and safety issues differ from men's.[25]

Current substance use should be the first target of intervention, since it interferes with a person's ability to maintain personal safety and with the accomplishment of adaptive life tasks. For instance, when using chemicals, judgment may be impaired so the person misses warning signals that a situation is becoming unsafe, such as a rape, or unprotected intercourse that leads to an unwanted pregnancy. Similarly, a person under the influence of alcohol or other drugs is unlikely to function well in school or at work, which can contribute to academic or economic difficulties. Drug use can also interfere with the process of grieving, making a successful mid-life transition or other necessary developmental life work, which creates vulnerability to later problems, including physical illness and depression.

The second concern would be the time a person first began using chemicals. For instance, a person who begins heavy use in adolescence fails to learn gradually to handle adult relationships and emotions through successive experiences, because the experiences are impaired by the chemicals. Heavy users of alcohol and other drugs since adolescence may be chronologically adult, but may have many adolescent emotional and behavioral characteristics, including an inability to assess risk or protect themselves from sexual or other forms of violence. They may not have learned to handle pain or relax in social situations without a chemical and may need to learn what "normal" reactions are, since alcohol or other drugs were used over time to avoid or reduce negative feelings.

Therefore, education should include the positive roles that pain, stress, anxiety, depression and other feelings perceived as negative play in indicating problems that need to be addressed. This information can help people resist the tendency to medicate feelings while they learn other ways to react to them. The understanding and skills gained through an educational approach will empower women, because education provides more options and imparts a sense of control for women over their bodies and lives. Knowledge of the role gender plays in their problems is especially important to women's recovery to reduce women's tendency to blame themselves.

Disinhibition, Learning, and Deviance Disavowal Theories

These theories have been invoked to explain unprotected sexual behavior, but have been especially prevalent in studies of violence—rape, incest and battering.[4,11] All offer explanations of the relationship between alcohol and other drug use, violence and other issues linked in this chapter that can be harmful to women, since the explanations can interfere with the recognition of multiple problems. These theories are also likely to reduce or increase individual accountability for alcohol- or drug-related behaviors. Since societal sanctions provide important motivation to seek help, anything that interferes with them can enable problematic behavior to continue.

Although not addressed much in the literature, these theories are likely to operate differently for women than men, since the very use of alcohol and illegal drugs is perceived to be more reprehensible for women. For instance, if "unacceptable" chemicals are involved, a woman may be blamed and punished for behaviors perceived as "normal" for a man. If acceptable (prescribed) chemicals are involved, people are far more likely to excuse women's problematic behaviors.

Disinhibition theories propose that behavior which is usually unacceptable socially and therefore suppressed, occurs because alcohol or other drugs reduce the inhibitions against that behavior. Studies suggest it is beliefs about the effects of alcohol that lower inhibitions, the cause being attributed to physiological, neurological or chemical factors.[26]

Therefore, negative behaviors are less likely to be considered intentional or as moral lapses, especially for men, and the individual is less likely to be held accountable for the actions (unless the very act of drinking or using drugs is perceived to be morally reprehensible, as it often is for women). Violence or pregnancy are believed to occur because normal neural inhibitions against assault or unprotected sexual activity are reduced by a chemical.

Beliefs about inhibition are probably active in Mary and Michael's understanding of their early sexual relationship (in which the alcohol use may have allowed them, especially Mary, to justify their behavior). It's not clear, but it is possible Michael deliberately plied Mary with alcohol to reduce her resistance to sex. This is a common tactic in acquaintance rape and some child sexual assaults.[27] In one publication, sixty-three percent of wives involved in marital violence reportedly were drinking.[28] The earliest episodes of violence in Mary's and Michael's relationship were probably also blamed on lowered inhibitions.

Learned behavior theories focus on the norms that regulate intoxicated behavior. They note certain behaviors are expected or accepted while "high" or inebriated that would be unacceptable while sober or straight. The situation or the circumstances are blamed for causing the behavior, not the physiology. For instance, behaviors exhibited by inebriated employees at an office Christmas party would be grounds for dismissal if they occured during an ordinary work day. Also, different environments and social contexts are perceived as appropriate for women and girls, different from those for men and

boys. The presence of a woman in some environments is perceived as deviant and she might be considered responsible for anything that happens to her in that environment (for instance, a gang rape in a fraternity man's bedroom, especially if everyone has been drinking). Numerous episodes in Mary and Michael's lives illustrate this type of thinking.

Deviance disavowal theory is related to learned behavior theories, but focuses more on how conceptualizations of drinking allow people to view an individual as "normal" despite unacceptable (deviant) behavior. For instance, if people perceive domestic or sexual violence to be a result of alcohol use, the person is not perceived as violent, but simply drunk. If only the alcohol use is seen as important, an observer is less likely to notice patterns in the violence, the control the violent person wishes or needs to exert and the choices that are being made in how, when, and with whom the violence occurs. These beliefs may also prevent a search for other factors that may be important in designing interventions (for instance, a learning disability or incest in an adolescent who drinks heavily and is skipping school).

Each of these theories has been used to excuse destructive behaviors and relieve people of accountability. People in a position to intervene can ignore behavior that needs attention if they view it solely as the result of alcohol or other drug consumption, or they can downplay its seriousness through a belief in deviance disavowal theories.

Changes in the definitions of disinhibition and of the behaviors treated as acceptable in certain situations can exert societal influence on the risks people are willing to take and the behaviors others will accept.

Mary, Michael and many of the others who knew about their problems illustrate how these beliefs shape people's responses. Many in a position to assist Mary interpreted Michael's violence as arising from problems related to drinking and other drug use. They tried to intervene with his drinking problem but did not hold him accountable for his violence. They focused on Mary's "codependency" but didn't recognize signs of her growing dependence on legal drugs or help her understand the ways her behaviors were adaptive within an impossible situation.

These beliefs also contribute to Mary and Sandra's reactions to their sexual abuse. Since they partially attribute their abuse to the alcohol consumption, they fail to see it it as a personal assault that should be punished and believe their behavior contributed to the assault.

Other Theories

Another cluster of theories suggests one or more of the problems addressed in this chapter contribute to the development of alcohol and other drug problems. One cluster concerns the consequences of childhood experiences and family-of-origin dynamics. A second asserts alcohol and other drugs are used to self-medicate stress, emotional or physical pain and/or as a coping tool for survival in difficult and painful situations. Others are specific to only one or two problem areas.

Family-of-Origin Issues

These theories are primarily concerned with incest and domestic violence, although the data also suggest relationships between family-of-origin dynamics, victimization and other problems. These include rape, adolescent pregnancy, school problems (including dropping out of school) as well as alcohol and other drug problems.

Growing up with domestic violence appears to have many detrimental consequences for children. These include physical and sexual abuse and neglect and psychological trauma. Self-destructive coping mechanisms include early sexuality, abusive relationships with older males and running away. Other consequences may be the assumption of parental roles, school problems, accidents, distrust of adults, alcohol and drug problems and suicide.[5,29]

Clearly, there are many families with both violence and alcohol and drug problems. However, while differences exist between families with alcohol or other drug problems and no violence and violent families with no alcohol and drug problems, the common denominators are probably inconsistent parenting, a lack of safety and the family's inability to help the child learn basic trust and interpersonal and emotional skills for adaptive coping. The severity of the effects probably depends on whether one parent, other adults or older children are able to attend to a child's needs and the age of a child when the family's situation becomes difficult. Whether other people or situations are able to provide a corrective experience for the lack of safety and nurturing and the unpredictability that so often accompanies battering may also be a factor.

Survivors of incest and other child abuse are also likely to experience other forms of violence. As adults, they often find themselves in violent domestic situations or in trouble with alcohol and other drugs.[8,30,31] Adolescent sexual assault victims have especially high levels of alcohol and other drug problems, as well as feelings of isolation, suicidal thoughts, low self-esteem, early sexual activity, accidents, school problems and sleep disturbances.[7,32] High proportions of women who seek treatment for addiction, including alcoholism, report incest or child sexual assault in their histories, as do adolescents who are heavy users of alcohol and other drugs.[10,33]

Coping and Self-medication

In most studies, women with alcohol or other drug problems report that their use began and often continued as a way of coping with pain—sometimes physical pain, but more often psychological and emotional. The pattern they usually describe is one of trying to contain or subdue negative emotions and thoughts so they can survive, often to meet responsibilities to their children.

Research on each of the problem areas finds examples of this pattern. For instance, children in domestic violence situations say their mother drinks to forget the beatings.[5] Some evidence indicates battered women may develop alcohol and other drug problems after leaving their assailant and trying to make it on their own. They report drinking as one way of suppressing feelings of depression and hopelessness.[34]

Incest survivors report drinking to help escape feelings, live with shame and guilt, block memories and fend off fear.[7] They also say they first got drunk to survive sex with their father and then to feel real when feelings had become anesthetized.[35] Adolescent school dropouts report early drinking and other drug use because of boredom and dislike of school and to escape emotional turmoil.[13,36] Pregnant teens report using drugs because they feel hopeless about their lives.[37]

Most statistics about drinking and other drug use to cope and self-medicate rely on self-report data. Men are far less likely than women to describe this pattern, and instead report they began using drugs to facilitate social situations and to feel "high." Both patterns are consistent with acceptable behaviors for each gender and may reflect women's and men's awareness of these gender-related norms, rather than "true" motivation. Men may also self-medicate, but may not want to admit they feel emotional pain and vulnerability, even to themselves. Women may like getting "high," but may only be able to accept using chemicals "medicinally," because of societal disapproval.

Even if gender-related reporting distortions occur, women in these studies are clearly reporting high levels of emotional pain and a belief that their use of alcohol and other drugs is a response to that pain. Some suggest the use of drugs may assist some women to survive impossible situations until other forms of coping become possible.

Primary prevention of alcohol or other drug problems which takes these connections into account could have several components. The most direct approach would attempt to reduce, through educational and therapeutic activities, the shame, guilt and hopelessness these problems often produce. The possibility that alcohol and other drug use assists with coping should at least be considered. If so, the woman should be able to reduce drug use substantially or completely after some work to allay the negative consequences of violence or other problems.

Another component of primary and secondary prevention could develop non-chemical ways of coping with pain and stress by drawing on recent research on women and stress.[38] Some of these focus on stressors that stem from the structure of gender relationships—those related to having less power, status, and financial resources. The likelihood of developing potentially maladaptive coping mechanisms, including the use of chemicals, can be reduced by helping to strengthen coping resources that build a sense of competence and offer social support.

Mary's alcohol consumption appears to occur in a coping pattern—she drinks when she is upset or frightened of Michael. Thorough assessment of her drinking patterns, drug use or other means of coping should be a part of the work with Mary. With education about the linkages between all these issues, active work on other ways to manage anxiety and fear, and positive movement towards financial security, Mary may find she no longer needs to drink or use drugs. If she cannot limit her consumption with support, especially when her stress is reduced, then direct alcohol and drug-specific intervention should be considered. Perhaps other alcohol- or drug-related factors besides self-medication have developed or been present throughout.

Poverty and Discrimination

Many believe that there are other factors that contribute to the development of all of the problems that are "linked" in this chapter. These factors are poverty and discrimination.

Data on the effects of poverty suggest it is not poverty itself, but many of its consequences that combine to create destructive situations. These include chronic uncertainties and responsibilities with inadequate monetary resources. These lead to an inability to fulfill role responsibilities, which can then lead to depression, low self-esteem, lack of hope or motivation and vulnerability to victimization or addiction. [39,40]

Interventions may need to incorporate these issues and the consequences they produce. For instance, alcohol-related problems, dropping out of school and violent behavior may all arise from profoundly low self-esteem and embarrassment about learning problems. Learning disabilities can arise from perceptual difficulties or low-quality teaching. If the learning problem is not addressed, it may prove difficult to have an impact on other problems.

Implications of Interrelationships

While the presence of one problem can create vulnerability to others, the nature of the causal linkages is often far from clear. In some cases, one set of problems clearly contributes to the development of others. In other cases, the presence of multiple problems may be clear, but their relationship may not be.

For instance, one study found that men who are violent when they drink are often also violent when they don't.[41] Alcohol and other drugs seem to increase the severity and frequency of the violence, but not whether it occurs. So, while the correlation exists between alcohol and violence, one does not appear to "cause" the other, at least not consistently.

Studies of rape and alcohol use demonstrate that while alcohol consumption is often present in a rape situation, men who drink heavily lose the physical ability to complete a rape. Rapes differ in spontaneity, either intensely planned, partially planned, or unplanned (impulsive). When a rape is impulsive, the perpetrator has often consumed alcohol, which may have acted as a disinhibitor.[9] In a planned rape, alcohol is often used to anesthetize the intended victim.

While teen pregnancy is often associated with dropping out of school, the factors that contribute to teen pregnancy and to dropping out of school are complex and alcohol and other drug use can be involved in multiple ways. As more studies investigate the nature of the interrelationships of life problems, more theories are evolving which may eventually provide clearer guidelines for interventions.[42]

Suggestions for Women's Centers

The evidence suggests several principles for women's centers:

1. *The correlation between all these problems and alcohol and other drug use suggests that each potential problem area should be thoroughly addressed and then carefully ruled out.* Usually, we address the single problem of concern to the type of agency for which we work and perhaps explore another problem if its presence is obvious or the participant expresses concern about it. Otherwise, we tend to overlook problems we do not anticipate. Alcohol and other drug use is implicated often enough in other problems that its presence and effects must be assessed routinely.

For example, in one study of women entering crisis agencies to deal with issues such as rape, domestic violence and displaced homemaker problems, more than 30 percent self-identified problems related to alcohol or other drugs. With some training, staff members identified even more serious alcohol and drug problems in an additional 10-15 percent of the women.[43] If problematic use of alcohol or other drugs is not present, all women who have experienced any of the problems discussed here are at risk of alcohol or other drug problems, so prevention activities are warranted.

Mary provides numerous examples of the consequences of one type of program not recognizing other problems. The alcohol and other drug programs that worked with Michael (and Mary) did not address the dynamics of violence in the relationship. Similarly, several women's centers missed opportunities to address the alcohol and drug issues in Mary's life.

2. *Any problems that are present need to be addressed, with no assumptions that addressing one will take care of another.* If one set of problems develops in response to another, once developed, they often continue after the conditions that "spawned" them change. Battering or incest may continue even after alcohol or other drug treatment leads to stable abstinence, unless the violent behavior is addressed. Conversely, violence may be difficult to control if problematic drug use continues.

More knowledge about causes and effects of particular problems may help a worker determine which issues to pursue first. Usually all must be acknowledged fairly early, even if some don't get immediate, extensive attention. Violence may not end until abstinence is achieved and both may need work before an early sexual trauma can be explored. The importance of the incest can be acknowledged earlier to validate its importance and reassure the person it will be dealt with at the right time.

3. *Learning about the linkages between these problems may require different kinds of staff development activities, and new inter-agency relationships and collaborative strategies to acquire the necessary knowledge and resources will need to be developed.*

Ethnicity, Race, and Class Issues

Some of the influences poverty has on other problems have already been discussed. But too often in research and writing about gender, differences that arise from culture, ethnicity or race are not recognized. Gender roles and role expectations exist within each culture, but are often different among diverse ethnic groups.

Ethnic norms will influence support systems available to a woman who experiences sexual violence. Religious beliefs and cultural values help shape the guilt and shame experienced by a woman who is assaulted or who becomes pregnant as an unwed teen. Cultural beliefs about the causes of hurtful events and the interventions that help reduce pain determine who is seen as a useful helping person and whether a person will readily seek help for a problem. Cultural beliefs shape attitutes about the importance of education.

Workers in women's centers need to develop ethnic-consciousness in their understanding of gender-related dynamics and expectations. This requires familiarity with the effects of one's own ethnicity and socialization and with one's reactions to others with different values and expectations. It also requires some knowledge of what is perceived as helpful or harmful within the other person's cultural and ethnic group.

Raising cultural issues can help keep a women's center staff person from imposing her own cultural values on another (unless it is appropriate to do so, to provide safety for a child, for instance). Non-conscious factors often perpetuate guilt, self-blame, or miscommunication. Once identified and discussed, their effects can be recognized and changed.

Systems Barriers to Addressing Multiple Problems

Alcohol and other drug treatment programs developed largely because existing health and mental health systems did not deal effectively with these problems. Developed by men, they have focused primarily on alcohol and illegal drugs. Women more often use legal drugs or combine them with others.

Society was interested in "treating" problems that occur more often in men than women—violence, accidents, productivity problems, absenteeism at the workplace and legal violations. Intervention programs were designed to address men's coping styles, such as massive efforts to protect self-esteem and sense of control. This focus aided men in not recognizing the consequences of their behavior and by externalizing responsibility for their problems. When concerns about women arose in social policy, program design and funding areas, they focused most often on pregnant women and the effects of alcohol and other drugs on the fetus. They tended to ignore the range of other problems addicted women experience or problems related to the use of alcohol and other drugs, such as depression, anxiety, low self-esteem, the likelihood of having been victimized by sexual or interpersonal violence and concerns about children. Since the body of knowledge was developed from work with men, treatment and prevention programs were designed for men and men's problems.

Research and programming reflected societal attitudes about gender, including the stigma associated with women who drank (and especially who became drunk) or who used illegal drugs. Prescribed drugs were not perceived as addiction problems requiring intervention, despite the massive numbers of prescriptions written for women. Concern about drug use increased as young people explored alternative consciousnesses through drugs. Volunteers and paid staff of the new drug crisis centers that opened made fewer gender distinctions.

Women's centers began in the 1970s as the Women's Movement raised consciousness about women's problems not addressed by human service agencies or legal procedures. Many were generic women's crisis centers with programs for violence against women (rape and battering) or designed to serve women's economic and emotional needs when they chose to live without a male. As norms about sexual behavior changed, concern grew about increasing rates of teen pregnancy and the consequences, especially when the mother decided to keep the child.

Reproductive rights became the focus of many women's groups. Recognition of child abuse expanded to include the frequency of incest and child sexual assault. Women's centers often led campaigns to develop more effective interventions and legal procedures to deal with these problems. Consciousness-raising sessions and a growing body of research began to confirm the prevalent woman-blaming and discounting pervasive in human services and legal procedures. Extensive social change began transforming laws and police and court procedures to reduce the re-victimization of women and children that often occurred when charges were pressed against male assailants. Funding was obtained for shelters and crisis services, more education, employment and emotional support for single mothers, including teen parents and "displaced homemakers."

Most of the feminist and women-oriented programs began in opposition to existing services, often with some legitimate cautions about working with health care, mental health, economic and legal systems that contributed to the exploitation of women. A similar distrust of other human service systems also continues in many alcohol and other drug programs.

Unfortunately for women experiencing problems complicated by alcohol and other drug use, the developing addiction fields were no more sensitive to feminist concerns than the systems they criticized for their lack of knowledge about alcohol and drugs. Also, feminists were all too aware that men's alcohol or other drug problems were used to excuse their behaviors, while women's use of alcohol or other drugs was used to stigmatize them.

Women's centers, especially those concerned with violence against women, often actively resisted recognizing that some women had problems with alcohol or other drugs. They were less willing to consider the effects that alcohol or other drug use in the family or in relationships might have on their current situation. This was viewed as another way to pathologize and blame women. Therefore, staff often had little knowledge about alcohol and other drugs and their effects, and little or no motivation to learn about them. Often, there was active resistance. That's why the women's crisis line worker doesn't consider the possibility of alcohol or other drug use when Mary calls sounding giddy and the domestic violence shelter indicates no

supportive response for examining her use of substances.

Today, there is more recognition within women's centers that alcohol and other drug problems are significant barriers to the empowerment of many women, and within alcohol or other drug programs about women's needs, but many obstacles remain to collaboration between chemical dependency programs and women's centers. Barriers are created by the different ways each system conceptualizes its work and goals, as well as the language each uses to describe key concepts and practices. One language tries to reduce rigid and maladaptive (often male) models of defenses and coping—such as, "I am powerless over alcohol and must take responsibility for my behaviors while drinking." Another focuses on strengths, societal interpretations of individual circumstances and helping women believe in themselves and their potential—such as, "I can control things that once controlled me."

Terms from chemical dependency work especially offensive to women's centers include "codependency" and "enabling."[44] Many feminists believe the term "codependency" stigmatizes women, especially given the connotations of the term "dependency" in societal stereotypes about women. The term "enabling" appears to assign responsibility for the drinker's behavior to the person who protects him from the consequences of his behavior. While these meanings were certainly not the intent of those who coined them, the way they are used in many treatment and prevention programs can be perceived by women as stigmatizing and blaming. Women's centers usually try to avoid negative labels and use words that convey power, hope, strength and commitment. A common view in alcohol or other drug programs is that denial is present when anyone fails to accept powerlessness and help from a higher power. The language of women's centers is often perceived as naive and as enabling continuation of drug problems.

If women's centers are to establish collaborative relationships with chemical dependency programs the languages used in each system must be made compatible. This may mean inventing new words with no negative connotations in either system. Each must be open to the other's perspectives and willing to grapple with the assumptions that underlie their language and style differences. Until this happens, a woman who encounters both systems must try to integrate their different advice. Too often, as with Mary, a woman must then compartmentalize her concerns and withhold information and questions from each agency.

If staff in women's centers examine how and why alcohol and other drug programs developed as they did, they may be able to approach collaboration with some understanding. The chemical dependency field is moving towards understanding how to identify and work with a broader range of defensive and coping styles.

Before this process is complete, a women's center must carefully assess treatment programs being considered as referral sources for women, *especially women who are survivors of violence.* How sensitive are they to issues of violence and to some of the victimization common in mixed-gender groups, or in a residential program? How willing are they to work with the center and exchange staff training sessions? What do women in the program say about their experiences there? Is the program willing to let the center sustain a relationship with the women referred?

If the answers to any of these questions are bothersome, but no other treatment alternatives exist, prepare the woman carefully for what she may experience there. Consider a non-residential program which can be less damaging than a residential one if neither is sensitive to women's needs. The center may then need to provide extra support and structure for a woman who really needs the intensity of intervention and the freedom from other responsibilities that are possible in a residential program.

Adolescence

Children often feel responsible for unhappiness in their families and believe they cause parental difficulties. In families with alcohol or other drug problems or domestic or sexual violence, this tendency is heightened and sometimes reinforced by parental statements. Two events of concern in Mary and Michael's story occur during adolescence. Understanding the key adolescent issues is critical in planning interventions for young women and girls in relation to early pregnancy and dropping out of school. A knowledge of adolescence promotes understanding of why these problems occur so frequently, how they are related to alcohol and other drug use, how to prevent them or to reduce negative effects once they have occurred. Alcohol and other drug use or misuse is also likely to begin during adolescence.[45]

Adolescence means massive changes—physical, sexual, cognitive, emotional, familial, social and political. In this society, it is a period without clear social value (except for preparing for later adult roles) and, except in some cultural groups, without a clear event or ceremony to mark transition to adulthood. Maintaining self-esteem can be difficult, especially for youth with little future hope and little investment or skill in secondary education. Extreme, rigid gender roles mark adolescence, when peer group norms and actions have much influence and parents less. Adolescents must learn to handle more physical strength, energy, sexual arousal and increased needs for stimulation and risk-

taking. Risk-taking, however, is heavily influenced by peer norms.[46]

Researchers once thought adolescence was always marked by high levels of stress and storm. Current research suggests this need not be the case, although this is generally a high-risk period for many teens. For those living with domestic violence, chemical dependency or other disruptive forces, or who have been victimized by incest, child sexual assault or other abuse, adolescence can be a particularly difficult and vulnerable time.

Even for children with a supportive, safe family environment, moods change quickly during adolescence. There is a shift of priorities with emphasis on achievement replaced or equalled by concern about popularity, especially among girls. Teens often struggle with personal, spiritual and moral beliefs and often become aware, intolerant of, or cynical about the hypocrisy, unfairness and inconsistency they perceive around them.

Elkind describes the teen as always playing to an "imaginary audience"—the anticipated reactions of others.[12] Because they are hypercritical and constantly self-scrutinizing, teens believe others also scrutinize them constantly and minutely. This leads to intense self-consciousness and despair about perceived shortcomings. Elkind also describes the "personal fable." This fable is a set of beliefs which leads a teen to believe his or her problems, hopes, joys and fears are unique and that what others experience is different. This can lead to feelings of isolation and loneliness or great hope and feelings of invulnerability. Therefore, besides behaviors adults see as "over-reactions," teens have difficulty assessing risk accurately. The personal fable can lead teens to engage in risky activities they would consider unwise before or after this period. For instance, Mary and Michael did not believe that pregnancy would happen to them.

Boys and girls differ in many ways during adolescence. The entire adolescent social organization of gender creates experiences and interactions for young women and men that sometimes overlap, but more often diverge and conflict.[47] Boys are encouraged to identify and develop adult interests, but girls' roles become more constricted.[25] By late adolescence, girls report more psychological distress than boys.[46] School achievement by girls drops during adolescence and career aspirations become more limited. Girls have a higher adolescent suicide rate than boys and more self-image problems.[47]

At least two sets of theories account for the relationships between adolescent pregnancy and problems in school. Here are brief descriptions of these theories, their implications for women's centers and intervention, with some examples from Mary and her family.

Problem Behavior Theory

This theory, espoused most strongly by Jessor & Jessor and colleagues, is closely related to others that consider social control, social learning and developmental theories that examine normative expectations and their effects.[48] They propose that any number of deviant adolescent behaviors correlate and either occur in sequence or become linked through their "rule-breaking" consequences. Some gender differences have been examined. When adolescent female roles become more restrictive, the normative prescriptions for girls in this society are narrower. Thus, one might expect the same behaviors in girls would be considered more deviant than in boys.

Various studies have found strong associations among "deviant" adolescent behaviors with somewhat different gender patterning. Comparing studies is limited since boys are more consistently asked about drug use, while girls are more often asked about sexual behavior. In a study done with boys only, early sexual behavior predicted school problems and several types of drug use, while early alcohol use predicted early sexual behavior.[49]

Experiencing violence is also associated with early alcohol use and school problems. The possibility of linking these events has the potential to stigmatize women, but could also help those working with women to assess the presence of other behaviors and situations. If this had happened, Mary's potential for developing alcohol and other drug problems and her high risk for a violent marriage might have been anticipated and intervened with earlier.

Reduction of Life Chances

Other theories suggest the use of alcohol and other drugs (and other potentially self-destructive behaviors) is more likely when a person's life chances are reduced. Without positive future propects, a young person is more likely to focus on pleasure and gratification now, including the use of addictive chemicals, with little thought to future consequences.

Numerous studies indicate that early pregnancy and dropping out of school reduce economic life chances and may create alienation and depression which are high-risk factors for developing alcohol and other drug problems.[37] Also, the added responsibilities and lower long-term education levels clearly limit a person's economic capacity. Mary's story illustrates how economic constraints limit what a woman sees as options when she must rely on her batterer's earning power.

Adolescent Pregnancy

Some studies state that 40 percent of adolescent girls become pregnant while still of high-school age. Many have families in which sexual abuse or alcohol pro exist.[50,51] Behaviors that may have helped their su vival in such families often leave young women vulnerable to men who promise to love them, and producing babies they believe will give them unco tional love.

As mentioned earlier, alcohol or other drug use lower inhibitions and lead to taking risks for all young girls. Some types of drug use can interfere with oral contraceptives and lead to pregnancy even when a teen is attempting to practice contraception. Some pregnancies result from incest. During pregnancy, alcohol or other drug use complicates a healthy pregnancy and can lead to abnormalities in the fetus. Teen pregnancy is linked to dropping out of school and often to reduced chances in later life. Poverty and rejection or alienation from her family further complicate an adolescent girl's situation.

Pregnancy prevention programs and teen mother programs need to focus attention on all of these issues. Models are developing which seem to improve the later circumstances of young women, but most do not give much attention to the role and impact of alcohol or other drug use.[50,52,53]

Dropping Out of School

Approximately 75 percent of adolescents complete secondary school and this percentage has not varied much for the past 20 years.[12] Almost half of students in school say they have been drunk at least once. Forty percent of heavy users say they do drugs with their friends and when they are bored or depressed. They say school is boring and only doing drugs is interesting.[13]

Few studies of dropping out of school have examined gender patterns. In those that have, girls appear heavily influenced by relationships with older boys in their use of alcohol or other drugs, sexual behaviors and school attendance.[54] Thirty to 40 percent of teen mothers drop out of school prior to conception.[50] Half to two-thirds of girls who drop out give pregnancy or marriage as the reason.[12] Other factors linked to dropping out are academic difficulties, irregular attendance, non-involvement in school affairs and attendance at multiple schools. Child sexual abuse is often present. Confusion about sexual identity and sexuality is also likely to be linked to dropping out.

Thus, preventing girls and young women from dropping out of school appears to be linked to the prevention or earlier detection of child sexual abuse and work on its negative consequences, as well as adolescent pregnancy and alcohol or other drug use. Other interventions should strengthen self-esteem, encourage relationships with boys their age, establish strong positive relationships with adults who actively support completion of school and develop a range of productive school-based activities. Many adolescent girls have no conception of a life apart from their relationship with an eventual male life partner. Mary, for example, had little sense of herself as a valuable person separate from her relationship with Michael. She also had a strong desire to leave home, given her fear of her stepfather.

The Consequences of Violence

Past or present violence can complicate the identification of, and work with, problems related to alcohol and other drug use and vice versa. Earlier, theory and evidence were presented about the relationships among alcohol and other drug use and three topics that involve violence—incest, rape (sexual assault) and battering (domestic violence). Another potential relationship between violence and alcohol and other drug problems exists—post-traumatic stress, both chronic and acute.

Post-traumatic Stress

Post Traumatic Stress Disorder (PTSD) as an anxiety disorder has been included in the latest psychiatric diagnostic statistical manual. Researchers and those who work with survivors of child sexual assault, rape, and battering—while they don't always name PTSD— all describe similar patterns of behavior consistent with those of other survivors of severe trauma. These include various ways of reliving the trauma such as flashbacks, nightmares, feelings of danger associated with particular stimuli, numbing or withdrawal from people or important activities and a range of other symptoms that include hyperalertness, sleep disturbances, guilt, shame and memory and concentration impairment.

This set of behaviors requires different reactions and interventions. General reactions in the past have laid major responsibility for the assaults on the victim. Thus, the assaulted child or woman was often described as behaving seductively or deriving secret enjoyment from the assault. A battered woman was thought to stay with her batterer to satisfy her masochistic needs. Many of these attitudes are still prevalent among those who are in a position to assist the survivors of these types of violence and within treatment programs for alcohol and drug problems.

An important focus for intervention with a survivor of violence is to identify ways in which behaviors have focused on surviving. The behavior may have served very important purposes earlier and recognizing them can lead to great reductions in the guilt and shame victims experience.

Healing from trauma requires experiencing the fear, horror and anger and facing the shame and guilt

survivors often feel when experiences are validated, then reducing or replacing these emotions with knowledge. If the victim was a child and the abuse repetitive, development may have been disrupted at the age abuse began and therefore adult coping mechanisms only partially developed. Interventions need to focus on helping the survivor identify more choices, feel more power and feel safe.

Many practices in alcohol and other drug programs may not allow women survivors of violence to feel safe. Many male-female interactions in programs—innocuous to someone with no history of violence—may be very frightening for a violence survivor. Aggressive reactions, seductive behaviors or confrontation, especially by a man (if her assailant was a man), can leave a woman trapped in fear and unable to recognize or practice more adaptive responses.

If a woman is not consciously frightened, she may still need persistent and careful work to feel confident expressing her needs—in fact, if her survival required adapting to others, she may not know her needs or feel that she deserves anything. She will automatically tell someone what she thinks they want to hear and be perceived as manipulative or dishonest when staff recognizes she told different things to different people.

When the violence recurs and the woman feels trapped, especially if the "captor" offers some kindnesses, some theorists propose battered women and incest victims develop characteristics resembling the "Stockholm Syndrome."[55] In this survival mechanism, the victim identifies with the threatening person, leading to confusing, paradoxical and contradictory responses of affection, loyalty and dependence, or fear, loathing and distrust. A strange symbiosis may develop, which can be difficult to sever. Strong positive relationships with others and education about the Stockholm Syndrome can help.

Victims of violence are also often re-traumatized by the agencies, persons and procedures they use to gain protection from their assailant. The treatment of injuries, evidence collection, questioning by police officers and prosecutors and the courtroom experience can all be very traumatic. When sexual or domestic violence is involved, if medical and criminal justice personnel are not well-informed about the dynamics of traumatic assaults or well trained in non-intrusive methods, they may generate further trauma. If alcohol and other drugs are involved, this process may be even more difficult.

A women's center may want to help develop training programs for staff in emergency health and criminal justice systems to avoid re-traumatization. Training programs should include information about the ways alcohol and other drugs affect perceptions and behaviors, so policies and procedures that diminish accountability for assailants or re-victimize women and children can be identified and changed. Careful preparation and coaching of the survivor, with active advocacy and support, is important to help her prepare for these experiences, give her some sense of control and minimize negative reactions. The advocate will also be able to identify needs for further training and policy and procedural changes.

Programs must also work consistently to change public attitudes and policies that allow violence against women and children to continue. Education in schools about unacceptable touching and acquaintance rape can support a child or adolescent to report violence and work on its aftermath. Education can help reduce the factors than may lead to rape and battering. Changes in legal, police, court and other practices may be necessary to protect victims from intimidation in court, to challenge disrepectful or dangerous news reporting practices, to ensure prosecution of perpetrators and deal with other situations that may arise in varied communities.

Also, unrecognized symptoms of post-traumatic stress are frightening to the person experiencing them and can look "crazy" to persons not experienced in recognizing them. Most women with histories of violence have accumulated a long list of psychiatric diagnoses and prescriptions for anti-anxiety and anti-depression medications, but often with little assessment of alcohol consumption or the effects of violence. Even experienced providers may have difficulty sorting through various "symptoms" related to alcohol and other drug use or withdrawal, post-traumatic stress reactions or other psychological, social or physical problems.

Time, patience, trial and error, great cooperation and trust are often needed to make these patterns clear. Meanwhile, the woman experiencing all these problems needs education, support and reassurance that her well-developed survival skills can be mobilized and refocused. If the violence is missed, however, she may receive more medications and "labels" and continue to live in unsafe situations.

Incest and Child Sexual Assault

As noted in another chapter in this volume and earlier in this chapter, child sexual assault is extremely common in the histories of women who experience the range of problems discussed. If the assault was recurrent, its effects can be especially pervasive and insidious. People describe drinking to prevent memories and fear and to feel more in control, or "real." Feelings of betrayal, self-blame or projection of anger against society can lead to many troublesome behaviors.

Numerous resources describe ways to work with incest survivors, although few focus on alcohol and other drugs.[35,56] A mother who is impaired by alcohol or other drugs may not protect her children and thus may be blamed more by them and others. Recognizing this pattern may assist mothers and children to reach some reconciliation. As alcohol and other drug use decreases or ceases, the survivor will be more likely to remember and feel the pain. This experience is necessary, but in the short term, an alcohol or other drug counselor must be prepared to recognize, reassure and work with what is uncovered or recovery will be sabotaged. Sometimes, work must be done to develop self-esteem and reduce shame before a woman can face giving up the only reliable "friend" she knows—her pills, bottle or needle.

Rape and Sexual Assault

Alcohol and other drug use contributes to risky situations, and is sometimes used to deal with the aftermath of rape or sexual assault. Most rapes are committed by male acquaintances of the same race as the victim.[57]

Women with alcohol or other drug problems are especially vulnerable to rape, as are victims of incest. Women in both categories are more frequently chosen as victims. Koss & Harvey report women with alcohol and other drug problems experience more and different types of rapes than other women and the duration of assault is often longer, probably because she resists less if inebriated or her resistance won't be taken as seriously.[9] Group rape is especially likely to involve alcohol or other drug consumption by the perpetrators, and the victim is often plied with alcohol to lower her resistance or to discredit her. Alcohol and other drug use can interfere with or prevent the work necessary for a survivor's recovery.

A large proportion of rapes are never reported. If a rape is not acknowledged in any way, it can undermine self-esteem and leave a woman vulnerable to other debilitating behaviors, including problematic use of alcohol and other drugs. Knowledge of alcohol's role must be incorporated into work with rape survivors—not to increase blame, but to assist in recovery and help prevent future rapes and chronic alcohol or drug problems.

Battering

If someone is predisposed to violence, it may occur more often when the person uses alcohol and other drugs and more serious injuries may be inflicted when the assailant has been drinking. In some cases, the woman's drinking is given as a reason for the battering.[58]

Those who work with batterers need to recognize that alcohol and other drug use needs to be assessed for everyone involved and active interventions developed. No assumptions should be made that violence will stop if alcohol or other drug use stops, or vice versa. Both problems must be worked on or one will undermine work on the other. Women's centers may need to educate alcohol and other drug programs about the need to address violence and battering, and to work with batterers' intervention programs to address alcohol and other drug use.

Alcohol or other drug programs are also unlikely to understand the degree to which a safety plan is important to a battered woman and her children—to protect lives, not just psychological safety. They may need specific information about why insisting on conjoint counseling is not safe, about child visitation and custody issues, about not disclosing addresses or allowing unsupervised visits—even to a father, if he is the batterer.

Safety and the treatment of alcohol or other drug problems may conflict, especially if the woman's behavior could lead to discharge from a shelter or treatment program. Some prior thinking about the ways conflict could occur, and how to handle it, may head off major problems. A battered women's shelter may need to revise its alcohol and other drug policies as staff learn more about the relationships of addictive substances to violence and the risk of future problems to residents.

Implications and Next Steps

The multiple linkages between alcohol and other drug problems and these five other problem areas illuminate the complexity often obscured when programs focus primarily on one problem. Many women's centers explicitly value holistic approaches. They assist a woman to develop an integrated sense of self that she defines for herself, rather than having someone else define it. Despite these beliefs, non-recognition of alcohol and other drug problems has hindered women's centers' ability to assist women to survive multiple problems.

Women's centers can also help develop new knowledge about how the use of alcohol and other drugs relates to the realities of many women's lives. The many questions and issues raised in this chapter should be key components of future agendas, both for service delivery and social change activities and for research.

References

1. Brownmiller, S. *Against Our Will: Men, Women and Rape*. New York: Simon and Schuster, 1975.
2. Stallard, K., Ehrenreich, B., & Sklar, H. *Poverty in the American Dream: Women and Children First*. Boston, MA: South End Press, 1983.
3. Garfinkel, I. & McLanahan, S.S. *Single Mothers and their Children: A New American Dilemma*. Washington, D.C.: The Urban Institute Press, 1986.
4. Coleman, D.H. & Strauss, M.A. "Alcohol abuse and family violence." In E. Gottheil, K.A. Druley, T.K. Skoloda, & H.M. Waxman (eds) *Alcohol, Drug Abuse, and Aggression*. Springfield, IL.: Charles C. Thomas, Publisher, 1983, 104-124.
5. Roy, M. *Children in the Crossfire: Violence in the Home—How Does It Affect Our Children?* Deerfield Beach, FLA: Health Communications, Inc., 1988.
6. Schetky, D.H. & Green, A.H. *Child Sexual Abuse*. New York: Brunner/Mazel Publishers, 1988.
7. Faller, K.C. *Child Sexual Abuse*. New York: Columbia University Press, 1988.
8. Crewdson, J. *By Silence Betrayed: Sexual Abuse of Children in America*. New York: Harper & Row, Publishers, 1988.
9. Koss, M.P. & Harvey, M.R. *The Rape Victim: Clinical and Community Approaches to Treatment*. Lexington, MA: The Stephen Greene Press, 1987.
10. Wilsnack, S.C. "Drinking, sexuality, and sexual dysfunction in women." In S.C. Wilsnack & L.J. Beckman. *Alcohol Problems in Women: Antecedents, Consequences, and Intervention*. New York, N. Y.: The Guilford Press, 1984.
11. Chilman, C.S. "Teenage pregnancy: A research review." In E. Howell & M. Bayes (eds) *Women and Mental Health*. New York: Basic Books, Inc. Publishers, 1981, pp. 325-339.
12. Elkind, D. *All Grown Up and No Place to Go: Teenagers in Crisis*. Reading, MA: Addison-Wesley Publishing Company, 1984.
13. Glassner, B. & Loughlin, J. *Drugs in Adolescent Worlds: Burnouts to Straights*. New York: St. Martin's Press, 1987.
14. Ackerman, R.J. *Children of Alcoholics* (2nd Ed.) Holmes Beach, FLA: Learning Publications, Inc. 1979, 1983.
15. Bepko, C. "The role of children in family treatment." *The Responsibility Trap*. New York: The Free Press, 1985, 198-232.
16. Black, C. *It Will Never Happen to Me*. Denver: Medical Adminstration Co., 1981.
17. Smith, A.W. *Grandchildren of Alcoholics: Another Generation of Co-dependency*. FLA: Health Communications, Inc., 1988.
18. Wegscheider-Cruse. S. *Another Chance*. Palo Alto, CA: Science and Behavior Books. 1981.
19. Woititz, J.G. *Adult Children of Alcoholics*. FLA: Health Communications, Inc., 1983.
20. Jesse, R.C. *Children in Recovery*. N.Y.: Norton, 1989.
21. Steinglass, P. with L.A. Bennett, S.J. Wolin, D.

Reiss. *The Alcoholic Family*. New York: Basic Books, Inc., Publishers, 1987.

22. Miller, B.A., Downs, W.R., Gondoli, D.M., Keil, A. "The role of childhood sexual abuse in the development of alcoholism in women." *Violence and Victims*, 2(3), 1987, 157-172.

23. Fox, R. *The Effect of Alcoholism on Children*. New York: National Council on Alcoholism, 1979.

24. Mondanaro, J. "The ultimate in female socialization: Women who love too much, codependents, and adult children of chemically dependent parents." *Women and Chemical Dependency*. Lexington Books, 1989.

25. Lott, B. *Women's Lives: Themes and Variations in Gender Learning*. Monterey, CA: Brooks/Cole Publishing Company, 1987.

26. Briddell, D., Rimm, D., Caddy, G., Krawitz, G., Scholis, D., & Wunderlin, R. "Effects of alcohol and cognitive set on sexual arousal to deviant stimuli." *Journal of Abnormal Psychology*, 87, 1978.

27. Ageton, S.S. *Sexual Assault among Adolescents*. Lexington, MA: Lexington Books, 1983.

28. Russell, D.E.H. *Rape in Marriage*. New York: MacMillan Publishing Co, Inc., 1982.

29. Jaffe, P.G., Wolfe, D.A., & Wilson, S.K. *Children of Battered Women*. Newbury Park, CA: Sage, 1990.

30. Browne, A. & Finkelhor, D. "Impact of child sexual abuse: A review of the research." *Psychological Bulletin*, 99, 1986, 66-77.

31. Finkelhor, D. *Sexually Victimized Children*. New York: Free Press, 1979.

32. Garbarino, J., Guttmann, E., & Seeley, J.W. *The Psychologically Battered Child*. San Francisco, CA.: Jossey-Bass Publishers, 1986.

33. Goodwin, J. *Sexual Abuse: Incest Victims and Their Families*. Littleton, MA.: PSG Publishing Company, Inc., 1982.

34. Coha, A. Personal information. Ann Arbor, MI: SAFE House, 1989.

35. Bass, E. & Davis, L. *The Courage to Heal: A Guide for Women Survivors of Child Sexual Abuse*. New York: Harper & Row, Publishers, 1988.

36. Filstead, W.J. "Adolescence and alcohol." In E.M. Pattison & E. Kaufman (eds). *Encyclopedic Handbook of Alcoholism*. New York: Gardner Press, 1982.

37. Wetzel, J.W. *Clinical Handbook of Depression*. New York: Gardner Press, Inc, 1984.

38. Thoits, P. Position paper. In A. Eichler & D.L. Parron (eds). *Women's Mental Health: Agenda for Research*. Rockville, MD.: National Institute of Mental Health, 1986, 80-105.

39. Belle, D. Women's mental health research agenda: *Poverty. Women and Mental Health* Occasional Paper Series. Rockville, MD: National Institute on Mental Health, 1986.

40. Seiden, A.M. Position paper. In A. Eichler & D.L. Parron (eds) *Women's Mental Health: Agenda for Research*. Rockville, MD: National Institute of Mental Health, 1986, 57-73.

41. Kantor, G.K. & Straus, M.A. "The 'Drunken Bum' theory of wife beating." *Social Problems*. 34(3), 1987, 213-227.

42. Gondolf, E.W. with Fisher, E.R. *Battered Women as Survivors: An Alternate to Treating Learned Helplessness*. Lexington, MA: Lexington Books, 1988.

43. Soler, E.G. & Dammann, G. "Women in crisis: Drug use and abuse." *Focus on Women*. 4(1), 1980, 227-241.

44. National Coalition Against Domestic Violence. "Chemical dependency, co-dependency, and battered women." Special issues of the NCADV *Voice*, 1988.

45. Braucht, G.N. "Problem drinking among adolescents: A review and analysis of psychosocial research." Rockville, MD.: National Institute on Alcohol Abuse and Alcoholism [DHHS Publication No. (ADM) 82-1193], 1982, 143-164.

46. Gove, W.R. "The effect of age and gender on deviant behavior: A biopsychosocial perspective." In. A.S. Rossi (ed). *Gender and the Life Course*. New York: Aldine Publishing Company, 1985, 115-144.

47. Bush, D.M. & Simmons, R.G. "Gender and coping with the entry into early adolescence." In R.C. Barnett, L. Beiner, & G.K. Baruch (eds) *Gender and Stress*. New York: The Free Press, 1987, 185-217.

48. Jessor, R. & Jessor, S.L. *Problem behavior and psychosocial development: A longitudinal study of youth*. New York: Academic Press, 1977.

49. Robins, L.N. & Wish, E. "Childhood deviance as a developmental process." *Social Forces*, 56, 1977, 448-71.

50. Dryfoos, J.G. "Schools get in the act: Pregnancy prevention programs and public education." *Equal Play: Sexuality and Sex Equity*, (Women's Action Alliance), VII(1), 1988, 3-6.

51. Press, M. "Sex and sex roles: What are we really telling kids?" *Equal Play: Sexuality and Sex Equity*, (Women's Action Alliance) VII(1), 1988, 9-10.

52. Gerrard, M., McCann, L., & Geis, B.D. "The antecedents and prevention of unwanted pregnancy." In A.U. Rickel, M. Gerrard, & Iscoe, I. (eds) *Social and Psychological Problems of*

Women: Prevention and Crisis Intervention. Washington: Hemisphere Publishing Corporation, 1984, 85-101.

53. Archer, E. & McGee, E. "Improving educational opportunities for pregnant and parenting students." *Equal Play: Sexuality and Sex Equity.* (Women's Action Alliance), VII (1), 1988, 31-32.

54. Howard, M.A.P. & Anderson, R.J. "Early identification of potential school drop-outs: A literature review." In M. Bloom (ed). *Life Span Development: Bases for preventive and interventive helping.* New York: MacMillan Publishing Co, Inc., 1980.

55. Graham, D.L.R., Rawlings, E., & Rimini, N. "Battered women, hostages, and the Stockholm Syndrome." K. Yllo & M. Bograd, *Feminist Perspectives on Wife Abuse.* Newbury Park, CA: Sage, 1988.

56. Gil, E. *Treatment of Adult Survivors of Child Abuse.* Walnut Creek, CA: Launch Press, 1988.

57. Russell, D.E.H. *Sexual Exploitation.* Newbury Park, CA: Sage, 1984.

58. Roy, M. (ed.) *Battered Women: A Psychosocial Study of Domestic Violence.* New York: Van Nostrand Reinhold Company, 1977.

19 Women and Legal Drugs

Susan Galbraith

"Legal drugs hold a special position in our society. Their use is considered legitimate and innocuous—especially the use of alcohol, prescription and over-the-counter drugs."

Legal drugs are the drugs most likely to be used by women. They are the drugs which are socially sanctioned and most acceptable for women to use. Although alcohol and tobacco are harmful legal drugs and their use by women presents critical health risks, the focus of this chapter is on major mood-altering legal drugs used by women that are less frequently discussed. Prescription drugs provide one of the few legitimate "highs" for women. They are particularly dangerous because women use them to self-medicate, to block out feelings of powerlessness, isolation and despair. Legal drugs are as dangerous as illegal drugs, and in some ways more dangerous, because they are perceived as "safe" and the media rarely focus attention on the risks associated with their use.

We don't have a great deal of information on the patterns of legal drug use among women and the problems these drugs create. Research and data collection has typically focused on men, their patterns of use and the impact of various drugs on their bodies. We have little research on legal drug use among women of color and low-income women. The misuse of legal drugs was once thought to be the domain of middle- and upper-class women who could afford psychiatrists. Some prevention programs, however, are reporting high rates of misuse among women in low-income communities as a result of doctors' writing prescriptions for women on Medicaid, sometimes in lieu of a thorough medical assessment. Despite the problem of inadequate research, there is some information on legal drugs that can give us a general sense of the potency of these drugs and the risks of their use for women.

Overview

Legal drugs are a regular part of our daily lives. There is a drug to perk us up, another to slow us down, one to help get us through the day and another to put us to sleep at night. Almost everybody uses them. In fact, many people don't even think of legal drugs as drugs.

Advertisers tell us our lives are improved by legal drugs. Thin, beautiful, sexy women drink and smoke. Experience tells us our lives may be empty with them. For women who develop problems or become addicted, the struggle to stop using alcohol, tobacco and prescription drugs is a long, painful and often private process, one which is never depicted in advertising campaigns.

Of course some drugs may help to save lives. But, there are those that can and do kill us. For instance, alcohol is responsible for almost 100,000 deaths each year.[1] Several international studies have indicated that alcoholic women have a significantly higher death rate from alcohol-related causes than alcoholic men.[2] Over seventy percent more women than men are seen in hospital emergency rooms because of prescription drug overdoses.[3] Lung cancer caused by smoking now exceeds breast cancer as the number one cancer-related cause of death among women.

The American public is flooded with information that glamorizes the use of legal drugs. These drugs are advertised on television, on radio and in magazines. Billboards, particularly in low-income neighborhoods across the nation, glorify the benefits of alcohol, the most destructive drug in our nation. Important public figures, sports stars and celebrities decorate our public transportation in ads which tell us we can't really be living without some kind of mood-altering drug. Ads for over-the-counter diet pills seduce women with their promise of beautiful, slender bodies. And, advertising in medical journals (and soon to be on T.V., with the relaxation of FDA regulations) promotes products to doctors to medicate the stress and strain described by so many women who come into their offices.

Legal drugs hold a special position in our society. Their use is considered legitimate and innocuous—especially the use of alcohol, prescription and over-the-counter drugs. Corporations producing these drugs wield a great deal of political influence and power which prevents adequate regulation and the dissemination of important consumer information. Our perception of legal drugs as safe is grossly misleading. It blurs the lines between use and problems. It makes it difficult for individuals to acknowledge when their use has become problematic. It perpetuates the myth that only "weak-willed" individuals become addicted. And finally, this false perception exonerates the multi-billion-dollar industries which produce legal drugs from any responsibility or role in the drugging of America.

Historical Perspective

Women have used alcohol and other drugs throughout the ages. This use has been condemned and condoned at different times. In Ancient Rome, the drinking of alcohol by women was strictly forbidden and women were actually stoned or starved to death for drinking wine.[4,5] In early nineteenth-century America, heavy drinking was common for both men and women. Alcohol was thought to be nutritious and there was an abundant supply of grain for cheap whiskey. The consumption of alcohol declined as other markets for grain supplies developed and with the advent of the Temperance Movement led by the Women's Christian Temperance Union (WCTU).[6] While the WCTU displayed the tremendous strength of women to organize and accomplish a goal, it failed to arouse concerns about the problems associated with alcohol use among women. The WCTU, concerned with drinking and drunkenness, defined these as male problems. Drinking was considered to be a problem of "fallen women" and prostitutes. Some have linked the lack of attention to alcohol and drug use by women with the previously strong middle-class image of women as virtuous and gentle.

Some drug use was legitimate and fashionable for women in the 1800s and patterns of prescription drug use were similar to those reported today. In the 1800s doctors prescribed opium (which was legal) to women for a range of problems defined as "female troubles." Lydia Pinkham's tonic was a widely used painkiller. One of the main ingredients was alcohol. The pattern of prescribing medications for women's problems created a large demand for drugs and a large pool of women with drug problems.[7]

Patterns of Use Today

Alcohol

Alcohol is the legal drug most often used by women and the one which creates the most problems. Because of its status as the most destructive drug being used by men and women in the United States, a complete chapter in this volume is devoted to alcohol.

Prescription Drugs

Women are much more likely than men to use and develop problems with legally prescribed drugs. The

National Institute on Drug Abuse (NIDA) estimates that from one to two million women have serious problems with prescribed drugs.[8] They are women from all racial, ethnic, social and economic backgrounds and women from all age groups. Most women who use legal, mood-altering drugs do so after receiving a prescription from their doctor. The initial prescription may be given to overcome insomnia, to calm "nerves," to kill physical pain or to control eating. Many women do not give any thought to the fact that their doctor's prescription may be addictive. Many prescription drugs—and particularly the minor tranquilizers—are perceived as being far more benign than they actually are. Women may unknowingly become physically and psychologically dependent.

Almost 60 percent of visits made to doctors' offices are made by women.[9] These visits are for both women and their children. Women are also more likely to see doctors when they're tense or upset. Thus, women are more likely to receive prescriptions for mood-altering and addictive drugs.

The facts about women and prescription drugs are startling:

- Each year, doctors in the United States write more than 121 million prescriptions for psychotropic drugs such as tranquilizers and sleeping pills. Over one-half of these prescriptions are written for women.
- More than 70 percent of all the antidepressant prescriptions written each year are written for women.
- Eighty percent of all the stimulant drug prescriptions—mostly for diet pills—are for women.
- Fifty percent more women than men are prescribed anti-psychotic drugs—the major tranquilizers—to treat illnesses such as schizophrenia.
- In a 1977 survey of persons over 65, conducted by the National Institute on Drug Abuse, nearly three times as many women as men reported using tranquilizers, sedatives and antidepressants.[3]

Of course, prescription drugs do have value. Some improve the quality of life for those with severe mental illnesses and some make a considerable difference for individuals who are experiencing both physical and emotional pain. Problems arise when drugs are improperly prescribed, when medication becomes a substitute for more costly interventions, when individuals are sedated in order to control behavior or when a person comes to rely on medication to deal with life's stresses and problems.

Problems with prescription drugs also arise from "self-medication." Women are much more likely than men to use pills to self-medicate, and to determine their own dosage and frequency of use without medical consultation. Women are also more likely than men to pressure their physicians to increase and continue their medications. This isn't surprising since prescription drugs provide one of the only legitimate "highs" or escapes for women.[5]

Women respond to prescription drugs in different ways at different times. Certain factors will affect an individual woman's response to a drug—her physical and emotional state, her previous use of drugs, her pattern of use of a particular drug and how much of the drug is still in her body. For this reason, a woman cannot be sure a mood-changing drug that acts one way in her body one day will react the same the day after.

The concept of "half life" is important to understand when focusing on the impact of prescription drugs on women's bodies. Half life refers to the time it takes for one-half of the original amount of the drug in the blood to leave the user's body. Different drugs have different half lives. For instance, Dalmane, a sleeping pill, has a half life of 108 hours. For Valium, a minor tranquilizer, it is 30 to 60 hours. So, if a woman is taking Valium every night, it will take several days for the drug to leave her system. If she adds other drugs to the equation, like alcohol, she will be ingesting a potentially deadly combination.[7]

Drug tolerance is also an important concept in understanding how drugs affect a woman's body. Tolerance refers to the way in which the body adjusts to a drug and then needs more of the drug to achieve the same effect. In other words, the more one takes of the drug, the more one needs. This pattern continues and doses must increase in order to achieve the same result. As the dose of the drug increases so does the amount of the drug that is remaining in the woman's system.

Drinking exacerbates the effects of many prescription drugs and presents a particular problem for women because women are more likely to use prescription drugs in combination with alcohol. Combining alcohol with minor tranquilizers such as Librium, Valium or Xanax is especially hazardous. Both alcohol and prescription drugs depress the central nervous system. The combination may make a woman feel good at first but may eventually cause a severe depressive reaction. Dual addiction often begins with drinking. Alcohol may increase feelings of anxiety and depression. A visit to the doctor for these symptoms may end with a prescription for tranquilizers. Women can become caught up in a vicious cycle—pills to counteract the bad effects of the alcohol and alcohol when the effect of the pills wears off. The combined effect of alcohol and tranquilizers is "synergistic"—it is many times stronger than the effect of either the alcohol or the tranquilizers alone.

There are some prescription drugs which, although valuable for some conditions, can be particularly harmful for women if not used with caution. These include minor tranquilizers, barbiturates, nonbarbiturate sedatives, amphetamines (stimulants and appetite-control drugs), narcotic pain-relievers, antidepressants and major tranquilizers.[10] Each of these is described briefly here.

Minor tranquilizers are prescribed to relieve anxiety and muscle spasms. There are two kinds of minor tranquilizers—the carbamate type (Miltown, Equanil or Meprobamate) and the benzodiazepines (Valium, Librium, Xanax, Tranxene, Ativan and Halcion). The benzodiazepines are also anti-convulsant drugs. Some of these drugs were introduced in the 1960s and became popular because they were thought to be effective and to carry relatively few side effects. Moreover, they were viewed as safer than barbiturates. One of the main advantages of the benzodiazepines over barbiturates was the wide margin of safety between the therapeutic dose and the lethal dose—it takes a larger dose of Valium to kill you than it does of a barbiturate. They are dangerous when taken in combination with alcohol or when taken daily over a period of time. Depending on the daily dose, they can be physically addicting within a few months.

Recently, great concern has been expressed over the effectiveness and safety of drugs like Valium and Xanax. While these drugs may give a sense of well-being, heavy users report erratic feelings including extreme anger. Withdrawal symptoms are prolonged and severe, and include feelings of shakiness and restlessness, inability to sleep, mental confusion, sweating and acute anxiety attacks. In some people, prolonged use produces similar symptoms. As a result of the highly addictive nature of these drugs, medical professionals are becoming much more cautious in prescribing the benzodiazepines. Many doctors now suggest the use of these drugs only for the short-term treatment of muscle spasms and anxiety.

Barbiturates include Nembutal, Seconal and Tuinal. These drugs were used for sedation and sleep. When taken in large doses they can produce coma, depressed blood pressure and death. Barbiturates are highly addictive and extremely dangerous in combination with alcohol, and physical withdrawal is severe. These drugs were often used in suicide attempts. Since Nembutal, Seconal and Tuinal are so dangerous, there has been a decline in their popularity, and they are prescribed infrequently. Phenobarbital, also a barbiturate, has been used effectively to control epileptic seizures and convulsions. Small doses of phenobarbital are also found in some drugs effective for the control of migraine headaches.

Nonbarbiturate sedatives are sleeping pills. One of the more popular was Methaqualone or Quaalude.

Withdrawal from the drug is severe. Although Methaqualone is no longer on the market in the United States, it can still be purchased in other countries under different brand names. The use of barbiturates or Quaaludes in combination with alcohol is extremely dangerous.

Amphetamines—diet or pep pills—are stimulants. They include Dexadrine, Benzedrine and Preludin. They are addictive. Amphetamines were manufactured and sold in large quantities in this country before the 1970s. The Food and Drug Administration developed stronger regulations for dispensing amphetamines because there were so many problems with addiction. Amphetamines are now legally prescribed only for narcolepsy (sleeping sickness), hyperkinesis (hyperactivity in children) and weight control. The use of amphetamines for weight control remains highly controversial. High doses of amphetamines can trigger confusion, violent and bizarre behavior and hallucinations. Long-term use can lead to serious medical problems, including brain damage, convulsions and coma. Deaths from amphetamine use have been reported. Withdrawal from amphetamines can lead to severe depression and, sometimes, suicide. For this reason, medical supervision of withdrawal is important.

Narcotics include Percodan (oxycodone), Demerol and codeine. They are used to relieve pain. They cause drowsiness and can be addictive both psychologically and physically. Withdrawal is uncomfortable and can resemble a bad case of the flu.

Tricyclic antidepressants (Elavil) and major tranquilizers (Thorazine) are important drugs for the treatment of severe depression, schizophrenia and other major mental illnesses. The use of these drugs in particular must be carefully monitored by a physician. Emergency rooms each year handle thousands of people with problems associated with antidepressant and major tranquilizer misuse. Women have far more problems with these drugs and often combine antidepressants with alcohol. The tricyclic antidepressants are drugs now frequently associated with suicide attempts. Some women are reporting extreme adverse reactions, including uncontrollable violent episodes, as a result of taking some of the antidepressants.

Over-the-Counter Drugs

There are many over-the-counter drugs including antacids, analgesics, antihistamines, vitamins and cough medicines. Some of these are safe. Others may not be. It is impossible to know who uses over-the-counter drugs or how the drugs are being used. These drugs are commonly sold in pharmacies and other retail outlets, and there is no system for regulating their purchase.[5]

There is some information which indicates that women may use more over-the-counter drugs than men, particularly women between the ages of 15 and 44. One study found that women were more likely to use stimulant drugs (diet pills) and that men were more likely to purchase drugs like No-Doz.[9] Programs that treat women with alcohol and drug problems have found that women report using over-the-counter sleep aids, diet pills, aspirin and Tylenol.

Conclusion

Women use alcohol and drugs for many reasons—to relax, to celebrate special occasions, to feel a part of the crowd, to ease pain and to feel more powerful. For all women, the use of alcohol and other legal drugs can become a problem. We now know that even small amounts of alcohol can increase a woman's chance of getting breast cancer.[11,12] We know that alcohol and drug use can create risks for women who are pregnant.[13] Combining alcohol and prescription drugs can be deadly. Withdrawal from prescription drugs, especially minor tranquilizers and barbiturates, can be prolonged and very severe.

All women need to take a close look at their own drinking and drug use. Legal drugs are highly seductive and women can grow dependent without intending to or realizing it. Some medical professionals may prescribe drugs without asking pertinent questions about a woman's medical history or her use of other drugs, or without warning the woman about potential dangers associated with her use of the particular drug being prescribed. The media, in addition to medical professionals, are sources of information for many health-related issues. They are not a reliable source for providing accurate information about legal drugs. Alcohol advertising is a perfect example. With the relaxation of FDA regulations regarding prescription drugs, we may see ads similar to those for alcohol before the decade is well underway.

Women need to ask some difficult questions of themselves and others: Am I taking this drink or pill to avoid an argument? Am I taking it to feel more comfortable with friends, for companionship? Do family members or friends ever express concern about my drinking or drug use? Do I ever feel guilty about my drinking or drug use? While legal drugs may provide temporary relief to ease stress or calm nerves, the long-term tradeoff can be very painful. Physical, social and emotional problems go hand-in-hand with regular, long-term drug use.

A very popular poster in women's treatment programs asserts "Silencing Women Isn't Helping." Alcohol and drugs anesthetize and silence. The line between harmless use and problems is a fine one—a line women cross over every day without knowing it.

Women with alcohol and drug problems are not

"other." They are our mothers, sisters, partners and ourselves. All women have a role to play in helping each other to identify when drug use has become a problem. It is important to begin with simple, supportive questions. It is also important to learn about the resources in your community. Recovery is possible and women of all ages, ethnic and racial backgrounds and economic means are beginning the process. Silencing women isn't helping and all women have a role to play in making sure that alcohol and drugs don't prevent women's voices from being heard.

References
1. R.T. Ravenholt, M.D., *Addiction Mortality in the U.S.*, National Institute on Drug Abuse, March, 1983.
2. Hill, S. "Vulnerability to the Biomedical Consequences of Alcoholism and Alcohol Related Problems." In Wilsnack and Beckman, *Alcohol Problems in Women*, NY: The Guilford Press, 1984.
3. Public Health Service. (1985). *Women's Health Report of the Public Health Service Task Force On Women's Health Issues*. (DHHS Pub. No. (PHS) 85-50206). Washington: D.C.: U.S. Government Printing Office.
4. Blume, S. (1986). "Women and alcohol: a review." *Journal of the American Medical Association*, 256, 1467-1470.
5. Gomberg, E. (1986). "Women: alcohol and other drugs." In B. Segal (ed), *Perspectives on Drug Use in the United States* (pp. 75-109). Haworth Press.
6. Lender, M., & Martin, J. (1982). *Drinking in America*. New York, NY: The Free Press.
7. Brenton, M. (1982). *Women and Abuse of Prescription Drugs*. New York, NY: Public Affairs Committee.
8. National Institute on Drug Abuse. (1989). *National Household Survey on Drug Abuse: Population Estimates 1988*. (DHHS Pub. No. (ADM) 89-1636). Washington, D.C.: Government Printing Office.
9. Burt, M.R., Glynn, T.J., & Sowder, B.J. (1979) *Psychosocial Characteristics of Drug-abusing Women*. DHEW Publication No. ADM 80-917. Rockville, MD: National Institute on Drug Abuse.
10. Prozac is a new antidepressant drug widely prescribed to both men and women. Some people are reporting severe negative reactions to the drug.
11. Willett, W.C., Stampfer, M.J., Colditz, M.B., Rosner, B., Hennekens, C., & Spaizer, F. (1987). "Alcohol consumption and the risk of breast cancer." *The New England Journal of Medicine* 316, 1174-1179.
12. Schatzkin, A., Jones, D., Zeigler, R.G., Harvey, E.B., Carter, C., Licitra, L., Dufour, M., & Larson, D. (1987). "Alcohol consumption and breast cancer in the epidemiological follow-up study of the first national health and nutrition examination survey." *The New England Journal of Medicine*, 316, 1169-1173.
13. National Council on Alcoholism. (1988). *Women, Alcohol and Other Drugs*. New York, NY: NCA.

20 Women and Illegal Drugs

Maria Vandor, Patti Juliana, and Rose Leone

"Women who use illegal drugs . . . are frequently seen as having a 'self-imposed addiction' and are often considered to be among the 'weak-willed.' This perception threatens to create different classes of substance abusers—those who are to blame for their problems and those who are not."

Like Dorothy in *The Wizard of Oz*, women who use illegal drugs are often put in the precarious position of wanting to click their heels three times to guarantee return to the safety and security of "home." However, nine times out of ten, these women just manage to scuff their shoes. In the United States, we have been raised to want to feel good—or at least not to feel bad. We take a magical potion, our problems are solved, and we can finally go home! Unfortunately, this conditioning can lead to poor choices.

Conservative estimates reveal that one out of every 10 Americans is dependent upon mood-altering substances, including alcohol. Addiction to substances affects both men and women. Drug and alcohol abuse in our society has become a problem of alarming proportions. Estimating conservatively, alcohol and drug abuse has become the third largest health problem in America. An estimated 8.5 million Americans are drug abusers and 10.5 million Americans are alcoholic.

Reasons for drug use, which may escalate to abuse, include relieving pain, stress or tension, influencing mood, enhancing social interaction, changing energy levels or promoting sleep. Drugs are also used to satisfy curiosity, to gain acceptance within a particular peer group and to achieve altered states of consciousness. One definition of drug abuse states that "[it] is the use of any substance in a manner that deviates from the accepted medical, social or legal patterns within a given society."[1]

Chemical dependency has increased steadily among women and for some drugs, such as cocaine, abuse by women is increasing more rapidly than is abuse by men. It is estimated that women make up 33-50 percent of all alcoholics and 20-30 percent of all heroin addicts, and that they are the primary users of barbiturates, non-barbiturates, sedative-hypnotics, minor tranquilizers, antidepressants, diet pills, non-controlled analgesics and controlled narcotics, not including heroin.

The 1988 Household Survey on Drug Abuse indicates that women in significant numbers are reporting the use of an illegal substance at some time in their lives. Of those surveyed, almost 35 percent of White women, compared to 39 percent of White men, reported using an illegal drug. Among Hispanics, almost 27 percent of the women, as compared to almost 38 percent of the men, reported using an illegal drug in their lifetime. Among Blacks, 29 percent of women, compared with 43 percent of men, said they used an illegal drug at some point in their lives.[2]

Women who use illegal drugs face a greater stigma. They are frequently seen as having a "self-imposed addiction" and are often considered to be among the "weak-willed." This perception threatens to create different classes of substance abusers—those who are to blame for their problems and those who are not. Women who use illegal drugs are condemned not only as being a failure for their weakness but also for not acting as the stabilizing force in family life. This is a difficult stigma to bear, since the quality of family life is almost always dependent on women. We often see families depicted in which the man is addicted or alcoholic, while the woman attempts to hold the family together. However, if the woman becomes chemically dependent, especially to illegal drugs, family life may disintegrate, since she is often depicted and perceived as the stabilizing force.

Drug use and abuse is often much more readily accepted by society if the person using is male. Denial or disgust are the most common responses to female addiction, especially if a woman is pregnant or has children. And yet, many women traumatized by domestic violence, sexual abuse, incest as children, illiteracy and homelessness may turn to illegal drugs in an effort to cope with feelings of helplessness, hopelessness, frustration and pain.

Most of what has been learned about illegal drug use relates specifically to drug use among men. There is a paucity of empirical data that reflect patterns of drug use, misuse, and abuse among women. Factors which may precipitate the use of illegal drugs by women are as diverse as the consequences. Physiological problems, psychological complications, socioeconomic factors and social role conflicts may predicate drug use and drug choice. The influence of the family is also a determining factor in patterns of use, abuse and recovery. It is important to remember that the causes and risks for drug dependence, whether it be to a legal or illegal drug, are not gender-specific. Addiction in women is essentially the same as addiction in men. Women show many of the same symptoms that men do. Women's experience of the consequences of drug use and of treatment vary greatly, however.[3]

All people use drugs for their initial benefits. Drugs can be a self-prescribed medication for feelings. For instance, stimulants, often used as aids in dieting, boost feelings of confidence. Barbiturates and tranquilizers used with alcohol can reduce anxiety levels. Cocaine use can enhance feelings of competency. Heroin use enables one to withdraw from life's problems and can result in feelings of security and calmness. Both legal and illegal drugs may also be used in combination with each other to enhance or counteract the effects of other drugs.

The initial reason for using illegal drugs may be to provide relief from uncomfortable feelings. However, continued use decreases early "positive effects" and replaces them with negative consequences. This discomfort can result in increased doses or in the use of other drugs to cope with the noxious effects of the drug originally used. For example, cocaine or crack may initially relieve feelings of worthlessness or powerlessness, but may eventually result in depression or paranoia. Continued cocaine use may cause feelings of shame. Increased use enhances the fear of incrimination, which often results in the need for increased doses of the drug.

Many women begin using illegal drugs as a means of empowering themselves. The drugs may help counter feelings of helplessness which may have begun as a result of childhood experiences of neglect or abuse. Despair, rage, and fear are all minimized by "hard" drug use.

Many users of illegal drugs share similar histories of parental deprivation or lack of familial integration. Their families have often experienced multigenerational problems with alcohol and drug abuse. Children raised in homes where a parent or parents are mentally ill may fear that the illness is inherited. When these children begin to experience feelings they cannot identify, they may turn to illegal drugs rather than be identified as "mentally ill" like their parents. As these children grow up, they tend to carry their problems with them, and drugs are often viewed as potent solutions to problems of daily living. They often enter adulthood with a multitude of problems and are in need of repair and healing.

Many environmental factors contribute to addictive behaviors. A study that compared drug-addicted and non-addicted women from similar socioeconomic backgrounds noted significant differences between the two groups. Nearly 70 percent of the drug-dependent women experienced early sexual abuse (before the age of sixteen). In the non-addicted women, fifteen percent had been abused sexually. Eighty-three percent of the drug-dependent women had a chemically dependent parent. Seventy-five percent of those parents were alcoholic. In contrast, thirty-five percent of the non-addicted women had a chemically dependent parent. The families of drug-dependent women had higher levels of family conflict and physical violence, and lower levels of family cohesion.[4]

Characteristics common to the childhood experiences of women with drug problems include chaos, unpredictability and inconsistency. Their homes often lacked security, safety, attention and nurturing. The parent was not able to fulfill the child's basic needs, and the child quickly learned to satisfy the needs of the parent in order to survive. The parent may also have experienced this same phenomenon with his/her parent(s). A cyclical pattern from childhood emerges that can influence a woman's use of illegal drugs. Surviving early sexual abuse or family violence often forces a young girl to experience feelings of fragmentation and to search for an escape. Where there is inner chaos, illegal drugs provide the illusion of feeling complete. The use of these drugs validates feelings of being outside social norms and expectations.

Sometimes, initial experimentation with illegal drugs is a way of expressing anger stemming from the deprivation experienced in childhood. Illegal drug use provides a potent means of shaming or disgracing parents who were hurtful. In some families, the use of illegal drugs honors a conspiracy of silence—as long as the user protects the family secrets, the family tolerates the drug use.

The family structure is instrumental in establishing the response to societal norms and expectations. While there has been significant progress in breaking down traditional gender roles, pressure to conform to those roles is often imposed by families. Dependence, passivity and compliance are still encouraged in women. Conformity to acceptable norms of behavior is enforced and reinforced. Women raised with these values move outside these norms when they use illegal drugs. The drugs quickly create feelings of pseudo-independence and reduce inhibitions. Women who are passive, withdrawn and conforming can express themselves—even in an exaggerated form—with the use of illegal drugs.

Illegal drug use places the user further outside societal norms. Behaviors that are directly related to the drug effects, as well as procurement activities, create a subculture outside the mainstream of society. The user is filled with new expectations and experiences a new sense of belonging and acceptance. The use of illegal drugs results in behaviors necessary to maintain an ongoing supply of the drugs. Theft, violence and prostitution are common activities undertaken to secure money with which to purchase drugs. Illegal drug use minimizes inhibitions and allows women to engage in previously restricted behaviors. The drug effects allow the illusion of expanded acceptable limits of behavior. Although the user develops relationships with those who conform to the new standard of behavior, the behaviors themselves reinforce feelings of being outside social norms and expectations.

For women, prostitution provides a way of earning money to maintain their habit. Despite sex role reversals, women in the drug culture are still protected by men. The changes of mores and inhibitions result in a greater freedom for sexual activity. At increasingly younger ages, women learn that sex can be traded for affection, popularity and, sometimes, for drugs. Pimps "protect" women who prostitute for drugs. Stories abound of women trading sexual favors for drugs at crack houses. Drug use and prostitution often serve as ways of replacing feelings of impotence with feelings of power.

Some women become dependent on their partners for drugs. Inadvertently, in search of someone who fills her need to be needed, a woman may join with a partner who provides drugs and also reinforces her self-loathing and feelings of worthlessness. Drug use may not have brought her to the partner, but it may become a part of her life. Sometimes the appeal of being with the partner is precisely the chaos or excitement of living "on the edge" of society. The woman can become trapped by her dependence on the drugs and on her partner. The fears she has about leaving the relationship and in establishing independence interfere with her efforts to "break out" of the relationship. Her use of drugs may temporarily reduce her fear. Feelings of depression and low self-esteem, which are common in female substance abusers, are reinforced by a double standard which often makes substance-abusing women undesirable partners in the eyes of their male peers.

Other consequences for women who use drugs should be taken into consideration. Addiction may cause delays in psychosocial development, depending on the age of onset of drug use. As a young woman comes to terms with her substance abuse and enters treatment, she must accomplish the developmental tasks of adolescence. She may be unprepared to negotiate in a world which expects more from her than she is capable of producing. The pressure to conform, in contrast to her feelings about her own capacity to do so, creates the potential for relapse.

If a woman has had children while addicted, she may be suffering from feelings of guilt or anxiety over the effects of her drug use on her children. Furthermore, she and her children may have become involved with child protective services agencies. Her children may have been taken from her, and she may be confronted with the task of negotiating with a large bureaucratic system. Involvement with child protective services may exacerbate her feelings of guilt, shame and incompetence unless proper and sensitive intervention is provided.

The treatment of women with substance abuse problems can be difficult and requires sensitivity. Many women may not seek treatment for themselves. Child Protective Services may have mandated that a woman seek treatment. A woman may enroll in treatment as a result of pregnancy. These motivating factors provide a unique opportunity for intervention, since, for some women, regaining custody of a child, or the health of their unborn children are key motivating factors to enter treatment. A mother will often do for her child what she would not do for herself. A woman may also tentatively approach treatment to get out of a dysfunctional relationship or as a result of her own poor health due to drug abuse.

Women who are in need of drug treatment services are also in dire need of health and medical care, housing and social services. In 1988, according to the most recent Analysis of State Alcohol and Drug Abuse Profile Data, only 22 percent of those entering publicly funded alcohol treatment programs and 33 percent of the drug program admissions were women.[6] In the past year, admissions for cocaine and crack (for both men and women) exceeded those for heroin. Very few programs are designed specifically for women.

Initially, a woman's commitment to treatment may be less than ideal and may require constant support. Treatment must include skill-building and assistance with concrete tasks that enable her to learn to live without using drugs. Moreover, a woman using illegal drugs needs an environment in which she can learn about the dynamics of addiction and can begin to trust others and herself. Most often, the factors which precipitated her drug use, combined with characteristics of the drug culture, have caused her to distrust others and rely completely on herself. She has learned that the world is not a safe place. It is critical that intervention and treatment staff working with women who use illegal drugs are not judgmental. Their approach must be a supportive one, so that women will stay in treatment, build self-confidence and learn the range of skills needed to maintain a drug-free lifestyle.

Treatment must be responsive to all the medical and social variables which complicate addiction and recovery for women. While methadone maintenance programs may encourage a heroin-free lifestyle, reduce the excessive exposure to human immunodeficiency virus (HIV) and help women have healthier infants, they do not address the range of social problems faced by many women who use drugs. Problems associated with support issues and access to food, housing and day care can be overwhelming to the recovering female addict. The chances for recovery are minimal when daily survival is at risk.[4]

Substance-abusing women need basic health and human care. It is suggested that well-baby clinics be revitalized. Outreach efforts in schools and community agencies need to be strengthened. Welfare and housing projects need to be upgraded. The reimbursement system needs to become more responsive. Providers of health, medical and social services need to learn that substance abusers are in need of many of the same services essential and available to non-abusers.

Treatment needs to focus on countering discriminatory practices against women who are poor and in need of education and employment assistance. Curricula geared toward women of color, extended families, women's issues and parenting skills are needed. Education on how to find and use services and how to negotiate systems needs to be developed. Treatment systems need to provide comprehensive services on-site, including prenatal care, gynecological services and birth control information.

In summary, drug abuse is a complex problem with symptoms ranging from minor physical or psychological difficulties to complete dependency, accompanied by physiological, psychological and social problems. To understand the impact of illegal drug use, it is helpful to become familiar with the specific effects of these drugs. Problems are most frequent with opiates, stimulants, marijuana and its derivatives, psychedelics and inhalants. The following is based on information in *The Well Adult*[1] and *Drug Free*:[5]

Opiates include heroin, morphine, meperidine (Demerol), pentazocine, talwin and codeine. It is estimated that between 5 and 10 percent of young city dwellers in the United States have used heroin at least once. Heroin addiction is actually a leading cause of death among urban males 15 to 35 years old. Heroin use usually begins with sniffing or inhaling, which causes a sense of peace, relaxation, relief from worry

and euphoria. Repeated use produces a tolerance that necessitates larger and larger doses to produce the same effects. Eventually, most users start to inject the drug, first subcutaneously and later intravenously. With each of the drugs classified as opiates, physical dependence ultimately develops—that is, withdrawal signs develop if the drug is not taken. These signs include anxiety, severe flu-like symptoms, perspiring and craving for the drug.[1]

Stimulants such as cocaine excite the central nervous system and give the user increased energy, confidence, euphoria and a sense of power. It is estimated that over 25 percent of the young adult population has tried cocaine at least once. Most often cocaine is inhaled in a powder form; less commonly, it is smoked or injected. A crystalline form of cocaine called "crack" has become widely available and is very inexpensive. The effects of ingesting cocaine persist for 20-40 minutes and are followed by a sense of letdown. In addition to the sense of euphoria, a person high on cocaine may feel restless, irritable and talkative. People who use the drug in large quantities may develop chronic feelings of paranoia and irritability and may use depressants such as alcohol to relieve these feelings.[1] In any form, cocaine can disturb the electrical rhythm between the brain and heart and cause potentially fatal seizures.[5] Stimulants create the illusion of increasing a person's energy and stamina by using up internal energy reserves. However, the stimulant effect of these drugs decreases each time they are used. The user needs more of the drug to maintain the status quo or to feel the drug's effects as intensely as the time before. After a while the system shuts down. Respiratory or cardiac arrest or the cessation of breathing can occur. Emergency-room crises caused by these drugs have increased dramatically in the past few years.[5]

Marijuana and hashish are mind-altering drugs which are both products of the hemp plant. They have been used for thousands of years. Marijuana is the most widely used illegal recreational drug in the United States. It is estimated that two-thirds of young adults ages 18-25 have used marijuana, and one-third are current users. The effects of marijuana are felt within minutes after it is inhaled, reach a peak within one hour and are gone within three hours. Effects vary widely with the dose, the user's personality and the social setting.[5] Reactions range from a sense of relaxation to giddy euphoria to anxiety. Perception of colors, sound and time may also be affected. Studies show that marijuana impairs short-term memory, and sometimes affects motor coordination, including driving. Continued use produces both physical and psychological tolerance to some degree, and cessation of regular use produces mild withdrawal symptoms of irritability and sleep disturbance.[1]

Psychedelics, a class of drugs that cause altered perceptions, have been used for thousands of years in religious rituals. Those most frequently used in the United States are LSD, psilocybin mushrooms, mescaline and angel dust (PCP). Of this group, LSD is the most potent. The effects include changes of perception, hallucinations, illusions, time and body-image distortions and mood changes. Common results are acute panic and paranoid, psychotic reactions.[1] Longer-term effects of psychedelics include flashbacks; times when the effects of the drug may recur spontaneously long after the drug has been used. Users of PCP may spend weeks, even months, under the influence of the drug and suffer in a state of psychological overdose before they return to normal thinking.[5]

Inhalants include amyl nitrate and nitrous oxide. They are used for sexual enhancement, mood elevation and relaxation. Adverse effects include heart palpitations and headaches.[1]

New Street Drugs[7]

Crank (as in "crank it up") is a common street term for crystal methedrine, an off-white powder which is a powerful amphetamine. Some of the street names for crank are Speed, Fast, Quick and Ups. Amphetamines are Schedule II controlled substances. They have some medical usages but there is a high potential for abuse.

Crank is a central nervous system stimulant, typically used to lift moods, curb appetites and increase energy levels. Tolerance to crank often leads to an increasing spiral of larger dosages. Although the use of crank does not necessarily lead to physiological addiction, psychological effects such as depression, anxiety and irritability may result from the cessation of use.

Ice is a common street term for methamphetamine, a powerful synthetic stimulant. Methamphetamine normally appears as a white powder. When sold as the street drug Ice, it resembles clear rock candy, rock salt or shaved glass slivers. The substance is also known by other names—"rock candy" and "Hawaiian salt." Methamphetamine is considered a Schedule II controlled substance. This classification indicates that there is a high potential for abuse. Like crank, methamphetamine can be snorted, injected or taken orally. However, when methamphetamine is processed into Ice, the substance can also be smoked like crack. In locations where Ice is popular, smoking is the most popular route of administration.

Ice is a central nervous system stimulant. It impairs mental faculties, produces elevated blood pressure, tachycardia and palpitations. The drug is also associated with dizziness, dysphoria, insomnia, tremors, restlessness and headaches. Prolonged use leads to tolerance, extreme psychological dependence and severe social

disabilities. Abrupt cessation produces extreme levels of fatigue and depression.

Ecstasy is a "designer drug," a synthetic substance usually made in clandestine laboratories. Ecstasy is a bitter white powder, chemically known as MDMA. The substance represents a combination of synthetic mescaline and an amphetamine. Some of the street names for Ecstasy are XTC, Adam, Euphoria and X. In 1985, Ecstasy was declared illegal. It is now classified under the Controlled Substance Act as a Schedule I substance (the most stringently controlled category).

Ecstasy functions as a mild hallucinogenic, mood-altering stimulant. Ecstasy is believed to be psychologically but not necessarily physically addictive. Some users of Ecstasy have admitted to bouts of uncontrollable paranoia and depression, even months after they discontinued its use. The long-term effects of Ecstasy are not well understood. According to the Drug Enforcement Agency (DEA), this substance has been associated with at least a dozen deaths since 1985. Recent animal studies indicate that MDMA reduces serotonin levels in the brain. Serotonin is a substance whose levels have been associated with affective disorders such as suicide, depression and manic psychosis.

Moonrock is the street name for crack "impregnated" with heroin. This combination allows users to smoke the two substances simultaneously. The smoking of heroin in conjunction with crack is popular because it serves to diminish the severe depressive state and some of the other adverse physiological and psychological effects associated with crack use.

Most crack users, particularly when they engage in prolonged periods of smoking, experience an intensified "crash" when the effects of the crack wear off. In an attempt to buffer this experience, crack smokers have attempted to use almost every possible drug in combination with crack. The three most common substances used for this purpose are alcohol, barbiturates and marijuana. Heroin use in conjunction with crack smoking is simply another attempt at "beating the crash." Crack smokers report that heroin seems to be an ideal substance to help mitigate the crack-induced "crash." Heroin is a highly effective painkiller and its effects last longer than crack. When crack and heroin are smoked together, they produce a "speedball" effect which results in a more mellow and longer-lasting high. The danger of an increase in the popularity of moonrock is that it may serve to create a new generation of heroin addicts.

Summary

The types of illegal drugs used by women are as diverse as some of the problems caused by their use. Problems ranging from early incest and sexual abuse to social isolation may lead to the experimentation and long-term use of illegal drugs. Multi-faceted treatment that addresses the psychological, social and physical problems encountered by women with drug problems is necessary. A supportive environment will lead to the development of autonomy and self-acceptance which is crucial for women's recovery.

References

1. Samuels, Mike, M.D. and Samuels, Nancy. *The Well Adult.* New York, 1988.
2. National Institute on Drug Abuse. (1989). *National Household Survey on Drug Abuse: Population Estimates 1988.* (DHHS Pub. No. (ADM) 89-1636). Washington, D.C.: Government Printing Office.
3. Ray, Barbara, Ph.D. and Braude, Monique C. *Women and Drugs: A New Era for Research.* NIDA Research Monograph, 1986.
4. Finnegan, Loretta, P., M.D. Testimony delivered to Committee on Labor Human Resources, Subcommittee on Children, Family, Drugs and Alcoholism held in New York City, 1990.
5. Seymour, Seymour B. and Smith, David E., M.D. *Drug Free: A Unique, Positive Approach to Staying Off Alcohol and Other Drugs.* Facts on File Publications. New York, 1987.
6. Butynski, Bill, and Canova, Diane. *State Resources and Services Related to Alcohol and Drug Abuse Problems, Fiscal Year 1988.* National Association of State Alcohol and Drug Abuse Directors (NASADAD) report to the National Institute on Drug Abuse (NIDA) and the National Institute on Alcoholism and Alcohol Abuse (NIAAA).
7. New York State Division of Substance Abuse Services, Street Research Unit. *Street Drug Alert: A Street Perspective on Current Drug Trends* (1989).

21 Living With An Alcoholic

Jean Kennedy Tracy, Ph.D.

"Maybe not the first time, maybe not the second time, but eventually, like Chinese water torture, a drop at a time, the drinking begins to wear away at our sense of value, self-confidence and ability to control our environment. We begin to feel isolated, frustrated, afraid and ashamed. And we begin to ask, 'Why is this happening? And what am I doing wrong?' "

For many women, living with an alcoholic or other substance abuser is like living on a roller coaster. The ride begins with great expectation. It's exciting and fun. It seems safe and at the same time intense, like the long slow climb up the first incline. Then comes the teetering on the brink and a rapid downswing followed by another climb, not as high this time. Then another rapid dip. Once you are on the track it seems impossible to get off. When the car levels off, you can catch your breath and feel relief and expectation again. The difference between the roller coaster ride and living with an alcoholic is that on the roller coaster you can see where you are going and know how long the ride will last.*

One woman describes her expectations and lack of awareness this way:

> For a long time I feared exposing my feelings and admitting that I was living with an active alcoholic who was getting sicker and sicker. I had no idea what was going on. When I married him I did not consider him to be a drinker. When I met him he was just out of the Navy. He went out and drank with his friends sometimes and told stories about getting drunk and doing wild and crazy things. But back then, I just thought that is what the guys did when they were not married. The belief that I held was that a good woman would be able to make a man stop doing that after they were married. If a woman was a good wife, her man would be a sober responsible provider for her and their children. That's what I thought then.

*Author's note: More women in the United States live with alcoholics than with men or partners dependent on other drugs. Alcohol remains the drug of choice in the U.S. and more men are alcoholic than women. The focus of this chapter, therefore, is on women who live with alcoholic men. Some of the same issues described affect women living with men dependent on other drugs. Some of the same issues affect women living with a partner of either sex who is dependent on alcohol or other drugs. And some of the same issues affect men who stay in relationships with alcoholic women.

When one person in a family abuses alcohol, the rest of the family members respond with a variety of behaviors which are meant to help them and the family system to survive. We operate in a somewhat delusional society which places a high value on keeping families at any cost. This places an unrealistic expectation on women to make a family work.

Alcoholism is still viewed as a shameful moral weakness. And our society still teaches women and children to judge themselves by what their spouse or parents do or don't do. We are judged by the accomplishments or failures of our family members, with little or no regard for what we ourselves do. The fear of what others will think leads to the need to keep what may be considered unsavory behavior secret.

Children who grow up in a family which tries to keep someone's drinking a secret, grow up with overwhelming feelings of responsibility and blame. Although the impact of living with an alcoholic is similar for both boys and girls[1,2] when they are young, gender-role expectations may complicate the way an adult female will learn to deal with an alcoholic partner. She is more apt to stay in the partnership and more apt to blame herself for all of the discomfort.

Living with an alcoholic reinforces the sexist cultural attitude that everything is a woman's responsibility or fault. As a child, she learns that to think of herself is wrong. She learns that her every action or lack of action may result in the drinker getting angry or becoming happy. She learns to try to control herself and everyone around her. She has often been physically or sexually abused and told it was her fault. As a result, she learned to disassociate (go into another world), deny reality and blame herself for the problems of those around her. She has learned to protect herself from expectation and disappointment. She may use substances herself to forget the pain.

On the other hand, a woman who grows up in a family with alcohol or drug problems may become an overachiever or a perfectionist who can never achieve for fear of failure. In either case, she will develop an extreme desire to attempt to control her world. Her world may include herself, her children, her partner, her fellow workers and her neighbors—everything and everyone who comes in contact with her and her environment, anyone or anything which may create a sense of surprise or the unexpected. In short, she may become a "codependent."

Codependency is a descriptive term for the set of coping mechanisms which started out as adaptive survival tools for people living with alcoholics and other substance abusers. Over time they become rigid responses aimed at trying to control themselves and as much of their environment as possible, in order to deny the shameful reality of their lives for which they erroneously feel responsible. These behaviors get reinforced by childhood learnings, a love for and desire to stay with the alcoholic, cultural values and norms, religious beliefs and/or financial need. It is preferable to think of this set of behaviors as a syndrome rather than criteria for the diagnosis of a mental illness.[3]

Women living with an alcoholic develop the disease/ dis-ease of codependency. What does codependency look like? The partner or family member of a substance abuser alternates between feeling that she is responsible for the well-being and functioning of everything in her family, and feeling helpless to control almost anything in her life.

While this chapter does not focus on the historical, political, or social aspects of the term "codependency," it is important to recognize that the term can be used as yet another way of blaming women for what happens to them as a result of our society's sexism, racism, and classism. We live in an addictive society[4] where recognizing one's own or other's maladaptive coping mechanisms is not okay. Codependency is not a gender-specific term. Men as well as women suffer from it. However, due to women's acculturation and financial dependence, they more often stay in alcoholic or drug-dependent relationships.

Because of the danger that women will be blamed, some feminist writers have commented that the term "codependency" once again tells women that if they change their behavior the alcoholic will change his or her abusive drinking behavior.[5] This is certainly not the interpretation of "codependency" outlined in this chapter. When a person is able to recognize her or his own maladaptive coping mechanisms and change them, it may or *may not* have an impact on the drinker's behavior. The point is, living with alcoholism or other substance abuse is oppressive. Codependence is a description of a syndrome or set of behaviors that arises as individuals attempt to survive in a dysfunctional family system within a dysfunctional culture. To

recognize one's own learned maladaptive behavior and take responsibility for it rather than blame someone or something else enables that person to begin to cope in a healthier way.

Jennifer describes codependency this way:

He had an alcoholic older brother. The family thought it was a secret. Everyone in the neighborhood knew it, but the family were first-class enablers. Of course I did not know what an enabler was then. I only knew they would bail him out no matter what his crime or what hardship it put on the family. The worst I remember was going to the jail with his sister to get the brother after he had been charged with drunk driving and improper sexual conduct with two minors. To the family and close friends he was someone to be pitied. He had lost his one true love. His life was hard. He just couldn't hold his liquor. He just wasn't man enough anymore because his girl had betrayed him and his work did not allow him to achieve his true potential. I too, began to keep the secret, to deny that anything out of the ordinary was happening. He was a good guy, he just drank too much sometimes. I felt sorry for him. I began to feel ashamed and to deny the seriousness of his problems.

Often women who live with alcoholics do not know the signs of alcohol abuse and alcoholism. In some neighborhoods and cultures heavy drinking is the norm. It is acceptable for people, especially men, to drink more after a disappointment or quarrel or to drink under pressure. Yet alcohol dependence develops with constant use of alcohol for relief of uncomfortable feelings like anger, sadness, fear, and disappointment. This pattern of use can result in an increase in alcohol tolerance. It takes more and more alcohol to get relief. With increased use of alcohol, people may begin to have memory blackouts and/or they may sneak an extra drink or two so that others won't know how much they drink. There is usually an urgent desire for the first drink, feelings of guilt and an inability to discuss this with anyone.   Jennifer describes her lack of awareness this way:

There were early signs of alcoholism which I did not recognize, mostly because I did not know they were signs. One of those was that weekends, parties, and dates were *always* occasions for buying and drinking a lot of alcohol. No occasion was complete without it. In fact, he would be nervous at first without it. I had never associated occasions with alcohol, but responded by feeling that my family was less sophisticated than his. I believed that something was wrong with me for coming from a lower-class, poor, unsophisticated family.

He would also tell me hilarious stories of when he had been drinking and did really crazy things which he could not remember. Of course, we did not call them blackouts. He was just so drunk he couldn't remember how much fun he had had. But everyone laughed and thought those unremembered times were the best. Oh, sure, sometimes he got in fights about silly slights and imagined insults. And sometimes he got really depressed.

The warning signals of alcoholism become more insistent, but often continue to go unrecognized as the partner or family member's own codependence progresses. The downswing into the crucial phase of alcoholism is heralded by an increase in memory blackouts, an inability to stop drinking when others do, drinking bolstered by excuses, grandiose and aggressive behavior, persistent remorse, promises and resolutions, failed efforts to control drinking, unreasonable resentments, a decrease in alcohol tolerance, loss of ordinary will power, work and money troubles, tremors, early morning drinking and physical problems. Most of these symptoms occur *before* the clear signs of alcoholism which our society usually uses to define an alcoholic.

Jennifer describes her husband's progression into alcoholism and her progression into codependency this way:

Then we got married. He became a sober and responsible husband and father. We had great ambitions for ourselves and I handled the money (a custom which was passed down from both of our families). I was not socialized to have alcohol around or to buy it for special occasions. Besides, we just couldn't afford it. During this time in our lives we were poor but happy. Some romantics would say we were happy because we were poor. That was not true. We were happy because we could communicate with each other, because we had mutual goals and values, and because we were not battling the active disease of alcoholism.

That changed. It started out at a Christmas party at the warehouse where he worked. He came home late, passed out in the bathroom, and left me to entertain our friends and relatives who had come to spend Christmas Eve with us in our new house. I stayed up and got the Christmas stuff ready for the kids. He apologized and was full of guilt and remorse. He would never do that again, he swore. And almost a year went by before he did. The next time it was a fishing trip with the guys. He came home from the mountains a day late. Not sure what he had done, remorseful and ashamed. He swore that he would not do that again.

I got accustomed to the irresponsible behavior whenever he went on special things with the guys or to office parties. After all, he was still a responsible husband and father most of the time. Wasn't it unfair of me to resent his "need to unwind once in a while"? And in the meantime, his ambition was paying off. He was being promoted. With each promotion came more money. It also meant more responsibility and more pressure. It also began the business lunches and dinners. We were now expected to do more entertaining in our home and as a couple. Our lives were full of special occasions. Our lives were full of pressures. He was now drinking more regularly. He could drink a quart of vodka in a day and a night.

He had begun to drink vodka because no one could smell it on his breath. He hardly ever had a beer anymore. It smelled too strong and his bosses might think he was drunk at work. I guess it was about then that I began to deny just how much he drank. I really did not think he drank much. I did get angry and try to find ways to get him to be more responsive to me and my needs. I did try to force him somehow to be the man I thought I had married.

He had changed and so had I. I had become so depressed I could barely function. This added to my fear of losing him. I blamed myself for all of his negative behavior. I felt unlovable and unloving. I began to see a therapist. I thought I was crazy. I just did not know at that time that all this anger, frustration, resentment, disappointment, fear and depression was related to the progression of alcoholism. I did not know that it was about him and his drinking. I blamed myself and so did people around me. I no longer was connected to my family and had no way to get validation. I was very confused.

Living with an alcoholic is a confusing and painful experience. For someone who has never lived with an alcoholic, the onset of the problem and its impact are as slow and as insidious as the progression of alcoholism itself. As alcoholism progresses, a personality pattern develops which is characteristically hostile and negative. This is especially so at home.

Included in this pattern is a tendency to be tense and depressed, aggressive or stubbornly quiet, perfectionistic and rigidly idealistic and oppressed by feelings of inferiority while secretly feeling superior. Alcoholics experience overpowering feelings of loneliness, isolation and self-pity. They may be self-centered and consciously or unconsciously defiant or rebellious. Finally, alcoholics become walled off in a world apart from others. As the alcoholic struggles with these patterns of behavior and the pain, resentment and rage that develop with them, he lashes out, withdraws, or otherwise acts inappropriately towards others.

The alcoholic's partner, family members and friends will react with hurt, disappointment, and anger. They become resentful of the person who is drinking who has let them down, who has made another "mistake." The very act of calling it a mistake is the beginning of the process of denial.

The drinking person will apologize and/or respond with anger at the person's reactions. This leads to self-questioning. "Why am I upset about this person drinking? It's a perfectly normal thing to do, something that almost everyone I know does." In our culture and in many cultures, it is considered perfectly acceptable for a man to go out and drink with his friends. It is one of the things that men are supposed to do. A good partner is expected not to be upset, jealous, hurt or disappointed when her partner does this. But we are. Maybe not the first time, maybe not the second time, but eventually, like Chinese water torture, a drop at a time, the drinking begins to wear away our sense of value, self-confidence and ability to control our environment. We begin to feel isolated, frustrated, afraid and ashamed. And we begin to ask, "Why is this happening? And what am I doing wrong?"

These questions, "Why is this happening? And what am I doing wrong?" lead us to ask "What am I doing to cause it?" This is reinforced by the alcoholic because as the disease progresses, he looks around for something or someone outside himself to blame for his behavior. On some level, the alcoholic recognizes that his behavior is not appropriate, is not loving. His behavior becomes a wall, a breach, a separation from his loved ones.

He begins to blame his problems on the woman and the children who live with him. And this insidious disease begins to take root in those people. He says things like, "If you hadn't looked at that man that way, I wouldn't have had to do what I did." As his inhibitions and his self-control lessen over the months and years of drinking, his temper may flare and his irrational behavior increase. He may begin to physically abuse his partner, to beat her, to shake her, to lock her in her room. He may begin to vilify her. As his sexual ability changes, he is often physically unable to maintain erections. He begins to doubt his own adequacy and so heaps scorn upon his partner and blames her for his body's reaction to alcohol.

For most women, the result of her partner's deterioration is to make her feel less attractive, worthless as a sexual partner and frustrated and unfulfilled as a woman. In some relationships with an alcoholic, the only time he is interested in sex is when he is drunk, when he may or may not be able to perform. Under the influence of alcohol, the quality of his sexual advances may be a turnoff for his partner, as well as another reason for his partner to blame herself. She vacillates between guilt, shame, self-blame and anger, and resentment and blame towards the alcoholic.

Women who live with alcoholics learn to distrust. They learn to take control, and feel inadequate in that control because they generally get criticized for it. Many people who live with alcoholics talk about an almost Dr. Jekyll-and-Mr. Hyde quality in the man they are with. They describe their partners as moving erratically from very loving and kind to angry and hateful. They begin to walk around as though the ground beneath them is made of eggshells, careful not to crack any or cause any disturbance.

Some alcoholics will become physically abusive. They will beat their wives or beat their children, or beat them all. In some families, the alcoholic becomes verbally abusive. An alcoholic may call his wife or children names and threaten to kill them. The verbal

and physical abuse is sometimes extreme. Other times it is subtle. Sometimes a woman's own protective defenses convince her that it's not so bad, that it's not really abuse. This denial is sometimes necessary because the woman does not have the resources to leave.

Jennifer describes her abuse this way:

> One time when we were out, he got drunk and wouldn't take me home. So, I went home myself. When he arrived later, he began calling me names and saying I didn't love him. Then he took hold of my shoulders and shook me. Then he threw me into the round mirror coffee table I had made and broke it. The next thing I knew, he had me on the floor in the bedroom. His hands were around my neck and he was choking me and shaking me. My head was hitting the floor. For a long time I didn't think of that as abuse. Probably because someone had called the police and they had taken him to the psychiatric hospital. How could it be abuse when he was just acting crazy?

In some families the alcoholic becomes sexually abusive with any or all of his children. Because alcohol lowers inhibitions and causes impaired thinking, the perpetrator justifies his abuse with irrational excuses. While under the influence of alcohol, he may imagine that sexual contact is the only way he can get love from or give love to his children. Sometimes he is just passing on what was done to him as a child. The cycle becomes one of abuse heaped on abuse and added to blame and guilt.

And so the people who live with an alcoholic take on his shame and his guilt. They feel helpless in the face of his drinking and his irrational or tyrannical behavior. Some women express their helplessness and impotent rage through physical illness. Their bodies, unable to take the stress, get sick. This illness adds to their feelings of helplessness and entrapment. They may continue to resist or deny seeing the problem as "his" problem and take it as their own. They may try to control it, placate it.

A bitter power struggle and subtle dance begins to develop between the alcoholic and his partner. Sometimes she tries to please him or hold her partner by drinking with him. She avoids the things she believes will result in fights, beatings, abusive name-calling, and even more drinking.

The alcoholic tries to control the world of his alcohol abuse. His partner tries to control herself, her children and everyone around her in order to try to control him. She tries to control his behavior so he won't drink, berate, abuse, abandon her or blame her for all of his failures in life. She tries to control him so that she will not be blamed for all his disillusionment.

Thus, a woman who lives with an alcoholic develops many defenses in order to survive. She denies how bad it is to live with him and focuses on the times when he is kind and loving. She sometimes imagines these times last longer than they really do.

A woman who lives with an alcoholic becomes so accustomed to taking care of everyone and everything around her that she becomes the person everyone turns to when they need or want something. She may not be able to say "no." She may sometimes feel taken advantage of. But it is difficult to change this pattern because it may be one of the few ways in which she feels good about herself. Her self-worth has been worn away. Her confidence in her abilities has been eroded.

Life becomes grim for the woman living with an alcoholic. She may deny her own pain. She may project blame for everything onto the world outside the alcoholic or onto herself. She may be physically ill. She may be depressed and feel hopeless. She may feel impotent rage. She may feel great despair. She may feel crazy. She may consider suicide. She is locked in a deadly struggle which she may find difficult to give up. So much of her energy may go into the struggle to control her environment that she can't imagine a life without that struggle.

Jennifer describes her confusion about change this way:

> After I was in therapy for a while, I began to understand that much of my depression was anger that I was using against myself. I was immobilizing myself. When I finally realized that I could not control anyone's behavior but my own, I was frightened. I had spent so much time focused on my partner that I wasn't sure who or what I was. I feared a life of emptiness if I let go of the struggle. I guess I was also a little afraid that I wasn't important enough to think of myself first and to make the decision to detach from my partner's drinking.

What can a woman do if she is living with an alcoholic? First, get all the information she can about alcoholism and codependency. Second, find a support group for herself. Al-Anon is an excellent source of support and understanding to help a woman recover from her own problems brought on by living with an alcoholic. Third, she may want to get into therapy with a registered substance/alcohol abuse counselor, psychiatrist, psychologist, or clinical social worker. She should make sure that the latter three have training in alcoholism and drug addictions and understand her needs. Fourth, she needs to learn to set goals of her own. Fifth, she needs to find ways to satisfy her own spiritual needs. And sixth, she may need to ask for help in obtaining independent financial support.

As the woman who lives with an alcoholic begins to understand alcoholism and the real physical, emotional, and spiritual pain that she, her partner, and other family members are in, she may wish to take steps to intervene in healthy ways with her partner. To do this, it is strongly recommended that she get assistance from a trained professional to plan a therapeutic intervention. She may also wish to talk calmly and assertively to her partner when he has not been drinking, explaining her concern for her partner's health and well-being. She may need to tell him just what her limits are in relation to his drinking. She will certainly need to *detach* from the actual drinking behavior—no more rescues, no more excuses, no more secrets about his drinking.

In the process of setting limits for herself about what she will and will not tolerate, some women may decide they cannot or will not live with an actively drinking alcoholic. Some women will decide they have experienced so much pain that they will not or cannot live with the alcoholic even if he responds to the help that is offered, abstains from drinking, attends a Twelve Step program, and seeks counseling. It is important for a woman to know that she has the right to make her own choice. It is, after all, her life.

It is a confusing situation for a woman who lives with an alcoholic. Often there seems no way out. But it is possible to survive the pain and devastation and become an even heathier human being as a result of fearlessly recognizing what is happening. The journey to helping oneself (and sometimes the alcoholic) begins with an important first step: recognizing the truth. The truth is that one lives with an alcoholic and that one is not in control of that other person's drinking. The rest of the steps can be taken one at a time.

References

1. Black, Claudia. *It Will Never Happen to Me!*, Denver: M.A.C., 1981.
2. Wegsheider-Cruse, Sharon. *Miracle of Recovery: Healing for Addicts, Adult Children & Co-Dependance.* Deerfield Beach: Health Communications, Inc., 1989.
3. Cermak, Timmond. *Diagnosing & Treating Co-Dependency: A Guide for Professionals Who Work With Chemical Dependents, Their Spouses, & Children.* Minneapolis: Johnson Institute, 1986.
4. Schaef, Ann Wilson. *When Society Becomes An Addict.* New York: Harper & Row, 1987.
5. Kanuha, Vallie. "Co-Dependency and *Women Who Love Too Much:* Helpful or Harmful to Battered Women?" Presented at National Coalition Against Domestic Violence Ntl. Conf., Seattle, 1988.

22 Children of Alcoholic and Drug-Dependent Parents

Sheila B. Blume, M.D.

"Although children of substance abusers are both male and female, the problems outlined in this chapter are of special importance to women for three reasons. First of all, women are assigned the primary child-caring role in our society. Second, some of the special problems of these individuals relate to drinking or using drugs by the child's mother during pregnancy. Finally, there is some evidence that children of alcoholic mothers are more severely affected than those of alcoholic fathers."

Introduction

In 1969, R. Margaret Cork, a social worker at Toronto's Addiction Research Foundation, published a book she called *The Forgotten Children*.[1] It was a study of 116 children whose parents suffered from alcoholism and it documented, often in the children's own words, the chaos and silent suffering of their lives. The title was a most appropriate one, since research on alcohol and drug abuse was still in its infancy in the 1960s, and research on the children born into these disturbed families was virtually non-existent. Worse yet, there were two fallacious assumptions made, that children of addicted parents could not be helped unless the parent sought treatment and that the children would recover automatically once the parents had stopped drinking or using drugs. Cork's study initiated the focus on the children as individuals with their own characteristic constellations of problems and their own needs for help. Interest grew slowly as this concern competed for scarce treatment and research resources, although the known familial nature of alcoholism made children of alcoholics the obvious target group for prevention efforts. The founding of the Children of Alcoholics Foundation in 1982 and its initiatives to review and stimulate sound scientific research in this area have facilitated this process.[2,3,4] The Foundation's critical review of the literature which identifies research needs and opportunities remains an important information resource.[2] The New York State Division of Substance Abuse Services subsequently developed a literature review covering children of substance-abusing parents, published in 1986, which provides an overview of knowledge and research needs relating to these children.[5]

Many creative researchers and clinicians have provided useful contributions to our knowledge of "addicted families." Some have pointed out that these families show similarities to other dysfunctional families and their children, for example, offspring of depressed parents.[6] However, there are sufficient unique characteristics in families of chemically dependent people to have given rise to a network of self-help groups, and also to a membership organization, the National Association for Children of Alcoholics.[7]

This chapter will very briefly summarize some current knowledge on the subject. The reader is referred to the two literature reviews[2,5] and other references cited for more detailed information.

Although children of substance abusers are both male and female, the problems outlined in this chapter are of special importance to women for three reasons. First of all, women are assigned the primary child-caring role in our society. Second, some of the special problems of these individuals relate to drinking or using drugs by the child's mother during pregnancy. Finally, there is some evidence that children of alcoholic mothers are more severely affected than those of alcoholic fathers.[8]

Table I lists the wide variety of problems that have been identified as more prevalent among offspring of addicted parents than in the general population. Such children, both during childhood and adulthood, are overrepresented in caseloads of virtually every health and human service system. However, the picture is not totally bleak. Many children from these families grow up to be competent and achieving.[8] In addition, the growing availability of appropriate treatment for these

Table I.
PROBLEMS OVERREPRESENTED AMONG COSAs

Fetal alcohol syndrome (FAS)
Other fetal alcohol effects (FAE)
Fetal drug effects
Neonatal withdrawal syndromes
Child abuse, neglect and incest
Behavior and conduct disorders
Attention deficit disorder/hyperactivity
Physical illness and injury in childhood

Depression and suicide in childhood and
    adulthood
Eating disorders
Antisocial behavior
Stress-related physical disorders
Marriage to an alcoholic or drug-dependent
    spouse
Alcohol and drug dependence
Compulsive gambling

adults and children has shown that their lives can be much improved.

In this chapter, for brevity, I will use COSA to abbreviate children of substance abusers, which includes children of alcoholics (COAs) and children of other drug dependent parents, and ACOSA to abbreviate adult children of substance abusers.

Epidemiology

Russell et al. estimate that approximately 28,600,000 Americans, 6,600,000 of them under the age of 18, are COAs.[2] This amounts to one in every eight Americans. No parallel figures are available for offspring of other drug abusers, but the New York State Division of Substance Abuse Services estimates that parents among methadone maintenance caseloads in New York State alone have 43,000 minor children. In 1984, nearly one in ten infants born in New York City were born to narcotic-addicted (including methadone-maintained) mothers.[9]

Genetic Factors

Research during the last 15 years has amassed increasing evidence that there is an inherited predisposition to develop alcoholism in some COAs.[3] This is not to say that alcoholism itself is inherited, since environmental factors including the availability of alcohol and a wide array of sociocultural influences and psychological factors are also important. However, even when adopted by nonrelatives and raised in homes free of alcohol abuse, COAs are at higher risk for developing alcoholism than non-COAs.[10,11] More than one hereditary pattern has been identified, and the interactions between genetics and environment are complex.[11]

These findings have led to a search for one or more biological markers of increased risk for alcoholism. Although differences have been found, none has yet been demonstrated to predict alcoholism.[2] The longitudinal studies needed to test such predictive utility take years to conduct, but some have been initiated. Studies of children or young adults with alcoholic first-degree

relatives (mothers or fathers) have shown differences in brain wave patterns, particularly event-related electrical potentials and, following a moderate dose of alcohol, less feeling of intoxication, less body sway, less change in hormone levels, and greater skeletal muscle relaxation.[2] Although most of these studies have been done in male COAs, recent research has found some similarities in young women with alcoholic relatives.[12]

Much less is known about possible genetic factors in drug dependencies other than alcohol. There is considerable evidence that the self-reported drug use of adolescents correlates with their reports of parental use patterns, particularly between mother-daughter and father-son pairs.[5] Drug dependence itself is also a major problem for COAs. For example, a 1985 study by Kosten and colleagues found that more than 20 percent of 638 adult narcotic addicts were COAs.[13] The authors also found that these addict COAs were more likely to show alcoholism, depression and antisocial personality disorder than other addicts. Whether these influences reflect nature, nurture or both, is not yet known.

Fetal and Newborn Effects

There are many damaging effects of alcohol and drug use on pregnancy, including spontaneous abortion, premature labor and a variety of obstetric complications. All of these complications are in themselves causes of fetal and neonatal death and morbidity. Anoxia and blood vessel spasm can lead to cerebral palsy and other disorders in the newborn. Low birth weight and prematurity are themselves newborn risk factors. In addition, however, there are both general and specific types of birth defects associated with alcohol and drug use in pregnancy, which by their nature are problems of COSAs.

The fetal alcohol syndrome (FAS) was described (actually rediscovered) in 1973,[14] and is now considered one of the three most common causes of birth defects with associated mental retardation in the United States. Features of FAS include: prenatal and postnatal growth deficiencies; central nervous system defects, including mental retardation, poor coordination, hyperactivity and learning disorders; characteristic abnormalities of the eyes and face which can be recognized in making a diagnosis; and a variety of other malformations involving the joints, heart, urinary tract and genitals. FAS is found in offspring of women who drink heavily throughout pregnancy. Other combinations of birth defects such as low birth weight and congenital anomalies that do not satisfy a diagnosis of FAS are referred to as fetal alcohol effects (FAE). These have been related to a wide range of levels of alcohol intake. Because no safe level of alcohol use in pregnancy has been established, women who are pregnant or planning pregnancy are advised to avoid all alcohol use. Current knowledge about FAS and FAE has been reviewed by a panel of the American Medical Association in the journal of the AMA, and the reader may find more detailed information in that publication.[15]

A recent follow-up study of 11 children diagnosed with FAS in infancy and childhood found that after 10 years, two of the children had died and the others continued to demonstrate severe disability.[16] Although much can be done to help victims of FAS and FAE, the basic developmental defects are not reversible. Prevention offers our best hope for the children of alcoholic mothers.

A number of studies have followed opiate-dependent mothers and their infants, including those in methadone maintenance programs. Although no syndrome comparable to FAS has been identified, lower birth weight, smaller size and disturbed behavior have been noted.[5,17]

An important problem in this group of infants is the neonatal withdrawal syndrome, which has been described for alcohol and sedatives, but is most severe in infants of opiate-dependent mothers, especially high-dose, unsupervised methadone users.[5] Infants undergoing withdrawal suffer agitation, irritability, difficulty in nursing and disturbed sleep. They also experience interference in their ability to establish the mother-infant bonding thought to be critically important for later development.[5]

Less information is available about specific birth defects caused by drugs of abuse other than alcohol. Lower birth weight has been associated with both tobacco and marijuana smoking.[5] Cocaine use has been linked to urinary tract malformations in one study[18] and also to abnormalities in newborn behavior.[19]

Nursing mothers have traditionally been advised to drink beer or ale as a folk medicine. Since alcohol passes into breast milk in the same concentration as into the bloodstream, and since the newborn is totally dependent on breast milk for nourishment, this practice is unwise.[20] Likewise, cocaine enters breast milk, and cocaine intoxication via breast-feeding has

been reported in an infant.[21] The best advice to nursing mothers is abstinence.

Problems During Childhood in COSAs

COSAs during childhood are at risk for a wide variety of physical, psychological and behavior problems. They use more family medical benefits[22], have more school problems[23] and are overrepresented in populations of abused and neglected children.[24]

Researchers have explored both factors important in the causation of health and behavior problems and protective influences present in those children who appear to escape such problems. For example, Williams studied child care patterns in 91 families with alcoholism in one or both parents.[25] She concluded that there were many problems, but that families with alcoholic mothers were most in need of help with parenting. Werner looked at characteristics of COAs who reached age 15 without showing significant physical or behavior problems, referring to them as "resilient" children because they had overcome significant risk.[8] She found that sons of alcoholic mothers had the highest problem rates among the COAs. The "resilient" children were more likely to have been rated outgoing, affectionate and "cuddly" as babies. They also were less likely to have experienced stressful life events during their first two years of life, including the birth of a sibling.

Clinicians have described typical rules of behavior in an alcoholic family (don't feel, don't trust, don't talk), and typical roles, such as family hero, lost child, problem child and family pet.[26,27] The family hero typically becomes a surrogate parent and overachiever. The lost child becomes introverted and escapes into fantasy, while the problem child or scapegoat misbehaves at home and school. The family pet tries to diffuse family tension through humor and often becomes a "class clown." In most affected families, individual children assume combinations of these roles as well as other behavior patterns, but these conceptualizations have proven useful in helping COSAs understand their own behavior.

Problems in Adolescence and Adulthood

ACOSAs experience the entire range of human psychosocial problems; of special interest are alcoholism and other drug dependence,[2] eating disorders,[28] depression[29] and a combination of traits sometimes referred to as "codependence."[30]

Some researchers have made a distinction between familial alcoholism and alcoholism which occurs in a person without any family history of the disease. For example, a recent study of 568 male alcoholics found that 65 percent had a positive family history of alcoholism. This group had earlier onset and more severe alcoholism with more medical, legal and psychiatric problems.[31]

Other "behavioral addictions" such as compulsive gambling[32] and bulimia[28] are also overrepresented among ACOAs. Depression and suicide are often related to COA status, both in adolescents and adults.[2]

Cermak has described the elements of a codependent personality disorder, which he conceptualizes as a distinct diagnostic category.[30] It includes problems in self-esteem, over-responsibility, fear of intimacy, "enmeshed" relationships, and a variety of other characteristics in the context of an ongoing relationship with an active substance abuser. Clinicians will find this concept useful in practice. Vannicelli has written an excellent textbook on group therapy for ACOSAs, which covers most of these issues.[33]

Although both male and female COSAs experience severe and persistent difficulties of the types noted in Table I, there are some problems that are particularly important for daughters of alcoholics and other drug abusers. Young girls are at special risk for sexual abuse, sometimes at the hands of their addicted parent, but often because the family's preoccupation with the parent's alcohol or drug problem leaves then unprotected. Early abuse and incest can contribute to severe emotional illness throughout life including multiple personality disorder, recurrent depression and anxiety disorders. In addition, the eating disorders—anorexia nervosa, bulimia and compulsive overeating—are commonly seen in female COSAs. Finally, young women COSAs are more likely to marry addicted spouses than their non-COSA cohorts. In spite of vowing never to marry "a drunk" or "a junkie" like Dad, such young women often end up doing just that. The man she marries is usually in the early stage of his addiction, and she does not identify his alcohol or drug use with the late-stage patterns she remembers or sees in her father. On the other hand, she relates to the "better qualities" her father showed (and she longed for) in her spouse. By the time the late-stage symptoms of his addiction occur, she is married to him and often has a number of children. She has also become invested in denying her husband's problem to preserve her own self-esteem, rather than admit she has married an alcoholic/addict. Thus the family cycle repeats itself.

Therapists and health educators dealing with women's health problems are in a unique position to intervene so as to break this family cycle. Special attention to COSA issues in prevention and treatment will help young women from addicted families make healthy choices in their adult lives.

Prevention

There are two major aspects of prevention in relation to COSAs. Adequate early intervention and treatment

for chemically dependent adolescents and young adults will spare their later offspring many of the problems of growing up in a dysfunctional family. However, such parents will need help with parenting skills, since they themselves are likely to have been raised in dysfunctional families. They must also help their children understand that if they are COAs, they may themselves carry a genetic predisposition to alcoholism.

COSAs and ACOSAs who are not alcoholics or drug abusers can also profit from prevention programs. By helping them to understand the effects of their early family dynamics on their current lives and to reinterpret childhood experiences in terms of the disease of alcoholism and/or addiction, such programs can improve present functioning. Learning to express and share feelings may help prevent later emotional problems. Alcohol and drug problems may be prevented by helping COSAs accept their increased risk for chemical dependency and teaching them techniques to resist peer pressure to drink and use drugs.

Treatment

The basic therapeutic needs of COSAs are listed in Table II. Meeting these needs for the millions of COSAs in the U.S. population may seem to be an insuperable task. However, as knowledge about COSAs is disseminated, real progress may be made in reaching those in need.

Two strategies are employed in trying to meet this need. The first, through professional education, strives to help those in the generic health, welfare and criminal justice systems become aware of the COSAs in their caseloads and adapt their treatment methods to meet their special needs.

The second strategy involves the development of specific services for COSAs, either as part of a family program adjunctive to the treatment of their substance dependent parents, or in a separate program for COSAs, whether or not the abusing parent is receiving help. Outpatient alcohol and drug treatment programs have begun to develop treatment programs for COSAs, and individual psychotherapists have learned to help these patients.[33] Self-help groups for ACOAs, many of them part of the Al-Anon Family Groups[34], and Alateen groups for teenagers provide a supportive social network as well as a program for recovery. Such self-help groups are often recommended by both generic treatment agencies and special COSA services as an ongoing source of help and support. All health and social service professionals, including the staff of women's centers, should become acquainted with the self-help groups available in the communities they serve. They have the potential of playing a vital part in the health and well-being of many women, their children and other family members.

Table II.
THERAPEUTIC NEEDS OF CHILDREN OF SUBSTANCE ABUSERS

Physical safety and protection
Physical health care
A trusting and trustworthy environment
Validation of feelings and experience
A supportive social network

Positive role models
Education about alcoholism and addictions
Assertiveness and stress management skills
Family intervention and family therapy, where
  feasible

Conclusion

This brief review of current knowledge concerning the offspring of alcoholic and drug-dependent parents has only scratched the surface of an important subject. Health professionals and public policy makers are just beginning to focus on the needs of this very large group. Research is sorely needed in many areas, but it would be particularly helpful to have data on the relative value of various prevention and treatment approaches now in use.

The American Society of Addiction Medicine, an organization of physicians with a special interest in addictions, has adopted a policy position statement related to this subject which can serve as directional guidelines for community action. It is appended to this chapter in the hope that other interested groups will join in the support of these measures.

References

1. Cork, R.M., *The Forgotten Children,* Toronto: Addiction Research Foundation, 1969.
2. Russell, M., Henderson, C., and Blume, S.B., *Children of Alcoholics: A Review of the Literature.* Children of Alcoholics Foundation, New York, 1985. (May be obtained from the Foundation—Box 4185, Grand Central Station, New York, NY 10163.)
3. *Report of the Conference on Research Needs and Opportunities for Children of Alcoholics.* Children of Alcoholics Foundation, New York, NY 1964. (May be obtained from the Foundation—Box 4365, Grand Central Station, New York, NY 10163.)
4. Blume, S.B., *Report of the Conference on Prevention Research.* Children of Alcoholics Foundation, New York, 1975. (May be obtained from the Foundation—Box 4185, Grand Central Station, New York, NY 10163.)
5. Deren, S., Children of Substance Abusers: A Review of the Literature, *Jour. Substance Abuse Treatment,* 3: 77-94, 1986.
6. Weissman, M.M., Gammon, G.D., John, K. et al., Children of Depressed Parents. *Arch Gen Psychiatry,* 44: 847-853, 1987.
7. National Association of Children of Alcoholics. Materials may be obtained from the organization at 31706 Coast Highway, Suite 201, S. Laguna, CA. 92677.
8. Werner, E.E., Resilient Offspring of Alcoholics: A longitudinal study from birth to age 18. *Jour Studies on Alcohol,* 47:34-40: 1986.
9. Deren, S., Parents in Methadone Treatment and Their Children. *Treatment Issue Report 450,* NYS Div. of Substance Abuse Services, Albany, NY, 1986.
10. Goodwin, D., Schulsinger, F., Hermansen, L. et al., Alcohol Problems in Adoptees Raised Apart from Alcoholic Biological Parents. *Archives Gen Psychiatry,* 28: 238-243, 1973.
11. Bohman, M., Cloninger, R., Sigvardsson, S. et al., The Genetics of Alcoholism and Related Disorders. *Jour Psychiatric Res,* 22: 447-452; 1987.
12. Lex, B.W., Lukas, S.E., Greenwald, N.E. et al., Alcohol-induced Changes in Body Sway in Women at Risk for Alcoholism: a Pilot Study. *Jour Studies on Alcohol,* 49: 346-356; 1988.
13. Kosten, T.R., Rounsaville, B.J., Kleber, H.D., Parental Alcoholism in Opioid Addicts. *Jour Nervous and Mental Disease,* 173, 461-469, 1985.
14. Jones, K.L., Smith, D.W., Ulleland, C.N., Streissguth, A.P., Pattern of Malformations in Offspring of Chronic Alcoholic Women. *Lancet* I: 1267-1271, 1973.
15. AMA Council on Scientific Affairs, Fetal Effects of Maternal Alcohol Use. *Jour Amer Med Assoc,* 249: 2517-2521, 1983.
16. Streissguth, A.P., Clarren, S.K., Jones, K.L., Natural History of the Fetal Alcohol Syndrome: A 10 Year Follow-Up of 11 Patients. *Lancet* 2: 85-91, 1985.
17. Chasnoff, I.J., Burns K.A., Buras, W.J. et al., Prenatal Drug Exposure: Effects on Neonatal and Infant Growth and Development. *Neurobehavioral Toxicology and Teratology,* 8:357-362, 1986.
18. Chasnoff, I.J., Chisum, G.M., Kaplan, W.E., Maternal Cocaine Use and Genitourinary Tract Malformations. *Teratology,* 37: 201204, 1988.
19. Chasnoff, I.J., Burns, W.J., Schnoll, S.H., et al., Cocaine Use in Pregnancy. *New England Jour Med* 313: 666-669, 1985.

20. Blume, S.B., Beer and the Breast-feeding Mom. *Jour Amer Med Assoc* 258: 2126, 1987.
21. Chasnoff, I.J., Lewis, D.E., Squires, L., Cocaine Intoxication in a Breast-Fed Infant, *Pediatrics* 80: 836-838, 1987.
22. Putnam, S.L., *Are Children of Alcoholics Sicker than Other Children?: A Study of Illness Experience and Utilization Behavior in a Health Maintenance Organization;* presented at the 113th Annual Meeting of the American Public Health Association, November 1985.
23. Knop, J., Teasdale, T.W., Schulsinger, F. et al., A Prospective Study of Young Men at High Risk for Alcoholism: School Behavior and Achievement. *Jour Studies on Alcohol,* 46: 273-277; 1985.
24. Famularo, R., Stone, K., Barnum, R. et al., Alcoholism and Severe Child Maltreatment. *Amer Jour of Orthopsychiatry,* 56: 481-485, 1986.
25. Williams, C.N., Child Care Practices in Alcoholic Families. *Alcohol Health and Research World,* 11: 74-77, and 94, 1987.
26. Black, C., Children of Alcoholics. *Alcohol Health and Research World,* 4: 23-27, 1979.
27. Wegscheider, D., Wegscheider, S., *Family Illness: Chemical Dependency.* Crystal, MN: Nurturing Networks, 1978.
28. Bulik, C.M., Drug and Alcohol Abuse by Bulimic Women and Their Families. *American Jour Psychiatry,* 144: 1604-1606, 1987.
29. Parker, D.A., Harford, T.C., Alcohol-Related Problems, Marital Disruptions and Depressive Symptoms Among Adult Children of Alcoholics in the United States. *Jour Studies on Alcohol,* 49: 306-313, 1988.
30. Cermak, T.L., *Diagnosing and Treating Codependence,* MN: Johnson Institute Books, 1986.
31. Penick, E.C., Powell, B.J., Bingham, S.F. et al., A Comparative Study of Familial Alcoholism. *Jour Studies on Alcohol,* 48: 136-146, 1987.
32. Lesieur, H.L., Blume, S.B., Zoppa R., Alcoholism, Drug Abuse and Gambling. Alcoholism *Clinical and Experimental Research;* 10: 33-38, 1986.
33. Vannicelli, M., *Group Psychotherapy with Adult Children of Alcoholics: Treatment Techniques and Countertransference Considerations.* NY: Guilford Press, 1989.
34. Literature Available from Al-Anon Family Groups, P.O. Box 862, Midtown Station, New York, NY 10018-0862.

AMERICAN SOCIETY OF ADDICTION MEDICINE, INC.

POLICY STATEMENT ON CHILDREN OF PARENTS SUFFERING FROM ALCOHOLISM OR OTHER DRUG DEPENDENCIES

A very significant proportion of the nation's population is affected by alcoholism or other drug dependency in the family. One in eight Americans is the offspring of an alcoholic parent. Of the 22 million children of alcoholics in this country, nearly 7 million are under 16 years of age. Many additional children are growing up in homes with drug dependent parents.

Current research indicates that these children are at special risk for a wide variety of physical, behavioral and emotional problems, both during childhood and in later life. Familial transmission of alcoholism has been shown to involve both genetic and environmental factors. In addition, prenatal alcohol and drug consumption can cause severe fetal damage, including fetal alcohol syndrome.

Because of societal stigma, ignorance and denial, these children often suffer in silence. As adults, they are unaware of the relevance of their parent's illness to their own distress.

Cognizant of these facts, the American Society of Addiction Medicine strongly recommends the following:

a. Professional and public education about the problems and needs of this group should be greatly increased.
b. Physicians in both pediatric and adult practice should inquire about parental and familial alcohol/drug dependency in every patient.
c. Physicians treating patients dependent on alcohol or drugs should routinely arrange for the evaluation of the patient's children, and for their involvement in the process of rehabilitation.
d. Health professionals should realize that the recovery of the parent may not be sufficient to lead to recovery in the child.
e. Children require attention to their own needs, conversely, professionals should be aware that the children of alcohol/drug dependent parents can be helped, even in the absence of parental treatment or recovery.

helped, even in the absence of parental treatment or recovery.

f.   All children and adults identified as offspring of alcohol/drug dependent parents should be evaluated, and services should be provided appropriate to their needs. These services should recognize the role of the parent's alcohol/drug dependence in the development of the child's problem, and provide for reinterpretation of their childhood experiences within the framework of the disease concept of alcoholism and drug dependence.

g.   Self-help groups for young and adult children of alcohol/drug dependent parents should be encouraged as an adjunct to treatment and personal development.

h.   Adequate health insurance and other third party payment should be provided to cover the costs of treatment for families of alcohol/drug dependent persons.

i.   Programs to prevent alcoholism, drug dependence and other illnesses should focus on the children of alcohol/drug dependent parents as a primary target group. They should include educating such children that they are not the cause of their parent's alcoholism or drug dependence and cannot cure it.

j.   Public and private support should be provided for research on both prenatal and postnatal effects of parental alcohol and drug dependence. Such research will lead to more adequate prevention and treatment.

k.   Interventions in families in which are found: child abuse or neglect, conduct disorders, child and adolescent suicide attempts, or alcoholism or other drug dependency in the children should always evaluate parental alcohol and drug abuse. Overall case management should always include specific treatment for alcoholism and other drug dependence when these are identified.

l.   Physicians and other health care providers should be aware of the resources available in their community for the care of children and adults who are the offspring of alcoholic or drug dependent parents.

m.   Student health programs in institutions ranging from elementary schools to universities should be particularly sensitive to this issue, and be prepared to identify, educate, assist and refer children of alcoholic and other drug dependent parents in need of services.

ADOPTED BY ASAM BOARD OF DIRECTORS
FEBRUARY 22, 1987

23 Issues for Homeless Women and Their Children

Rita Zimmer and Maryanne Schretzman

"When one talks with a homeless mother, she describes a life of poverty and substandard housing, a history of incest or child abuse and neglect, family violence and alcoholism and drug abuse. . . . [The women] walk down welfare hotel corridors surrounded by drug dealers, buyers or indifferent security personnel. The atmosphere is one of incessant danger and threat, similar to that of a combat zone."

For years, many homeless women with an alcohol problem ended up on "skid row," where there were few treatment options. A homeless woman, like her male counterpart, was White, divorced or separated, and in her mid-40s or early 50s. She was a mother whose children were with family members or in foster care. She had many physical problems due to homelessness, lengthy alcohol abuse and lack of treatment.

Research has amply demonstrated that homelessness both aggravates chronic conditions commonly found among housed populations, such as diabetes and hypertension, and increases the prevalence of other conditions, such as respiratory and peripheral vascular disorders. The abuse of alcohol has its own debilitating effects causing health problems among these women, such as cirrhosis of the liver, anemia and gastrointestinal bleeding. In fact, recent research seems to indicate that females are at higher risk for these alcohol-related pathologies than the male drinker.[1]

In the 1980s, changes occurred and we began to witness a significant increase in the number of younger women and children who became homeless. Figures provided by the National Association of Community Health Centers, Inc., indicate that between one million and three million of the nation's total population are homeless. In these surveys, it is estimated that the median age of the homeless population is in the late twenties even if children are excluded.[2]

In New York City, female-headed single-parent families are currently the largest growing segment of the homeless populations. The typical homeless family is a mother between the ages of 18 and 32 with 1-3 children. About 95 percent of the family homeless population is believed to be non-White. By 1988, the number of homeless families had grown to 5,000. In the

1980s, the number of single homeless women also continued to grow, from about 200 to over 1,000. The reasons for these increases are varied, but the most common answers women give when asked how they became homeless are: the loss of affordable, decent housing (during the 1970s), fire, unsafe conditions in their former housing, gentrification, eviction and "doubled-up living"—living with a number of other people and without the security of a lease. A large number of homeless families live in congregate shelters, where many individuals sleep in one room, share bathrooms and eat in large dining halls. Over the course of one year (1987), 11,800 people passed through emergency shelters in New York City.[3] Homeless families also live in welfare hotels, where a family has only one room, sometimes with a private bathroom, but with no kitchen or other private space. The hotels can hold up to 450 families and are located in neighborhoods without adequate schools, playgrounds, shopping or community social services. In the last few years, the trend has been towards non-profit organizations creating transitional residences for anywhere from 4 to 120 families. These transitional programs are better managed, offer a larger variety of services on site and emphasize rehousing families into permanent apartments, facilitating the families' transition into a new and sometimes hostile community and maintaining contact for 6 to 9 months to prevent families from becoming homeless again.

It may be two to three years from the time a woman and her children become homeless to the time they live in permanent housing. A typical scenario follows. A woman starts out in a congregate shelter. After two or three months, she is shuttled from hotel to hotel, where she will stay for two weeks at a time. Eventually (but it may be six months or more), she will end up in a welfare hotel for between one and two years. If she is lucky, she may leave the hotel and go to a non-profit transitional residence like the one described earlier. The hotels, in addition to their undesirable locations, are run for profit and, therefore, have minimal security. The management is reluctant to give up any space for use as a day care center or for health, educational or social services. When they do allow space for these activities, it is at a high cost and after a great deal of advocacy and community pressure. All kinds of illegal activities from pornography to prostitution and drug selling flourish in the hotels, and women and children live in constant fear for their safety and sanity.

A homeless mother describes a life of poverty and substandard housing, a history of incest or child abuse and neglect, family violence and alcoholism and drug abuse. She has frequently quit high school in the 10th or 11th grade because she became pregnant, and has had minimal work experience or job training. She has been on public assistance for anywhere from 6 months to ten years and, without adequate education or job training, sees little hope of getting off welfare in the near future.

We have described a woman in crisis whose severe pressures are compounded by the fact that she is homeless. From her history, it's natural to expect that she sees alcohol and drugs as a means of temporary solace. The availability of substances is not a problem and the peer pressure to drink and use drugs is a fact of life.

Although there are no hard data available, the incidence of alcohol and substance abuse among the homeless is thought to be at least three to six times greater than that in the general population.[4] Given the severe stress of the homeless condition, this is not surprising. It is common in our contemporary society for all segments of the population to rely on some form of drug to cope with difficult adjustment problems. The daily life of a homeless woman, often with dependent children, is usually a spiral of cumulative stress and pressure.

Becoming homeless is a major event. It has been noted in the literature that, for women, specific life events have been associated with the onset of alcoholism.[5] In contrast, this does not seem to be the case with men, whose drinking problems are not associated with specific life events. It becomes important, therefore, in the treatment of women, to establish connections between life events, feelings and drinking behavior.

The course of addiction is also more accelerated in women, and their physical deterioration occurs sooner than in men. This becomes more acute in the lives of homeless women, who show an above-average inci-

dence of liver damage, hepatitis, hypertension and other health problems. The progression of the disease of alcoholism or drug dependency vastly accelerates for homeless women, and their vulnerable condition places them at risk of being victimized by traumatic events such as rape, physical violence and the loss of their children.

The abnormal ambience of welfare hotel life is a constant assault. It almost self-perpetuates an increase in complexities for women. Often, the only illusionary relief from the grim reality becomes alcohol and/or drug use. This creates further problems for women who must rely on various social agencies for money. Women with children receive money from Aid to Families with Dependent Children (AFDC). Single women receive funds through general public assistance. The cost of alcohol and drugs creates a significant strain on their limited financial resources and leads many women into dangerous situations as they search for immediate "solutions." It is not uncommon for a woman to share or "rent" her room for extra funds to a hotel drug dealer who then moves in with her and her children. Women and their children are often at risk of violence from the drug dealer. She is also prey to loan sharks. To secure an immediate loan, some women will use their Medicaid cards or AFDC cards as security. To redeem their cards and pay off the loans (whose interest accrues daily), women are forced into prostitution or drug-related activities. Thus, the conditions of homelessness and poverty often increase the use of drugs and alcohol, which in turn creates a spiral of seemingly insurmountable problems.

The condition of homelessness places a woman in a very restricted world. Homeless women are either bussed to shelters, where some of the security guards may themselves deal drugs (according to many women), or else they walk down welfare hotel corridors surrounded by drug dealers, buyers or indifferent security personnel. The atmosphere is one of incessant danger and threat, similar to that of a combat zone. For both men and women addicted to alcohol and drugs, the hotels and shelters constitute a subculture that makes any attempts toward sobriety extremely difficult. The tendency is to look to drugs for relief from anxiety and desperation.

Homelessness, for the majority of women who experience it, is a profound shock. Most of the women never thought this could happen to them. Even when they find themselves homeless, they cannot believe it. Life has been pulled out from under them, and there are no set skills for dealing with this unanticipated reality. Many of these women find themselves in a state of profound isolation.

This isolation serves to cut women off from family and friends. They no longer live in a community of churches, schools and other social supports. They no longer have elders as role models or a sense of family or culture. Because of her isolation, a homeless woman's addiction can often progress significantly before there is any intervention. People in more stable environments may have concerned family or friends to encourage treatment and appropriate health care. This is not the case for the homeless woman who is isolated from her support system. The homeless subculture lacks the supports that can help women control or arrest their alcoholism or drug dependency.

Homeless women with alcohol or drug problems are doubly stigmatized. Society has always viewed the female alcoholic more severely than her male counterpart. The state of homelessness is another "failure" for the women who experience it.

Many alcohol- or drug-dependent women form attachments to homeless drug-dependent men, who often share their single rooms with the women and their children. Many of these men place these women at increased risk for HIV infection and other sexually transmitted diseases. In addition, the profile of the alcoholic woman is changing due to homelessness. Most treatment centers, prior to the 1980s, saw women in their 40s. Now the alcoholic woman seeking treatment is much younger and her condition more difficult. Her alcoholism is compounded by addictions to other drugs.

Our experience indicates that, initially, homeless women often seek help in order to reclaim their children or from fear of losing them, or because of crack addiction. Women do not perceive their alcohol abuse as a problem and they have to be shown how it contributes to their difficulties. It may be most accurate to view the homeless woman who is chemically dependent as polydrug addicted. The most commonly used chemicals are crack, alcohol and marijuana. It is not unusual for some women to use alcohol to regulate the intensity of a crack-induced "high" as well as the after-effects of the drug.

Crack, a smokeable form of cocaine which is readily available at low cost, often becomes the drug of choice. At present, it is unclear whether the incidence of drug use among homeless women would be so high if it were not for the highly addictive nature of crack. Other factors which account for the pervasive use of crack are the purity of the drug and its route of administration. Smoking the drug, in addition to providing a rapid and intense high, appears to the user to be less dangerous and less invasive, much like having a cigarette.

Although the effects of crack may vary, it is known that the user experiences a sense of euphoria and power. These experiences are welcome in a daily reality of poverty and homelessness. For many women, the loss of control and the loss of self-esteem have often been the by-product of struggling with the prolonged stress of living in welfare hotels. Continued crack use is often a seductive "aid" to bolster self-esteem and ward off depression.

But the abuse of crack quickly becomes another problem rather than a coping mechanism. It leads to alarming increases in child abuse and neglect, emotional problems, criminal activity and other forms of antisocial behavior and unemployment. It may lead to the need for foster care. It undermines women's pursuit of educational skills and vocational training, and contributes to the loss of public assistance and other entitlements due to failure to keep appointments.

One of the most devastating effects of crack is on the children. Studies have also indicated possible health hazards for children living with crack-smoking adults.[6] A small welfare hotel room filled with crack smoke can cause major developmental difficulties. It is essential that infants and children living in these environments receive early intervention and individual attention.

Barriers to Treatment

Our work with homeless women has made us aware of a multitude of obstacles which make it difficult for many women to seek help. The problem is further complicated by the unique circumstances of the homeless. The adult population in welfare hotels is almost 95 percent female and overwhelmingly Black or Hispanic. A large majority of these women are single-parent heads of households.

Barriers to treatment are compounded by discrimination based on race, sex and class. All too frequently, minority women's double victimization in a racist, sexist society has meant fewer resources and the absence of choices. Conscious and unconscious negative attitudes displayed by some service providers often result in a woman's inability to trust or bond with the service providers.

Denial of alcohol and drug abuse is endemic among people in need of help. For homeless women, crack and alcohol abuse are not viewed as serious problems. They are instead viewed as a way of coping with more "important" stresses in life, such as lack of housing, unemployment or the difficulties of dealing with single parenthood and poverty. These women are often the primary caregivers for their children, and it is not unusual for them to deny addiction problems for fear that their children will be taken away from them.

At present, most homeless women have no appropriate child care services available other than foster care. Many mothers fear they will not be able to regain custody of their children once they have surrendered them to the foster care system. Consequently, women who want to keep their children find it almost impossible to go into hospitals for detoxification and rehabilitation, or to use halfway houses and long-term inpatient care facilities. Other child care services, such as infant-toddler programs and crisis nurseries, are reluctant to accept a child when the mother needs hospitalization for detoxification.

As indicated earlier, most of the women living with their children in welfare hotels are young, impressionable and isolated. Since the hotel milieu is often frightening, strong peer relationships are formed for support. The women share child care and past and present experiences together. For some, it is through these relationships that they are introduced to the use of crack and excessive alcohol.

The life of a hotel mother is a round of appointments—visits to welfare, possible housing resources, picking up children and medical appointments. These appointments and tasks often involve long waiting periods. Unfortunately, many drug treatment programs demand a rigid attendance structure that effectively prevents this population from attending consistently. Women are frequently discharged from these treatment programs without having received care or follow-up.

Finally, many service providers are overwhelmed with the magnitude of the problems that confront homeless women. Their priority is to solve the crisis at hand. This may be lack of food, hot water, clothing or diapers. Many lack the training to deal with alcohol and drug problems. Unconsciously, service providers may not give sufficient weight to the drug and alcohol problems of these women. They may view these problems as a sign of weakness or as a "nervous problem." This perception leads some to make referrals to local mental health clinics where the women may be treated with more drugs. These clinics may not have professional staff with expertise in substance abuse, and referrals that would help women abstain from alcohol and drugs are often not made.

Treatment Model

The key component in successfully engaging and treating homeless women with alcohol and drug problems is to address the multiplicity of problems that cause stress in their lives. This includes the anxieties of child care, medical problems, housing and unemployment. We believe that addiction treatment for homeless women has to incorporate, at the very least, three areas of expertise: chemical dependency rehabilitation, family/child treatment and medical services.

The treatment should fit the environmental, social and psychological needs of women and be consistent with the racial and cultural characteristics of the population. This means viewing alcoholism and drug addiction among homeless women as a response or coping mechanism to other "bigger" problems. This

treatment method allows for a connection to be made between sobriety and an enhanced life situation, and focuses on these problems as an essential part of treatment.

Women In Need, a program for homeless women and their children located in New York City, realizes that in order to best serve the needs of homeless women, the agency must be cognizant of the multiplicity and interdependency of the problems characteristic of this population. To date, traditional substance-abuse treatment modalities have proven ineffective in working with homeless women and their families. Clients may fail to keep appointments, or if they do, fail to come consistently. Traditional treatments evolved from a model that was successful in reaching a primarily White, often middle-class, male population. Traditional techniques usually focus on addiction and subsequently deal with other problems when the addiction has been arrested. This is viewed by women as impractical, since they simultaneously need to feed and house their children while coping with their addiction problems.

The preferred modality for treating men is group counseling, which has proven to be highly effective. It has been our experience, which is supported by the literature, that women initially prefer individual counseling to deal with their problems. Women want privacy when they begin to talk about their children, homelessness, depression, economic and medical problems, battering, loss of social supports and of significant others. Also, given the range of their current problems, many cannot be solved initially in a group, such as calls to Child Welfare Agencies, foster care or medical care.

In spite of the harsh conditions of shelters and welfare hotels and the chaos of their immediate lives, the needs of their children often provide a deep motivational urgency for many women. It is the hope of making better lives for them that leads women to attempt to get help and sustains them in persevering in their struggles for a better way of life. What they may not do for themselves they will often do for their children.

Treatment strategies need to address specific issues of homeless women and children. Substance-abuse treatment centers that provide child care and child treatment, medical treatment and a range of support services seem to attract homeless women. The female substance abuser has significantly different patterns of use as well as social and psychological needs that have not been effectively met by the male-oriented treatment model focused solely on addiction. Furthermore, the children of addicted homeless women need to be given equal care in treatment planning. Some of the problems we have encountered in working with these children are short attention span, difficulty in moving from one activity to another, excessive crying or tantrums, delayed language development and hyperactivity. The children often have health-related problems such as asthma, ear and respiratory infections and eating and sleeping disorders. To avoid incorrectly labeling these children, it is important that staff who work with them are not only early childhood professionals but also cognizant of the problems of homelessness and addiction. An on-site children's center can address the care of the children and also provide a safe environment where parents can learn parenting skills and where mothers and children can share positive activities together. When the children's program is an integral part of the total treatment program, the recovery process is strengthened for the entire family.

The homeless woman comes to treatment with her children of her own volition. Her financial entitlements are not contingent upon her attendance. She is not "coerced" into treatment, as is the case for many women without children. However, as previously stated, the women's children often become their primary motivation to seek treatment. Therefore, sensitive treatment models need to focus on these issues, since they are a priority for the client. Thus, at Women In Need, we don't wait until a woman has attained a certain level of sobriety to place her in groups not directly related to substance abuse, such as parenting, relationships and housing groups.

As a consequence of their homelessness and addiction, these women have not been around people they trust nor do they trust themselves. Many of these women have had traumatic sexual experiences with males in their lives and have a high degree of rape and incest in their histories. They also seem to find it easier to divulge intimate details of their lives to a woman. In a non-judgmental setting that ensures privacy and safety, a climate is created whereby the homeless woman can slowly begin to experience a trusting relationship with her counselor.

Many traditional treatment models of alcohol and drug abuse may view a person's insistence on talking about problems of daily life as a "resistance to treatment," or another defense to avoid her problem with addiction. With homeless women, these issues are often at the root of her problem and not irrelevant ploys. In traditional treatment models, using her children as an excuse for not coming to treatment may be seen as a form of "denial" or "rationalization," when in fact the woman is aware that to seek help may be jeopardizing her rights to parent her children.

Women In Need's comprehensive outpatient program is tailored to meet the special needs of homeless women and women with children. We have found that when we are able to satisfy the concrete needs of our clients during the initial stage of treatment, a supportive and trusting relationship can be established. Every effort is made to coordinate with other providers, such as Child Welfare Agencies and AFDC. We provide food, clothing and other necessities for the women and their children whenever possible. We adjust treatment schedules for women according to their varied appointments.

It has been our experience that the technique of confrontation regarding the woman's alcoholism or drug dependency has been counterproductive. We believe that many homeless women already feel an abundance of remorse, shame and guilt. The major problems of homeless women who are alcoholics and drug abusers are not denial and delusion, but what to do about their dependency and where to go for help. We have found it to be therapeutic for the women to write letters to their elected officials about the discrimination they have experienced. It is important that homeless, addicted women find "a voice of their own." It is important for the experiences of these women to be validated and not denied in order for the treatment process to begin.

References

1. *U.S. News and World Report*, "Why Liquor is Quicker for Women," Jan 22, 1990, Vol. 108, No. 3, p. 13.
2. "The Health Needs of the Homeless: A Report of Persons Served By the McKinney Act's Health Care for the Homeless Program" published by The National Association of Community Health Centers, Inc., Sept. 1989, p. 1.
3. "Home is Where the Heart Is: The Crisis of Homeless Children and Families in New York City," A Report to the Edna McConnell Clark Foundation by Janice Molnar, Ph.D., Bank Street College of Education, March 1988.
4. Lubran, Barbara G., "Alcohol Related Problems Among the Homeless: NIAAA's Response," *Alcohol Health & Research World*, Spring: 4-6, 73, 1987.
5. Beckman, L.J., and Amaro, H., "Patterns of Women's Use of Alcohol Treatment Agencies," *Alcohol Health & Research World*, 9 (2): 15-25, 1984/85.
6. "Passive Freebase Cocaine (Crack) Inhalation by Infants and Toddlers" in *AJDC*, Vol. 143, p. 25, Jan. 1989, by David A. Bateman, M.D. and Margaret Heagarty, M.D.

24 Advocacy: Prevention Strategies and Treatment Services Sensitive to Women's Needs

Christine Lubinski

"Alcoholism and drug addiction reinforce the second-class status of women in our society by rendering women incapable of self-actualization and unable to take concrete steps, individually or collectively, to improve the quality of their own lives or of women generally. Alcohol and other drug problems have political ramifications for women, as well as health, safety and social ones."

Sound public policies and the availability of services to meet the special needs of women are dependent on the advocacy efforts of women. This is a fact of life in the women's movement and has been since its inception. Whether the issue has been domestic violence, rape, breast cancer or child care, women have joined together to bring the issue to public attention and have fought for new policies and services to meet the needs of women. This is no less true of the issue of alcohol and other drug problems among women.

A commitment to integrate alcohol and other drug prevention programming into multi-service women's centers brings with it the added responsibility to advocate on behalf of prevention and treatment services and policies in the best interests of women who have, or who are at risk for developing, alcohol- and other drug-related problems. Advocacy is not new to women activists or to women's centers. The new charge will be the development and inclusion of alcohol- and other drug-related issues into the ongoing advocacy agenda of women's centers.

Advocacy in this area is no simple matter because women with alcohol and other drug problems are a doubly stigmatized population. If they are women of color or economically disadvantaged, the problem is further compounded. Alcohol and other drug problems have historically been viewed as male illnesses both by the alcohol and drug abuse field and by the public at large. Consequently, there is widespread denial of both the nature and extent of alcohol and drug problems among women. Prevention and treatment policies and

services are generally based on assumptions that men are the target population because men are the population at risk. Further, services and policies are likely to be based on White cultural assumptions with little sensitivity to the special cultural values and needs of ethnic minority people. The growth of the private treatment system and a corresponding reduction in public support has also generally contributed to a reduction in access to treatment for individuals who are not insured or underinsured, while treatment opportunities for middle-class White males have expanded.

Another major challenge to advocates is the historical reluctance of national, state or local women's organizations to address alcohol and drug problems among women as a component of their agendas. There are undoubtedly a number of complex reasons for this and there is no reason to believe that education and encouragement cannot turn this issue around. Women activists, like everyone else, have been exposed to very limited information about the nature and extent of alcohol and other drug problems among women. Because of widespread discrimination against women in virtually every aspect of American life, the list of issues to address is long and laborious.

Many women's groups have simply not had the time to take on the alcohol and drug issue and have not been convinced that it should have a high priority in their work. The process of education and advocacy invariably carries with it a compelling need to assess one's own drinking and drug use as well as the drinking and drug use in one's own home and family. This can be a threatening and frightening prospect in a culture where alcohol and other drug problems are pervasive.

Women's organizations tend to be economically constrained and sectors of the alcoholic beverage industry or the pharmaceutical industry could be a significant source of financial support. It has been a truism in the alcoholism field for decades that financial support from the alcoholic beverage industry invariably translates into avoidance of advocacy on alcohol issues, whether or not the funding has formal or informal strings attached. Women's and minority publications frequently have difficulty attracting adequate advertising revenue to make ends meet, and are notorious for their dependence upon alcohol and tobacco advertising to meet their budgets.

While all of these issues present potential reasons why women's organizations might choose to avoid alcohol and drug issues, none of them are insurmountable. Good advocates are effective, in large part, because of their level of knowledge of the opposition. In this case, the opposition is not simply the alcoholic beverage industry, pharmaceutical companies or bureaucrats reluctant to fund comprehensive services for women. The enemies are also attitudes and practices which impede efforts to organize a constituency to address these issues.

Recovery Services for Women

A critical part of the process of creating an alcohol and drug component of service in a women's center will be identifying and forming linkages with already existing alcohol and other drug services in the community. It is not unlikely that this very activity will begin to generate focal points for advocacy activity. Women's center staff and volunteers may discover, either through initial fact-finding or when referrals of women to services actually begin, that services are either inadequate or non-existent. Obviously, the success of the identification and referral component of the alcohol and drug program depends in large part upon the responsiveness of community-based services to the needs of the women referred by the center.

In some cases, centers may have the resources and capabilities to respond directly to gaps in services. It might be feasible for the center to offer child care services to women involved in outpatient treatment in the local area. Meetings of Alcoholics Anonymous, Narcotics Anonymous or Al-Anon which are dominated by Black, Latino, Native American or lesbian women can often easily be initiated at center sites, as components of afternoon or evening activities. Gender and culturally appropriate detoxification, treatment and aftercare services, however, will generally fall outside the purview of a community-based women's center. Advocacy at the local, state and perhaps even

the national level may be necessary if the alcohol and other drug services needs of women's center participants are to be met.

The ability to successfully advocate for increased services will be strengthened if the center is recognized as an authoritative voice for the needs of women with alcohol and other drug problems in the community. It is important, at the onset, to inform local and state officials about the nature and content of the program. Prior knowledge about the program and center activities in the community will add credibility to the center's arguments for new services.

The next question, of course, is where does the funding come from—and this question may generate a variety of answers. State funds, supplemented by federal dollars, are the major source of funding for public treatment services. In some cases, the state alcohol and drug agency funds program services throughout the state directly. In others, the state agency apportions funds to counties and municipalities and decisions about spending funds are made at that level.

Federal legislation enacted in 1984 required that states spend 5 percent of their federal alcohol and drug funding on new and expanded services for women. In 1988, this "set-aside" for women was increased to 10 percent. Because of this federal requirement, the implementation of the 10 percent set-aside in a given state is an obvious potential funding source for women's programming. States have interpreted and implemented the set-aside in a number of ways with dramatically different results. A National Council on Alcoholism and Drug Dependence (NCADD) study of the implementation of the set-aside indicated that states which pooled 5 percent of their funding and utilized a request-for-proposal process to finance women's programming were much more likely to experience a tangible increase in women's services than states which did not.[1] In a large number of states, programs receiving public funding were simply directed to utilize five percent of their allocation on women. In those states, there were few tangible gains made in women's services.

In the Anti-Drug Abuse Act of 1988, a new demonstration program was created within the Office for Substance Abuse Prevention (OSAP) to provide funding for programs which offer prevention, early intervention and treatment services to pregnant and post-partum women and their infants. This program was generated from the national recognition that there are significant barriers to gaining access to alcoholism- and drug-treatment services for women generally, and pregnant women in particular. Funding for this program and for other treatment services to be funded through the National Institute on Drug Abuse was increased in 1989.

Unfortunately, it took the high visibility of crack addiction among pregnant women and a flurry of prosecutions of pregnant addicts for drug use during pregnancy to induce policymakers to increase substantially the funding available for prevention and treatment programs for pregnant women. Many women involved in advocacy for alcoholic and drug-dependent women have felt that if there had been a stronger network of prevention and treatment programs for all women with alcohol and other drug problems, this serious crisis in care for pregnant addicts might have been avoided.

Decisions made about the expenditure of public dollars, state or federal, are a matter of public information. A phone call or visit to the state alcohol and drug agency should provide clear information about how funding decisions are made, what programs currently receive public money and how the 10 percent set-aside is being implemented. Women in the community who are current providers of alcohol and other drug services to women are also an excellent source of information about state and local politics on the matter of women's services. Local and state NCADD affiliates and some local Junior League chapters may also provide useful information as well as advocacy support to any effort to enhance services for women. Local politicians who have a vested interest in enhancing state and federal support for services in their community can also be cultivated as powerful allies in efforts to attract additional public funding for community-based services for women.

The recent enhanced federal commitment to wage a "war on drugs" has generated significant increases in revenue to states for prevention and treatment efforts. By establishing credibility for the center's program through the establishment of relationships with the media and with local officials and by building coalitions with other organizations and individuals in the community and throughout the state, advocacy efforts to increase funding for women's services have a very good chance for success. Community and institutional denial of the existence of alcohol and other drug problems among women, coupled with the absence of an organized constituency to advocate for services, have been the major stumbling blocks to establishing women's programs. The very existence of a vital new program at the women's center, coupled with some basic advocacy activities, offers the ingredients for success.

Prevention

Prevention strategies hold the promise for dramatically reducing the incidence of alcohol- and other drug-related problems among women. Alcohol and other drug problems are public health problems. Historically, no public health problem has been adequately addressed simply by treating its victims. A public health approach which addresses agent, host and environment is necessary if we are to achieve real reductions in the incidence and prevalence of alcohol and other drug problems in our communities. The agent, of course, is the drug itself. The host is the individual or group of individuals. The environment is community attitudes, practices and policies which can either nurture or discourage alcohol and other drug problems from manifesting themselves.

Women offer a tremendous untapped resource for leadership on prevention initiatives. Research indicates that women respond more positively than men to health and education measures pertinent to their own health and that of their family members. Women are more likely to seek professional advice on health-related matters. Polls designed to measure public opinion on alcohol policy changes including requirements to label alcohol with health information, restrictions on alcohol advertising and increases in alcohol excise taxes, all indicate higher approval rates from women than from men.[2] Moreover, although alcohol and drug abuse by women is a significant problem, women still tend to use fewer drugs, including alcohol, and to use them less frequently than their male counterparts. An exception is the high incidence of prescription drug use among women, frequently used in combination with alcohol. In addition, recent anecdotal information from treatment agencies indicates that women may be addicted to crack in numbers comparable to men. Generally speaking, however, female drinking practices provide a much safer model for appropriate alcohol use than do male drinking practices.

Women clearly have a vested interest in leading efforts to reduce alcohol and other drug problems. It is common knowledge that alcohol, for example, does more damage to female bodies than to male bodies, after less drinking and after shorter durations of drinking.[3] Women are frequently and profoundly victimized by alcohol and other drug problems. Alcoholic and drug-dependent women report high levels of sexual abuse, including rape and incest.[4] Women are also subject to victimization at the hands of their partners with alcohol and other drug problems. Alcohol and other drug use are often co-factors in episodes of domestic violence.

Alcoholism and drug addiction reinforce the second-class status of women in our society by rendering women incapable of self-actualization by undermining women's ability to take concrete steps, individually or collectively, to improve the quality of their own lives or of women generally. In short, alcohol and other drug problems have political ramifications for women, as well as health, safety and social ones.

Too often, prevention in this arena is exclusively defined in terms of alcohol and other drug education curricula in the school system. Prevention efforts targeting women are usually ignored entirely, except as they might relate to the female role of mother and primary caretaker of children. The initiation of alcohol and drug prevention programs in multi-service women's centers provides important opportunities to educate women about alcohol and other drug problems, to identify women already experiencing problems with alcohol and other drugs and to cultivate advocates for the development of prevention programs and policies which will serve the best interests of the public health.

There is a great deal which can be done in the policy arena and at all levels of government to create an environment more conducive to prevention goals. Education is obviously a critical tool, but we must look at all sources of education and information about alcohol and other drugs.

Health and safety warning labels on alcoholic beverage containers and warning posters at points of purchase for alcohol provide an important vehicle for accurate health information to consumers. A national coalition effort of over 100 national organizations, led by the National Council on Alcoholism and Drug Dependence and the Center for Science in the Public Interest, was successful in facilitating the enactment of a federal warning label law for all alcoholic beverage containers. All bottles and containers labeled after November 18, 1989 must bear the following message:

GOVERNMENT WARNING: (1) According to the Surgeon General, women should not drink alcoholic beverages during pregnancy because of the risk of birth defects. (2) Consumption of alcoholic beverages impairs your ability to drive a car or operate machinery, and may cause health problems.

Local coalitions across the nation have been quite successful in efforts to enact warning poster legislation warning women of the risks of drinking during pregnancy. In some cases, these coalitions have then turned their attention to address other alcohol-related problems in their communities.

The current environment is dominated by messages which promote, directly and indirectly, alcohol and other drug use. Alcohol advertising in the broadcast and print media and on billboards now provides the greatest source of alcohol education for American consumers. No other information source can possibly compete with the $1.3 billion spent by alcohol producers each year.[5] To ignore the power of advertis-

ing is to render our own educational efforts virtually ineffective. Alcohol advertising must be discussed and demystified. By doing so, the very potency of the ads' influence on our attitudes and our lives is diminished.

But discussion and analysis of alcohol ads is clearly only a partial solution. Not only do ads color our views about intoxication, alcoholism and the appropriate role of alcohol in daily life, they also operate to censor vital media coverage of the social and health consequences of alcohol use in our society. The financial dependency of the broadcast and print media on alcohol advertising revenues clearly generates media reluctance to address alcohol issues. Moreover, the proliferation of alcohol ads taints with hypocrisy the so-called "war on drugs," heralded by the media and the politicians.

The National Council on Alcoholism and Drug Dependence has joined with hundreds of consumer and health groups calling for equal time for health and safety messages when alcohol ads are aired on the broadcast media. NCADD also supports the expansion of health and safety warning labels to broadcast and print advertisements. As the alcohol industry and its advertisers increasingly target women, alcohol advertising becomes a ripe issue for feminist action. While equal time may be the ultimate national goal, action can be initiated at the local and state level on a number of fronts. Letters to women's magazines expressing concern about the number of alcohol ads and the very limited attention to alcohol and drugs as health issues for women is one place to start. Community organizing to reduce or eliminate billboards which advertise alcohol in the community may also be an effective strategy, particularly in neighborhoods dominated by ethnic and racial minorities where such billboards are most prevalent. Challenges to specific companies protesting ads which are particularly offensive to women may produce positive responses from an industry interested in winning the goodwill of female consumers.

Other community-based efforts might address the price and availability of alcoholic beverages as major influences on the level of alcohol problems. "Ladies' Nights" which offer female customers reduced drink prices only serve to encourage heavy drinking among women. Educating local restaurant and bar owners and proposing alternative promotional strategies could pay off. Advocacy for tax increases on alcoholic beverages serves to reduce the overall level of consumption of alcohol and alcohol problems. In some cases, advocates have been successful in channeling some of the additional revenue from tax increases into alcohol and other drug prevention and treatment programs. Initiatives to expand outlets for the sale of alcohol to grocery stores and other retail establishments are frequently aimed at increasing the availability of alcoholic beverages to women. Women have the opportunity to take a leadership role in opposing these initiatives.

Many of the policies outlined would affect the entire population of drinkers. It is also important to realize that targeted prevention activities must be culturally appropriate and must incorporate the particular values of the population to be addressed. It is obvious that the special needs and concerns of women have frequently gone unaddressed. But there are also a number of different subpopulations of women, all with their own lifestyles, cultural values and unique problems. Women's centers, with their wealth of experience in addressing issues of concern to single-parent women, older women, lesbians, Blacks, Hispanics, and others have an invaluable role to play in crafting alcohol- and drug-prevention messages, programs and policies which speak to the many concerns of all of these groups of women. This expertise will serve to enhance the work of the larger alcohol and drug community while meeting critical needs of women at risk for alcohol and other drug problems.

As we enter the last decade of the twentieth century, efforts to prevent and treat alcohol and other drug problems among women are marked by important recent victories as well as alarming incidents of discrimination and barriers to quality care. The warning label victory brought basic information about some of the risks associated with drinking to American consumers on the container itself. The effort to label alcohol also elevated public recognition of alcohol as a drug. There is increasing interest on Capitol Hill in addressing the constant promotion of drinking on the public airwaves through alcohol advertising. Unfortunately, the Food and Drug Administration may relax regulations governing the advertising of prescription medications on television. Just as we may be poised to reduce or balance alcohol advertisements, we could be faced with the direct marketing of tranquilizers to television viewers. Vigilance will be critical if gains in prevention are not to be undermined by new losses.

A status report on the availability of alcoholism and drug treatment for women is also a case of mixed reviews. There are undoubtedly more gender-sensitive treatment programs of all sorts in the nation than ever before in history, and there are finally some important initiatives to offer child care to women with dependent

children. But treatment options for women have not begun to keep pace with the need for services, particularly in the public sector where women who are underinsured or uninsured seek services. AIDS and crack addiction have intensified and complicated the issue of addiction in women. Drug-addicted women, especially if they are poor, pregnant or mothers, are being scapegoated by the very service-delivery systems that are responsible for their needs, but cannot begin to meet them. Hence, we see the prosecution of pregnant addicts for "child abuse" or "delivering drugs to a minor." It is not unusual for public hospitals or other social service agencies to make the call to the district attorney's office.

The complexity of alcohol and other drug problems among women, especially poor women and women of color, make us all important players in the days to come. Fundamental issues of racial, sexual and economic equality are closely intertwined with the issues of access to treatment. Corporate control of public information and its impact on the health of women and their children is one cutting edge of prevention for the next decade. We must all play some role in ensuring that public policy in this arena is progressive and humane.

References

1. National Council on Alcoholism. (1987). *A Federal Response to a Hidden Epidemic: Alcohol and Other Drug Problems Among Women*. New York, N.Y.: NCA.
2. "Alcohol Warnings Favored: Ad Age Gallup Survey," *Advertising Age*, April 9, 1990.
3. S. Hill, "Vulnerability to the Biomedical Consequences of Alcoholism and Alcohol-related Problems," in S. Wilsnack and L. Beckman (eds), *Alcohol Problems in Women*. New York: The Guilford Press, 1984.
4. S. Wilsnack, "Drinking, Sexuality and Sexual Dysfunction in Women," in S. Wilsnack and L. Beckman (eds), *Alcohol Problems in Women*. New York: The Guilford Press, 1984.
5. "Total Media Spending Drops 3.9% As Brewers Increase Outlays to $900 million," Impact, vol. 19, nos. 16 & 17, Aug. 15 and Sept. 1, 1989.

About the Authors

Miriam Aaron, M.P.A. is the Statewide Coordinator of Intervention and Prevention Program Performance for the New York State Division of Alcoholism and Alcohol Abuse. Her background includes degrees in nursing, sociology and public administration, and she is a certified employee assistance professional. She has extensive experience in the promotion, development and operation of occupational health and employee assistance programs and has published numerous articles and a textbook chapter on these topics. Ms. Aaron's concern with women's issues has been expressed in various activities, including the coordination of a governor's Task Force on Fetal Alcohol Syndrome and teaching a course on women and alcoholism at the Rutgers Summer School of Alcohol Studies.

Marilyn Aguirre-Molina, Ed.D. is an Assistant Professor in the Department of Environmental and Community Medicine of the University of Medicine and Dentistry-Robert Wood Johnson Medical School in Piscataway, New Jersey. She is also an Assistant Professor of Public Health within the Graduate Program in Public Health. Her teaching focus is on the public health aspects of alcohol and other drug problems and community health education. She is a National Fellow of the W.K. Kellogg Foundation, studying the political economy of Latin America and its implications for health. She is Principal Investigator of a grant from the Department of Health and Human Services, Office of Minority Health and is a member of many national boards and committees, including the Latino Council on Alcohol and Tobacco and the Executive Board of the American Public Health Association. She was founding director of the Advanced School of Alcohol and Drug Studies at Rutgers University. She and her husband are writing a book on the health status of Latinos in the United States. Her master's and doctoral degrees are in Public Health Education from Columbia University in New York City.

Sheila B. Blume, M.D. is Medical Director of the Alcoholism, Chemical Dependency and Compulsive Gambling Programs at South Oaks Hospital. Dr. Blume earned her medical degree with honors from Harvard Medical School. She is clinical professor of psychiatry at the State University of New York at Stony Brook, and Director of The South Oaks Institute of Alcoholism and Addictive Behavior Studies. Formerly medical director of the National Council on Alcoholism, she was also New York State Commissioner for Alcoholism under Governor Hugh Carey, from 1979 to 1983. Dr. Blume was appointed by President Jimmy Carter to the National Commission on Alcoholism and Other Alcoholism-Related Problems. An international expert on the topics of alcoholism, women and alcohol, and children of alcoholics, she is also a consultant to several foreign countries. She is a Certified Alcoholism Counselor.

Stephanie S. Covington, Ph.D. is an internationally known speaker, trainer and clinician specializing in programs on women and addiction, dysfunctional families, sexuality and building healthy relationships. She received her degrees from Columbia University and The Union Institute, and has served on the faculties of the University of Southern California, San Diego State University, and the California School of Professional Psychology. She has published numerous articles and recently co-authored the book *Leaving the Enchanted Forest: The Path from Relationship Addiction to Intimacy*. Her new book, *Awakening Your Sexuality: A Recovery Guide for Women*, will be published in 1991. She has appeared on the "Sally Jessy Raphael" and "Geraldo" television talk shows, and on numerous radio and television shows throughout the country. Her private practice is in La Jolla, CA.

Laura Derman, M.S.W. received her Master's degree in Social Work from the University of Michigan and an M.P.H. from the University of California,

183

Berkeley. She worked for fourteen years as Director of Consultation and Education for the Women's Alcoholism Program of CASPAR, Inc. In that role she developed programs, facilitated client groups, and provided consultation and training on issues of women and substance abuse. She is currently at the Boston AIDS Action Committee, developing mental health resources for people affected by HIV. She is a mother of three young daughters.

Norma Finkelstein, Ph.D. received her M.S.W. from the University of Michigan and her doctorate from the Florence Heller School, Brandeis University. She has worked in the field of addictions since 1972. She is the founder and creator of the Women's Alcoholism Program of CASPAR, Inc., where she served as Executive Director from 1975 to 1989. She is currently Director of a new federally funded demonstration program, The Coalition for Addiction, Pregnancy and Parenting. She is the mother of four children, including two step-children, and was a single parent for eight years before re-marrying in 1980.

Susan Galbraith, M.S.W. is a consultant specializing in alcohol and drug issues and women. She is the Director of the Coalition on Alcohol and Drug Dependent Women and Their Children, which is committed to preventing punitive actions against pregnant women with alcohol and drug problems and to enhancing prevention and treatment efforts. She was a consultant for the Women's Alcohol and Drug Education Project of the Women's Action Alliance and assisted in the editing of this book. She worked for the National Council on Alcoholism and Drug Dependence as an advocate, and has worked in direct treatment with women with alcohol and drug problems and their children as a counselor and administrator. She is currently working with women's shelter providers in Washington, D.C. to organize services for homeless pregnant women with alcohol and drug problems.

Anne Geller, M.D. was born in England and graduated from Oxford University with a Bachelor of Medicine degree. She trained in Neurology and Psychiatry at New York University division of Bellevue Hospital. She did a post-graduate fellowship in psychopharmacology at Albert Einstein College of Medicine and for several years did research on drugs and behavior, receiving a Research Career Development Award from the National Institute of Health. In 1977 she re-entered clinical medicine and joined the staff of the Smithers Center of St. Luke's-Roosevelt Hospital in New York City, becoming Chief in 1979. Dr. Geller has published both in basic research and more recently on clinical issues. She is a member of the Board of

Directors of the American Society of Addiction Medicine and is on the Editorial Board of the Journal of Substance Abuse Treatment. She has a special and personal interest in the area of Impaired Physicians. She is on the Physicians Committee of the Medical Society of the State of New York and is a board member for the Office of Professional Medical Conduct.

M. Jean Gilbert, Ph.D. is an Applied Medical Anthropologist who received her doctorate from the University of California, Santa Barbara. Her most recent work has focused on alcohol use among Mexicans and Mexican Americans. She was a National Institute on Alcohol Abuse and Alcoholism Scholar in Hispanic Alcohol Studies at the University of California at Los Angeles from 1984 to 1989. She is currently conducting health care management research for Kaiser Permanente in Los Angeles.

Sandie Johnson, M.A. is a psychologist and writer who has worked for over 14 years in various aspects of the alcoholism field—research, program and materials development, and counseling. As a data analyst with the Alcohol Epidemiological Data System, she published a national study in 1978 on cirrhosis mortality among American Indian people. She has worked in prevention materials development at the National Clearinghouse for Alcohol and Drug Information. For over 10 years she worked part-time as a counselor in a county alcoholism program. She is the author of over 20 publications and resides in Potomac, Maryland.

Patti Juliana, A.C.S.W. is a social worker experienced in the fields of child welfare and substance-abuse treatment. This unique combination of experience affords her a critical perspective on the effects of substance abuse on the family. She is currently the Director of Children and Family Services at the Albert Einstein College of Medicine—Division of Substance Abuse, where she is responsible for the programming that addresses the special needs of parents who are patients in drug treatment programs and their children. The program provides a multidimensional range of services for parent, child and family, designed to improve family life and break the cycle of substance abuse and related problems.

Jean Kilbourne, Ed.D. writes and lectures on alcohol and cigarette advertising, the image of women in advertising and other topics. The award-winning films "Killing Us Softly," "Still Killing Us Softly," and "Calling the Shots" are based on her lectures. She has written on these topics and has been interviewed by many magazines and newspapers, including *Time, Newsweek, Forbes, The Christian Science Monitor,* and *The New York Times.* She has been a frequent guest on radio and television programs, including "The Oprah Winfrey Show" and "The Today Show," and she has been consulted by ABC and CBS news, "20/20," and "Nightline." She has also been consulted by the U.S. Congress and the Surgeon General. She is a Visiting Scholar at Wellesley College, is on the Board of Directors of the National Council on Alcoholism, has chaired the Council on Alcohol Policy and is on the National Advisory Committees of the alcohol education projects of both the Junior League and the Women's Action Alliance.

Robin A. LaDue, Ph.D. is a licensed clinical psychologist. She works in private practice and is involved with research in Fetal Alcohol Syndrome. She is a member of the Cowlitz Indian Tribe and has worked in several Indian communities. She has served on numerous committees regarding the provision of services to Native veterans and other minority populations.

Rose Leone, C.S.W. has worked in the substance abuse treatment field for over twenty-four years in a variety of positions, from counselor to supervisor to administrator. She also has been a private practitioner for over fifteen years and has an office in New York City. She has published a number of articles and is in the process of publishing her first book. In addition to being a Certified Social Worker, she is a Certified Rehabilitation Counselor.

Christine Lubinski, M.A. has served as Director for Public Policy for the National Council on Alcoholism and Drug Dependence in Washington, D.C. since 1983. Her extensive advocacy efforts on behalf of alcoholics, drug addicts and their families have included initiatives to improve prevention and treatment policies sensitive to the needs of women and their children. She played an instrumental role in the adoption of national legislation requiring states to utilize a portion of federal funds for new and expanded services for alcoholic and drug-dependent women, and helped to spearhead NCADD's initiative to create a national Coalition on Alcohol and Drug Dependent Women and Their Children. She worked to initiate this broad-based national group in the hope of creating a powerful opposing voice to those who respond to the pregnant addict with criminal prosecution, termination of parental rights and proposals for forced sterilization.

Lynne C. McArthur, M.A. is the AIDS Coordinator for the New York State Division of Alcoholism and Alcohol Abuse. She is a co-chairperson and co-founder of the New York State Women and AIDS Project, an

organization that focuses its attention on women who are affected by HIV disease. She is an advisory board member of the Women and AIDS Resource Network in Brooklyn, New York and the Women's Alcohol and Drug Education Project of the Women's Action Alliance. She has a B.A. in Political Science and Master's degrees in Education and Library Science, all from the University of Michigan, Ann Arbor.

Juana Mora, Ph.D. received her doctorate in Sociolinguistics from Stanford University in 1984. She has specialized in research on Latinos and alcohol consumption patterns and problems and has done ethnographic research on alcohol behaviors and norms among Latino couples and families. She was an Associate Research Scientist at the Prevention Research Center in Berkeley, delivered alcohol services for Latinos as the former Executive Director of *Zona Seca,* in Santa Barbara, California and as a planner in the Los Angeles County Office of Alcohol Programs. Her interests include the changing patterns of alcohol consumption among Latino women; public policy, advertising, and the role of the alcohol industry in the promotion of alcohol in Latino communities; and community planning and organizing to prevent alcohol-related problems in Latino communities. She is currently a Research Associate at the Chicano Studies Research Center at the University of California, Los Angeles where she is conducting a research project on alcohol use patterns among Mexican American women and related lifestyle factors.

Kary L. Moss, J.D. is a Staff Attorney with the American Civil Liberties Union Women's Rights Project, representing women charged with child neglect and felonies because they used drugs or alcohol while they were pregnant. She is currently the lead counsel in *Elaine W. et al. v. North General Hospital,* the first lawsuit challenging the exclusion of pregnant women from alcohol- and drug-treatment programs. Her publications on this subject include: "Legal Issues Raised by Drug Testing Post-Partum Women and Their Children," *Clearinghouse Review,* Vol. 23, No. 11 (March, 1990); "Recent Update," *Harvard Women's Law Journal,* (April, 1990); and an article co-authored with Dr. Wendy Chavkin published in *Christianity and Crisis* (June, 1990). She is also the Co-Chair of the Law and Policy Committee of the Coalition on Alcohol and Drug Dependent Women and Their Children. In addition to her law degree, she has a Master's degree in International Affairs.

Suzanne E. Ostermann is Executive Director of the Alcoholism Council of California, a state affiliate of the National Council on Alcoholism and Drug Dependence. She has over fifteen years of experience in alcoholism services, and has served on governmental alcohol and drug advisory boards and as a volunteer for women's recovery programs. For the past five years, the focus of her work has been in public policy and advocacy on behalf of alcoholics, other drug addicts, and their families. In 1988, she co-founded the National Association of Women in Alcoholism and Other Drug Dependencies (NAWAODD) and is currently co-authoring a non-traditional Twelve-Step Workbook with Brenda Underhill.

Beth Glover Reed, Ph.D. is an Associate Professor of Social Work and Women's Studies at the University of Michigan at Ann Arbor. She received her doctorate in Community and Clinical Psychology. She was program evaluator for the W.O.M.A.N. Center, a research-demonstration project providing services for women with drug problems, and was Principal Investigator for the National Institute on Drug Abuse-funded Women's Drug Research Project, which collected information on women in treatment from 25 programs and studied the special needs of women and how to meet them. She is editor or author of many publications on topics of relevance to this book, including a two-volume set entitled *Treatment Services for Drug Dependent Women*, published by NIDA. She is Chair of the Board of the Domestic Violence Project/SAFE House, a program for battered women and their children, and is on the Advisory Council for the Assault Crisis Center. Both programs are in Ann Arbor, Michigan. Within the areas of Women's Studies and human services, she has been especially interested in the structure and dynamics of all-woman social systems and their implications for leadership and administrators.

Paula Roth, M.A. is the director of the Women's Alcohol and Drug Education Project at the Women's Action Alliance. She has worked in alcohol and drug prevention and treatment programs for twenty years and has been a consistent advocate for improved services for women. She was Prevention and Education Officer at the national offices of the National Council on Alcoholism and was the founder and director of an award-winning model outpatient treatment program for rural women, funded by the National Institute on Alcohol Abuse and Alcoholism. She has presented at national and international conferences on prevention and education strategies for both women and youth, including a conference for health and government officials from five Latin American countries and an international congress on women. She has been a consultant to drug-free, methadone maintenance and alcoholism programs, appeared on local and national television and radio, including the Cable News Net-

work, and been interviewed by magazines and newspapers, including *The New York Times, El Mundo, Vogue, Harper's Bazaar* and *New Woman*. Several of her articles on alcohol, women and youth have been published. Born in New York City, she has traveled extensively in Latin America. Her degree from Goddard College, Plainfield, Vermont, is in Female Psychology.

Sue A. Russell, M.S. After spending several years as a Christian missionary in Africa, she returned to the United States to pursue a lifelong interest in theology. It was out of the process of becoming the first woman to obtain a Master of Divinity degree from her seminary that her feminist consciousness came to maturity. Finding opportunities for further development scarce within the confines of the church, Ms. Russell chose to pursue a career in psychology. She is presently a doctoral candidate and National Institute on Alcohol Abuse and Alcoholism research fellow at the University of North Dakota.

Maryanne Schretzman, M.S.W. was born and raised in Brooklyn, New York. She received her Master's Degree in Social Work from Hunter College. She has worked extensively in the areas of family and alcohol treatment and is the Director of the Women In Need Alcohol and Drug Clinic. The clinic is designed specifically for homeless women and women with children, and is the only clinic in New York City that provides day-care on site. Ms. Schretzman is also the treasurer of the Association of New York City Alcoholism Programs. She is a member of the Emergency Alliance for Homeless Families and Children.

An-Pyng Sun, Ph.D. received her doctorate from the School of Applied Social Sciences, Case Western Reserve University, Cleveland, Ohio. She is a Certified Social Worker in New York State and was affiliated with Chinatown Alcoholism Services, an alcoholism center in New York City, for over two years. She has been engaged in research concerning Asian immigrants and substance abuse and has presented numerous papers at national conferences. She is currently teaching a course entitled "Family Issues-Substance Abuse" at the University of Bridgeport in Connecticut.

Ashaki H. Taha-Cissé, B.A. is an African American public health educator, community health activist and women's advocate who has developed and implemented innovative national and community-based multicultural women's health initiatives in the United States, West Africa and the Caribbean. For more than fifteen years, she has worked to empower African American women. She served on the Executive

Committee of the National Black Feminist Organization, consulted to the New York Urban League on drug treatment issues for women, consulted to organizations on battering, rape, incest and multicultural education issues and was Project Manager for a multicultural AIDS risk reduction initiative for the National Hemophilia Foundation. She has edited several publications on women and education and is currently the Associate Director of the Women's Alcohol and Drug Education Project at the Women's Action Alliance. She holds a Bachelor of Arts degree from Sarah Lawrence College and is a candidate for a Masters of Public Health degree from Hunter College in New York.

Jean Kennedy Tracy, Ph.D. is a licensed clinical social worker. She has lived and practiced psychotherapy in Maine for twenty years. She developed a pilot rural Rape Crisis program funded by the National Institute on Mental Health and served for eight years as clinical consultant to Skyward, a rural women's outpatient alcohol treatment program. Both programs are in the mid-coast region of Maine. Her current clinical interests include women's issues, substance abuse, treatment for adult children of alcoholics and working with adult survivors of sexual abuse.

Brenda L. Underhill, M.S. is Executive Director of the Alcoholism Center for Women in Los Angeles, a comprehensive, community-based alcoholism recovery and prevention services program for women. She is a faculty member of the Chemical Dependency Studies Program at the California Family Studies Center in North Hollywood, California. She has over fifteen years' experience in the alcoholism field and was recently published in *Alcohol, Health and Research World* and *Alcoholism Treatment Quarterly*. She is a member of several national boards of directors, serves on committees for the California State Department of Alcohol and Drug Programs and is Co-Chair of the Los Angeles County Women's Coalition on Alcohol and Other Drug Services. In June of 1989, she was appointed to the Treatment Committee of the Governor's Policy Council on Alcohol and Drug Abuse of California. She is a Certified Alcoholism Counselor.

Maria Vandor, M.S. is Coordinator of Children and Women's Services for the New York State Division of Substance Abuse Services. Her career with the Division has focused on the development of services for special populations. Since 1984, she has directed the Division's response to substance-abuse treatment for women and children. A graduate of New York University School of Education, she holds Master's degrees in both Special Education and Remedial Reading, and has

completed post-graduate courses in administration and supervision.

Ellen Weber, J.D. is Legislative Counsel for the National Policy Project at the Washington D.C. office of the Legal Action Center of the City of New York, Inc., a non-profit public interest organization whose purpose is to provide legal advice and assistance to former drug and alcohol abusers, persons in treatment for addictions and the many programs and agencies which assist in their rehabilitation. Ms. Weber has been a staff counsel with the Center since June, 1985, and in November, 1988 became the legislative counsel for the Center's National Policy Project. She staffs the Center's Washington, D.C. office, which focuses exclusively on federal public policy relating to alcohol, drug and AIDS issues. Prior to joining the Center, she served for five years as a trial attorney with the Civil Rights Division of the U.S. Justice Department.

Sharon Carlson Wilsnack, Ph.D. received her master's and doctoral degrees in clinical psychology from Harvard University and studied as a Fulbright Fellow at the University of Freiburg, Federal Republic of Germany. She is a professor in the Department of Neuroscience, University of North Dakota School of Medicine. She is presently conducting a 10-year longitudinal study of drinking and problem drinking in a national sample of women and is co-editor of the recent volume *Alcohol Problems in Women: Antecedents, Consequences, and Intervention* (New York: Guilford Press). She serves as a consultant and Review Committee member for the National Institute on Alcohol Abuse and Alcoholism and for several national organizations concerned with women's health.

Dooley Worth, Ph.D. is Consulting Anthropologist to the Department of Epidemiology and Social Medicine at Montefiore Medical Center, where she is conducting research on the links between sexual behavior and drug use and AIDS with female heroin and crack addicts. In addition to her work with Montefiore, she is a consultant to other organizations working with chemically dependent women. She is currently working on a book on women and drug treatment.

Rita Zimmer, M.P.H. was born in Detroit and raised in upstate New York, and received her Master's degree in Public Health from New York University. She is founder and Executive Director of Women In Need, a seven-year-old, non-profit, multiservice agency dedicated to the needs of homeless women and their families. The organization operates a preventive child welfare program, an alcohol clinic, child care services, an outreach program and, in the summer, Camp WIN. Ms. Zimmer is on the board of the Coalition for the Homeless and a member of the Emergency Alliance for Homeless Families. She is one of the three recipients of the 1988 Josephine Shaw Lowell Award of the Community Service Society for being a woman "who has demonstrated that one person can make a difference" and the Brooke Russell Astor Award for being "an unsung New York hero who contributed substantially to the enrichment of the City" in the fields of Civics/Community Service/Culture, Education or Literature.

Index